ONE BRIDGE TO LIFE

ONE BRIDGE TO LIFE

WILLIAM SAMELSON

Eshel
Books

Washington • Baltimore

ISBN: 978-0-945938-02-6
Library of Congress Control Number: 2008937437

Printed in the United States of America

ESHEL BOOKS
8600 Foundry Street
Savage Mill Box 2043
Savage, Maryland 20763
800-953-9929

For my mother Bela, and my sister Felusia that they may not have died in vain, I lend my voice. . . and to the unsung heroes of all wars, the Righteous among Nations. . .

—W.S

There is a land of the living
and a land of the dead
and the bridge is love,
the only survival,
the only meaning.

—Thornton Wilder

Preface

This book is a tribute to life, not a capitulation to death. It is a triumph of love over hate; a victory of faith in humanity over despair.

Man-made circumstances forced upon my childhood and adolescence a life full of anguish and terror, resulting in the loss of my loved ones and my own imprisonment in Nazi slave-labor and concentration camps. After six-and-a-half harrowing years, I was liberated by the U.S. Armed Forces under the command of General George S. Patton Jr. from the concentration camp Colditz, a branch of Buchenwald.

It has taken four decades to cleanse my soul from Nazi hell. Unable to find a voice with which to express my anguish, I remained mute. At times I even envied the dead martyrs of Hitler's war against the Jewish people, my brethren. During those years, that anguish did not subside since I realized more and more that the lessons of Buchenwald might have been in vain.

Then the day came when I knew that the only way in which I could exorcise that hell was to become the voice of the victims. To accomplish this, I embarked on a task of study and contemplation, which enabled me to gain distance from the pain and also to purge my survival guilt. This became my life's guiding purpose.

The story which unfolds on these pages is the result of many sleepless nights, countless pads, and innumerable trips to the past, as I traveled roads I had tried to avoid for so many years. I was forced to reweave again the tapestry of all those lives so dear to me and cut so short by the scythe of the assassins.

In the darkness of that memory, however, there shone a faint light: the actions of a few who have been called the Righteous Gentiles. My story would not be complete without recognizing those who helped save Jewish lives or who died while trying.

While this work is dedicated to the silenced victims of Nazi bestiality, it must also serve as a reminder that an occasional kindness occurred among the captors, even some betrayals among the victims. In hell there were no simple answers.

May this book serve as a challenge to humanity: to remember that life is the answer to death and love is the answer to hate.

January 1989   *William Samelson*

Prologue

Only a few months ago, I enjoyed life as a student at K.S.U., a university boasting one of the most beautiful campuses in the nation. Now, dressed in the olive khakis of an American G.I., Pfc. stripes on my sleeves, I am on my way to Seattle, Washington; a stopover between here and Korea.

As a member of the famed 3rd Armored Division, I am shipping out overseas, part of the United Nations "police action for the containment of Communist expansion in Asia." All of us at Co. "C" understand little, if anything, about geopolitics. During the sixteen weeks of basic training we were taught, in the quickest way possible, the art of killing which we were now prepared to practice on our enemies.

At the age of twenty-three, I am the "elder" of our outfit. My buddies jokingly refer to me as "pops", of which I am exceedingly proud. Little do they know, but their "pops" has lived several life-times already, and not all too pleasant ones at that. Moreover, I have a strong feeling that there is nothing ahead of us so frightfully difficult that this body of mine would be unable to sustain. After all, I've been there before. Only this time it is different; I go willingly, for "God and country."

These last few months, things progressed so rapidly I was at first unable to pause and think of the consequences. The fever of right-eous indignation had gripped all my senses, and I did not mind being inducted into the Armed Forces. I love my adoptive country dearly since my arrival here in the year 1948, and I recall the excesses of our arch-enemy from personal experiences.

As the convoy inexorably approaches our destination, I suddenly encounter mixed feelings. What only weeks ago seemed like an exciting adventure, assumes now the dimensions of a new reality.

"Why me again?" I ask silently, but I quickly realize that I shouldn't be asking such awkward questions which not even God is inclined to answer.

The "other" War was scarcely over. Wasn't that "other" War enough of a lesson to be remembered? Hadn't I been taught severely enough?. . .

. . .All of a sudden, we are hit by heavy small arms automatic weapons, rocket granades, and mortar fire. Under the blanket of bombardment, the Communist troops launch several massive ground assaults. Our division lines are broken, but we beat the enemy back after heavy casualties.

I am crouching inside my "living grave", the foxhole, which I share with my comrade Joe Perna from Havana, Cuba. Joe keeps firing his M-1 rifle as if it were a turkey shoot. The noise is overwhelming. I tremble and pray. In the dim light of the kerosene lamp I can make out the pretty features of the Cuban dancer on the entertainment page of the magazine Joe's parents sent him the other day. I can't make out the caption. It's in Spanish. Joe's language. But I can surely appreciate her smile, her taut, sensuous flexing body. By God, I think to myself, when all this is over, I'll. . .

Joe doesn't let me pursue my thoughts. He reloads the rifle, looks my way, and grins. "You still gawkin' at the pretty *senorita*, do you?" He grins.

"Sure thing. I'd much rather look at her than at you, you ugly bastard."

"You got religion, Bill?" He asks, disregarding my insult.

"I sure do." My eyes look toward heaven. "Don't you?"

"Hey, my good buddy, we all do, one way or another. Specially in times like these."

"He's got to help me through this mess, Joe. He's got to!" I shout through the din of gun rattle. "I promise you this, Joe. When we get out of this dump in one piece, I'll marry that little Cuban number. I swear!" I point at the picture.

"Sure, you will, Bill. You and a dozen other guys." Joe reloads again. "Anyway, I won't hold you to it, buddy. Everybody makes big promises when they're about to piss in their pants from fear."

"I mean it, Joe. No kidding." I sound defensive. "I like that pretty face and the gentle features. Soon as we're out of this hole, I'll write her, you'll see. Soon as it's over, the good Lord willing."

"It's okay to think about the Lord in a time like this, but He's up there and I'm down here, and the gooks keep coming like they was invited, so I got to defend what's mine." He pats the rifle endearingly. "Like they say, 'the Lord helps them that help themselves.'" Joe squeezes off another round. "Okay, Bill, it's your turn."

"Why in hell do they always come at us in the dark of the night?" I shout through the din of battle. I throw a last kiss at the little dancer and tuck the magazine into my breast pocket.

"If you was them, would you want to get shot at in daylight?" Joe asks with the familiar smirk on his mischievous face. There is a roar of approaching waves of men, a kind of ritual death chant, accompanied by the sound of bell-like instruments. "Here they come!" Joe shouts, shooting into the crowd of weirdly swaying apparitions. As soon as they fall, others climb over their fallen bodies, continuing the never ending procession.

The rocky, windswept hills of the west bank of the Yalu river soon turn into a burning, exploding inferno.

"I want to live!" I scream as loud as I am am able to under the circumstances, knowing full well that no one hears my outcry. . .

. . .now, cradled in my mother's arms, I am a young boy in my native Piotrkow, Poland. The family gathers round the radio in the living room of our modest apartment, listening to the broadcast from neighboring Germany. We hear marching music and we hear the hoarse but frightful voice of a man; he shouts obscenities with the shrill, threatening tone. We understand German, Russian and Polish in my parents' home; my father being of German descent, my mother of Russian parents, and the children, Roman, Felusia and myself, speak Polish as well, for we were all born here. I can hear the man's voice clearly:

THE JEWS ARE OUR MISFORTUNE! THEY MUST BE EXTERMINATED LIKE VERMIN! GERMANY IS FOR THE GERMANS ALONE! WE MUST HAVE MORE LIVING SPACE! ON TO THE EASTERN TERRITORIES! THEY BELONG TO THE THOUSAND YEAR REICH!

"I love you, mama." My arms tighten around my mother's neck, and I kiss her on the cheeks. They are moist and they taste salty.

"Mama loves you, too, Vilusiek." She speaks endearingly. Little Felusia is also in tears, following my mother's example. Only Roman, the eldest of the siblings, looks on valiantly.

"There's nothing to worry about, children." My mother says reassuringly. "Daddy won't let anything happen to us." I adore my mother, and I know there is absolutely nothing in the world my father can't handle. It feels wonderful to have the love and strength of our dear parents at this critical time.

But my father stands in the doorway dressed in his reservist's uniform. "Papa! You mustn't leave us now! Please, papa!" I cry.

"There's a war on, my son." He says embracing all of us. "I'll be back soon. Don't cry, children." He implores. There are already sounds of airplanes above, the agonizing whining sounds of falling bombs, and then the earth trembles under the powerful explosions. "Take care of your mama!" I hear father's voice from a distance.

He's gone now. My mother shelters me in her arms, Felusia clings to her garment tenaciously. "Remember, children," I hear my mother's voice clearly, "remember your roots and love one another. You'll be better able to bear the burdens of life." Suddenly her face becomes a blur, a figment of my memory . . .only her resonant voice echoes clearly from the great distance of time. . .

. . .My name was Vilek then; it seems such a long time ago and yet only one generation has scarcely come and gone. It all began when I was ten years old. We had heard that Jewish synagogues were being burnt to the ground in Germany, our neighbor to the West. In November 1938, I was living with my family in the Polish province of Upper Silesia, cradle of our country's coal and steel industry.

My father, Henryk, a tailor who struggled by any measure in my childish understanding, was able to provide for the family our daily necessities and occasional luxuries. Only the latter had always been rare exceptions. We were happy just to get by from day to day, and there was no accumulation of wealth to speak of. Oh, my mother did have a meager piggy bank, which she kept hidden in the cupboard. The "bank" was a simple cookie jar where she deposited any "excess" household coins for "her children," as she used to say to us, and for that eventual "rainy day."

My mother, Bela, was an extraordinary woman, accustomed to hard work and dedicated to her family. My brother Roman was twelve, and our little sister, Felusia, was four.

Some of our friends had already left for parts unknown even before the recent developments in Germany. Now, panic had begun to flutter the hearts of the Polish Jews, and they spoke of countries I had never heard of except in travel brochures and exotic novels: Mexico, Australia, Brasil, Argentina, Paraguay, and Uruguay. However, the most desirable refuge was that cradle of liberty for all people, the United States of America. But America was a dream accessible only to those who had relatives or friends there who would claim them by filling out the documents of support called "affidavits," or to the well-to-do who needed neither.

My father was honorable and he was far too proud to beg, but after many arguments with my mother, some of which became quite heated, she finally persuaded him to write to his cousin Mickey in Brooklyn, U.S.A.

I remember how sad I felt to have witnessed my parents' anguished arguing over whether or not to write that first letter to America. Seldom in the first ten years of my life had I seen or heard my parents address one another in anger, and never to shout at the top of their voices. They had always followed a strict rule: 'never to display their worst in front of their children.' But now, powerful emotions had played havoc with their reason and deep concern had temporarily displaced decorum. Even so, the joyful anticipation of a possible American journey eased considerably the burden of my sadness. And so, the letters began. . .

PART ONE

Mr. Mickey Meyerson
187 Powell Street
Brooklyn, N.Y., U.S.A.

May 14, 1939

Dear Cousin Mickey,

It has really been a long time since I last wrote you, and I must tell you that many things have happened here since then. We thought of you very often and planned to write, but in the rush of the day and scarcity of time we had never gotten to it.

We hope that this letter finds you and Fay, Victor and Isaac, in the best of health and that your business is coming along successfully. My shop is bustling with work, and I have had to hire extra help even though Beta's helping me most of the time. We're all fine, thank God. Roman was Bar Mitzvah in January. It must have slipped your mind or you would have surely sent him a card as you always do on the occasion of the children's birthdays. Vilek will be eleven come September, and Felusia will be five years old come next month. Please, if you could find a spare minute, write them a short note.

The children keep talking about America. They show the postal stamps to everybody. It's a source of much pride and joy for them, and they are the envy of their friends.

There has been a lot of talk about this man Hitler in Germany.

He makes hysterical speeches over the radio about taking back German territories from Poland, and soon. Something about the Treaty of Versailles and the great injustice to the German nation. Most of us here think Hitler is serious. After all, in March the Nazis took Czechoslovakia, and nobody lifted a finger to stop them. What do I tell my friends? Is America going to stand by and let Hitler take over? France and England promise to fight on our side, but they always look after their own interests first. Who can blame them?

With all the customers we have, there's little money coming in because everyone's holding on to their cash. We can't refuse to do the work, hoping that things will soon come to normal.

Love to all of you. Write soon.

Your cousin Henryk

* * *

1

Pan Henryk S.
Modrzejowska 3
Sosnowiec, Poland

June 12, 1939

Dear Cousin Henryk,

Your letter arrived on Friday a week ago, and I didn't have a chance to reply sooner because Fay was hospitalized for gall bladder complications since the end of May. She was released yesterday, feeling better, thank God. She's recovering well and gaining strength.

I'm sorry to have missed Roman's Bar Mitzvah. You can imagine how hectic it's been over here. Please convey our congratulations to the boy. I'm sure he'll bring you andBela much joy. Mazal tov. Get him a nice gift for the enclosed $5.00.

We read the newspapers and listen to the radio broadcasts about the mess in Europe. I still think Hitler is just blowing off steam. That's politics, you know. He's not going to attack Poland. America wouldn't stand for that. Can you imagine? We have a German Bund right here in New York. The gall. Brownshirts marching down Fifth Avenue! Lucky there are enough Jews hereabouts to give them a good fight. That's democracy at work! Fay's worried because Victor, our fourteen year old is getting into street fights as well as our eleven year old Isaac. I'm afraid she'll suffer a setback.

So, you can see, we have our own problems here. Needless to say, I'm sorry you're passing through a crisis. I pray God things will come to normal soon for all of us.

Our love to all of you.

Your cousin Mickey

* * *

Mr. Mickey Meyerson
187 Powell Street
Brooklyn, N.Y.,U.S.A.

June 17, 1939

Dear Cousin Mickey,

Bless you for your quick reply. We're all happy to hear about Fay's convalescence. Be sure to tell the boys to be careful. If the Bund is anything like the Nazi stormtroopers here, they play for keeps. It's a matter for the law, so let the police do their job.

Roman was so happy you remembered him! Thanks! It was more than enough. We'll keep some of the money for a rainy day. Mickey, I'm sorry to tell you that the situation here is deteriorating in spite of the assurances of our allies. The

Nazis provoke border incidents, claiming that our soldiers killed their border guards. Big lies sound like truth. The Swiss Commission believed them. It's frightening.

0Without making this letter too long, I want to come straight to the point: Jews are leaving Poland as fast as they can get exit visas. Without relatives in America, they're fleeing to many other countries, mostly South America. People are running for their lives, Mickey. No exaggeration.

Please hear me, Mickey, if you can't get the affidavit for the U.S.A., then send us about one thousand dollars. For that money we can get visas for Australia. I'll return the money to you as soon as I start working there, I swear! Don't let us down! Time's running out!

Love to all of you from us. Let's hear from you soon, please.

Your cousin Henryk

* * *

Pan Henryk S.
Modrzejowska 3
Sosnowiec, Poland

August 3, 1939

Dear Cousin,

I've been trying to see my way through this thing, and I can't. There's very little I can do for you right now. Fay's sickness has taken the very last dollar out of our savings. My heart cries out to all of you. I'm especially anxious for the children, but. . . what can I say? Money doesn't grow on trees even in America, contrary to common belief. There's no cash on hand, and we need to replace some old furniture badly. We have other expenses as well. By the way, have you tried the relief organizations there? Maybe they can help.

Henryk, I'm terribly sorry that it has to be this way. We spend sleepless nights just thinking about you. It's no use. I know you are anxious to hear from us, so I won't delay this any longer. Love to all.

Cousin Mickey

* * *

Mr. Mickey Meyerson
187 Powell Street
Brooklyn, N.Y., U.S A.

August 20, 1939

Dear Mickey,

The interview with the relief organization was wasted time. There was a queue of hundreds asking for help. The official wanted to know how much money I've brought. When he found out I have none, he showed me the door.

We've got to have the money immediately! Please, Mickey, we need your help *desperately! It's not like I'm asking for a handout. You'll get your money back, I promise! They need tailors in Australia, and I'll get a good job as soon as we land there.*

I hate to burden you with our troubles, but we have no one else to turn to. God help us, our lives are in your hands. Remember, whatever your decision, we love you just the same.

Your cousin Henryk

P.S. Enclosed is a recent photo of the children.
* * *

Pan Henryk S.
Modrzejowska 3
Sosnowiec, Poland

August 30, 1939

My dear Cousin,
Wings of urgency must have caused your letter to get here so fast, and I want to reply immediately. I still don't go along with those who say that Hitler's about to invade Poland. But Fay and I decided to do everything possible to bring you all to America. True, we're crowded in our small apartment, but we'll all manage somehow.

Victor picked up the necessary papers from Immigration. First thing tomorrow, the affidavit will be on its way. In a week from now it should reach our embassy in Warsaw. You've worked hard all your lives and now you'll have to leave all your belongings behind, but your safety comes first. Forgive me for hesitating before. Hope we can make it up to you.

We loved the children's photo. Wish you had sent one of you and Beta. Well, anyway, we'll see you here soon in person. We wish you a happy Rosh Hashanah which is around the corner. May we all be inscribed in the Book of Life, amen.

Your cousin Mickey

* * *

The mailman made a special effort to deliver the envelope to the Meyersons personally. It was Saturday, and they had returned from the early services at the old synagogue. The mailman examined the envelope curiously. There were many seals stamped in German, and he couldn't make out what they said. He knew the letter had been returned from Poland. He was making sure it got back into the hands of the sender.

Mickey stood in the doorway turning the envelope every which way and trying to read the significance of the stamped messages. He was unable to understand it even with his knowledge of Yiddish. His heart beat violently at the sight of the swastika emblem staring at him.

"Who was that, Mickey?" Fay's voice came from the living room and startled him momentarily. He walked toward her without haste. As he approached his wife, he extended the arm which held the letter.

"It got there too late, Fay. God help us all." He buried his face in the palms of his huge hands and sobbed convulsively. Had he been able to read one of the stamped messages beneath the eagle clutching the swastika, he would have known. . . "whereabouts unknown"

—*"Adressat unbekannt".* . .

1

"For the love of God, Henryk. Everyone's going somewhere!" My mother insisted during one of my parents' frequent discussions. "Where, Bela? Where can we go?" My father kept asking, almost hostile. "Who's going to help us?" He looked at my mother with that worried look of his so easily recognizable in the past few months. "I've done what cousin Mickey had suggested in his letters. You were there, they practically threw us out of the HIAS office. How could they treat us like that?"

"Hush, Henryk, the children."

"It's much better for them to know what's happening, Bela. How much longer can we deceive ourselves? The truth is, we have no-where to go." He paused, clearing his throat. "We are all alone. Every door is shut in our faces. Here in Europe and elsewhere." He looked at the three small children listening attentively, and he cleared his throat again, this time a bit longer. "It's almost the end of August, Bela, and we're still here. I don't like it. I don't like it at all." He repeated, shaking his head helplessly.

"Perhaps we should go to Piotrkow for the time being?" My mother suggested cautiously. "It's away from the border, and we can temporarily stay at my parents home. At least until this whole thing with the Germans is solved." She thought for a moment. "Besides, they may never get that far. Why, it's smack in the middle of Poland."

"Go, go with the children, Bela." My father said. "I've got to report to my reserve unit on Wednesday."

"That's a day after tomorrow!" My mother shouted. "Why haven't you told me sooner?"

"I just learned about it this morning myself. There wasn't any chance to postpone it. I tried." He hesitated. "I knew it would come to this. I didn't expect to be called in this soon, but I knew that it was inevitable." He pulled her tenderly to himself.

"We'll send the children ahead," my mother offered, "and I'll stay behind."

"No, that isn't a good idea, dear." He kissed her on the forehead. We have seldom seen our parents in such a display of affection. That in itself was strange, in addition to their open dispute. It added to the gravity of the situation. "No, Bela," he continued. "You must go with the children. The war can't last forever." He hesitated. "If there is one at all." He added.

There was momentary silence. Then, my mother spoke:

"If that's what is best, dear, then that's what we'll do."

Suddenly, my father left the room. He kept clearing his throat all the way to the bathroom. He closed the door behind him, and he let the water run for some time. When he had returned to the living room after having washed his face and hands—he was still drying himself with a small towel—he motioned me to approach.

"Velvele," he addressed me by the endearing Yiddish diminutive, "you are old enough now to be entrusted with an important errand." He paused. "You've been a good boy in the past and fulfilled many important tasks. The one I'm going to ask you to carry out now will be unlike all the others and by far more important."

It was the first time in my memory that my father had taken me into his confidence, and I was frightened. With a trembling voice, he continued: "Now let's see, where was I?" He rubbed his hands together. He always rubbed his hands together when he lacked words. "All right, then, I'll tell you about our plans first. Afterward, you'll get a chance to ask all the questions you want to ask. Is that all right?" He looked anxiously at me.

"That's fine, daddy."

We sat near the living room window, and the sun shone through it making the room bright and happy. Sitting on my father's lap, I felt the joy of life surge through me. I had the awareness of some important task facing me. Without knowing what it was I will have to do, all I could think of was that task. Nothing else mattered. Not my past, nor the present. Only the future had any meaning.

My whole being concentrated on the goal of fulfilling that task: not to disappoint my parents, especially my father. He continued to tell me about the journey I would embark on with my little sister Felusia; about Piotrkow and our grandparents; about all the wonderful things we were going to do when we reunited some day. It made me feel very important, my father confiding in me like that.

"Why must we leave?" I asked. "Why don't you come with us?"

"Try not to ask so many questions, Vilek." My father sighed heavily. "We're doing the best under the circumstances."

"Then, why can't you tell me the truth, daddy? Don't you think I'll understand?" I was nearing tears. He hugged me powerfully, nearly taking my breath away. Then he let out another sigh and exchanged one of those meaningful glances with my mother. "All right," he started, "I'll tell you the way it is, Vilek. We're sending you and Felusia ahead because we want you to be safe."

"But. . . I still don't understand." I insisted.

"Have patience, Velvele." My father pleaded. "Let me come to the point, and we'll see whether you'll understand." My father cleared his throat loudly, like he always did when he lacked words or tried to collect his thoughts. "It's like this, son," he started again, "let me first tell you a little story." I waited patiently, not daring to interrupt, sensing the anguish he was experiencing, and my skin developed goose-bumps in places my father could not see.

"When I was a young man, I wanted to break away from the old traditional ways, and I left my father's home to search a new life for myself and your mother. We came to this city long before you were born. First came your brother Roman; two years later you were born, and six years after that, Felusia came to us. Things were good for us, and we were happy together."

"Then why must we change that now?" I couldn't refrain from asking.

"Because there are ugly things happening now, and your mother and I are concerned about your safety." My father sighed again. "So we're sending you back where we came from."

"Daddy, do you think some day we're going to be able to be like everyone else?" I asked suddenly, and my father looked at me in complete silence.

"You want me to tell you what I really think, Velvele, don't you?"

"Yes, daddy."

"All I can tell you now, is that your mother and I love you all very much," my father kissed me on the forehead, "and that we want you to be safe." He paused painfully. "I can't predict the future, but right now it looks like we'll have to separate for awhile."

"Where are you going, daddy?"

"I don't know that either, Velvele." He squeezed me tightly and kissed me on both cheeks. Unaccustomed to such an effusion of affection from of my father, I naturally thought the worst of the situation. I trembled with the anticipation of things to come, and my father tried his best to assuage my anxiety.

"In a day or two, your mother will follow with Roman. She needs to help me settle a few things here, you understand, don't you?"

I listened silently, afraid if I spoke I'd be in tears.

"When this is all over," my father continued, and I didn't understand what he meant by "this," "I'll follow, too." He added without meeting my eyes, and I knew that he suffered unspeakable doubts himself. "You'll take the 2:30 train for Katowice. Your mother and I will be greatly relieved to know that you and Felusia are both on it." He blew his nose loudly. "Your mother will travel with you as far as Katowice where you'll board the train for Piotrkow. You'll be on your own until you arrive at your grandparents." My father stopped, and his eyes asked my mother whether she had anything to add. She nodded.

"Meanwhile, remember to practice your violin, Velvele." She said.

My father hugged me powerfully, virtually crushing my bones in his hold. I didn't complain, feeling rather secure and good in his embrace. Suddenly, he let go of me and turned to go. "God be with you, my children." I heard him say. He closed the door behind him, giving us no time to argue or ask any further questions.

It was fear mixed with excitement. We were on our first journey alone! My little sister Felusia and I. I felt important, after all, it was I who was responsible for my sister. Early in the morning we were up preparing sandwiches and packing small necessities. By mid-day, we were ready for departure. It was a dreary, cold August day. Some men came to our door to inquire about my father, but he had gone somewhere, my mother told them "he'd return later," she said, and they left. My mother's eyes were reddened and all puffed up, and I knew she must have cried all night. Things were happening too fast, and she had wished they'd slow down somewhat. But they didn't. The men returned a few minutes later.

"Please tell your husband to report immediately. . ." I overheard them say. Then I heard the word "desertion" and "military" but not the words in between. My mother assured the men everything would be fine, and they left without saying goodbye.

"Where'd daddy go?" I asked while my mother was pulling a scarf around my neck and a woolen ski cap on my head. My face was scarcely visible.

"He went to Krakow on business." She replied.

"Did the men want to hurt daddy?" Felusia asked.

"No, my dear." My mother assured the little one. "They're friends of your daddy's. Whatever gave you such a strange idea?" My mother held back her tears, and I could sense that it was a struggle.

"You mustn't ask too many questions, Felusia." Roman stepped in taking the little one by the hand. "Can't you see mama's busy and wants you to help?" He held her coat, and Felusia slipped into it, then the scarf and cap. "Just do what mama tells you to do and leave the questions for some other time." Felusia observed her eldest brother with much admiration. He'd always been good to her and came to her defense during her frequent battles with me. She would miss him.

One hour before the train's departure, we already sat on the platform awaiting our train. "Never saw that many people traveling this time of the year." My mother remarked more to herself than anyone. There were multitudes milling around, some aimlessly, but others were silently sitting on and around their bundles, waiting.

The train was hours late. Railway traffic had seldom been on time before, but the present delay was even greater. The mass of people crowded into the partially occupied compartments, yelling directives and shoving one another.

Suddenly, we heard a voice calling from one of the windows: "Bela! Over here! Bela!" It was my father's boyhood friend from Piotrkow, Max Mandel. "Come quickly!" We ran toward the open window of his compartment. My mother handed Max our luggage, then Felusia and I went through the window as well. Soon, my mother joined us in the compartment, as we sat next to Max' small son Hayim and his pretty niece Nora.

My mother was out of breath. "It was a godsend, I tell you, a miracle to find you here!" She exclaimed, breathing heavily. When they told her they were going all the way to Piotrkow my mother's miracle had grown considerably.

"And we'll be happy to look after the children." Nora said. She was chatting happily with me, her arm over my shoulder, and I felt very comfortable. Nora's long brown hair brushed against my cheeks occasionally, and I inhaled the scent of a mild parfume. I was quickly falling in love with this sixteen year old girl. Feelings of unexplainable pleasure invaded my soul, and I felt a special warmth in the pit of my stomach when her deep brown eyes looked into mine with a reassuring smile. Soon, her protective embrace and the monotonous rocking of the train conspired to put me into an innocent slumber.

On our arrival in Katowice, there was more shouting and shoving as people were seeking to accommodate themselves for whatever destination. Finally, our train for Piotrkow was ready to leave the station.

"Kiss grandmother and grandfather for me." My mother was trying to sound casual but there was a tremor in her voice.

"Don't worry, mama, I'll take care of myself," I sounded as adult as I was able to be under the circumstances, "and Felusia also." I quickly added.

"I know you will, my darling," my mother held back her tears, "after all, I'm counting on you."

"I love you very much, mama." I said, hugging her with all the strength of my arms.

"I love you, too, my darlings, both of you." She hugged Felusia, kissing her on her lips and cheeks, and then me again. "Mind your brother, Felusia, you hear? Mind your older brother." Felusia nodded, smiling, and her pudgy round face was even rounder and pudgier. My mother held us both in a long embrace as the train began to move. She stood on the platform, then walked along the side the moving train as it accelerated. Soon she was left behind, standing there (and I knew she was in tears now) and waving her clean, white kerchief. We waved at her from our window, until only a small dot remained in the distance.

"Come, let's play charades!" Nora captured our attention. Nevertheless, the excitement of the play did not ease the pain of parting from my mother, nor from listening to the cadence of the wheels hitting against the rails. Their persistent melody heralded the ever-increasing distance from my parental home.

During the night, our train pulled into Czegstochowa. Two young soldiers, backpacks, rifles and all the military paraphernalia, climbed into our compartment, and the occupants made extra space for them by squeezing tightly together. The young warriors were loud and arrogant, a bit drunk. They took up most of the bench in front of ours, laughing and joking with the passengers and making terrible eyes at Nora which made us all very uneasy, expecially Max Mandel. Both Max and his son Hayim wore fringed garments of the Hasids, and both wore earlocks.

"We're going to fight the Krauts! Eh, yid? Fight the Krauts for you!" They laughed raucously as they pulled Max' earlock. Max squinted his eyes in pain but did not raise his voice in protest. Neither did the rest of the passengers. Some snickered among themselves, others sat quietly, pretending to sleep.

"Fighting the Krauts for you deserves special consideration, don't you think, Jew?" The one called Yanek chuckled while pulling Max' beard. Max was silent. "Cat got your tongue, eh?" Yanek tormented the man. "It isn't right we should get our heads blown off for you, while you stuff your coffers full of gold and jewelry. Is it now?" He turned to his companion. "I say that calls for a special favor, don't you think?" He was looking directly at Nora and her arm tightened around my shoulder. Nora's face showed no fear, but her arm trembled when Yanek approached. "Come on, Marek," the first soldier urged his companion. "Surely, the Jewish slut wouldn't mind a little kiss for the hero." He bent over Nora, his arm extended. She turned her head.

"What's the matter, Jewess, too proud to talk to a soldier, eh?" Yanek jeered.

"Maybe if we cut your daddy's earlocks, you'd come around and be nice?" Marek joined his comrade. If only my father were present. I wished silently. He'd show these ruffians. I looked at Max Mandel and I felt the fear inside him. It was a fear built up over centuries of torment suffered at the hands of our countrymen, the Christian Poles, who had never been able to accept any Jew in their midst.

"Hey, Marek, never mind the Jewish slut." Yanek took a large swig from the bottle, then handed it to his comrade. Marek followed suit, then both laid down the full length of the bench, pushing all passengers to the floor. Moments later both snored loudly and we let out a sigh of relief.

Within the hour, the train pulled into the train terminal in Radomsko. Our two soldiers hurried with their gear out of the compartment. Nora heaved a sigh of relief.

"This is where we get off," Yanek called from the platform. "Aren't you sorry to see us go, little Jewess?" He mocked simulating a Jewish accent.

Marek approached Nora, leaned over trying to touch her breast. I stepped between her and the soldier. "You leave my sister alone," I said in an unmistakably Polish accent. The soldier laughed uproariously. "Look, Yanek! We've got a fucking Jew hero!"

"Hey, maybe we should put a soldier's uniform on the little Jew?" Yanek suggested. "He might give us a hand chasing the Krauts to Berlin?"

"Please leave, and let my sister be." I said bravely. "She did you no harm!"

Surprised or humored by my challenge, Marek left the compartment throwing a kiss in Nora's direction. "Keep it for us, little Jewess!" He called from the platform.

"Next time we meet, you'll be ready for us, eh?" He made an obscene gesture with his index finger, and Nora turned away blushing.

"That was a brave thing you did, Vilusiek." She hugged me. "That was a very brave thing indeed." She repeated. I felt one foot taller as I happily nestled against her breasts. We talked late into that night, and Nora satisfied my childish curiosity concerning her journey to Piotrkow. It seems, her parents had arranged a match (sheddach) for their daughter, even before her birth, with their lifelong friends, the Rabinowiczes. The Mandels had pledged their first daughter in marriage to their friend's first-born son. It was bashaert, even though the two families had separated in search of a livelihood; Nora's father had joined his brother Max's fur business in Sosnowiec; the Rabinowiczes had moved to Minsk where carpentry was thriving.

As tradition demanded, Nora was informed about her "betrothal" on her thirteenth birthday. She accepted her destiny placidly, as did the women in her family before her on many occasions. Now, even though her parents were no longer alive—they had perished in a terrible train wreck several years back— she was on her way to Piotrkow to fulfill that promise made so long ago.

"Only with my mother, I dared argue the merits of marrying for love." Nora confessed to me. "But she would always insist that love came long after the marriage vows were taken, and oftentimes never." She paused, as if reflecting on the merits of her mother's pronouncement. "Respect for one another and a fierce mutual loyalty are by far the two essential virtues in marriage, my mother insisted."

"And you accepted their condition, Nora?" I asked not without disdain and a propensity for stubbornness.

"It's my parental wish." She said simply. "And I must obey."

At the railway station, upon our arrival in Piotrkow my grandparents met us, uncles and aunts, cousins, and even some dear friends. There was rejoicing but there was also some sadness at parting from our friend Nora. Grandmother thanked the Mandels for their help with "the children."

"We'll be seeing you soon," Nora said holding my hand in hers.

"You must come to visit," I kissed her on the cheek. At the time we had no way of knowing that our paths would cross very soon indeed.

On Friday, September 1, 1939, at 5 o'clock in the morning, the German bombers flew over Piotrkow. It was my first taste of the *Blitzkrieg*. I saw soldiers running to some fortifications they had prepared nearby and, soon, heard the rat-ta-ta-ta rat-ta-ta-ta of the machine-guns. There was a trail of smoke in the sky above, and we rejoiced, until someone said it was one of ours shot down by the attacking *Stukas*. This was also our initiation into the efficient air raids of the German divebombers.

Moments later, the machine-gun emplacement flew sky high; a direct hit of the enemy's bombing skill. But we continued to hear the chattering of other guns from the direction of the old armory.

Then, the sirens wailed letting the people know that they should run for their lives and seek shelter in the trenches which the government had dug previously for that purpose. They were called 'air-raid shelters,' and they appeared in the shape of the letters U or T with no covering above and one entry which also served as an exit. They were eight feet deep and about three feet across; the dimensions of an average grave.

The wailing and hooting of the sirens and factory whistles only added to the confusion. People spilled into the streets, children cried frightened, men cursed, and the womenfolk tried in vain to retain calm.

Grandfather insisted that we were safer in our bedroom than out on the street, so we followed him under the bed: first grandfather, then Felusia whom I followed tightly, and last grandmother who embraced two feather pillows, in her belief that if a bomb went off on top of us the pillows would serve as a buffer against splinters and thus save us from harm.

The raid lasted over an hour and the old armory was in total ruin. Glad to be alive, the people marched wearily back to their homes. I was very quiet. The fires were burning into the night, and the whole horizon had been lit up like from fireworks on a national holiday. In the silence of the night, my thoughts traveled across the great ocean to my relatives in Brooklyn, America. Do they believe us now? I wondered. . .

It was still a little time before dinner, and Isaac had brought the paper for his father to read.

On that Friday, September 1, 1939, which we had spent in the air-raid shelter in Piotrkow, The title page of the *New York Times* read in bold extra large letters:

GERMAN ARMY ATTACKS POLAND; CITIES BOMBED, PORT BLOCKADED; DANZIG IS ACCEPTED INTO REICH.

For the benefit of his listeners, Mickey proceeded to recite the various headlines across the top of the page:

BRITISH MOBILIZING—HOSTILITIES BEGUN—FREE CITY SEIZED—HITLER ACTS AGAINST POLAND—WARSAW REPORTS GERMAN OFFENSIVE MOVING ON THREE OBJECTIVES—HITLER GIVES WORD, ACCUSES WARSAW OF APPEAL TO ARMS—HITLER TELLS REICHSTAG "BOMB WILL BE MET BY BOMB"—SOVIET RATIFIES REICH NON-AGGRESSION PACT—BRITISH CHILDREN TAKEN FROM CITIES.

Mickey went on for a few more minutes reading here and there between the lines and skipping to the more important items. When he finished, he put down the paper and took off his glasses to wipe them clean. They were all steamed up, and he was unable to continue. Fay and the two sons listened in silence. They sat without saying a word even after Mickey had stopped reading.

"They must be there by now, Fay." He spoke almost in a whisper. "Lord, forgive us."

"Now, Mickey, don't go blaming yourself for something you couldn't have helped anyway." Fay admonished her husband. "Even mighty England is atremble."

"No, mama, that's not true." Isaac spoke for the first time since those letters had been written to Poland. He had kept to himself most of the time since then. "England isn't trembling. It just makes sure that all the children are safe and out of the cities."

"The children, think of the children, Fay." Mickey moaned.

"There's nothing you can do about it now, Mickey. Pray to God for their safety." Fay continued to move her lips in prayer while the others rummaged through the paper eager to find some encouraging news.

Looking out the window, we saw a large cloud of smoke toward the east side of the town, the area where the military arsenal was situated. I listened to the bells of the fire trucks and people shouting, "The town's on fire!"

Down the street, there were several policemen leading a handcuffed man between them dressed in a priest's cassock. I tugged my grandfather's coat.

"A real spy, grandfather!" I said excitedly. "They caught a spy!"

"I knew there was something sinister about this sudden air-raid," my grandfather said.

"What would they want with a priest, grandfather?" I asked.

"He's not a priest, Vilek. He's a spy dressed up as a priest." My grandfather said with the authority of an expert. "No priest would spy for the enemy." Grandfather immediately went on to tell me about World War I, the way he always remembered it and as I have heard it from his mouth many times. While I listened to my grandfather, I watched the small figure in a priest's cassock, walking rapidly and hunched over with his hands cuffed behind his back. He looked nervous and thoroughly beaten. He walked with a slight shuffle, eyes peeled to the ground. The handcuffs must make it terribly uncomfortable for him to move forward, I thought to myself. A mob of children soon circled the small group with the prisoner, snickering and spitting in his face.

"Dirty traitor!" They shouted. "Nazi pig!" They spat and threw rocks and the policemen walked along indifferently. Pity had crept into my heart.

Will he be shot by a firing squad? Will they blindfold him? I wondered. I had learned from spy movies that he had a choice. They'd even offer him a cigarette.

"How will he die, grandfather?" I asked. "Will he have a trial?"

"Makes no difference, my boy." My grandfather became suddenly pensive. "One thing is certain, Velvele. He's as good as dead."

Grandfather fell silent and the crowd had moved from our view. I knew not to disturb him when he was that way. I put my hand into his and squeezed it affectionately. He became melancholy, and for those tense few moments heightened by thoughts of death we forgot our differences. In total silence, a mysterious bond was tied between two disparate generations, a world apart yet unified by the solemnity of man's ultimate destiny. "I love you, gramps." I said softly and hugged him as I never did before.

My maternal grandfather, Srulko Stybel, was also known in the shtetl by the nickname *Malpo* (the monkey) because, I guess, he had partially earned a living by entertaining people. He played the fiddle at all kinds of socials, and he was also a barber by trade. As a barber, he was often called on to administer herbal "cures" and soon became known throughout the entire area for his great skill as a *feltscher*, a sort of 'witch doctor.'

Srulko was almost seventy years old, but one couldn't tell from his youthful appearance. Anyway, no one would believe it due to his extremely active life. My grandfather was a devout Hasid and a great scholar of the Mishnah. Of slight stature, he sported a goatee and a splendid Franz Josef mustache which were very much in fashion. The handle-bar was an especial source of pride, and he spent hours grooming and cultivating it.

Grandmother Rachel was a wigmaker. Hasidic hygiene dictated that women shave their heads. She wore one of her wigs herself, and I was astonished at seeing her remove it before bed time exposing a completely shaven skull.

"Why is grandma's head shaven?" I asked my grandfather.

"So that she can wear a wig." He replied. He was reluctant to talk about issues concerning the Law.

"Why are you not permitted to cut your own hair?"

"Because it's the Law." He replied.

"Is there one Law for men and another Law for women?" I asked to my grandfather's great annoyance.

"The Law is the Law, Velvele, and you ask too many questions."

"You always taught me to be inquisitive, zeyde." He liked to be addressed by the Yiddish equivalent for grandpa. I looked him straight in the eyes, he smiled knowing that I wouldn't let him off easily.

"We can question everything *except* the Law, Velvele." He emphasized "except," and the discussion had come to an abrupt end.

They were decent and kind people, Srulko and Rachel, my maternal grandparents. They walked their quiet lives without harming anyone, never a problem that couldn't be resolved by looking into the Law. Respected in their community and by their Christian neighbors, my grandparents pursued an honest existence, endowed with that special dignity which comes with birth and cannot be learned or acquired through experience.

"Respect people and revere life, my boy," my grandfather liked to remind me during his better moments, "and remember also to practice on your violin. Music is one of the finer things in life." He prided himself of the fact that his favorite grandson had inherited his musical talents.

There was plenty of food for supper the night following the bombardment. My grandparents made a ritual of eating even the smallest morsel of food. First, there was a prayer of thanksgiving; a lively conversation followed. Each meal episode was another lesson. Grandmother called these lessons 'memory capsules.' She said to us: "Paint a picture in your mind, children. And when later years come around, you'll have something to fall back on."

"But what if our pictures are sad, grandma?" I asked.

"Sad or happy, they make up life." My grandmother answered. "Remember, and learn." Early next morning a messenger arrived from the Jewish Council of Elders. "There's a meeting tonight at the synagogue, Srulko." He announced. "Can we expect you there?"

"Haven't I been there each time you've called a meeting?" Srulko challenged the messenger, Isaac, the shtetl *gabbah,* Yiddish for 'keeper of the house of worship.'

"Of course, *rav* Srulko." The gabbah hastened to add. "A meeting of elders wouldn't be a meeting without you." He knew how to get on my grandfather's good side. Srulko smiled satisfied.

"Go, Isaac, and tell them I'll be there."

The patriarchs of the Jewish community met regularly under the present leadership of the wealthy produce merchant Haskel Warszawski. But this was not going to be a 'regular' meeting. The elders gathered in the sanctuary of the Great Synagogue of Piotrkow to deliberate on an important issue: what to do in case of another bombardment.

"Szpitalna Street was razed. The old artillery barracks and the arsenal have gone up in flames." Warszawski announced solemnly. "The arsenal workers were the first war fatalities in Piotrkow."

"Anyone we know?" Someone asked.

"Some Gentiles."

"That's all?"

"Fortunately, the buildings on Szpitalna were vacant." Warszawski added. "Many Jewish families live there, you know."

"Praised be the Lord."

"Amen." All said in unison.

"That isn't what we came to discuss," the *gabbah* interrupted. "We came together to decide who would be assigned what shelter when the bombing starts up again."

"All right, then, we all know that the *mikvah* has the thickest walls of any building in town. The basement is as solid as a fortress. There's water, and there's heat. In a word, it's the ideal place to wait out any earth shaking event." Warszawski spoke in a sing-song of the Hasidim.

The *mikvah* was the community ritual bathhouse. Not unlike the ancient Roman bathhouses, the mikvah boasted massive rock walls and a sufficient supply of water from its underground wells. Everyone agreed, the bathhouse would make an ideal air-raid shelter. There was only one problem: there were about four thousand Jewish families in Piotrkow, while the *mikvah* could barely hold three hundred people. How to accommodate the remaining fourteen thousand seven hundred persons?

Felix Rabinowicz, a young man newly arrived from Minsk, suggested a solution: "In Minsk we drew lots for the *mikvah*, even in normal times."

Lots were drawn, and alternate shelters were provided for those who had not drawn the mikvah. The community took care of its own.

"Anyway, who can tell where the bombs will fall?" Someone remarked.

"We're all in the power of the Almighty, blessed be He."

"Amen." Resounded in unison.

"May God be with us all." Rabbi Lubianski intoned, "He alone holds our fate in His hands." The rabbi added, but he was glad to have drawn the *mikvah* for himself and his family.

My grandfather had drawn the *mikvah* lot, but looking at him one would think he hadn't. "Rachel, start packing," he said to my grandmother on his return home, "I've drawn a lot for the *mikvah*, and that's where you and the children must move tonight."

"Aren't you going with us, gramps?" I asked with concern.

"No, my child," he said softly. "Come what may, I'm going to die in my own bed."

"You're not too old to revere life, gramps." I reminded him. The old man was silent. Grandmother put up a good argument against grandfather's obstinancy. All to no avail. Once Srulko had made up his mind, it was impossible to sway him. The argument would end with my grandmother weeping while my grandfather stomped his feet obstinately to the delight of the busybodies next door. Again, my grandmother gave in with a few words of warning:

"Remember to run down to the cellar when the raid comes."

"I'll die in my own bed, Rachel." Was my grandfather's reply.

We were gathering a few essentials and a lot of bedding when we heard the now familiar humming of the airplanes. Moments later, the house shook in its foundations.

"The Stukas are here!" I yelled. I was frightened. I had quickly learned to recognize the characteristic sounds of the dive bombers.

We hurried down to the cellar. Even my grandfather skipped several steps at a time. As the tremors approached, sirens were wailing everywhere. It was night and the whole horizon was lit up in spectacular flashes and fires. We lay in the cellar, Felusia and I between our grandparents who put pillows and bedding on top of us. But I didn't believe that my grandparents had too much faith in the safety of the bedding because, as we lay there on the barren floor, they kept praying to the Lord without interruption. "Pray, children, pray." They encouraged us. "We're in the hands of the Lord."

Between prayers, I heard the neighbors complain about an antiaircraft emplacement on the rooftop of the ancient castle. We heard the sound of the machine gun—which proved ineffective against the raiders—followed each time by a powerful quake.

Sustained bombardment lasted more than an hour, and a great deal of damage was done. My pulse throbbed with excitement. It was an emotion I had never experienced before, and I was unable to explain my subsequent actions. I ran out into the open before anyone could caution me. There were people already on the street, calling out names, adults holding on to impatient children who kept asking questions without response.

Some of the people looked around for more secure shelter, others were searching for their kin. The surprise attack caught many unawares. By now, it was no secret that the destruction was the work of the newest and fastest attack-bombers. They swooped down on us from nowhere, catching many pedestrians on their way from work as well as some strollers taking advantage of the nice weather.

Dead were everywhere. Bodies of men, women and children lay strewn about in great disarray. As I looked at their faces, I saw in most evidence of surprise; a puzzling, questioning grimace caught at the moment of death. Others lay mortally wounded, crying out for help, moaning with pain, with head wounds or limbs torn from their bodies. Blood was everywhere on the pavement.

At first, I tried to resist the reality of the abhorrent picture, make myself believe it was only an illusion, my eyes and my senses playing tricks on me. Soon, however, the truth became inescapable. Those were clearly the mangled bodies of people, my friends and neighbors. I looked at them in shock and bewilderment, trying to fight the oncoming nausea. The sight got the better of my will, and I vomitted violently in the midst of all the carnage.

Buildings were on fire, many from their foundations all the way to the rooftops. Some were smoldering ruins. The acrid smell of sulfur was everywhere. That's what bombs are made of. I thought to myself. That smell, and the smoke that filled the air, brought shouts of "gas" among the hysterical people. The initial warning must have come from one who was familiar with World War I. Frightened, I ran home, breathlessly reporting to family and friends what I had seen. Were it not for the worry I had caused concerning my safety, I might have caught a few well-deserved licks on the seat of my pants. Everyone was relieved, and the punishment was quickly forgotten.

"Don't you ever do a thing like that, young man." My grandfather admonished, and I blushed silently.

"Let this be a lesson for all of us." My grandmother said. "We must pack up and leave for the mikvah this very minute."

"The castle gun emplacements are gone now, so I'll be safe here." My grandfather was happy he could now give a valid excuse for staying behind. Nobody argued. We gathered our belongings and set out for the nearby *mikvah*.

Grandmother covered our heads with pillows and told us to walk quickly without looking at the destruction around us. "Don't look Felusia! Look up straight, little one!" She urged my sister, gently holding on to the tiny hand and pulling her ahead. My grandmother kept praying and Felusia cried, frightened. The Red Cross appeared on the scene, busily collecting the wounded and the dead.

On the sidewalk, to our left, there lay a woman clutching two infants to her bosom. All three were burned to a crisp. "Don't look, children!" My grandmother warned, but it was too late. We saw the frightful sight, and it was etched forever into our memory.

We reached the *mikvah*. Preceded by the humming of the aircraft, the earth shook again with violent explosions. The Stukas were back for another raid, and they struck with formidable force. The feeble ticking of the anti-aircraft guns mixed with the detonations of the bombs. The earth trembled mightily under the impact of this man-made earthquake. First, we would hear a loud and persistent whistle as if a heavy object came hurtling through space, then followed a loud bang that shook the earth all around us. Some of the bombs exploded a good distance away. Others hit very close to the mikvah. But the whistle we heard hovered imminently over our heads or so it seemed. We expected a bomb to fall on our heads and we made sure the pillows sheltered us throughout.

"What's going to happen to the dead people?" I asked my grandmother.

"They'll go to heaven to protect us from all evil." She replied.

"Will they, grandma?"

"They will. Don't you doubt that, child."

I wished I could have believed my grandmother, but the whole idea of heaven and protection flew out of the window with the first air raid and the infants that burned to a crisp. Still, to be on the safe side, I couldn't shake the feeling that maybe there is a remote chance that such things really happen; I left myself open to doubt. Another raid was in progress, and I prayed silently to those heavenly spirits.

The *mikvah* had no windows. We searched for "our" place in candlelight. All sorts of people were already there: Jews, Christians, a few local Gypsies, even the family of Min Lee, the Chinese grocer. Seems that no one was turned away, even though they hadn't drawn lots. The *mikvah* was filled to the very last corner, every inch of it there were people bedded down for the duration of the bombardment. Our friend, Shlomo Zaplocki, saved us a small spot in the corner next to his family. We were close to the wrought iron staircase leading to the ritual baths below and therefore in the line of great traffic, but my grandmother didn't complain. She bedded us down on the earthen floor, trying to make us as comfortable as circumstances permitted.

"Now, try to get a little sleep, children." She said, having finished her task. We closed our eyes, but we were unable to fall asleep. The walls of the *mikvah* shook repeatedly, people prayed, fear and excitement mingled to form an element of suspense. By now, I had learned to accept the unexpected. Was that part of life? I dared not ask my grandmother, for she had enough on her mind already. I promised myself to ask my mother, if I remembered.

The worshippers addressed their gods in different languages, expressing remorse about one thing or another, making assurances and promising change. After all, it isn't everyday one listens simultaneously to so many tongues. Surely, God must have many assistants and interpreters keeping Him forever informed about the activity of His subjects.

"Why did these people commit all those wicked deeds, grandma?" I asked in a hushed voice, noticing that Felusia had fallen asleep.

"I don't really know, my dear boy. I don't know." My grandmother replied.

"Now, they ask forgiveness, grandma."

"They feel remorse, child."

"Do you think God listens to us, grandma?" I persisted.

"Are we not a people exiled and persecuted?" She responded with her own question.

"I. . .I guess." I said unconvincingly.

"Are we not hated by most people?" She asked again.

I was silent, nodding my head without comprehension. I was suddenly reminded of an appalling incident that occurred not long ago; the first time I had made the discovery of what it is like to be hated for no apparent reason. Until that day I didn't know how intense that hatred was.

It happened while I was on the way home from school. A small group of my Christian schoolmates approached. As a precaution, I stepped from the sidewalk onto the street.—I remembered my mother's distant admonishments to stay out of trouble—and I had sensed trouble just looking at those boys.

My apparent humility didn't appease my adversaries. The gang fell upon me, and I had no recourse but to defend myself. Amused adults cheered with no intention to stop the fight. It was the first time I had heard the expression "dirty Jew" shouted, though I knew I was as much a Pole as they. My father left home to join our Armed Forces, and the language we spoke at home was Polish. That was the first time, too, I had learned what it meant when some-one was an "anti-Semite."

My face was soon covered with blood streaming from my fractured nose. Only then did they have enough. "Filthy scum!" They called after me, as I walked away. "Jew, go to Palestine!"

The nose kept on bleeding, but my soul was scarred forever. It hurt to be called "dirty Jew" when I always considered myself a "clean Polish boy."

"Is it not true that misery like everything becomes a habit, when you've lived with it for a long time?" My grandmother startled me out of my rev-erie.

"I don't know, grandma." I answered honestly.

"The Jewish people began their wailing with the final destruction of the temple in Jerusalem. Ever since that day, we address the Lord with much worry and suffering. It is written in our faces. God looks at us from on up high and asks his angels: 'Who are these wretched people?' And His angels reply: 'They're Your chosen people, Lord.' The Lord becomes angry. 'Go on!' He shouts at His helpers. 'Give them all they ask for! I can't bear to look at those miserable faces any longer!'"

Grandmother Rachel was a simple woman. She made up simple explana-tions for complex issues. I wasn't satisfied with my grandmother's explana-tions, but I wasn't going to challenge her. That would surely hurt her feel-ings. I decided to wait and ask my mother just as soon as she arrived in Piotrkow.

"So you see, Vilek," my grandmother concluded, "God orders, and His word is obeyed instantly." She hugged me to her bosom and kissed me on both cheeks. It felt wonderful to be hugged and kissed by my grandmother.

Though I wasn't able to accept my grandmother's story, I was still amazed that with all the havoc raging on the outside, she was able to regard the world with a healthy sense of humor.

The bombardment lasted five days and four nights, but it seemed much longer than that. We were about to run short of food supplies, when the tremor of the exploding bombs was joined by heavy artillery bombardment.

"Grandma, can you hear?" I asked her excitedly. "Now, there is ground artillery as well." She looked at me puzzled.

"So? What does that mean?" She asked, more to humor me than out of curiosity.

"Don't you know, grandma? It means that the Germans are advancing on the ground as well." I was proud of having remembered the lessons of history. World War I was fought on our soil. That was only twenty years ago. A little more than a hundred years had gone by from the time the grand French Armies under Napoleon passed this way. Napoleon was a great artillery general, and cannons were the main implements of destruction for him. There were no planes then, so artillery had to fulfill their function as well.

"Why must some people always look for ways to destroy others, grandma?" I felt that my grandmother owed me this one.

"It's the way God in His infinite wisdom tests his creations." She replied. Now it was my turn to be puzzled.

"So all this is only a test, grandma?" I asked. "Those poor people who died in the bombing; the burnt bodies of the infants, all that was only a sign that God was testing us?" The humorous twinkle in my grandmother's eye was gone. She looked suddenly very sad, and I could not guess whether her sadness was for me or for all those others who were no longer among the living. Whichever it was, I made a silent oath that someday (if I should be destined to remain alive) I would dedicate the remainder of my days to probe into the obscure nature of these things.

"We are not to question the ways of our Lord." My grandmother concluded. I had heard that argument before, and I learned to accept its ultimate though imperfect resolution. My silence told my grandmother that I understood her predicament. She let out a sigh of relief. The matter was closed.

When the whistling and explosions had stopped, it became so quiet that it had seemed all life had ceased. We speculated on the significance of that silence. The optimists maintained that the enemy had been repulsed; the pessimists knew that it was all over for us. The enemy was knocking at our doorstep.

Suddenly, we heard urgent voices behind the massive *mikvah* door. No one dared step forward to ask who it was on the outside. In the midst of all that, the Stukas returned and the bombardment resumed. The earth shook again, and the explosions came closer than before.

"For God's sake, let us inside!" The voices pleaded in Yiddish, and I thought I recognized the woman. But I remained crouched against the wall, paralyzed with fear. "Grandma, make them open the door!" I begged, for I now clearly recalled Nora's voice as the one begging entry. "It's our friend, Nora! The one from the train!"

"You can't be too sure, child." Grandmother trembled. "It could be anyone out there. We ought to be careful. Better leave things the way they are."

"I can tell it's Nora's voice. I'm sure it is, grandma. You remember Nora, don't you, grandma, the girl who helped us out on the train from Katowice?"

After some more pleading, Shlomo Ganev Zaplocki, the grocer, unbolted the door, with a loud prayer on his lips and let the desperate group inside. It was Nora, her uncle Max Mandel, and his son Hayim.

"Hear oh Israel, the Lord our God, the Lord is one," the congregants prayed in gratitude for the safety of the newcomers.

I ran to Nora, she hugged me and kissed my cheek. I had fallen secretely in love with the beautiful girl, though I realized she was much too old for me. Her chestnut hair fell freely down to her shoulders. The deep brown eyes spoke kindness and innocence. I placed my arms round her waist, my face close to her, almost touching her breasts, and I inhaled the sweet scent of her body, wishing she were five years younger.

While her uncle Max was busy sharing the long awaited news of the outside world, I led Nora toward my grandmother who promptly thanked the girl for having helped us on the train and offered to share our modest corner of the mikvah with the new arrivals. Nora nodded gratefully, and I was glad.

Max Mandel came to the *mikvah* in search of a minyan on the occasion of his son Hayim's barmitzvah. On this day, Hayim was to become an adult, in keeping with the age-old Jewish ritual. Max came from an air raid shelter on Marszalkowska Street, a predominantly Gentile part of town, where he was unable to gather the required ten adult Jews for the minyan. That was when he had decided to take the risk of running over to the *mikvah* during a lull in the bombardment. When things became quieter they came running.

Down the narrow steps to the ritual baths, I observed the preparations for the barmitzvah ceremony to sanctify Hayim Mandel. A makeshift altar, two suitcases covered over with a prayer shawl, waserected in the middle of the large hall. Shlomo the grocer donated two candles, prized items because they were becoming scarce. The candles were lit and placed in the middle of the altar. Men, wearing their prayer shawls, assembled in prayer around the makeshift altar. The women stood in a group apart, their heads covered in festive headgear, praying in harmony with their men. Orthodox tradition insisted on the separation of the sexes during worship. The Law had to be obeyed.

The worshipers' swaying figures threw sinister shadows onto the wall. I looked on fascinated, but the strange ceremony seemed solemn and frightening. I saw Hayim's diminutive figure, totally enveloped in the ceremonial prayer shawl. In the flickering candle light, the boy looked terribly frail and tiny for someone thirteen years old. He seemed hesitant, perhaps afraid, and I was glad it wasn't me in his place.

The ceremony began. Isaac the *gabbah* led the congregants in prayer with all the dignity of his position as the keeper of the temple.

"*Borchu et Adonai hamvorah, Baruch Adonai hamvorach leolam vaed. . .*"

"I now accept my faith and the faith of my fathers with all the responsibilities attached thereto. . ." Hayim intoned in his clear boy's soprano.

For the first time in his life, Hayim put on the sacred phylacteries, the *t'filin*. He placed one on his forehead and the other in the pit of his elbow. The small cubes contained excerpts from the Torah and Hayim would repeat the ritual for the rest of his life during worship. They were an integral part of the past and the present, as they were to become Hayim's strength of the future. The worshippers swayed to and fro in rhythmic Hasidic chant and clapped their hands to its cadence. Time fused past and present into the mysterious proceedings of that memorable evening; the chanting and clapping and the bombing continued.

"*Mazal tov, mazal tov.*" "Good luck, good luck."

The Bar Mitzvah ceremony had taken the better part of the night as the ground continued to tremble. But the initial fear of the unexpected had by now lessened, and the ceremony had an uplifting effect of those present. We had scarcely realized during those hours of celebration that it was already the tenth day we had been in hiding.

The ceremony had come to a close, and the participants rejoined their families. Felix sat down silently nearby.

"Just for a while." He said with a shy smile. He seemed pensive and depressed. His dark eyes shone out of their deep sockets reflecting the candle light. I strained to observe this man who had come to us as a stranger and now became one of us. He stood tall among native Poles; his six feet and four inches towered above the rest. He was lean and muscular, and I imagined his physical strength to be great. He seemed to be in good health, yet since the time I had first laid eyes on him he seldom cracked a smile. He took life seriously and expected others to act likewise.

There was a mystery surrounding this stranger I could not quite explain. Like at this very moment, crouching against the wall without saying a word to anyone, immersed in thought and making me feel that I'd feel very bad if I dared to break that silence.

"Were you ever barmitzvah, Felix?" I couldn't resist asking.

"I was. My family insisted." He said softly. "It's such utter nonsense." He got angry for no apparent reason. "No one matures through ceremony." He was excited. I suspected that he was trying to show off for Nora's benefit, though I didn't understand why anyone would want to do such a thing. I observed her from the corner of my eye and caught her hanging on Felix' lips admiringly. It was all so puzzling to me, and I resolved to remain silent.

Anyway, nearby explosions interrupted Felix' performance. He got up from the floor and walked away without a word to anyone. I heard him muttering to himself, and I felt a sudden pity for him. He was the typical man in the middle; distrusted by all those who didn't understand him, feared by those who did, persecuted by both.

It was a dark but unquiet night. We lay still, Nora and I, arm in arm and body to body. It was pure innocent closeness. Outside the sky was crimson with the multitude of fires and the earth shook often.

2

The bombardment stopped. The ground rested. We waited patiently expecting a resumption. The people lit candles and chanted prayers. By now, anxiety had sculptured furrows on the faces of the elderly.

"What do we do now?" Someone asked.

"We must be patient." A voice responded.

"We must wait."

"Wait? Wait for what?"

"Just wait. Time will tell."

A learned rabbi once said that there is perhaps one cardinal sin: impatience. Because of it we were driven out of paradise, and for the same reason we cannot return. I looked at Nora lovingly, and she squeezed my hand in return. I knew that this part of my life would remain for me full of sunshine and happy feelings in spite of the dark and sinister sounds.

We waited one whole day and nothing happened. I suddenly began to worry that a bomb might have landed on Zamkowa and brought it crashing down on my grandfather's head. I missed him terribly, and thinking myself safe and my grandfather in danger of his life accentuated my longing for the dear old man. But there was not much at present I could do about it. Waiting was becoming a way of life for us all.

"Why not get out and take a look around?" A voice suggested, and I thought I recognized Felix. "We can't stay here idle forever."

We kept silent, fearful that we might be called on to venture outside.

"Who'll be the first?"

The men looked at each other in the candle light, none having the courage to challenge the other nor to volunteer. Families clustered together, seeking security in closeness and common concern. I saw Felix unbolt the heavy *mikvah* door, and I ran to join him. Moments later, I breathed the stagnant air of the defeated town.

All that remained of some houses were mere skeletons or only a grotesque chimney as a sole reminder of erstwhile domesticity. Now and then, an entire wall stood solidly, without apparent support, as if miraculously left intact. Plumbing pipes wound their way to former bathrooms and kitchens. Solitary sinks and bathtubs hung in mid air.

Here and there, detachments of the once proud Polish Army units, now *Kriegsgefangene*—prisoners of war—stripped of their military insignia and guarded by the invaders, marched by mourned by their countrymen who stood silently on the crowded sidewalks with tears in their eyes.

The German's won! I suddenly realized. Our soldiers are prisoners, and the invader is victorious!

Our own soldiers looked unhappy and apologetic. They didn't sing war songs as they shuffled on in the middle of the road through the dust and rubble. They looked weary and hungry, and their once shiny uniforms hung from their bodies in shreds. Some walked on crutches, and others were helped by their comrades, now and then looking with fear at their captors who marched alongside the prisoners. To think that only a few weeks ago we were able to believe in the invincibility of the Polish Army.

Most of the Germans were very young and fair, rosy-cheeked, smiling with a happy appearance. They were wearing remarkably clean and well-fitting uniforms of a grey-green color. They held rifles and automatic weapons at the ready, aimed at the column of their P.O.W.'s. As I came very close to one of them, I noticed that he wore a belt secured by a buckle with a nice inscription on it: *Gott mit uns,* which meant "God is with us." I remember thinking that soldiers who wear such buckles with God inscribed on them can't be all bad.

The Germans walked with a cadence to their step; a lively gait of self-confidence. I thought to myself: What am I going to tell the others waiting in the *mikvah*? Surely, they must have guessed the truth by now? I was unable to think of anything that would soften the blow.

Soon, children appeared and followed alongside the invaders, begging for handouts. The *Wehrmacht* men seemed kind tossing candy or an unusual looking coin into the crowd. The children scrambled for the "charity," and it was then I'd learned that there was no reward for the slow and the weak.

The results of the *Blitzkrieg*—the lightning war—were most heavily felt by the homeless. They wandered forlorn, seeking shelter and salvaging whatever their buried property and mounds of debris would yield. Some sat resignedly in the rubble of their erstwhile homes, stunned and unable to mourn.

On the surface, the town seemed tranquil. The silence of smouldering ruins was only occasionally disturbed by human outcry. I passed the public square in front of the great Cathedral where the air raid shelters had been dug only a few weeks ago. Crowds were gathered while some workers labored feverishly digging at the entrance. Seems that the trenches had been converted into a common grave for many who sought its safety. "Any victims?" Someone asked.

"Many. Buried alive. Didn't have a chance." Another voice said.

"Didn't they tell us it was safe?"

The diggers tried to make their way into the trench at the far end where the entrance used to be. As they approached their goal, bodies were visible, piled on one another as though trying to get out into the open, expression of terror on their faces.

"Why dig up their bloody bones?" Someone asked. "Why not let the dead lie buried?"

The remark shocked and saddened me. How could anyone say such a thing? I thought to myself. It was then I learned that some people have no reverence for the dead, nor do they respect another's grief.

From a distance, I could see my grandfather waving at us as we approached our home. "Grandpa!" I rushed into my grandfather's arms and my happiness had no bounds. I gave him a powerful hug.

"Careful, Velvele, or you might accomplish that which the enemy had been unable to do." He smiled, and I knew he was equally pleased to see all of us.

One of the German garrisons established its quarters in the ancient castle around the corner from Zamkowa 20. We were already experiencing a shortage of food; bread and potatoes were sold at outrageous prices on the black market which only the affluent could afford to pay.

"What are we going to eat, grandma?" I asked, looking at the furrows of worry on her forehead.

"We'll manage, my dear." She murmured in response. "Don't you worry, Vilek, we won't starve."

My grandfather went up to the attic where he had hidden a large box full of worthless rubles from the time of the czarist occupation of Poland. He brought it down with him, counted the money several times and said proudly: "If only the Russians had come instead of the Germans, we would be rich today." My grandmother shook her head benignly.

"How many times have you wished for this worthless paper to turn into money?" She asked. "Don't you know by now that things don't go backward? What's gone is gone, Srulko. So why don't you throw the rubles away. They might get us into trouble with the Germans."

My grandmother was thrifty as ever, counting her meager savings and apportioning a certain amount to each day. With the expected arrival of my mother and Roman any day, additional resources would be needed. My grandparents bickered about the "additional mouths to feed," and the hardship that was sure to come.

The twentieth of November, 1939, had come. The sun rose on a cold winter morning, and the earth was covered with a thick blanket of snow.

Winter could be very unfriendly in those parts of Poland. Thus far, temperatures had only reached a harmless minus fifteen degrees Celsius. There was no significant windchill, and the morning was pleasant by our standards.

I was on my way to the well, the yoke across my shoulders, two buckets hanging one on each side. The well was about three kilometers away from our home, but it was the only source of fresh water for the neighborhood. On my way back, I took the longer route through Marszalkowska Street which took me by the front gates of the castle. I stopped to rest, released the buckets and straightened out my back. The sentry's eyes peered through the narrow slits in his ski-mask and his breath steamed from beneath the wool into the open air.

I raised my hand high into the air in the familiar Nazi salute. "*Heil* Hitler!" I said crisply.

"*Heil* Hitler!" The sentry responded.

I stomped my feet and swung my arms around my back to keep circulation and shake the stiffness out of my joints. The sentry came toward me.

"Are you German?" He asked in his language.

"My father's German." I lied. "We're from Upper Silesia. "My mother's only half German."

"Oh, you're *Volksdeutscher!*" The sentry's attitude became friendlier, and I was happy that he didn't inquire into the whereabouts of my father.

"Is there anything I could do here to earn a little food?" I asked.

"*Ja.*" A second sentry joined in. "You have a pretty sister? You know, woman, pretty woman?" He made a hand gesture I didn't understand. "We want fucky-fucky, you know? Yes?" He laughed uproariously, but I failed to understand the meaning of his request even though he accompanied it with explicit gestures.

"I have a sister," I informed them innocently. "She's seven years old . . . well, not really seven. . . going on seven." I stammered, embarrassed to have added six months to my sister's age. There was another burst of hilarity.

"Go home and come back when she's older!"

My first acquaintance didn't laugh. He scolded his companion with his eyes before turning toward me.

"*Ja,* we must find something for our landspeople." He said cheerfully. "We mustn't let you starve. After all, we have come to liberate you. We're fighting for you, aren't we?" He paused, measuring me from head to toe. "You're awfully small for your age, aren't you? Haven't your folks been feeding you properly?" He winked with his left eye. I smiled. "Say, you haven't told me your name."

"Vilek. . . really it's Wilhelm. They call me Vilek here."

"We'll call you Wilhelm, okay? And for short, we might call you Willi. Good?"

"That's fine with me." I responded smiling. "All I want is to earn some food for the family. I want to work."

"Hey! Hans!" The guard called a passer-by, a tall, rather heavy-set private. "Take this young fellow to see the corporal. He's looking for a job. He's German." He explained my presence to his comrade, then he turned to me again. "Go with Hans Müller, he'll take you to our corporal." He spoke in German. I remembered the salute before turning to go.

"*Heil* Hitler!" I extended my right arm its full length.

"*Heil* Hitler!" Both men responded. "Come along!" Müller commanded brusquely. I left my yoke attached to the two buckets of water in front of the guardhouse and followed behind Müller.

We walked through the arched corridors of the ancient castle. In the course of history, those arched, musty walls have housed many invaders. Each had come to devastate the fertile valleys of Poland, to kill its men and rape its women. Hostile armies had trampled the fields under the hoofs of horses and the feet of soldiers. Most of them were driven back, others had crossed this country; the gateway to the West and to the East. But the old castle was host to the victor and the vanquished alike.

My guide knocked respectfully at a door marked *Unteroffizier* Boost. "Come in!" A voice told us to enter. Inside, Corporal Boost sat comfortably in an old rocking chair, a pipe between his nicotine-stained teeth, reading a newspaper.

"What have we got here?" He inquired with a friendly smile.

"*Heil* Hitler! *Herr Unteroffizier* Boost, begging your pardon," private Müller saluted his superior, "young Willi here wants to work for us. Found him begging outside." Müller stood at attention, so did I. I didn't like the term he used to describe my inquiry.

Boost stood up reluctantly. He responded to Müller's "Heil" with a common greeting. "Thank you, Müller, that'll be all." Müller snapped another "Heil" at his superior, raising his arm in the Nazi salute, and I flinched at the sudden thud of his boot heels as he brought them together with a violent movement. He made an impeccable about-face and left the room. Boost followed the soldier with his smiling eyes until the latter closed the door behind him.

The corporal was a tall, skinny man. He wore his uniform well, he was neat, but not overly meticulous. A crop of unruly blond hair covered his rather large head. His hand was gentle when it rested on my shoulder.

"You'll shine our boots, wash dishes, and clean up the place in the evenings." Boost said, smiling. "Can you do all that? Will you be our houseboy?" He paused, as if measuring me from head to toe. "You know, that can be too big a job for a little fellow such as you." Though he grinned encouragingly, his deep blue eyes expressed genuine concern. I knew this man was the enemy, but I was unable to dislike him. My conscience dictated caution, but some mysterious voice inside me told me to trust him.

"Yes, I know, *Herr Unteroffizier*, but I want to earn some food for my family. I'm not afraid to work and I cannot afford to be idle." He smiled again.

"Very well, then," Boost said, "come along and I'll explain your duties and introduce you to my comrades."

He went on ahead, and I followed. We entered the room which he occupied along with seven enlisted men. They were all part of the food-storage and transportation detachment, the *Verpflegungskompanie*, an impressive long name to describe a simple task. Boost was the corporal in charge.

The men were in the middle of a meal when we had entered. The first to see Boost jumped to his feet and yelled "Attention!" Everyone stood at attention, arms outstretched toward the ceiling, shouting a brisk "*Heil* Hitler!"

"At ease. Relax, men." Boost seemed amused. "I want to introduce this fine young man, Willi, to you." He pointed in my direction. "I hope he'll lighten our burdens of this campaign. Willi is our new orderly." He used the word *Hausbursche*.

There was a murmur of approval and satisfaction, and I was glad to have been welcomed in that fashion by the invaders. I couldn't wait to return home and tell my grandparents not to worry about my mother's and Roman's arrival. We'll manage.

Leaving the premises of the castle, Boost pointed to an ornate inscription on the massive wall. It read: LA GUÈRRE EST UN GRAND MALHEUR in large bold letters. And then, more to himself than to me, he murmured. "The war is a terrible calamity for all, the victors as well as the vanquished." He kept repeating the sentence over and over, in a quiet voice, all the way to the guard house.

When I left him on that day, he casually mentioned that as time went on I would become better acquainted with the rest of his men. "Sorry, there wasn't time for you to get to know each of the men. In time, you will, I'm sure."

"I hope I can serve them well, and perhaps they'll like me." I responded.

"That they will, my boy." He assured me.

There were not many among the invaders of the likes of Ernst Boost. He was a good-natured man from Leipzig in Saxony, awkward at playing a fierce

Nazi, scarcely aware of knowing what it was that had brought him to Poland. I had learned that his wife Hannelore managed their small hardware store while he was away, with the help of his two teenage daughters, Margot and Helene.

Ernst did not make it further than the sixth grade in school. He had taken over the management of the family business from his father-in-law when he was only nineteen. One does not need a college education to run a hardware store. The first child came one year into their marriage, the second following soon thereafter. They were a happy couple, though prosperity had a way of eluding them.

Now, he was away from home for the first time of his married life. One day, he had received an official-looking letter, and the notice inside had instructed him to appear *mit sauberer Unterkleidung* (with clean underwear), at ten o'clock in the morning on Friedrichstrasse 10, the regional induction headquarters. He did as instructed. Ernst was a simple, law-abiding man.

I had quickly learned that there was one in that room who believed in the Third Reich and his *Führer*. His name was Karl Fritzke. Blond and blue-eyed, he was a member of the NSDAP—National Socialist Workers Party—and proud of it. Because the others in the unit felt he had been planted among them by the Gestapo, they dared not speak their mind in his presence.

Karl was a native of Borna, a small town not too far from Leipzig. He was the son of an industrial worker, unemployed since World War I. From his early youth, Karl was taught to hate the Treaty of Versailles and its perpetrators, the wealthy Jews. When he had reached his fifteenth birthday, Hitler came to power. Karl joined the Hitler Youth, because it was fun. He was given a fancy uniform with a swastika armband. He liked the mass rallies at midnight with the flaming torches, and his pulse rose to a crescendo when he marched to the sounds of the powerful brass bands and the drummer corps. Karl Fritzke was thankful for the new job the Führer created for his father in the reactivated munitions factory. He sang *Deutschland, Deutschland über alles, über alles in der Welt*—Germany, Germany over all, over all in the world—to the strains of the Haydn melody which often brought tears to his eyes.

Hating the Jews was only a pastime for Karl, until he was told that he must hate this prime "enemy" of his fatherland and all of mankind with as great a passion as his father hated the Treaty of Versailles. Although Karl himself didn't put the Jewish homes and businesses to the torch, he didn't protest when others did during their nightly orgies. And, when his own Hitler Youth troop ransacked a Jewish home, he confiscated what was rightfully his, in keeping with Hitler's solemn promise to his people. Especially pleasant were the book-burning rallies on cold, wintry nights. The bonfire warmed the area, and the sparks reached very high, almost to the second stories of the houses, as more books were thrown onto the dancing flames. "Burn the Jew books!" Was the cry of the group leader. And in their enthusiasm, the young vandals managed to throw volumes of Schiller and Goethe, Leibnitz and Hugo along with Heine, Dostoyevsky and Dumas onto the pyre where they fused into a great pile of ashes. No one bothered to ask: Why Leibnitz? Why Goethe?

On my return home, I was greeted at the doorstep by my little sister: "Mama and Roman are coming!" Felusia exclaimed happily. She hadn't been that excited in weeks. When I had told them about my own good fortune, my grandmother, so seldom happy these days, announced with a glowing smile on her face: "Everything's going to be fine, just wait and see."

They stepped off the 1:25 p.m. from Czegstochowa. I picked themout in the vast crowds spilling onto the platform, and I ran toward them.

"Mama!!" I threw myself into my mother's arms, and we hugged and kissed very long. Roman got his share of affection from my grandparents. Srulko snickered and twisted his mustache, which he did when he tried to cover up his stirred emotions. They didn't carry much luggage, and we left the platform arm in arm in a happy mood. The word "father" had not been mentioned for fear that the magic of the moment might be shattered and lost forever. As we were leaving, I looked around me and I realized that things were not as they used to be. Not long ago this very same train had brought Felusia and me to Piotrkow. Was it the same railway station where we had gotten off the train?

The grotesque web-like steel dome above our heads had been bent by the heat of the fires which raged here not too long ago during the blitzkrieg. Gone was the hustle and bustle of the happy travelers, and absent were also the conductors' voices urging the passengers, in their native language, to board or disembark the train. Missing were the voices of excited children, now silent on the urging of their parents or guardians, fearfully looking over their shoulders to spy an enemy agent charged with maintaining the "new order." A dark cloud of foreboding had descended on all of us, and the absence of dear ones had become images of longing and anguish.

Walking arm-in-arm, I looked at my mother. I was startled at the changes I had noticed. There were so many wrinkles on her beautiful face, sculptured into those serene features. And that heavy chestnut hair of hers, so vibrant and pure as I had remembered it, now streaked with silver, all too obvious, due to the natural hue of brown surrounding it.

"My darlings. . ." she wept with joy, "how skinny you've become. . . have you been attending school?" She asked hastily, to change the topic and without expecting a reply. "Have you practiced your violin?" We walked home from the station, and she kept on talking and asking questions without respite, afraid that we might have some of our own to ask. We were together again, and nothing else mattered.

3

As winter turned to spring, unusual things began to happen. I was able to read cause for concern from bits and pieces of conversations I had overheard, spoken in hushed voices, nevertheless indicative of a state of upheaval. One day, my mother could no longer hold it within.

"They can't do that!" she cried. "I absolutely won't let them!" My mother was refering to the new decree of the local German occupation authorities barring all Jewish children from attending public schools. "I must see Jerzy," she was referring to the principal, Mr. Rzeszewski, "he's an old friend. He won't let us down."

"It's no use, mama." Roman tried to reason. "We're not the only ones expelled. All non-Aryans met with the same fate."

"What's a non-Aryan?" Felusia asked.

"Never mind that, my dear," my mother hastened to change the subject. "I'll see the principal. Things will get straightened out."

"We are non-Aryans." Roman replied to Felusia's inquiry. "We are Jews, and we are inferior to the Aryans, says Hitler. So are the Gypsies and our Chinese friends, the Lees. And as such, we are subject to special new laws."

"What are they trying to do to us, mama, aren't we human?" I asked. She looked at me sadly, without words.

My mother could not be dissuaded. Her two boys in tow, she asked to see the principal of our school. Mr. Rzeszewski graciously invited us into his office. A long time friend of the family, he couldn't have very well refused to hear her out. He listened patiently, his hands folded in front of him on the desk, as my mother extolled the virtues of her two sons.

"They're excellent students and they've never given you any cause for dismissal," she concluded.

"You know how terribly unpleasant it is for me to let them go, my dear Bela," the principal responded. "I have known Vilek and Roman since they were little boys. But there's really nothing I can do. These are the orders from the occupying forces, and I have to enforce the new law. I hope you can appreciate that. Can't you?"

"Aren't you at all afraid, Jerzy?" Mother addressed the principal by his first name. "Aren't you even a bit concerned that some day, when all this is over, you'll be called to account for your actions?"

The principal smiled with embarrassment. "I can't think that far ahead, my dear Bela. All I know. . ." he paused suddenly as if to reflect on his statement, ". . .is that I have a job to do. And the truth is, that if I won't fulfill my duty, I'll be replaced by someone who'll do the job." He spread his arms in a gesture of helplessness and stood up, indicating that the audience was over.

"May God have mercy on you," my mother said, gathering us up and ushering us out of the principal's office. She held her tears bravely until we were outside where she finally let go. "We'll just have to make the best of it, children. We're not going to sit idle and fall behind in our school work."

Soon, underground classrooms sprung up secretly all over the shtetl. Teachers and parents volunteered their time and services so that the children could continue their formal schooling without delay. Things were "normal" again.

At least, we thought, they were.

A crowd gathered in front of Shlomo's grocery store. The grocer had donated a large board, on which important official notices were put up by the occupation authorities for immediate public attention; the Germans called it *Bekanntmachung*. This one bore the impressive stamp of the Third Reich and the endorsement of the Gestapo's Seventh Bureau; a fierce black eagle clutching the swastika. Isaac the Gabbah translated:

PUBLIC NOTICE!

Mandated by the *Führer* and by the order of the Area Commandant all Jews will wear an identification arm-band on the right forearm displaying the Star of David. The armband must be white and the star blue. This order is effective immediately. Jews found not wearing identification will be severely punished.

December 11th, 1939

"What's going on here?" Someone asked the Gabbah.

"Something new for us, a star," he replied with concern.

"Is there reason to worry?"   .

"You can be sure it's nothing g. . ." He caught his tongue in time. People were becoming aware of the newly created breed of informers in their midst. They began to feel the effects of the new regime even in their own community; in their own homes.

"A star, the mark of Cain." Someone said.

"To the contrary, the streets of Piotrkow will soon resemble Hollywood," someone said jokingly, "you'll see stars everywhere." No one laughed.

The newly established Polish militia personnel were relentless in their pursuit to implement the rules laid down on December 11th. Motivated by incentives ranging from a half liter of vodka and a two-pound spicy sausage to monetary awards, they delivered violators to the Seventh Bureau, none of whom was seen or heard of again. The disappearance of so many people in a short span of time was noticed by the community, and inquiries were made by the Council of the Elders. The Gestapo denied knowledge of the captives' whereabouts.

"Communist Jews are crossing the Soviet border every day," the Gestapo official grinned. "We can't stop them. No matter," he added, "we'll soon catch up with them in Moscow." His office comrades laughed raucously at the quip.

The Council representatives dared not mention that some of the identi-fication armbands had been ripped off the sleeves of the victims by their Gentile countrymen who delivered them into the hands of the Gestapo. Yet in spite of the generous bounty offered for the head of a Jew, the treachery of the informers as well as the fatal consequences, the Jews risked their lives each day as they ventured into the countryside to negotiate a few potatoes or the luxury of a fresh egg.

On leaving home in the morning, I took off the armband and tucked it safely into my pocket. I knew what to expect for this singular crime, but losing the job meant a calamity of equal proportions. This was a great source of worry for my mother. But she managed to hide her thoughts from me. In the distant past, when things were still "normal," one look into my mother's eyes was enough to reveal to me her feelings. As time passed, she had learned to disguise her feelings by sending the wrong signals. As it would happen, I was quick to pick up on her deception or emotional cover- up and learned to read the correct signs in order to detect sincere emotions.

The most reliable source was her forehead; no matter how hard she had tried to put on a "happy face," her forehead would tip me off by drawing into wrinkles, pointing to the fear and concern she felt for us all.

"Wish you wouldn't try to hide your fears from me, mama." I said one morning before leaving for the castle. She drew me close to herself, kissed my cheek and asked: "Let's keep it as our own little secret, Vilusiek, all right?"

"If you wish, mama." I replied, clinging to her bosom. "But you mustn't worry needlessly, mama. Corporal Boost won't let bad things happen to us." I meant what I said, for I ascribed more power to the corporal than he possessed.

"He must be a kind and decent man, your corporal Boost," my mother said, letting go of me.

"He is, mama." I hastened to say. "Wait till you meet him. You'll like him too."

"I'm sure I will, if you feel this way about him, Vilusiek," she hugged me once more. "Only, do be very careful, will you?"

"I will, mama, I promise." I called already from the street.

Soon, we added another word to our vocabulary: *Judenrein*, which meant "clean of Jews." One of the great promises Hitler had made in his book *Mein Kampf* was to rid the world of Jews. "Jews," he said, "were vermin and had to be exterminated." Those were his very words, and they were already becoming a reality in Piotrkow. The Seventh Bureau continued with their systematic deportation of the intelligentsia men. Most of them were rounded up during the night "for resettlement into work camps," they were told. Families that were left behind, would be reunited with their loved ones "at the earliest possible time." They waited.

The shtetl elders had received orders from the authorities to form a *Judenrat*, Jewish Council. When established, the Council would consist of fourteen Jews, and those Jews would govern the shtetl for their masters, the Germans. The catch was that only those who could pay for the privileged position would be called on to serve. As long as their wealth was unspent, the Council members would enjoy a "privileged" status while having become willing collaborators in the administration of Nazi cultural and Jewish Programs.

"I said no! Do you understand? N-O!" Srulko shouted. "Don't count on me!"

"Srulko, the time is here for you to start thinking about your family." Shlomo Ganev Zaplocki pleaded with my grandfather about contributing to the "cause" and becoming a member of the Jewish Council.

"If you live long enough, you'll have a chance to learn that those you considered your dearest friends are total strangers." Srulko chanted his response in the fashion of the learned.

"What do you mean by that, Srulko?" Shlomo asked, puzzled.

"What I mean is that I curse this day on which you have come with such an offer to me, thinking that I'll accept." Srulko continued his singsong response. "And I'm wishing it wouldn't be you who asks that I betray my own people."

"You're taking it all wrong, Srulko." Shlomo sounded hurt. "I could have gone to others before I approached you; there are many takers, Srulko. Do you know what's happening? Wake up, my friend! It's a matter of life and death!" Srulko listened to the man quietly. Shlomo went on. "Warszawski himself sent me to see you. The community holds you in great esteem,

Srulko. We need you on the Council. That's why I'm here, for no other reason."

"You need me to do the German's dirty work. That's where the dog lies buried." Srulko used one of the ancient proverbs to cut across hypocrisy.

"Don't be a fool, Srulko." Shlomo argued. "The truth is, if you don't join us, someone else will. Someone less esteemed in the community and without a trace of scruples."

"A fool I may be, my old friend," Srulko said softly, "but a fool with honor and integrity. You want to use me in dealing with our people. I've heard that people are becoming suspicious of your activities, and you must find some decent folk to cover up the filth of the Council's politics. I'm not the person to do this. I feel sorry for you and the others. How terribly burdened you must feel in your conscience. I will not become your accomplice. Please leave now, and don't come back. I'll try to forget we ever discussed this topic."

"Think again, Srulko." Shlomo tried vainly to intercede for his cause. "Think of your family, your grandchildren, Srulko. Some day you might wish you'd have followed my advice." Shlomo talked quickly, avoiding my grandfather's glare. What he did not mention was that the Council members carried the authority to arrest and deliver their brethren into the hands of the Gestapo. Shlomo did not tell my grandfather how many Jews had already been delivered by the militia for transport and labor in parts unknown. On leaving, he offered Srulko a handshake, and Srulko ignored it.

"You go on thinking about helping your family any way you know how, and I'll attend to the welfare of mine the best way I can." Srulko was composed now. "As for the honor you meant to pay me, I appreciate your effort, not your motives. I cannot see myself as a clerk of any kind. Too many bureaucrats are all official and no heart. And in my humble opinion, the most despicable character is that of a bureaucrat without a heart; he'll commit murder in the name of his office. Be careful, Shlomo, you're beginning to sound like one yourself." Srulko reflected briefly. "And as for me and my family, please don't concern yourself. I've relied on the Almighty's will far too long to place my destiny in the hands of the Gestapo. What the Blessed One will destine for us, is going to happen, no matter what I'll do; if it is bashaert, so let it be. It is written."

"One more thing, Srulko." Shlomo stopped in the doorway. "I don't want you to say I haven't warned you."

"If you must."

"Every day, there are more refugees arriving here from the West. German Jews." Shlomo called the refugees in the derogatory manner *Yekkes,* as they were commonly known among the Polish Jews. "Families are coming by the trainloads. They need housing. They have influence with the Germans because they speak their language. They'll use that influence against us, Srulko."

"If they knew their countrymen as well as you imply, Shlomo, then why are they here? Why aren't they in their own homes, attending to their own business?" Srulko was in an argumentative mood. "Besides, I can't see the connection between the original purpose of your visit and the *Yekkes*." Srulko turned to go.

"Let me tell you the reason, Srulko," Shlomo continued in a trembling voice. "The German Jew arrived in our community and we received him as best we could under the circumstances. Did he deem proper to appreciate our help? Did he shake the hand we offered him as brethren?" Shlomo paused for effect. "On the contrary, the *Yekke* arrived here filled with an air of superiority. He has forgotten his Jewishness, and in his state of assimilation, he holds us responsible for his own exile. Do you know what I heard them say? Do you want to know?" Shlomo looked challengingly at my grandfather. Srulko was silent.

"I'll tell you anyhow." Shlomo went on, "They especially blame the Hasid, you and me, for their own falling out of favor with the Nazis. I wouldn't be at all surprised if the *Yekke* believes the Nazi stories about the Jewish conspiracy to take over the world. It is clear that the *Yekke* is more German than he is Jew. I can bet my life he'll try to show his loyalty to the Reich at our expense. Yours and mine, Srulko. Are you willing to risk that?" Shlomo caught his breath. He had used his strongest argument, and now he looked at Srulko anxiously,

"I will not worry about a few *Yekkes*, and you exaggerate their influence."

"What, then, are you concerned with, Srulko?" Shlomo asked bitterly.

"I'm particularly worried about my self-respect, Shlomo. Furthermore, I refuse to pay with someone's misery for my temporary safety. When the Almighty, blessed by His holy Name, will deem fit to punish me for my many imperfections, He will do so without the permission of the Council, I'm sure. And I'll accept my destiny with dignity. That's all I have to say to you."

As may have been expected, Shlomo left my grandfather a defeated man. Not because Srulko had refused to join the native mercenary force of hirelings and informers, but because from then on Shlomo was unable to delude himself about the purpose of joining the Council. He was familiar with the Gestapo's simple prison psychology; use the Jew to betray the Jew, and the promise of life was all too tempting to refuse the offer to serve. Shlomo knew it was like a pact with the devil himself; only the devil delivered on his promises. There was no quitting the services of the Gestapo. Were it not for his attachment to life, Shlomo might have turned honest.

Grandmother Rachel seldom expressed her views. It was not "fitting" for her to do so. She was a woman in the tradition of the Hasidim; revered her husband and family; performed her many duties with dedication and self-effacement. Filled with excessive humility, she suffered silently, ready to sacrifice herself without the slightest protestation.

So much the more, everyone listened astounded when suddenly my grandmother spoke up at suppertime. Her voice quivered with great emotion. "God sent a new curse on us, Srulko." She said. "There are rumors we'll be locked up in a ghetto, with sentries and barbed wire around us to keep us in."

"Old wives' tales! Be quiet, woman! Don't blaspheme!" Srulko was more surprised than angry. "If it's the will of God that the Jew must live in a ghetto separated from the Gentile, then so be it."

"And how do you suppose we'll get to the market if it is outside the ghetto? If we can't buy food from the *Goyim*, then what do you expect me to put on the table at dinnertime?" Grandmother lamented.

"Our Lord will provide." Srulko repeated stubbornly. "No use arguing about it."

My grandmother fell silent. I spied a tear rolling down her cheek as she quickly wiped it with her index finger. Had he seen it, Srulko might have taken it as a display of weakness and a distrust toward the Almighty.

Almost one year from the outbreak of the war, the Jewish population of Piotrkow had grown from the 15,000 to approximately twice that number. Refugees from the West, mainly from Germany, flocked into the area in Poland the Nazis annexed and called General Government. The newly created administrative area was under its Governor Hans Frank in the city of Cracow. From there, on August 5th, came the newest decree: the ghetto.

We woke up surrounded by coils of barbed wire strung all round one section of the shtetl, sealing it off from the rest of the city. Every few yards, Lithuanian and Ukrainian sentries guarded the new compound. They were now part of the SS establishment.

My heart sank. Daily, those Jews who until now lived outside the new wall, were herded into the ghetto. Some, we have heard, didn't make it that far. They were taken to the stock yard, loaded into freight-cars, and taken somewhere; no one could guess where. One whole week went by, and I remained home for fear I would endanger Corporal Boost.

"He must know it by now, mama," I almost wept, confessing my deepest fears to my mother.

"He has known it for a long time, dear Vilusiek," my mother assured me. "It didn't take much guessing to establish that fact. It didn't matter to him before, and surely won't matter to him now."

"How am I going to continue, mama?"

"Corporal Boost will think of a way, dear," my mother said.

"Meanwhile, don't you worry yourself sick."

Just as my mother predicted, Boost found a way to continue my employment at the supply company. Private Müller was sent one morning to fetch me.

"You can take that rag off your sleeve now," he said as soon as we went past the Lithuanian sentry at the gate. "Out here, you're one of us. Orders from corporal Boost. I nodded, tears glazing my eyes. He knew, after all. I thought to myself. I looked at Müller and he smiled reassuringly. He was a bear of a man with goodness to match his size. We walked silently a few moments. Suddenly, as if in afterthought, Müller said: "They told me at home I'd be sent to Poland to fight Communism. That's why I enlisted. They didn't tell me I'd fight children and women." He patted me on the head, and I looked up at him, his honest grey eyes now winking at me mischievously

I kept my job as orderly of the supply company. Each day, as I approached the ghetto gate, I showed the sentry my work pass. As soon as I left the ghetto premises, I tucked the armband into my trouser pocket. I knew that my presence at the castle endangered Boost as well, but I didn't have the courage to quit work. The way things were, Boost wouldn't remain in Piotrkow forever. Lithuanian SS in black uniforms and the silver skull on their collars kept arriving in increasing numbers.

"What do you think Uncle Mickey's family is doing right now, mama?" I asked, thinking of my distant relatives.

My mother was hesitant. She was always hesitant when she was startled. "I really couldn't tell, dear." She said sadly. "I don't know what their habits are nor do I know what time of day it is in America."

"Is it very different from ours?" Felusia asked.

"Yes, baby," my mother continued patiently, "when it's daytime here, it must be night over there and they must be eating supper."

Or, maybe they're in the movies?" Felusia suggested.

There were questions pressing into my mind, but I noticed my mother's reluctance to continue on the subject, and I remained silent. The evening ended up in prayers, as usual, but I went on daydreaming about America. Do they also suffer shortages of food? Are they digging air-raid shelters in their parks and streets? What sort of news releases do they read?

Uncle Mickey had taken Isaac and Victor to a matinee performance at the movies. The newsreel had come on, projecting disturbing headlines onto the screen:

Jews are being resettled from Western Europe's Nazi occupied territories eastward. Trains overcrowded, people leaving homes and belongings behind. Old men and women beaten by SS guards. Children crying. The *Führer* conducting a great rally at Nuremberg. Thousands of cheering Germans. Banners with swastika emblems adorning the crowd. . .

On leaving the theater, Uncle Mickey picked up the *New York Times*. He found no better news there:

NAZIS ATTACK LONDON AGAIN AT NIGHT; BRITISH ROUTE PLANES IN DAY FIGHT. NAZI RAIDERS AGAIN BOMBED LONDON LAST NIGHT. . .AGAIN THE DIN OF GUN FIRE AND EXPLODING BOMBS RESOUNDED IN THE CITY AS THE NAZIS PRESSED ON WITH THEIR AERIAL ONSLAUGHT, WHICH HAS SPREAD DEATH AND DESTRUCTION IN EVERY QUARTER OF LONDON, FOR THE FOURTEENTH CONSECUTIVE NIGHT.

"My God! Look!" He pointed to the date on top of the front page of the *New York Times*. "September 21, 1940," he read. "It's Vilek's birthday." He remembered.

"Rumors have it that the British are suffering great casualties through Nazi air-raids. Hitler took Denmark, Belgium and France in one swoop." Felix held his face in the palms of his hands. We were having a Friday supper to which he had been invited at Nora's request.

"Perhaps it's only propaganda spread by the Nazis themselves." My mother suggested.

"You mean, the 'big lie'?" my grandfather chuckled. "I wouldn't put it past them."

"Unfortunately, the news was broadcast by the BBC. My Polish contacts heard it only yesterday." Felix said in a whisper.

"In that case, the damage might be bigger than they care to admit," my mother said. She was resolute, seemingly deriving strength from adversity. I looked at her lovingly. I'll help you, mama. My eyes spoke to her. She understood.

"We're in for a long, cold winter, children," my grandfather said, and the humorous twinkle disappeared from his eyes.

That night, under the featherbedding which I had pulled over my head to muffle the sounds, I cried bitterly. When I wiped my tears, I had made myself a promise to remain strong; to form alliances but not be dependent on them. Our staunchest allies had failed us in spite of the historical bonds that tied the countries together. I've learned a great lesson which I would remember in the days to come.

Corporal Boost was very supportive, as always. He was able to read the worry in my face, and he suggested that we make the market rounds a day earlier than usual. "I know we customarily shop on Saturdays, Willi," he said with his typical grin, "but I don't suppose it would do any harm to change the routine. I'm sure no one will notice."

I understood. In a way, this would test the waters for both of us. The peasants were a shrewd lot. They were bound to react to the recent developments, and Boost wanted us to meet their challenge head on.

During our weekly visits to the vegetable and fruit market, I acted as Boost's interpreter. The corporal would point out a product and I would bargain with the farmers. It wasn't unusual, here and there, a peasant would become suspicious of my knowledge of German; he'd point at me and utter the only German expression he had learned: "*Jude!* Jew!"

At moments like those, Boost would stare at the peasant without saying a word. I wanted to run and hide, never to return. But Boost would turn to me and smile reassuringly: "They have learned to denounce much better than they speak their own language." I looked at his smiling face, and we walked on without responding to the peasant's accusation. My gratitude had no bounds.

We've completed our shopping while it was getting dark. On the edge of the square there was a man selling hot buns. He had set up a makeshift stove on the base of several bricks, with a fire inside that kept shooting sparks out into the air. Some people stood round the stove, warming their hands while waiting to be served.

"Want one?" Boost asked. We came closer. The scene brought memories of long ago—a country fair, a little boy led by his father through the crowded grounds, vendors hawking their wares, much excitement—tears welled up in my eyes. I smiled tearfully when Boost handed me a steaming hot bun. Silently, I wished I could share it with the others at home. He understood my hesitation. "Here, take a few home with you." He held out a bagfull, and I took it from him thankfully.

Christmas was upon us. The second Christmas of the War. I sat beside Boost in the arched hall of the medieval castle, and we listened to almost three hours of the *Führer's* speech. He shouted and his followers responded with shouts. It was not too difficult to understand why they were carried away by their leader's charismatic frenzy. He was the fulfillment of the dreams they had harbored since their defeat in World War I.

A loud murmur went across the room at the conclusion of the *Führer's* speech with the familiar phrase: "Next Christmas, at home!" The orchestra intoned with the national anthem, "Germany above all else in the world," and the rallying masses shouted in unison "*Sieg Heil!*"

Another rally came to a conclusion. The room was silent. If they believed the *Führer's* promises, they didn't let on. Those who would express skepticism bit their tongues. They didn't want any trouble with the Gestapo, and Karl Fritzke was all too ready to oblige.

Hanukka coincided with the Christmas holidays. To celebrate the festival of lights, the underground teachers conceived an idea with which to break the despair of the ghetto inhabitants. Even as Hitler was delivering his fiery oration in Nuremberg, the Piotrkow ghetto celebrated its first artistic "bazaar." The event took place in the Joseph Hertz Auditorium, and the proceeds were to aid the needy. As one of the teachers, my mother was radiant in her enthusiasm.

"We must never forget the needy!" she exclaimed. "And even in our moment of need, we remember those who cannot help themselves!" She was ecstatic. There reigned a general state of euphoria, we all helped with the organizational chores, and all of the students displayed their best works.

The event culminated with a theatrical presentation, songs and dances from the past and present and, of course, the singing of the Jewish "national anthem," the *Hatikvah*.

Following the conclusion, the participants and the public spilled into the streets of the ghetto, discussing among themselves the community's great cultural event; the "art fair." No one took the time to worry that this was to be the first and only such event to take place in the Piotrkow ghetto. All that mattered, was the present.

My mother's arm was around my shoulder as we slowly treaded our way home. "Why hasn't anyone mentioned our dear teachers, mama?" I asked. "They worked so hard to put the fair together."

"The teachers know they're appreciated, dear," my mother assured me. "They need no public recognition." She smiled happily. I was glad she hasn't yet forgotten how to smile. What she didn't tell me, was that the identity of the underground teachers was a closely guarded secret. "But I want to tell you, Vilusiek, how very proud you've made us all with your fine rendition of the violin concerto." She kissed me tenderly.

Much later into the War, I would often return to those happy moments, the smile on my mother's face, Felusia and Roman clapping their hands in delight, our relatives and friends chatting excitedly, stimulated by their one most singular possession: imagination. They were experiencing an evening at Covent Garden and Carnegie Hall put together in one. The memory of that evening was to carry my spirit beyond the most inscrutable prison boundaries.

The ghetto population grew. Trainloads were unloaded each day; most of them from Germany, but there were also Jews from other countries. The new arrivals were assigned quarters within the congested ghetto, and conditions have become intolerable, in a large degree due to the incompatibility of the tenants with their hosts.

The ghetto Council maintained an accurate census. New arrivals were recorded; health, age and, most importantly, property. The militia was especially punctilious concerning the latter before assigning new quarters. By the time the refugees had gotten settled, few had been left with any means of support.

When my grandfather heard that refugees might be assigned to share our home, he was beside himself. "They're not going to deposit one of those assimilated German families in my home!" He shouted at the top of his voice. To my grandfather, all German Jews were "converts."

"Now, Srulko, these are poor, homeless people." My grandmother said softly. "They need shelter, and we have space to spare, so why not let a good family from among those defeated people live with us? I'm sure they'd do the same for us."

"A good family? Did you say a good family?" Srulko mimicked his wife, waving his arms in an outrage. "There aren't any good families among the converts! They're worse than the Gentiles!"

My grandfather was not alone in this view of the German Jew. Most of the Eastern Jews were orthodox but the Piotrkow Jews were ultraorthodox. To them, any Jew that was less than a Hasid must have been a convert. The Hasid's appearance was unmistakeable; the earlocks, fringe garments, the beard, all these had become the targets of persecution by Hitler Youths and the SS who roamed the ghetto in search for victims. Beards were cut with dull-edged bayonets, and beatings were common daily occurrences. The Hasid had come to feel that he was suffering for the transgressions of the impious intruders, the converts.

"If you think I'll turn the other cheek, you're wrong!" Srulko shouted at his wife. "We'll just see about that! They're not going to share my home!" With that, my grandfather slammed the door on his way out.

"One of these days, he'll take it off its hinges." My mother remarked, referring to the abused door.

My grandfather's second cousin on his mother's side, Joseph Lazar, was a man of considerable influence at the SS and Gestapo headquarters. He made custom-fitted boots for the administrative head of the ghetto, Sturmbannführer Paul Schröder, his lovely wife Eva, and the two children, Egon and Bert; the first one thirteen and the other eleven years old.

Joseph's dealings extended as far up the SS hierarchy as the all-powerful Brigadeführer, the district Commandant headquartered in Lodz. Higher than that, the modest aspirations of a humble shoemaker did not venture to soar. With each pair of boots he had made, Joseph reached a greater degree of influence. At one time, he was quite possibly the most influential Jew in Piotrkow. Indeed, his influence eclipsed all of the money the Council could put together.

"Why do you think I have them eating out of the palm of my hand?" He boasted. "I've got the skill and the leather. The Nazis worship their riding boots. For them, it's a source of authority and power." Joseph was sure he'd enjoy the influence for as long as there was a demand for his skill provided, of course, that his masters would keep on supplying him with the special calf hide when his own private stockpile becomes exhausted.

Who else but Joseph could help to move in the Mandels with us? My grandmother suggested the idea, and Srulko agreed. He'd go to see his cousin, although he hated to ask favors of any kind, especially where the Nazis were involved. This time, my grandfather had no alternative; it's either ask a favor or have the "converts" move in with us. The Mandels would fit very nicely into our home; they were haymesh, "our" kind, and they had no place of their own. I was looking forward to sharing my room with Nora and Hayim.

"All right, Srulko, all right," Joseph interrupted Srulko's emotional outburst. "I'll see what can be done about it."

"Look at him! The big shot! He'll see what can be done!" Srulko shouted again. "You sound more like your clients each day. You even wear their kinds of footwear, Joseph. You already look and act like them, too!" Srulko spat violently.

"Calm yourself, cousin Srulko." Joseph tried to assuage the old man. "There's no reason to be insulting. I said I'd do my very best."

"You'll have to do better than that, Joseph!" Srulko exclaimed.

"You must promise me here, in the name of our departed grandfather of blessed memory, that the Mandels will move in with us immediately." He lowered his voice. "You'll do it for the times I used to change your diapers; for the times I rocked you to sleep when you yelled like a spoiled brat, which you were; for the. . ." Srulko might have continued, were it not for Joseph's solemn promise to do what he asked.

The Mandels moved in with us. They were grateful, and we were all very pleased. The Nazis were happy, too. Uncle Joseph had made two pairs of brown, calf-leather boots; one pair for the *Sturmbannführer*, the other for his wife Eva. Joseph regretted the sacrifice of the last of his finest stock of calf-hide; he had intended to use it when, as he used to say, "a real emergency arose."

As time went on, we realized that our grandparents had made the right decision. The Mandels, Nora's uncle Max and her cousin Hayim, were quiet but cordial people whom we grew to love as our very own. My grandfather was especially pleased because Max Mandel belonged to his Hasidic circle. They met to study the Talmud, and I witnessed some heated scholarly sessions as the Hasidim argued the intricate points of the Law. At first, I could not understand those bearded scholars, unconcerned as they were about the daily goings on. In time, I grew to appreciate and cherish those sessions during which these mild-mannered men have come to exemplify human dignity in their quest for the ultimate truth. I grew accustomed to their singsong dialogue and I absorbed what I understood of the ancient wisdom.

Soon, I became familiar with the Hasidic songs, zmeeres they called them, and I joyfully joined in at the culmination of each study session.

They were simple, peace-loving men. In their unique thirst for knowledge, the Hasidim had tried to assert the claims of the heart as opposed to the dictates of the mind. They zealously pursued their struggle against excessive legalism and intellectualism. Theirs was a simple faith. It was an enviable shield against the swastika. For the Hasid, it was never sufficient to merely indulge in the interpretive commentary of the Mishnah or the Gemarah; they took it upon themselves to reinterpret the famous passages, as only tsaddikim—the wisest of the wise—were permitted to do. Listening, I learned, and I remembered.

The snows have come and gone, and spring was here again. The ghetto population had grown uncomfortable, and I was looking forward to my daily chores at the Supply Company, leaving the congestion behind me.

"Today, we shall feed the horses, Willi." Boost suggested. He knew how much I loved the animals, and he enjoyed the expression of happiness he saw in my face, as we fed and watered the animals. I mounted Frika, my favorite chestnut mare, and Boost took photos.

"I'll send the snapshots home to mama and our daughters, Margot and Helene. They'll be happy. They'd always wanted a brother, you know. Now, they'll have one."

"I'd like that very much." I said without hesitancy.

"I had always wished for a son, Willi. Two tries, and two daughters." Boost chuckled as he examined my face with careful scrutiny. I remained silent. "For now, I'll be your papa," he laughed. "Until your real father returns, of course." He added hastily, observing a cloud of sadness coming over me.

The following day, I brought Boost home for a visit. My grandfather was beside himself with rage, but he knew to conceal it. He took my mother aside to the other room, while I showed my guest our family photo album. I heard my mother arguing with my grandfather. Boost must have heard them as well, but he didn't let on. Finally, my mother appeared, her eyes red, but otherwise calm.

"Please, have some tea." She placed a cup in front of Boost. "I'm so sorry the place isn't a bit more tidy for your visit."

"Please, don't worry yourself about such small details." Boost tried to reassure her. "You've done quite well under the circumstances." She smiled. I thought it was a happy smile. I hadn't seen my mother smile in a long time. I was glad Boost was good to my mother. They made small talk, and I listened with interest. I wanted them to become friends.

Boost had become a frequent visitor at our home, and people talked about him and my mother. Grandfather Srulko was furious.

"The shtetl is buzzing about you and the German." He shouted.

"They say that you're a whore, Bela! A whore!" He repeated. "My daughter, comforting a German!"

"Do you believe what people are saying, father?" My mother cried.

"I don't know what to believe anymore."

"Since when do you care about people and their gossip?" She challenged the old man.

"This is altogether different, Bela." My grandfather insisted.

"You're bringing the enemy into our home."

"If he's an enemy, then who are our friends?" She asked.

"Convince me that he's helping out of the goodness of his heart." He challenged.

"And if I say, he does?"

"Then, I'll believe you, Bela."

"And you won't listen? Won't believe the gossip?" My mother agonized.

"I'll believe you, Bela. I must." My grandfather embraced his only daughter. The matter was closed.

It was May, 1941. On the morning of the sixth, on my way to the castle I noticed powerful movement of the Nazi war machinery headquartered in Piotrkow. The tank motors were revved, ready to move out, black crosses on their turrets and a large SS that resembled lightning.

I found the Supply Company quarters already vacant. They were no doubt preparing to join the movement, and I had a feeling that this day was going to affect my life significantly.

Boost came toward me quickly, his usually cheerful smile was gone from the sensitive face. He was carrying a large cardboard box. "We're leaving, Willi," he said quietly, his eyes glazing over. "Orders from the *Führer*." He smiled now. "You'll take this box home with you today."

"I can see that something is happening." I said without looking directly at him, ready to weep. "Do you know where you're going?"

"East, Willi, you mustn't tell anyone." He paused. "*They* wouldn't like that." He emphasized *they*, and I thought I saw him glance over his shoulder. I was quiet. I understood.

I wanted to continue talking as if nothing was happening, but I kept getting swept away by the flood of my thoughts; memories of the past nine months, the good as well as the unpleasant.

The Supply Company, and with it Boost and my temporary security, were leaving the castle. The supply wagons were all hitched up. There was my lovely Frika, beating the pavement with her hoofs and impatiently neighing as if aware of the goings on. Boost took me aside.

"Memorize this address, my son: *Eisenbahnstrasse* 134 in Leipzig." He paused. "That's my home and yours, remember it well. You're always welcome." He hugged me powerfully after having made sure that no one was watching. "Promise to look me up after this madness is over. Promise me Willi. And take good care." He pleaded.

"I'll do my best. I promise." I said quietly. "You must take care of yourself, too." I said. "And Frika, yes?"

"I will, Willi, I promise." He said. "Have faith. Better days will surely come, my boy." Boost whispered quietly, while the column began to move, "and when they do, Willi, we'll start up again on equal terms. Perhaps then, my boy, it will be you who will come to my aid, who knows?" He was talking quickly, as if to himself, trying to race against the turning wagon wheels.

"You'll be coming back this way, Ernst." I called him by his name for the first time and it brought a smile to his face. I'll be waiting, and there'll be many things I'll have to tell you. You'll come, won't you?" It was my turn to ask for his return.

"Please, Willi, for this one time of our farewell, call me 'papa' Ernst. Just this once."

I could see that he was holding back his tears, and I was having a difficult time keeping a dry eye myself. "I'll miss you terribly, papa Ernst." I said.

"Keep all those good things in your heart, my son." He spoke quickly as the merciless formation was gaining momentum. "Keep them, and they'll give you strength in the struggle ahead."

"I'll never forget you, papa Ernst!" I repeated his name lovingly.

"Remember!" He squeezed my hand gently and then let go, pushing me aside. He jumped onto the driver's seat next to Pvt. Müller. I ran along for a while, shaking Müller's hand. "God bless you, my boy." The big man said. He, too, choked with emotion. One more handclasp with Ernst Boost, and soon the column disappeared around the corner of Zamkowa Street past the ancient castle.

Slowly, the large carton of provisions in my arms, I walked home. A lit cigarette butt was thrown from one of the wagons. I picked it up mechanically and without knowing why. I puffed the aroma of the tobacco deep into my lungs. My head became momentarily lighter and my whole body seemed to float like an inflated balloon. I suddenly took ill, my stomach contracted violently, and I had to sit down at the curb feeling faint. The spasm brought tears to my eyes and I retched terribly. It set me coughing and spitting violently, a sharp pain driving its full force into my skull. All I could think of now was that my breakfast had been wasted, and I threw the remainder of the cigarette butt away in disgust.

I would be careful about forming attachments in the future. Too many things happen in war, unexpected things, and none are conducive to lasting friendships. It was especially painful to let go of the one person I could depend on in this time of great need. I could not help but wonder how the family would get along now without the help of Corporal Boost. I felt a profound emptiness following his departure.

In a queer way, I was also glad that he had left before things got worse. Soon, I realized, it would have become difficult for Boost to keep up our relationship. I was almost glad that he was spared this embarrassment. Now he was gone, and I was determined to go on, to survive.

Though we heard rumors during the past few weeks of an impending change, we were still shocked at waking on a hot June morning to find ourselves cut off from the outside world by a tripple layer of barbed wire. A new contingent of Lithuanian and Ukrainian SS had been busy during the night uncoiling the fence, and now it wound around the ghetto, leaving only one exit on Warszawska Street. The wire coils were laid one on top of the other so densely that it seemed all of the land had given birth to a new plant; an endless fence of sharp, jagged strings of steel that brought on a renewed mood of fear and panic.

Until now, many were allowed to leave the ghetto premises to go to work for the German masters, provided they complied with the curfew and wore an armband. Now, only individuals like Uncle Joseph, with special skills and materials, continued their trade and were on privileged status with the SS. He was issued an exit pass by the Gestapo, and from time to time was able to supply the family with sorely needed food. But his resources were limited, and there was his own immediate family to feed.

Then, one day, Joseph's supply of cow-hide ran out and with it his influence with the Gestapo. He was now one of us, confined to the ghetto and looking forward to collecting on the debts he had accumulated during his days of influence.

The first signs of typhus appeared in July. It was an unusually hot summer, and the ghetto population had grown beyond all expectations. Up until then, the plague was what we read about in the Bible. The real epidemic was an altogether different thing. In its second week, Hayim came down with a terrible fever. Nora and my mother did all they could to halt the rising temperature. Tirelessly, they laid cold compresses on Hayim's forehead, but the fever wouldn't let up. He was delirious most of the time, especially during the night, with only brief moments of lucidity. There was sickness all around us. We feared the worst, but we dared not seek medical help for fear of a quarantine. That would mean isolation from everyone and certain death.

The only funeral carriage in the shtetl was overburdened, and we could see common droshkys delivering the wooden boxes containing the dead to the cemetery outside the ghetto. In fact, the only ones to receive a permit to leave the ghetto were the dead. Even that had to be conducted under the cover of darkness, because the Council and the ghetto authorities tried to keep the epidemic a secret.

There was a typhus case next door at the Naibergs. Their only son, Moniek, came down with a fever overnight. Roman and I were Moniek's kheder companions. Soon after we had learned of Moniek's becoming ill, both of us came down with the dreaded disease.

"Am I going to die, mama?" I asked in a moment of consciousness.

"What a silly question!" My mother exclaimed with a faint smile on her weary, aging face. "In a few days from now you'll be well again. A week later, you won't believe this ever happened."

Mother and Nora cared for the three of us tirelessly, keeping down the fever. Grandmother consulted Srulko's witchcraft feltchering and poured an assortment of herbal brews down our throats. Throughout our ordeal, we feared that someone would denounce us to take possession of our apartment if we got quarantined. People have been known to resort to this sort of action as conditions had become progressively worse.

I drew some comfort from my mother's confidence, but I found it hard to believe that the plague could be dismissed with a mere shrug of one's shoulder, as if to say, "this is all too stupid; it can't last long."

My mother's blind optimism ultimately triumphed. After almost two weeks of battle, the fever was gone as mysteriously as it had struck. The silence of the ensuing night was disturbed by the recurring wailing of the mourners around us; a solemn reminder of the continuing epidemic. Their lamentations mingled with the feverish outcries of the stricken, the crackling bursts of automatic rifle fire, and the wild laughter of the Lithuanian sentries.

Announcements became less sporadic as the new office of the District Commandant managed to establish liaison with the Council by means of local authorities. Important announcements were usually transmitted from the Commandant's office through the new ghetto commandant

Sturmbannführer Meier. He, in turn, communicated his mandates to Warszawski, the leader of the Council. So it was that the new "law" concerning the ghetto population was announced by Warszawski during the regular Council meeting:

"From this day on, only working parties will be permitted to leave the ghetto premises, and then only if accompanied by the Militia. The curfew will be more stringent, 0500 to 1700, to be exact. Anyone found on the street past that time will be shot on sight." He sounded formal and made no personal comments concerning the bulletin he had just read.

"It's an affront to human dignity!" My grandfather nervously paced up and down the room, shouting at his cousin Joseph. For the first time since the resettlement into the ghetto we began to feel hunger. As our food supplies dwindled, my mother tried desperately to provide food a day at a time. There was little money left us, and the black market prices soared. Roman had been able to smuggle some food into the ghetto as other "Aryan-looking" Jews had done. But with the erection of the barbed wire wall and the multitude of sentries guarding the perimeter, this became virtually impossible.

"The *Sturmbannführer* said to me, 'Joseph, you are a damned good Jew, fact is I often regret you weren't born an Aryan. I can confide in you, can't I? I'll tell you now that we'll have rigid controls over the ghetto—we can always tell a Jew by his Semitic features, it's scientific, you know—outside he'll be shot on sight. Death is the only penalty feared by people. No matter how miserable they are, they want to go on living.'"

"Nobody can tell that Roman's a Jew." I interjected. "He looks Aryan, talks Polish without an accent, and they don't know him well enough in town."

"That's where you're wrong, my boy." Joseph smiled sadly. "The Gestapo has informers among our own people. They've succeeded in turning brother against brother."

"But what if one is not denounced by an informer?" I insisted.

Joseph hesitated for a moment, and with sadness in his voice, he went on. "The Gestapo knows all there is to know about us. They'll catch a suspect and they'll administer the genital test. That'll show them whether or not he's a Jew."

"What's a genital test?" I asked.

"I hope you'll never have to learn what it means, any of you."

My mother was frightened, Roman was defiant, and my grandfather kept on pacing back and forth wearing down the floor. I still didn't understand what was meant by "genital test," but I was to find out about it sooner than I had expected.

As a force of habit, people had become accustomed to gather in front of the Council office on Szpitalna Street where the Army barracks used to be. News traveled fast in the ghetto. And when we heard that a crowd was gathering in mid-afternoon, curiosity prompted Roman and myself to join.

The SS in their black uniforms, the silver SS skull on their starched collars, their guns at the ready, surrounded the entire block. Several Gestapo officials led a prisoner into the building, his wrists manacled behind his back.

"They've caught a Jew outside the ghetto!" People whispered.

"Poor bastard!" Someone close by said.

"First one. They're sure to make an example of him. He's as good as dead."

Warszawski came out of the office to greet the Gestapo arrivals. "Must be important." I whispered to Roman. "Be quiet, Vilek, they might hear." He warned.

There were rumors that an exemplary trial was to be held, for all to see and hear.

"Anyone we know?" Someone asked.

"Never seen him before." Another voice remarked.

"Must be a newcomer. A total stranger." The first voice said.

Driven by curiosity, we joined the spectators in the large Council hall where the "trial" was being held. The prisoner was of average height and of slight build, rather insignificant looking and not at all heroic. Above his upper lip, he was barely showing a shadow of a mustache, and his eyes were surrounded by dark circles as though he had spent a sleepless night. From his youthful appearance, I had guessed him to be no older than twenty-five. He kept on talking, knowing that his life depended on his power of persuasion, assuring his "judges" that he was innocent.

"I'm not a Jew! I'm not a Jew!" He kept repeating in a plaintive voice. When this did not elicit the desired response, he resorted to stronger arguments. "Why, it's totally absurd, this accusation. Not only is it absurd and unfounded, but it's an insult. I'm a Catholic! Have been all my life! My family is Catholic! Whoever accused me of being a Jew is a preposterous liar!" The judges regarded the man with cold, implacable eyes. It seemed, once the Bureau had made up its mind to make an example of someone, they would pursue their course; guilty or innocent.

The man pleaded with his eyes. And when reason had told him that there was no mercy among his judges, he hid his face in the palms of his hands and sobbed quietly.

Sturmbannführer Meier looked forward to what was promising to become an unusually entertaining session of the "court." It was obvious from the grin on his face. The Gestapo photographers were present, ready to record every detail of the proceedings. Meier himself would be the prosecutor. The crime demanded the best. As it was, being the highest ranking officer on the tribunal, he would have the privilege to pass final judgement. Meant to impress his superiors at the Bureau, this entire show might entitle Meier to a long overdue promotion in rank.

The large hall of the Council office held approximately one hundred and fifty people. *Sturmbannführer* Meier was seated at the center of the long conference table, flanked by two Gestapo officers of lesser rank. Behind them stood three Lithuanian SS with their automatic weapons drawn. Now, the prisoner was told to face his judges. Still manacled, his head bent low, he stood before them. Warszawski stood to his left, and an interpreter on the right.

Meier was busy taking notes on a small pad, while the arresting officers reported the events. The prisoner stood silent, seemingly resigned to his fate. Meier ignored the frightened man while preparing his "case." He finished writing and stood up, facing his audience. He pointed at the prisoner, speaking in a solemn, well measured tone of voice:

"This Jew was apprehended today outside the ghetto limits. It happened in broad daylight, in violation of the Judenrat order that no Jew is to leave the ghetto without a proper permit." He looked atthe silent crowd, eager to see what effect his statement had made, since he had cleverly maneuvered the Council into complicity with the Gestapo. "This Jew," he continued, "did not wear an identification armband. He was challenged by the authorities, but he chose to make a run for it. He was apprehended by one of our men. Now, he must be brought to justice. You all know the law and what it means to disobey it." His cold green eyes rested on the accused whose lips were moving rapidly in prayer.

Meier went on, telling the assembled how reprehensible it was for one delinquent individual to jeopardize the safety of a community. He read his notes in a monotone voice, in the usual involved style employed by his people, and the interpreter was extremely careful in his translation. Meier outlined the charges with the greatest care.

"You must answer to the following charges: first, leaving the ghetto premises without authorization; second, trying to conceal your identity; third, refusing to respond to the challenge issued by the arresting officer; and fourth, deliberately endangering the safety of your people." Meier pronounced the charges with the familiar cadence of marching troops, especially when he enumerated "first, second, third, fourth," which sounded almost like a sergeant drilling his command. His concern for the well-being of the ghetto population sounded almost convincingly genuine.

The prisoner must have realized that his fate lay in the hands of the well-mannered Gestapo official. He must have been thinking of ways to convince his judges of his innocence. But his spirits must have sunk as he gradually understood that his judges were determined to use him as an example. The news of his trial and subsequent punishment would serve as a deterrent for would-be escapees from the ghetto. Meier's voice startled the prisoner out of his thoughts.

"The prisoner will state his name!"

"Franek Piecha." The response was almost inaudible.

"Speak up! Speak louder!" Meier ordered sternly.

"My name is Franek Piecha."

"Where were you apprehended, Franek Piecha?" Meier's cold eyes pierced the frightened man.

"I was. . . I was. . ." The man stammered and I could feel his anguish. By now, he had been the victim of twenty-four hours of ceaseless interrogation by the Gestapo, and I knew how difficult it must have been for him to respond accurately to the questions put to him and to recall the sequence of events past. He hesitated, not remembering the exact location and the events leading up to his confinement and trial.

Slowly, Franek Piecha told his accusers how he got off the train from Lodz, having arrived in Piotrkow to visit with his aunt, Mrs. Bosiacki. He walked toward the droshky stand. He was looking forward with delight to a refreshing cool bath and a change of clothing.

It was then that he heard a voice clearly shouting "Jew! Jew! As the voice came closer, he suddenly realized it was he who was being pursued. He got frightened and ran, was apprehended and manacled, and found himself in the midst of a jeering crowd of hostile people. He protested, but one formidable kick to his left thigh had caused him to stumble onto the pavement. His bag had been ripped from his shoulder, and he was promptly taken to the Gestapo headquarters by two Lithuanian SS. "The rest is common knowledge." Franek concluded. "If you don't believe me, you can check with my parish in Lodz. Father Sowiecki will testify I'm no Jew."

It was a dreadful night Franek must have spent in the basement cell of the Seventh Bureau jail. He could not have understood why he was there, after having explained his identity and presented his identification papers and travel permit. Every citizen carried identification papers these days. And one had to apply for a traveling permit to go anywhere within a twenty-five kilometer radius from one's home. Franek was a God-fearing Christian and a solid citizen. His father, Dr. Olek Piecha, was formerly Professor of Pathology at the University of Lodz, but had since fled to Russia and from there to England. There, he had joined up with the Polish Armed Forces in exile.

At first Franek must have been afraid his arrest and his father's excape were inextricably bound together. He shrunk into himself as though a thousand eyes were scrutinizing him. The spotless Gestapo uniforms and their shiny boots intimidated him. Above all, he was tired and annoyed. He had always been aware of his Semitic appearance. Even as a small boy during Christmas festivities in grade school he was always his classmate's choice to play Judas Iscariot, the betrayer of Jesus. For that he had been nicknamed zyd—Jew. It had always been the source of much anguish to him; an aquiline nose does not make one a Jew, does it? He asked himself silently.

It might have occured to him that his friends would come forward to testify in his behalf. None did, and Franek must have feared that this might only further implicate him as well as his friends. His lips continued moving in silent prayer: "Merciful Virgin Mary," so it went, "give me strength and courage to keep my family and friends out of this terrible nightmare."

"Speak up! Answer the question!" The sound of Meier's voice returned Franek to reality. "Tell the assembled where you were at the time of your apprehension!"

"I was near the railroad station."

"What were you doing near the station?" Meier continued relentlessly.

"I was walking toward the droshky stand."

"Now then, were you aware that you were not permitted to leave the ghetto without special authorization?" Meier was especially pleased with the use of the word "authorization," and he repeated it for the benefit of the assembled before the prisoner could respond.

"Did you have an official permit from the authorities to leave the ghetto premises?"

"No, I did not," replied Franek with a disconcerting lack of equivocation, "I didn't realize that I needed one." He was almost able to project a certain degree of joviality, for which the statement might have been accepted under different circumstances. Here, no one appreciated the humor.

"And it didn't occur to you that you might be apprehended and brought to justice?" Meier emphasized the last word of his question.

"Frankly, no," replied Franek with all sincerity, "I had no reason to fear apprehension. I'm not a Jew!" He mustered all his strength and courage to enunciaate the latter.

"Did you not run away when you were challenged as a Jew?"

"I might have run, I might not have. I can't remember exactly." I studied Franek's face and I saw signs of resignation. He must be at his wit's end, I thought, and I was reminded of the old adage "those whom the gods will destroy, they first make mad." Meier, too, was sufficiently a judge of men to sense the imminent breakdown.

"If you are innocent of the charges brought against you, if you are not a Jew, then you will let the court examine you. In keeping with the law, you must submit to the genital test." Meier's statement had a conciliatory tone, as though he, too, were fed up with the proceedings and wished an end to them. In an instant, the prisoner replied affirmatively: "Yes, of course I will." And as he uttered his consent, his eyes bulged in terror, for he must have realized, with the suddenness of death, that he had been circumcised as an infant—"for sanitary reasons," they had said. After all, he was the son of a doctor.

Franek Piecha's fate was sealed. He was hanged in the middle of the market square, now called *Umschlag Platz*, across from the ancient synagogue. His limp body was left on display for a total of forty-eight hours; a sampling of Gestapo justice for all to see, for all to remember.

The Jews considered Franek's death an oddity, a kind of "poetic justice." Anecdotes spread among the community as a result of the trial. People whispered to one another, "Frank laid down his life for our cause, and he wasn't even a Piotrkover Jew." They said. "He was the first Gentile in the shtetl memory to give his life al kiddush hashem, for the sanctification of His Name, and he wasn't even entitled to a proper burial and a *kaddish*."

I listened to the stories, and I wondered whether Franek's soul was going to return and mingle with the souls of our own departed.

The night following the Piecha trial, the Seventh Bureau received orders to begin the "resettlement" of the Jews. The occupied territories were to be free of Jews or *Judenrein*, as the Nazis called it. The units responsible for this task came under the strange-sounding name: *Einsatzgruppe.*

A column of trucks, loaded with Lithuanian SS, drove through the ghetto streets in the early morning. The trucks came to a halt on Silna Street, and the eager mercenaries piled out rapidly onto the street. Disciplined efficiency was the essence of the operation. As they started toward the various homes, their assignment became obvious. From behind the safety of window shutters, we watched and listened terrified.

The sound of Meier's voice could be heard throughout the ghetto as he announced through the bull-horn: "You have ten minutes to come out! You are being resettled East and you will work for the Third Reich! Leave your belongings, only take essentials! You will be supplied all you need on your arrival to the work camp!"

"Ten minutes he gives them to take the essentials." Max said bitterly. "How can they think of their belongings when they're being clubbed into the trucks?"

"God's hands will strike him down." My grandfather said, and I hoped it would happen soon; before they came for us.

Neighbors were quickly rounded up and herded into the street. Most of them were only half-dressed and not altogether awake. On occasion, the hunters stopped long enough to molest the more attractive women and young girls. Those who resisted were quieted with the butt of a rifle. The hunt went on for several hours as we looked on helplessly. Shouts of pain and anguish resounded as homes were looted and women were violated.

I was helpless with rage. Along with the Mandels, our family huddled quietly behind the curtains of the living-room windows. Only one block away, our friends and acquaintances were being driven from their homes, robbed and raped, but we remained passive, terrorized by the mere thought that the search might not end on Silna Street. We prayed that God would permit the invaders to be satisfied with their booty and leave us in peace.

"God Almighty in heaven." My grandmother prayed. I hope they won't come for us."

"Whatever happens," Mandel whispered to Nora, "we mustn't doanything to antagonize them. If we'll leave them alone, they'll leave us alone too," he reasoned.

I regarded Nora with much affection. She was truly beautiful. In her devotion and modesty, she had become dear to all of us. Secretly, though, I admired her feminine beauty. God, not her, don't let them lay their hands on her. I prayed silently. The mere thought of the enemy desecrating her unspoiled beauty had caused me unspeakable anguish. And in my anxiety, I had visualized the worst.

"Remember," my grandfather was reading aloud, "our sages tell us to live, as they say: I call heaven and earth to witness against you this day, that I have set before thee life and death, the blessing and the curse; therefore choose life, that thou mayest live, thou and thy seed. . ."

"*Jude verrecke!* Jew drop dead!" We could hear the SS shouts above he recital of the prayers in our hideout. But even worse than the sound of the enemy's raucous laughter was the guilt that we were to carry with us henceforth as a helpless people.

Following the first *Einsatzgruppe* there was a queer silence which prevailed on the streets of the ghetto; a silence louder than the shouts of pain and agony which filled the air during the previous night.

The invaders had come closer to their professed goal; Piotrkow was well on its way to becoming *Judenrein*.

An image of a world so near in time, yet already becoming like a legend from the past, had just come to me. The other day, little Simchah, the Shohet's eleven year old boy, was caught leaving the ghetto without his identification armband. *Simchah* had always been slow to understand things. He was not altogeter feeble-minded but he was not like the other children. There was talk about his mental retardation, but it was only talk. Simchah was a harmless boy, not into mischief, quiet and obedient to a degree of his consciousness. No matter how many times he had been told to remember the armband, its importance had never quite impressed the boy. And now, as he faced his antagonists, Simchah grinned from ear to ear, oblivious to the seriousness of the situation. He was clearly unable to comprehend what the fuss was all about and why he had become the center of everyone's attention.

The crime carried the death penalty. Even as he was being led to the execution, he did not understand why. The noose around his thin boy's neck, he was handed an order by one of his executioners, an Estonian SS, on which the verdict was written. The boy glanced at the paper uncomprehendingly and asked: "Please, what is this little paper?"

Many of the assembled wept. I gripped my mother's hand tightly, and she gave me a special look of reassurance. But Simchah was hanged on that day in the market square, and his frail body swayed grotesquely from the thick rope. He was the second example of Nazi ghetto justice; a lesson to be remembered. Simchah was the Hebrew word for "joy." I knew then that things would not change easily for me, despite my mother's patient reassurances. Weeks would turn into months, and nothing would change.

There were persistent rumors. There was fear. Above all, there was congestion and the constant anxiety of the ghetto mind. With overall conditions becoming worse, laughter and happy songs were rarely heard. That was a bad sign, because the Jewish people were a joyful, musical people. Occasionally, we still heard the Hasid's chant, as he sang praises to the Lord God or the kiddush on Sabbath eve. Not even the constant rattle of the SS automatic rifles was able to disrupt the majesty of the Jew's prayer.

Soon, a new song was born in the ghetto. It was hummed by anyone able to carry a tune. Like all things in war, it appeared suddenly, spawned by misery and nurtured into life by our longing and hope. It was called Where Can I go?

Where, oh where can I go?
When every exit is shut.
Where, oh where can I go?
When everywhere stands a guard.
Where, oh where can I go?
I am told to stay put.
Wherever I might turn,
They tell me "Jew, stay here,
And return to your lot!"

It was an old question. There were ghettos in the past. I recalled the story of Purim and the cruel Haman. There was also the story of the Jewish bondage and suffering under the great king Rameses II of Egypt. How much simpler and less painful it has been to tell a story than to experience it? I thought silently. The stories were old, but the reality was imminent. We prayed for a Moses to utter the famous words: "Let my people go!"

We needed a miracle. And while we waited for it and prayed, there was more fear, there was more congestion, and there were black rumors. And in all the fear and congestion, in sickness and in the scourge of death, amid the rumors of imminent doom, there resounded the haunting melody as it reverberated from every spiral of the barbed wire fence: Where, oh where can I go. . ?

4

Weeks and days merged. Were it not for the love we shared we might have entered into a state of despair. The feeling of love and belonging had kept us going and thinking of a better future.

Hunger was now becoming a permanent state, constantly present in our minds as it was felt in the pits of our stomachs.

It did not come as a surprise. Our money was finally and irrevocably gone. Having used up her piggy-bank savings, my mother now tried to find buyers for her linen or the fine feather bedding which we would scarcely miss, but unfortunately everyone was trying to sell and nobody wanted to buy. Sadly, the Christians, when approached about buying, laughed cynically saying: "Why should we pay you? Soon we'll get it for free."

There was still some demand for silver, but my mother held onto hers, which she had hidden in a special place in the attic, because it was an anniversary present from my father and she would not part from it. Not this soon.

"Can you imagine? What do they take me for? Ten zlotys they offered me for three sets of linen." My mother cried.

"Calm yourself, child," my grandmother consoled her, "we'll get by."

"Ten zlotys! We could hardly get a pound of potatoes for that amount of money. That's only one meal. One meal for three sets of linen!" My mother was inconsolable.

"Quiet, Bela, the children." My grandmother gestured toward us.

"No matter. It's time they knew. The money's gone and we'll have to act accordingly, all of us."

"Let's take out the silver, Bela." My grandmother suggested.

"We can sell my violin." I said, holding out the case to my mother. With an expression of utter dismay, she cried: "I won't have it! Now look what you've done!" She reproached my grandmother.

"But, mama," I interrupted. "I won't have time to get much use out of it. With work in the glass factory and all things considered. Besides, we can always get another violin when things change."

"No, Vilusiek, and that's final." My mother was resolute. "You'll practice as much as time permits. You know how rusty you get when you miss a day's practice."

"Yes, I know, it might as well be a year."

"Children, children, don't argue over nothing." Grandfather Srulko stepped out of the bedroom, carrying in the palm of his hand a small blue and white metal box, with the familiar map of Palestine on one side and the inscription "make the wilderness bloom" on the other. Nearly every Jewish home carried such a box. Children and adults alike contributed so that some day the Jews might redeem and reclaim the land of Israel.

"We'll use what we saved." He declared sadly.

"No! You mustn't, Srulko!" My grandmother was aghast.

"Israel can wait, we can't." My grandfather responded calmly. "If we starve, it won't be good for anyone. This, I feel, Israel wouldn't want to happen. It is our holy duty to survive. And if these meager savings which we have here can help us even toward one meal, then we are obliged to spend it in good conscience. I'm sure Israel will be, no matter what happens. And, the Almighty, blessed be He, will forgive us, for He is kind and merciful."

"Srulko, this is sacred money." My grandmother insisted.

"Let me have the key, Rachel." He addressed his wife by her given name only during moments of crisis. "Let me have the key, I say, we'll replenish all we have taken if we survive, and if we don't, I'll be the one who'll answer for it when I'm called before our Maker."

Reluctantly, my grandmother handed over the small key. She looked away when he turned it and opened the box, emptying its contents onto the tablecloth. He counted the small coins. "Nine zlotys and thirty-five groszy," he said loudly, for all to hear. There was much sadness in his voice. "It wouldn't have purchased much land in Israel anyhow."

Rachel ignored Srulko for one whole week after his sinful deed. The charity money provided us with one inadequate meal, and my mother's special silverware was sold soon thereafter.

"What's going to happen after all this is gone?" My mother didn't really expect anyone to reply.

"I have an idea!" Grandfather exclaimed, "it's high time I paid another visit to our cousin the shoemaker!"

I was delighted at the prospect of visiting with Aunt Sabina and Uncle Mihas. I had carried a special fondness for their daughter Devorah for as long as I could remember. A year younger than myself, she was my frequent playmate since our arrival in Piotrkow. As time went on, we had become separated by curfews and restrictions, but the cordial relationship continued during our infrequent get-togethers.

On one occasion, we were in our attic hiding place, I proposed to my pretty cousin. "Will you marry me, Devorah, when we're both grownups somewhere in America, away from these hateful people?" She closed her eyes tightly and made a wish and a promise. "I will, Vilek. When all this is over, I shall marry you." We had often talked about America and Hollywood, the great stars of Cowboy movies and their torrid love affairs. It was our dreamworld, equally as unattainable as were the distant stars and gallaxies. Our escape.

"Remember, Devorah." I had taken advantage of her eyes being shut and sealed the pledge with a kiss on her lips. She did not withdraw. "I'll remember," she said, and we were happy together.

Uncle Joseph had become a frequent visitor to our home on Zamkowa 20. It seemed unusual that he would spend so much time away from his own family. He did not come emptyhanded, and the food he brought for us was always welcome. He especially remembered to shower Nora with gifts. In fact, it had become clear that she was the primary reason for his frequent visitations.

In spite of the hardship, Nora had grown more beautiful with each passing day. She seldom ventured outdoors for fear that she might attract the attention of the plundering militia. Many ghetto women had daily fallen victims of the SS and their mercenaries.

When on occasions Max Mandel would admonish her for staying out longer than necessary, Nora promptly replied: "I can care for myself, so please, don't treat me like a child."

"Your mother entrusted you to my care, Nora, and I worry regardless how old you are. I don't distrust your ability to take care of yourself. Under normal circumstances, you could. But we don't live under normal circumstances; vultures are out there looking for prey, and I worry."

"If it'll make you feel better, Uncle Max, I'll be in before curfew." Nora complied and Max gave her a look of gratitude.

Max knew that force had become synonymous with the law. No one dared question the behavior of the SS bureaucrats and their mercenaries. They ransacked with impunity. Shot Jews dead in the street from the guard towers which were erected by Jewish labor and tortured men, women, and children at a drop of a hat. The new "law" protected them.

Wednesday night was Jewish Council assembly night. My grandparents left for the meeting. My mother and brother Roman went along. New work regulations were to be discussed, and Roman was an able-bodied "adult" at fourteen, affected by the new laws.

Felusia was asleep; Hayim and I were busy preparing our humash portion for next day's school session. Nora was reading by candle-light. There was a knock on the door. It was Uncle Joseph. As usual, he didn't come emptyhanded.

"Shouldn't you boys be in bed now?" He asked.

"Just as soon as we've done our homework, Uncle Joseph."

"Hurry up, then." He sat very close to Nora on the couch. They talked about things in general, and we couldn't concentrate on our task. "I've had a very successful week, Nora." He said. "Just think, I made three pairs of boots; two are for the *Brigadeführer* and one for his wife." He paused and I saw him move closer, almost touching Nora's shoulder. I didn't like that. But it was Joseph, and he brought food, and we needed food. Nora seemed unimpressed. He continued: "I was treated to several glasses of Schnaps before they called the staff car to take me back to the ghetto. I'm like this with the *Brigadeführer*." He pressed his index and middle fingers together to illustrate his close relationship with the SS chief.

"Joseph's drunk," I whispered to Hayim, "let's leave the room." We excused ourselves to seek quiet in the bedroom. Although we had closed the door behind us, we could hear the boisterous voice of Joseph coming through.

"Nora, you're a beautiful woman." There was a moment of silence, then I could hear her voice objecting very strongly.

"You mustn't, please." There was a struggle, as if she had tried to disengage herself from his hold. "Let go of me, please!" She pleaded.

"Please, just a little bit," he said. His voice had an unpleasant hissing sound. I opened the door a crack, and I saw Joseph reaching into Nora's breast. I could see fear on Nora's face. It was inconceivable that Joseph would dare to make an attempt at seducing the girl. Caught by surprise, she did not resist. Joseph mistook her hesitation for acquiescence. "I've waited for this moment with all the passion and longing, my little beauty." He embraced her very tightly, kissing her on the lips and letting his right hand search the warmth of her thighs.

"Please! Joseph, let go! You're not feeling well." She pleaded.

"Please, go home."

Joseph must have suddenly resolved that he would have Nora whatever the price. He lunged forward, placing his large body on top of hers. He tore the garments from her trembling body, and Nora screamed. I ran up to them, standing there fascinated by the mysterious struggle. "Do something, Vilek! Call someone! Help me!"

I began pounding his back with my fists, barely making an impression. Then, he looked back at me, released his hold on his victim and slapped her twice across the face. "You little hussy! Go ahead and keep it! Keep it all for them!" He stood up, tidying up his clothing. "And don't come running for help to your Joseph when the SS comes to fuck you, you little bitch!"

Nora blushed, glancing in my direction. I wanted to tell her that she needn't blush in my behalf. I was familiar with such expressions, though they were still puzzling to boys of my age.

Joseph stumbled over his own feet as he rushed out of the room. We could hear his hurried steps all the way down the wooden staircase. Exhausted from the encounter, Nora sat sobbing on the floor. Dispassionately, I picked up her torn garments which lay scattered about the room and helped her put them on. She was momentarily in a daze, but quickly regained her composure.

"We mustn't tell about this," she pleaded. "Do you hear, Vilek, no one must know what happened here tonight."

"You needn't worry, Nora." I said reassuringly. "I swear I won't tell!" I kissed the tears from her cheeks, though their saltiness felt uncomfortable. "Hayim's asleep, so is Felusia. No one will know.'

"I've made Joseph angry, and he won't bring food any longer." She cried. "My Lord, what have I done?" She seemed weary, and for the first time, I felt pity for her.

"You mustn't cry, Nora." I held her hand in mine. "He's no better than those he works for. It's just as well if he stays away from now on." There was anger in me. "Besides, let's wait till we hear what they decided at the Council meeting. We have gotten along without Joseph before and we can do it again." I spoke more out of spite than sense. We would miss the occasional provisions Joseph brought us; both Nora and I had realized that much.

When morning came, we learned that all able-bodied men of the ghetto between the ages of twelve to sixty were to be inducted into forced labor detachments. The two glass factories, Kara and Hortensia had increased their production of bottles for drugs and beverages, and were short of manpower. The peacetime output of the two factories had always been impressive, but with the occupation and the Nazi war effort, their output had to double.

Soon after the Nazi occupation had begun, factory workers briefly enjoyed perferential treatment for meritorious work. However, as the enemy grew stronger and more arrogant, the governor's patriotic enthusiasm as well as economic wisdom imposed annoying innovations on Polish labor. "Longer working hours, greater productivity and a freeze on pay." The governor announced.

Gestapo agents and informers staffed all production lines, and SS guards were posted throughout the two plants. The enemy was in control. There were protests, but they were quickly put down. It was one of the severest winters in memory and there was nowhere to go. The howling Siberian wind blew in from the East and snow covered the countryside. Nature shrunk unto itself, and so did man. We lacked coal to fire our stoves and everyone stole what wood there was. Wooden fences and staircases had begun to disappear. The water we carried from our well was frozen into cubes by the time we returned home.

I was never able to understand why it was we filled the buckets with water to the brim, but when we thawed the ice, only half of it was left. "It's one of nature's miracles, Vilek." My grandfather joked. "Some day, you'll understand this mysterious partnership between nature and man; what she gives, she gives grudgingly, and then she takes half of it away." He smiled, and I knew he was in one of his rare moments when he didn't allow his wit to become dimmed by the gathering storm.

Spring ushered in an epidemic of runaways from the two factories. Polish workers left their jobs, and no one knew where they had gone, except for the rumors that young people were joining up with the growing resistance. For each man gone from his post, one Nazi war function remained unfulfilled and the total war effort suffered.

The Gestapo was furious. They knew that with each abandoned work station there was one more saboteur in the Polish forests. The Germans were swift to strike back. Urgent announcements were posted everywhere in public view. If a worker were to desert his post, the worker's family would be held responsible and pay the consequences; severe reprisals took place immediately culminating in death by public hanging.

Even as the announcements were posted, more workers did not report to their factory duties. In defiance of reprisals the ranks grew. At the Kara and Hortensia glass factories machines stood idle, diminishing production as well as the *Sturmbannführer's* chances for promotion. He was Rinehardt Schröder, a man of humble origins who came up through the SS ranks due to his stubborn belief in the *Führer* and a bureaucratic tenacity for detail. His superiors assigned the task to Reinhardt, because he was, in their eyes, "the best man for the job." He would not fail them, he swore. Now, Schröder's only preoccupation was the training of unskilled labor so that production might be pushed upward in an attempt to partially redeem himself in the eyes of Berlin.

It was then, in utter desperation, that the commandant conceived the idea of a "working Jew." The idea grew. Jews were mobilized into a ghetto workforce, and every able-bodied individual was to be drafted. Only the very old and children below the age of twelve would be exempt.

Ghetto workers were selected at random. Shifts were established around the clock. The foremen came from faraway places in Germany to supervise, and were called "efficiency experts." Their task was to whip the undisciplined ghetto inhabitants into an orderly and highly efficient labor force in the service of the Third Reich.

"All you'll get is a loaf of bread and five pounds of potatoes a week?" My grandmother lamented over the combined rations of the three woring "adults" in our household; Max Mandel, Roman and myself. "We won't starve, but we won't live on it either."

"It's better than not getting anything." Roman remarked.

"And they expect you to work on Sabbath, too?!" My grandfather shouted. "You're only boys, and they force you already to commit a great sin against the holy commandments! I'm not going to let it happen!" He paced up and down the room.

"Be reasonable, daddy." My mother pleaded. "They could do worse than that."

"Yes? And what's worse than desecrating the Sabbath?" Srulko fumed.

"The boys could disappear, like all the others did," my mother said softly, "and we wouldn't know where they've been taken to." Srulko stopped pacing. "Besides," she added, "there must be some kind of exemption on the strictness of the Sabbath Law in the Talmud to deal with emergencies such as this." I thought, I noticed a twinkle in her eye.

"I'd say, there must." My grandmother hastened to add. "And if there isn't, Srulko, you and your Hasidim might want to think of one very quickly." She paused, noticing a frown on my grandfather's face. "Circumstances, after all, aren't the same any more." She concluded almost in a whisper, as if to herself.

The Hasidim searched the Talmud, and they did their souls as well. They argued late into three nights in succession. At last, a compromise was reached. It was one of those typical solutions which I had been accustomed to hearing during their past sessions. This time, however, it was a matter of the gravest importance; the salification of the Sabbath. The *gabbah* expressed the decision of the Hasidic leaders. He swayed to and fro, his strong fingers caressing his abundant beard. He lifted his eyes to heaven as he spoke:

"It is written that God, blessed be He, completed the creation of the universe on the sixth day. And so, in His infinite wisdom, He declared the seventh day a day of rest; the Sabbath." The gabbah paused, to clear his throat, and continued. "But it is also written that life is even more sacred than the Sabbath; life is more precious than any commandment. Indeed, if there be no life, there be no observance of His holy commandments." The *gabbah* paused again and took a deep breath. This time, he looked around at the assembled, as if to challenge the last existing thread of opposition. There was silence.

"Thus, in His infinite wisdom, the Almighty, blessed be He, grants us permission to labor on the Sabbath if it means saving a life in doing so." The speaker implored the heavens again, "Gotyenu," he addressed God with the endearing Jewish name, "forgive us, but we must save the lives first, so we may be privileged to observe Your Sabbath in some future time." The argument was closed. I marveled at the flexibility of the Law.

Herr Seemann and *Herr* Förster were the new civilian administrators of the Hortensia Glass Works. No one knew where they came from, nor did we know whether they were part of Department IV-D-4, the dreaded section of the Gestapo responsible for deportation and emigration. On the day we had been formally inducted into our new status of forced labor, we stood at attention, carefully measuring our new adversaries as they readied to address us. *Herr* Wolfgang Förster stepped forward and shouted an order, thereby establishing his superiority as the camp's Deputy Commandant. There was silence. He ascended the makeshift rostrum. He was a man slightly over forty years of age, his curly blond hair allowed a clear view of his scalp at the back of his head. He was of medium height but stoutly built. He had the frame of a grizzly bear and probably the strength to go with it.

Our attention centered on Förster's massive structure, his cloud-gray eyes, the silver-handled riding whip which he tapped against his spotlessly clean boots as he talked. He tried to be funny, but his audience did not respond to his type of humor. This increased his awkwardness and the tempo with which he kept on whipping his boot. It had also earned him immediately the nickname golem, the idiot.

"Jews!" Förster exclaimed. "You will work now for the glory of the Third Reich. We expect you to work hard, and you'll get good treatment. Work will continue around the clock; three shifts, each eight hours long. You will have a half an hour rest period during each shift. In payment for your work, the council will be given provisions for the ghetto. Any individual who will do outstanding work will receive special benefits. We are generous with hard-working and loyal people."

"Did you hear that, Roman? He's generous." I whispered. "It won't be so bad after all."

"Quiet there!" Förster's associate, Herr Hans Seemann, shouted into the crowd. "This is another thing you'll have to learn, *verfluchtes Gesindel!*" He addressed us with the German equivalent of "damned rubble." "You'll have to keep your mouths shut when you're spoken to by your superiors!"

Initially, it was Seemann who had attracted our attention. He was the younger of the two, approximately thirty-four or thirty-six years old, and his small, cunning eyes measured our ranks incessantly, as though searching for something or someone. He had a way of making you feel terribly uncomfortable. The ugly scar on his right cheek lent him a repulsive as well as a frightening aspect. Knowing the Deputy Commandant to be a bafoon, his second-in-command earned our immediate respect as the man to watch and avoid. He was respectfully nicknamed *mamzer*, the bastard. In time, Reinbold Seemann would prove to be that, and much more.

Neither *golem* nor *mamzer* had ever before been vested with such absolute authority. Their newly acquired awareness of being masters over the lives of so many inferior beings overwhelmed them. This was their first opportunity to realize their full potential. They dedicated their energies to whipping people into order.

That night, my grandfather and I had a serious talk. He talked to me about the recent past, and made no illusions about the future. As he talked in a brief flash of memory, I recalled little Simchah, the Shohet's youngest, sensitive but feeble-minded son, who wandered out of the ghetto without an armband on his sleeve and paid for this terrible "crime" with his life; I thought of his mother going mad after the hanging of her little boy, and it brought tears to my eyes.

Things were deteriorating rapidly, with no improvement in sight. First, there had been the identifying armbands with the star of David, so we took great risks to pass as Gentiles, facing the penalty of death for removing the armband. Many defied the order to steal a moment of freedom and dignity. Then came our isolation from the rest of the world, as truckloads of barbed wire was wound around the ghetto periphery, with Lithuanian, Latvian and Estonian SS sentries posted to guard the Jews. They had our carpenters build the guard towers, and one large gate on Zielna Street in the central point of the ghetto. Now, we had entered the newest phase: forced labor.

"What's next, grandpa?" I asked.

"Who knows, my boy, who knows." My grandfather mused. "The enemy thinks up clever ways in which to make us suffer, but you must take thins as they come, Velvele," he paused. I was pleased my grandfather called me by my Yiddish name, for he had used it only on very special occasions, "life's burdens never lighten, we simply learn to live with them as time moves on."

I understood. It was one of those rare occasions when my grandfather and I were in harmony. I was deeply preoccupied, and my grandfather knew. He would not pry into my secret worries, but his eyes had told me that he would listen if I felt like confessing.

"When I worked for the Supply Company, there were some Gentile boys my own age. They lived in the neighborhood of the old castle, and they came to the fence begging for scraps of food."

"Well, that's nothing to worry about, is it?" My grandfather encouraged me to go on.

"I had always managed to save something for them. Some became my friends, others envied me and suspected all along that I was a Jew." I paused, and he smiled encouragingly.

"So there are always people who'll envy others and try to find fault with them. Thank the Almighty, blessed be His name, that you're not one of them."

"You're missing the point, grandpa." I wanted to avoid sounding impatient, "passing for a *shaygets*," I used the Yiddish expression which meant a Gentile boy or ruffian, "had its advantages. I enjoyed the freedom of movement in their company. I could walk proudly on the sidewalk, without having to duck the blows and elude the rocks of other gentiles. I was a lion among lions."

"That you'll always be, my boy." My grandfather couldn't refrain from interrupting.

"That's not all, *zayde*," I used the Yiddish for grandpa which he loved so much. "No, that's not all of it. Don't you see, zayde? As long as I was in their company, no one dared to call me dirty Jew! I was one of them, I passed for one of them."

"So? What worries you now?"

"You still don't get the point, *zayde*?"

"No, but I'm curious."

"Well, tomorrow will be the test. On the way to Hortensia, the guards will march us through the section of town where my friends live. I know they won't miss the parade. They'll line the sidewalks to see the dirty Jews led to forced labor."

"You must walk proudly, my boy. You must walk with dignity, and no insults will touch you."

"That'll be very hard, *zayde*. You see, some of those who had defended me will suffer along with me tomorrow. And those who had pointed their fingers at me will triumph. It'll be humiliating for my friends. Is that justice, grandpa?"

"Leave justice to the Almighty, my boy, and be strong. He will not let you down. You must always believe that, and you'll be fine."

"I believe it, grandpa." I said, but the tremor in my voice betrayed lack of conviction. It wasn't that I had my doubts about the existence of God. I thught to myself. I was more preoccupied with things affecting me here on earth than whith those of a heavenly nature. I dared not share these thoughts with my grandfather, for he would surely become very angry. He showed little, if any, tolerance for lack of faith.

The day was here. I was leaving my mother and the others at home to spend my first day at work. I read great concern in my mother's eyes. She must have been particularly worried about my education. No one could tell for how long we would have to forget the world of scholarship. Perhaps, too, she wondered about her "little boy's" ability to cope with this new task. We hugged, and she admonished: "Do what they say. Stay out of trouble. Do well in your new task." She let go, and the three directives had become my principles for survival. The column of workers started out for Hortensia.

I walked between Max Mandel and Roman. My grandparents prayed and my mother turned her head so I wouldn't see her tears. I kept deep in the ranks, hoping to blend into anonymity. I dreaded facing up to my adversaries. The crowds were there. I saw them from the distance as they lined the sidewalks.

They shouted obscenities and some of the children threw rocks at the marchers. "*Jude! Jude!* Jew! Jew!" They yelled the German word they'd learned so well. "The filthy Jews are coming!" Someone yelled. "How do you like to carry the cross for a change." Another added.

There were those who stood silently, and we thanked them in silence. And there were some who shed a tear for us, and we wept with them.

There was the ancient castle on Zamkowa Street. What memories it brought to mind. I wished Boost were there right then. He would know what to do. But Boost was gone, and I was going to face my friends alone. I prayed for courage.

From some distance, I saw their faces. My heart pounded violently. Like a pursued animal sensing danger, I knew that things were going to happen on that day that had never happened before. I kept praying and wishing that it were all over for me quickly, with as little pain as possible. But as in most nightmares, time passes exaggeratedly slowly: one. . . two. . . three. . . four. . . one. . . two. . . three. . . four. . . I measured the cadence of our steps. At last, we were marching past the "reviewing" stand.

They were all there jeering. There was Tadzik, Yanek, Zbyszek, Mietek, and all of the others. Some children held whips fashioned from tree branches. Encouraged by the indifference of the elders, they whipped those in our ranks nearest to them. They hadn't seen me at once. "*Jude! Jude!*" They made grotesque faces at us, laughing and mimicking. An old woman spat in our direction: "Curses on you, Jews!" She said loudly. "You had it coming!"

Eventually I was noticed.

"See the filthy Jew?!" Mietek shouted with glee. "What did I tell you?! He's a Jew, a filthy, rotten Jew!" He addressed the others triumphantly. "Now it's in the open! He lied to all of us, but he can't deny it now, can he?!" Mietek was in his glory, and against all reason, I felt shame and guilt of having had to lie about my being a Jew. Mietek's words kept reverberting in my mind: "He made fools of all of us, the filthy Jew, he did!"

Tadzik looked at me in disbelief.

"Tell him it's not true, Vilek!" Tadzik implored. "You shouldn't be wearing an armband! Take that rag off and come over here with us! You belong over here, Vilek! Tell them it's all a mistake!"

I was fearfully silent. My ears were filled with the sounds of angry, accusing voices. I saw hostile faces, hateful eyes, and though my body sustained the punishment of physical abuse, I felt no pain at all.

For this moment alone, I had wished that I were not a Jew. I wanted to take Tadzik aside and explain to him how I felt, but there was no time and there was nothing to explain. What had set us apart was that I was as much a Jew as they were Gentiles.

Suddenly, something inside me snapped, and I pushed my way through the formation before anyone could stop me. I plowed into my tormentors, and I ran. And as I ran, I tore the armband from my sleeve; tore it into small shreds and tossed it behind me. I have committed not one, but two cardinal sins in full view of witnesses all too willing to testify against me. All that didn't matter for the moment. What mattered was the exhilarating feeling of freedom from humiliation and the restoration of one small shred of my self-esteem. "You are a human being, and you must always walk with your head raised high and with your God-given dignity to guide you, no matter what." My grandfather's words echoed through my mind.

I heard shouts of "halt!" and the sound of pursuing boots on the pavement. Now, I could only think, I must get away, I must get away. The tips of my lungs were burning, and I was out of breath. Here, I redoubled my efforts, but they caught up with me easily.

Blow upon blow landed with an uncanny accuracy. I was kicked onto my upper body until my ribs felt like cinder. Someone picked me up, only to toss me down onto the pavement with great force. With each strike, the pain was less and the world around me reverberated with the sound: "*Jude! Jude!* Jew! Jew!"

There was darkness and light and the colors of the rainbow. Then, there was a sudden emptiness, as if the world had ceased to be. I felt myself falling into an endless chasm, and the pain ceased also. And during this semiconscious state, between being and not-being, I thought I heard a voice that sounded familiar, it could have been Tadzik's voice.

"He's still our friend." The voice spoke. "He'll always be one of us." I did not mind the derisive laughter of the others, for I knew that one had remained my friend. He was a friend of Vilek, the Jew. That was all that mattered.

Later, at home, I kept repeating to myself: "It isn't as though you have been smashed to bits, you know. There's only a bruise or two here and there and a sting of pain."

"Why were they angry at me, mama?" I asked my mother who tried to comfort me. "What have I done to make them hate me so?"

"You mustn't think that way, Vilusiek." She caressed my aching shoulders and massaged my back. Think of Tadzik and his loyalty to you. It far outweighs the behavior of all the others."

"I'll try, mama." I said unconvincingly.

"Time's the best healer, Vilusiek," my mother murmured the old cliche, patting my head, "before you'll get to be twenty-one, the hurt will be long gone and forgotten."

I listened half-heartedly. I tried today to imagine what would happen tomorrow and asked myself: "What evil will tomorrow bring?"

Time and hard work did exercise some healing effect on my bruises, although pain had found its way deep into my soul. Days grew inscrutably long and increasingly wearisome. Gradually, I was beginning to accept my fate.

Among themselves, in subdued voices, the Jews attempted to lighten their burden by ridiculing their enemy. Anecdotes and jokes abundantly circulated the ghetto, although the macabre humor failed to inhibit the success of the Nazis. My own escape was to dream of America, and my thoughts traveled to my American relatives full of questions I was unable to answer. . .

. . ."Now look what you've done!" Fay yelled at her cringing husband. "He's only fourteen, and he wants to join up! Stubborn like his father!" Mickey was helpless when Fay carried on like that.

"What can I do?" He tried to reason. "He's got a mind of his own."

"It's all your fault, Mickey! You and 'your let's wait' attitude!"

"The more I try to talk sense, the more determined he gets." Mickey was afraid to argue with his wife. Deep inside, he knew that she was right. He did have a tendency to be cautious. It was a weakness which had always allowed him to defer decisions to Fay. Why should it be different now?

Isaac's gotten into his head that he was going to join the Army. At fourteen he could pass for seventeen. The boy was mature in every way. Through the newspaper articles and the movie newsreels, the boy has grown to hate the Germans with a passion. The Bund rallies in Manhattan added fire to his hatred. He wants to fight the Nazis even though America's not at War. Mickey thought silently observing his wife.

"And you'd better tell him to stay out of the street fights, Mickey." Fay admonished. Isaac has returned home with cuts and bruises on several occasions, and she feared one day he might be seriously injured.

"You can only try to reason with a big boy like that, Fay," Mickey said sheepishly. "After all, you don't throw a man his size over the knee any more."

"Mark my words, Mickey," Fay went on, "that boy of yours will be big trouble." She had a way of making Isaac her husband's responsibility when the boy became a cause for worry. "Victor never gave us half the trouble at thirteen."

"Okay, okay, I'll have a talk with the young man when he gets home from school." Mickey promised.

"It'll take more than talk, Mickey." Fay insisted. "The boy's never forgiven you for letting down your relatives in Poland. He's still brooding about them, don't you know?"

Mickey left the room. He couldn't face his wife when the subject of Henryk and the family came up. Why did she have to keep reminding him. Wasn't it her mistake as well?

Nora came down with the fever at the worst possible time. Rumor had it that we could expect an *Einsatzgruppe* action at any time.

"We must get a doctor." My grandmother said.

"And risk quarantine?" My mother reminded her.

"She's burning up with fever." My grandmother tried to maintain composure. "It's typhus again. And we haven't any broth left to give her."

The tell-tale signs were there. With warm weather upon us, the sickness returned. A dark red rash of elevated spots appeared all over Nora's body. My mother and my grandmother took turns in applying cold compresses to lower the temperature. It subsided during the second week of Nora's illness, but on the ninth day Nora became delirious again. She screamed with terror, such was the force of the demons within her, and it took both my grandfather and max Mandel to hold her down. My mother frantically applied the wet towel and repeated mechanically: "No one will harm you, little one. We won't let them harm you."

"I don't want to go! I don't want to go! Don't let them take me!" Nora pleaded in the monotonous wail of the sick.

"You're staying right here with us, my baby, and we're not going to leave you." My mother placed another compress on Nora's forehead. Eventually, Nora slept.

"There's nothing we can do but wait and pray. The fever must break soon," my grandmother spoke from experience.

Everyone stayed up through the night with the delirious girl. When morning came, we were greeted by a faint, but determined demand: "I'm hungry." My grandmother was right. The last bit of fever had wrestled the sickness from Nora's body.

A special prayer of thanks was recited to acknowledge God's boundless mercies. "Blessed be He, amen." There would be no quarantine, no arguments with the bureaucrats from the Department of Health. We were prepared for Nora's demand. Special foodstuffs were kept on hand for her convalescence purchased with our remaining resources on the black market. We were happy to relinquish our share so that she was properly nourished. Now, we had no money left, but we didn't mind.

Soon, Nora recovered, more beautiful and incalculably stronger for having experienced partial death. The Hasidim rejoiced and sang praises to the One and Only.

Strange were the ways of the Lord. Just as we began to rejoice about the newly given life, Tadzik's engineer father returned from one of his runs north-east. "There's a camp hidden in the forest; smoke's billowing out of the chimneys that you can smell for miles around, sort of sweet and nauseating." Tadzik said, pausing.

"Go on, go on." I urged my friend.

"He heard loud screams. Like pain and anguish coming from the camp. He said it must be a death camp because he comes with a full load and always leaves empty. It's a death camp, all right." Tadzik repeated sadly.

I listened to my friend in disbelief. "You must tell them, Vilek!" He urged. "Tell them all!"

"First, we must make sure it's true." I said hesitantly.

"My father saw it with his own eyes. And he heard the screams. And others were there with him, not far from where it all happened." Tadzik went on. "When he asked one of the guards what was going on in there, the guard, a Ukrainian SS, just laughed and said: 'We're making soap in there. Can't you smell it?' This is how my father knew the terrible truth." Tadzik concluded gravely. "Only empty freight cars came back." That night, on my return home from the shift, I told everyone what I'd heard. They listened, didn't say a word, and they didn't believe a word of it.

Suddenly, my mother spoke: "After all, their soldiers wear God's name on their belt buckles, don't they?" I looked at her, and I saw an expression of hope in her eyes.

"Besides, they are such a cultured and proper people, truly civilized," my grandfather hastened to add, and I wasn't quite sure that I should have caught a trace of sarcasm.

"Truly, a nation of poets and thinkers, governed by law and justice," my grandmother concluded with an assertion intended to allay our doubts and presentiments.

I listened to my elders, and my spirit was instantly uplifted. What I did not suspect then was that the laws of the Third Reich had already been changed to reflect the thinking of the Führer; his brand of justice was a mere consequence of these laws.

Meanwhile, my whole body began to "look" hungry. While I washed my face one day, I made a startling discovery: as I ran my fingers over my skin, I was able to feel each bone. The skin was drawn tightly over the bones, and I was able to distinguish each and every one of them. It was only then I looked carefully at the faces of those near me; they, too, assumed the appearance of hunger.

5

Work at the Hortensia was at full capacity. The intensity of the heat made us forget the fear of hell.

By now, all Jewish property was confiscated. It was common practice for the Lithuanian guards as well as their SS superiors to loot the ghetto shops. The shopkeepers, although frightened, frequently consoled themselves after the ransacking, "Well, at least they left a little for the next time! And they forgot to give me a beating!"

The looting continued. The Commandant issued an order forbidding guards and soldiers to enter the Jewish sector without special authorization. Still, the plundering continued. Our home had been spared at first, but early one morning, the Lithuanians surprised us. They called it "confiscation of enemy goods." I observed my grandfather, fearing a fatal outburst of his uncontrollable temper. Srulko had by now gotten accustomed to the unpredictability of the enemy. If he hated, he didn't show it. Quite the contrary, he was trying to seem jovial as he carried his cherished belongings onto the waiting truck. He made humorous remarks in Yiddish about "those ignorant hirelings," and I prayed that no one understood.

The hirelings were systematic about their task, and not at all ignorant. They plundered from house to house and took whatever valuables they could find. The loot ranged from bedroom and dining room furniture to dismantled lavatories.

Things might have continued in their customary way, were it not for Isaac, the *gabbah*. Rumor had it that he had committed the fatal error, shouting for help when the plundering Lithuanians broke into his store during the night. His cry was silenced with a few shots. Neighbors wondered in fear, but dared not break the curfew to investigate. It was only on the following morning, the old temple-keeper was found slumped in the corner of his store, a large puddle of blood had gathered around his body, his eyes open wide with terror and incredulity.

News of the *gabbah's* murder spread within the ghetto community in record time. Isaac was prominent; after all, only a select few were members of the Council. Warszawski lodged a cautious protest with the Seventh Bureau. "The authorities would investigate and punish the guilty," he was assured.

The temple lost a faithful servant and we a loyal friend. Only a few days earlier the old man had suffered a severe beating at the hands of a band of Hitler Youth. They knocked out his upper bridge, and he lost the ability to chew. "At least, he won't have to worry about a new set of dentures," my grandfather remarked, and I became skeptical about his sense of humor.

The Bureau didn't keep its promise to the Council. If anything, the situation worsened, and the hopelessness touched off a series of suicides. The first in the ghetto. An unheard of occurrence in the Piotrkow community among its Jewish inhabitants. "Life is sacred." I heard the echo of my grandfather's admonishment. "Taking a life is a cardinal sin; another person's or one's own, regardless of circumstances."

Isaac's son, Yulek, swore to avenge his father's murder. He had been seen lately in the company of some young people who were not at all the Hasidic types. "No good will come of it, I'll tell you that much." My grandfather said. "He'll get himself in trouble, and he might antagonize the enemy. If he wants to honor the memory of his dead father, he should stay away from troublemakers."

"See how much good it did for poor Isaac," my grandmother remarked, more to herself than to my grandfather, but he picked up the thread of her remark, alarmed that it was made in my presence.

"That was an accident!" He raised his voice. "Do you understand? An accident!" He looked at me with great concern. "And in no way an excuse to follow the example of these accursed barbarians."

"Grandpa, why is it wrong to defend one's life when it's being threatened?" I asked.

"To defend it is one thing, but to kill for it is another." He replied without answering my question.

"But if to defend means to kill, shouldn't there be some provision in the Law to decide which life is more sacred; yours or his?" I insisted, and my grandfather showed signs of impatience. I knew it immediately because he began to twist the ends of his mustache in his own nervous manner.

"The Law is explicit, my boy. And life is sacred. All the rest must follow and the Law must be observed." He repeated stubbornly. I knew not to press the point further. There were things, after all, not to be argued. I thought to myself. Where words failed, deeds would speak for themselves.

Infrequent though they were, some days went by without looting or other forms of harrassment. When they did occur, the Jews wondered what would come next, but no one behind the barbed wire of the ghetto regarded the enemy as a benefactor. We were grateful for the smallest of mercies, but we knew the enemy was only planning new ways to torment us; waiting for the right moment to implement his plans.

Peace was of short duration. Rumors had intensified about the newly created camps to which thousands of Jews were being transported. Names, such as Treblinka, Sobibor, Majdanek, and Auschwitz were on everyone's lips. We heard these names uttered in whispers that filled us with anxiety and fear. But no matter how vivid the rumors, verified by an occasional escapee, eye-witness or a Christian friend, people were reluctant to believe.

"What will it take?" Felix asked. "If you won't believe it, then how will the outside world believe in the bestiality of the Nazi Reich?" Felix argued with the Hasidim.

"I can't believe that man can be this cruel to others of his species." Max whispered.

"I wish it were true, Max. But the Nazi doesn't believe we're human!" Felix was at the end of his patience. "To the Nazi, we're vermin! What do you do with vermin?" He waited for the other's response, but it didn't come. "I'll tell you, if you won't have the courage to admit it. You exterminate vermin, that's what you do!" Felix shouted. He turned quickly and ran out the front door. I could hear his hasty, nervous steps all the way down to the street.

"This one will cause trouble someday, too. Mark my words, he will." My grandfather shook his head, pointing after the young man. I didn't know what to make of my grandfather's words, but I had begun to feel an intense sympathy toward Felix and a strong inclination to follow his example of resistance.

Roman and I were now seasoned glass blowers at the Hortensia. We had made progress increasing our skills and gaining the respect of our superiors as well as our Christian co-workers. We were particularly fortunate to have earned the friendship of our immediate supervisor *Herr* Amadeus Edelmann. He reminded me of Boost in his easy-going manner and friendly smile. I liked him right away. Besides, I was partial to Mozart.

No one knew much about Edelmann. He seemed to be a man in his late forties, and the moment he appeared he attracted attention. He was a slim tall man, still young, with brown hair, green eyes but his face was creased like that of an old man. "That's because he worries too much," Roman whispered. The harbor city of Rostock on the Baltic Sea was his home until his arrival at the Hortensia. He dressed in simple gray khakis of a factory worker, and were it not for the Nazi Party button above his breast pocket one could have taken him for a common laborer.

Edelmann showed fairness in his relationship with the workers under his supervision, Jew and Christian alike, oftentimes stepping in to prevent harsh treatment at the hands of an overzealous foreman or guard. This had earned him the nickname "Jew-lover," though no one dared express it within ear-shot of the engineer. After all, he was protected by the Party emblem, and there was a mystery surrounding his background which had everyone guessing about the nature of his assignment at the Hortensia.

Edelmann had found ways to smuggle leftover food from the foremen cafeteria. On those occasions, he would call Roman and me to his office. "Get those two Jews over here, immediately!" He ordered his assistant. There, in the sanctuary of his quarters, we enjoyed the food without arousing the suspicion or envy of our co-workers. In addition, we took some of it home to feed the family.

The Poles despised us because our employment threatened to deprive them of their traditional livelihood. They ignored the fact that we had no options. "Never mind them," my grandfather used to say. "They're looking for an excuse to justify their deep hatred of the Jew. You must do your best. Your life depends on it. Theirs doesn't."

Even *Herr* Förster seemed more relaxed lately. Each day he would stand at the factory gates to receive the column of ghetto laborers. As we marched past him, he would spit into the palms of his hands, rub them briskly together, then grin his own inimitable smile. "Work Jews!" He shouted, laughing uproariously, "or we'll use you for soap!"

Our work had become more precious to us each day, because we realized that our very lives depended on our usefulness to the Nazis. We were laboring under "delusions or reprieve," believing that conditions would ultimately improve for they could not grow worse.

Tadzik Bosiacki had joined the Hortensia workforce back in April. I was happy to have him close again, for he had remained a good friend. He kept bringing me news about the strange happenings in those near and distant places to which Jews were being transported daily in box-cars, never to be seen again. "I will tell you," he whispered fearfully, "my father takes them there everyday, to the cities of death. Last time is was a place called Maidanek."

The Jews were forbidden by law to communicate with the Poles. When we talked, we did so only in secret and on rare occasions. One day, as we were leaving the assembly line, Tadzik whispered, "I've got to talk to you. It's important. The usual place, next break." It sounded urgent.

I had been waiting for my friend only a short while behind the great furnace—our customary meeting place—when Tadzik emerged out of the surrounding darkness. My fears for him and myself made the waiting seem much longer.

"I want to tell you things myself," he began, "before you'll hear it from others, because not all the things you'll hear will fit the truth."

"Go on, I'm listening." I urged him on. He hesitated a moment as though trying to find the right words. He avoided my eyes, as he continued.

"You see, Vilek, we're going to become Germans. The whole family, all of the Bosiackis will be *Volksdeutsche!*" He spoke quickly, like a person trying to relieve himself of a heavy burden. "Something about being Aryan." He added.

A painful silence followed. Finally, I spoke.

"How can you become Germans when you've been Poles for generations? Why Tadzik?"

"Things are changing, Vilek. It's not only our family. Many Poles, like ourselves, will soon be taking the oath and become naturalized Germans, *Volksdeutsche*. Maybe as early as next week." He paused.

"What's more, they're going to change most street names. And all the kids will learn German in school, can you believe that?"

I was aghast. "But. . . but. . . how did all this happen?" I stammered.

"All I know is that the District Director General sent out notices to the Railroad Commission last week. The supervisors were informed that people employed in key positions would have to be Germanized. My father's chief engineer, you know. He wasn't happy about all this, but there's no other way, if he wants to keep his job." Tadzik looked at me concerned. "You understand, don't you, Vilek?" He pleaded. "It doesn't change a thing between us."

"Well. . . yes. . ." I was hesitant. "In a way, I understand."

It was the morning of Sunday, June 22, 1941, and Mickey was anxiously awaiting the paper. Isaac had run down to the corner, and now *The New York Times* was spread before them on the table:

Hitler begins war on Russia, the headlines on the front page began, with armies on march from Arctic to the Black Sea . . . Mickey held his face in his palms, and Isaac continued to read:

As dawn broke over Europe today the legions of National Socialist Germany began their long-rumored invasion of Communist Soviet Russia. . .

The boy continued reading, but Mickey seemed dazed. "They're in for it now. . .they're in for it. . ." He muttered to himself. Monday's headlines weren't any better:

Smashing air attacks on six Russian cities, clashes on wide front open Nazi-Soviet War; London to aid Moscow, U.S. delays decision. Germany's attack on Russia is regarded by the State Department as convincing proof that *Reichsführer* Hitler plans to dominate the world. . .

"What are we waiting for?" Isaac exclaimed, "Why doesn't President Roosevelt and the Congress of the U.S. declare war on the bastard?"

"It's not easy to declare war, son." Mickey said softly, still in shock.

"It's easy enough for Hitler, even with his non-aggression pacts." Isaac said stubbornly.

"I just hope our president doesn't make the same mistake I made." Mickey whispered to himself.

"The Nazis have to woo the Poles now that they're fighting the Bolsheviks." My grandfather said on hearing the news about Tadzik's family. "Hitler's gone berserk. He can't win with either of them. It won't be long now before the Reich collapses." He concluded.

"The order had come from the Director General of the occupied territories, *Herr* Frank in Cracow." "The Third Reich," it stated, "must recover Aryan elements of mixed blood and language and welcome them into the fold of their national origin."

As a result of that proclamation, many different categories of German "nationals" had been introduced. Some of the "new Germans" were regarded as "safe" and "loyal," others were initiated on a "trial" basis. Attractive inducements had been offered, regardless of origin, to win over as large a portion of the native population as possible.

"Isn't it unusual how the Gentiles have traditionally distrusted each other, even hated one another," my grandmother remarked.

"There's one thing that unites them: the hatred and persecution of the Jew."

Nothing unusual about that, my dear Rachel," my grandfather said. "They're still holding us responsible for the crucifiction of their Savior."

"But that happened so long ago," I said, "surely, by now they might have forgiven?" I thought for a moment. "Besides, those were different circumstances, different people."

"Not at all. . . not at all. . . my boy. . ." my grandfather was in an argumentative mood. "Our friends had made up their minds to stop the progress of time, at least, as far as the Jew is concerned. And, that must be the reason why they spend so much energy hating us." He concluded sadly.

As far back as I could remember, the peasants had been the most virulent foes of the Jews. This was not in the least attributable to their lack of formal education. Our Polish intelligentsia was a perennial sufferer from antisemitism as well. Education was no obstacle.

"In actuality, the Jews are a blessing to the Gentiles." My grandfather said with a twinkle in his eye. "Why, had it not been for the Jew, our friends would have been constantly at each other's throats. If we're gone, who'll be their scapegoat?" He asked himself. "And they tell us to leave and go to Palestine!" He shook his head incredulously.

I met Tadzik at our hideout behind the great furnace on the following afternoon. We heard steps. Moments later, *Herr* Förster emerged. He was so very close to us, we could almost touch him. We held our breaths for fear that even the slightest sound might betray us.

Soon, we saw a shapely female form approaching our Camp Commandant. She was silent and walked quickly toward him. They stood together, whispering, but we heard every word of their conversation. Suddenly she fell quiet, irresolute, as if filled with some inner suspicion. She looked at her companion curiously, then glanced over her shoulder as if to make certain no one else was present.

"What do you want?" She asked.

"You!"

"Here? Now?"

"Yes!" Förster's voice was hoarse with desire. Their silhouettes playing against the furnace light had lent them both a sinister appearance.

"No!!" She hissed. "Not now! Not here!"

"What do you mean?" He sounded somewhat puzzled, unaccustomed to being rejected.

"Just that! Not here and now!" She repeated, sounding more composed.

"Then, say when!"

"I'll let you know when I'm ready and no sooner than that, do you hear?" Her voice had a coquetish sound to it. Förster grabbed her arm rudely and pulled her to himself.

"You'll do as I say!" He was the master now.

"Let go!" She tried to free her arm from his firm grip. "Let go, you're hurting my arm!"

"Then. . . you'll do it. . . right now?"

"No! Not now. . . not ever! You pig!" She jerked her arm away in sudden fit of strength. He caught her by her wrist.

"You come with me right now!" His voice was hateful, authoritative. He lead the woman away from our earshot. She resisted meekly. "I say you must come this very moment, Bronia! Do you understand?" He paused. "I've waited long enough." With his free hand, he slapped the woman twice across her face. She turned violently, but we had gotten a good look at her. It was Bronia Kotek, Tadzik's cousin on his mother's side. Firmly in Förster's grip, she followed the man quietly.

"The bitch!" Tadzik hissed. "Wait till uncle Marek hears of this!" Suddenly, I recalled what the men were saying about Bronia Kotek; about her "asking for it." I was too young to understand what she was "asking for," but I recognized that Bronia was a very attractive eighteen-year-old woman. She, too, must have been aware of her "assets." In fact, she was the flirt of the glass factory and seemed pleased with the effect she had on men. She dressed for the role. The transparency of her outer garments teased the men in daylight as well as against the bright flames of the great furnace in the factory.

As if on purpose, Bronia wore nothing under her dress. Her shapely figure was exposed to all who cared to look. She was an assistant inspector of glassware, and she crossed the yard frequently.

Every man in the factory desired Bronia. Small wonder that Herr Förster had had ample opportunity to observe and develop an appetite of his own.

"I can do things for you, my little one." He was overheard saying to the young woman during one of his factory "inspections."

"Perhaps you can, *Herr* Förster," she responded, giggling. He followed very close behind her, and she drew her long blond pony-tail over her shoulder with a sharp movement of her body. Her attractive, full breasts, did not escape Förster's appreciative eye. "Some other time, *Herr* Förster. Come back some other time," she dared to dismiss the commandant.

But *Herr* Förster was not one to be discouraged easily. "It's good to have a friend in the right places who can help when times get really tough." He said, his eyes boring into her.

"I'm sure, it is," she replied without glancing at him. "I'll remember that."

"You must come soon, *Liebchen*—darling—." He used the language of the conquerors, the language of authority, of the superior who would not tolerate denial. It was his right to take anything he desired. He made certain Bronia understood.

There were large wooden crates for carrying glassware stacked behind the great furnace. The area was dark even during dayshift, and a person could get lost among the rows of crates.

Holding the woman's wrist, Förster dragged her toward the crates, and she followed now without a word of protest.

"What's going on, Tadzik?" I asked in a hushed voice. They were getting close to where we had been hiding and I was frightened.

"Shut up, Vilek, you want them to hear?"

The woman fought quietly but desperatley against his searching strong fingers. *Herr* Förster held her tightly with one arm around her slim waist. With the other, he bent her over backward till she lay stretched out on top of the crate. It squeaked treacherously under the weight of the two struggling persons, as Bronia continued bravely in her attempt to escape from under Förster's massive frame. During the ensuing tense moments, in the dim light coming from the great furnace, we observed the most mystifying drama.

"Please, *Herr* Förster, you're hurting me." Bronia pleaded.

"Please, let me go." He paid no attention to her complaints, but grunted, as he labored his way to her, murmuring unintelligibly, sounds resembling animal not human. He tried, with his free hand, to unbutton his fly, but was unable to accomplish this simple task under such demanding circumstances.

After a brief struggle, Förster released the woman from his hold, quivered excitedly and let out a sigh of relief. I saw a grin of guilt on his bloated face. He looked at the woman with his keen reddish eyes that gleamed in the dark like two sinister chinks.

Bronia pulled away scornfully, but not before he managed to slap her brisquely across the face, making her reel backward. He had to do that, it was obvious, if only to show a shade of condescension and contempt for a person of inferior station and culture than his own. He was almost pleased now, judging from the silent whimpering of his victim.

"The slut! To him she sold herself! She had it coming, the whore!" Tadzik cried, as we ran into the yard. We separated before I was able to respond. After all, it was not as simple as Tadzik put it. Förster had a lot to do with it, I knew, but I wondered how Bronia's family was going to look at it when Tadzik gave them his version of the events. Life was puzzling. I had seen its many faces without having reached manhood as yet.

The newest order from the desk of the Commandant of the ghetto forbade any man to grow earlocks and beards; for sanitary reasons, we were told. To the Hasidim, this was a major crisis; their very life was in jeopardy.

My grandfather seldom left the house from then on. Grandmother Rachel made him stay indoors, for fear he'd run into "law enforcers."

"They'd have to kill me to shave my beard!" He shouted in his helplessness.

"That's exactly what they'd do." My grandmother asserted.

"Father, please shave it off, for our sake." My mother pleaded.

"The Lord will not think any less of you if for once you'll comply with the Commandant's wishes and stay alive."

"It's not a question of being forgiven, my child." My grandfather replied. "The Lord, blessed be His Name, is merciful. He forgives even the converts and derelicts, but does that mean that I must become one?"

Grandfather kept his earlocks and his full beard; he wore fringed garments and remained under self-imposed house arrest, like most of his Hasidic friends. From then on, I missed the daily discussions, learned arguments, and their happy chants.

Following the Commandant's proclamation concerning German "nationals," there was a surge of applicants showing interest in serving the Reich. We were amazed to learn how many "genuine Aryans" had lived among us. There were plenty of them. Soon, as they received their second-class citizenship, bands of brownshirted youths prowled the ghetto streets, searching for ways in which they could prove worthy of their newfound station. These erstwhile Polish youths wore swastika armbands; fancy daggers hung from their belts with the ominous letters "H.J." carved on ornate ivory grips.

Nearing curfew, I spotted a gang of Hitler Youths approaching a bearded man, a Hasid who must have left the safety of his home by necessity. They were about to amuse themselves at his expense.

"Over here, *Jude!*" they shouted. "Don't you know the law?" The man walked on, but the raucous group caught up with him and blocked his way. He was at their mercy. I came closer and, to my terror, recognized the Hasid as Nora's uncle Max. I also knew some of the Hitler Youths from earlier days; the days I fed them scraps of food from the Supply Company at the ancient castle. There was Heniek Popielski, whose new name had become Heinrich Aschengruber. And there was Adam Niski, now Adolf Klein, and Piotrek Kowalski who had been named Peter Schmidt, to please their new masters. The gang circled the Hasid with their daggers drawn.

Heniek was their leader, the oldest and the strongest of the band. He stood by, as his underlings shouted abuses and kicked the defenseless Hasid who knelt before them. They pulled and pinched his beard and tore the earlocks from both sides of his temples. Max screamed with pain, and his entire face was soon covered with blood which gushed out of his fractured nose. The greater his pain, the louder the Hasid's shouts, the more boisterous the goons had become.

"Heniek! Stop them! Heniek, they'll kill the man!" I suddenly shouted. "It's my friend they're beating!!"

I knew the punishment for addressing a uniformed Hitler Youth, but in view of the intolerable circumstances I forgot caution. All I knew was that I must stop them, else they might kill Max Mandel.

The gang was startled at the sound of my voice. The beating subsided for a moment. Heinrich, too, was astonished to hear someone pronounce his "Christian" name. He looked at me, came closer, but he did not strike. I knew then that he must have recalled those days he stood begging at the castle fence on Zamkowa Street. He turned to his comrades.

"Let the dog go!" Heinrich Aschengruber spoke with the voice of authority and self-confidence. Released, Max ran. He was running from Sodom, and there was no looking back.

"Why must you do such things? Why do you beat up on defenseless people? He hasn't done you any harm, Heniek."

"The law must be obeyed," Heinrich answered, "and no one can change that."

How odd. Here is a man inflicting pain in the name of his law. And the person who was running for his life, chose to suffer because he insisted on observing his own law. I suddenly remembered my grandfather's response whenever I solicited explanations regarding observances: "The Law is the Law," he'd say, "and all else is subordinate to it."

For the first time in my life, I had learned that Law does not imply Justice.

"You don't have to enforce it, do you?" I muttered, still unable to grasp the complex idea. I have known Heniek as a Polish boy whom I helped when he was hungry, with whom I shared my food. Now, all of a sudden, he is Aryan, and I am someone inferior.

"We're the law now, Vilek, and you'd better remember that." Heinrich paused as if to reflect. "I'm now where I belong, with my *Vaterland*, and I must do all I can to make myself worthy of this honor."

I looked at him, and he looked away. We both knew the abyss of our separation. And just as he started to walk away, he turned toward me and stopped. "This time I remembered you, Vilek, and I repaid you in full. If we should meet in the future, you must not address me in public. If our paths cross, it will be as German and Jew; I shall treat you accordingly."

My reason had told me over and over again that this wasn't happening at all, it was a nightmare, couldn't be real. I tried to talk but I choked and no sound would come out. We stood in the middle of Adolf Hitler Street, which not long before had been Pilsudski Street.

"I leave you now, *Jude*, you must obey if you value your life. *Heil* Hitler!" Raising his right arm, he shouted the world-shattering salute, turned around smartly on his heel, and left me standing in the street aghast and hurt.

At home, I received a hero's welcome. Everyone was on hand to celebrate my "bravery." Nora's was the most welcome demonstration of gratitude.

In the midst of enemies, beneath the swastika—the ancient amulet for long life, good fortune and luck—which had now become the symbol of evil, we found that nothing could lessen the pleasure of a slight squeeze of a hand, a kiss, and a fond embrace or a simple smile. Love's magical powers made us immune to the realities of the day.

It was a clear night, and we went up to the rooftop, Nora and I, as we often did when we sought privacy. We sat there in complete quiet. I couldn't guess her thoughts, but mine were filled with plans for the future. A future I had dreamed of long ago. How I would become a violinist, a doctor or a scientist, and cure the ills of this world with my skills.

"I've missed hearing you practice the violin," Nora suddenly said, and I was sure she had read my mind. That, too, was once a dream. Everyone in the family admired my talent, but my grandmother claimed that playing the violin wasn't a practical profession. "Just look at your grandfather," she'd say, "you don't want to entertain people at weddings for the rest of your life, do you?" I disagreed, but I didn't dare contradict her. I loved my grandfather's music and his sense of humor. And others liked it as well; he made people laugh, he made them happy. What's wrong with making people happy? I asked silently. And why shouldn't I be able to combine the skill of medicine with that of playing the violin? I didn't argue about things with my grand-mother. It wasn't the right thing to do.

"Haven't felt like it, lately." I answered Nora's question.

"But you must, Vilek, you must make music even when you don't feel like playing." She said softly. "It's still the only sane thing around." She pulled me close to her and I inhaled the sweet odor of her body. She was silent for a long time, and then, as if reaching somewhere into the distant past, she recited the words from the work of an American writer . . .

"There is a land of the living and a land of the dead and the bridge is love, the only survival, the only meaning."

6

Days turned into weeks, and weeks into months. Nothing remained the same. Things changed for the worse each time we had picked up the courage to hope that, somehow, we might resume life with a semblance of normalcy. Only my mother, in her infinite optimism, kept repeating to her children: "Things cannot go on like this forever, my dears, soon they'll get better. They're bound to improve." She spoke these words over and over again, as if trying to convince herself.

During the first days of December 1941 they took cousin Joseph away on a transport. It was bitter cold, when two Gestapo agents came for him during early morning hours and dragged the groggy Joseph out of his deepest sleep onto the yard where a Gestapo staff car was waiting. "They need good boot-makers where you're going, Joseph." They told him, and that's the last aunt Sabina heard. The Gestapo wouldn't allow goodbyes, and all Sabina and Devorah could do was wave at the disappearing car.

We sat listening to Aunt Sabina's account of that fearful night. "It was like a nightmare," she cried, "they were dragging him away like an animal led to the slaughter. He tried to tell them who he was. . . it was all a terrible mistake. . . he was the *Sturmbannführer's* bootmaker. . . but they only struck at him harder. . . as if to silence him. One of them jeered 'You've outlived your usefulness, Jew!,' and they laughed. 'The leather's all gone,' they spat at Joseph, 'you stole half of it, swine, and now you'll pay!' They continued to beat him, until he bled from his nose and his ears. . . oh my God. . . how they beat him!" She tried to continue but her sobbing became too violent and she couldn't go on. My mother comforted aunt Sabina in a tender embrace.

"Then, I tried to stop the bleeding with a wet kerchief, but one of them pushed me to the floor." Sabina reflected for a brief moment.

"Merciful God, I had just realized that we hadn't had time to say goodbye!" She wept.

"Please, Sabina, dearest, calm down." My mother pleaded. "You'll make yourself sick. Think of your children," she reminded the sobbing woman, "you must be strong now, for Devorah and Michael." The mention of her children calmed aunt Sabina.

"I can't go back there!" She suddenly exclaimed. "As they were leaving, one of the Gestapo officials shouted 'keep your door open, Jewess! We'll be back for you tonight!' I can't go back there!" She wept again.

"We won't let you go back there," my grandfather assured her.

"You and your children have a place here with us." He paused. "It can't be any more crowded than it already is." He held Sabina in his arms and kissed her tenderly on the forehead.

My grandfather's display of tenderness surprised me, but I was delighted with his decision. My cousins would share the corner of the bedroom with Hayim and me, and we would have good times together. In spite of my infatuation with Nora, Devorah still remained my favorite. I knew I loved her because of those large brown eyes surrounded by dark circles, which were always plagued by a look of sadness. I knew Nora wouldn't mind; she would love both of us dearly.

Christmas would soon be here, and my thoughts were with Ernst Boost and his Supply Company frozen somewhere into the Soviet landscape. Earlier in the week, Hans Müller, the gentle giant from Boost's outfit, came through Piotrkow on his way to his native Saxony. He sent word through Tadzik: "Ernst is okay, though we've been stuck in the mud and then frozen into icicles in Russia." Tadzik quoted Müller.

"But why's Müller going home and not the whole outfit?" I asked.

"Because only the wounded have that privilege." Tadzik replied.

"Müller's hurt?"

"I'd say he is. His right leg was amputated up to his knee. Shrapnell, you know." Suddenly Tadzik grew pensive. "You'd better go now, Vilek. We mustn't be caught meeting like this. You understand. Things are getting tough out there. Everybody's watching everybody. I was about to leave when he reached to his pocket. "Here. . . wait. . . Müller brought this for you from Boost." He handed me Boost's silver bracelet. His tenth anniversary present from Hannelore and the girls. I knew Boost wouldn't part with it without a good reason, and I was worried.

"My Lord. . . " I started to say something, but Tadzik had already disappeared behind the crates. I was left alone in the glimmer of the great furnace, turning the bracelet in my fingers, admiring the fine craftsmanship. There were the initials "E.B." etched into the precious metal, and I ran the tip of my index finger over them. I knew how much Ernst had treasured this gift from his wife and his two daughters. Why would he give it up just now? I asked myself silently. Quickly, I put the bracelet into my pocket, but my heart pounded with an eerie premonition.

They were tell-tale warnings when laughter was no longer heard in the ghetto, and the Hasidim stopped singing their happy songs after the Sabbath meal. Music froze up along with nature as it died on the lips of the Hasidim. The Jews were now selling their most prized possessions, and the Poles profitted from their desperation. I found out that the going price for a violin was five pounds of potatoes and a jar of lard; scarcely enough for a meal. If only our American relatives knew?

"Papa! Mama! Look!" Isaac spread the *New York Times* on the table for his parents to see. The headlines of the December 8th issue read:
Japan wars on U.S. and Britain; makes sudden attack on Hawaii; heavy fighting at sea reported

Isaac went on reading:
Sudden and unexpected attacks on Pearl Harbor, Hono- lulu, and other United States possessions in the Pacific yesterday by the Japanese air force and navy plunged the United States and Japan into active war. . .

"War! Papa!" Isaac exclaimed excited. "Did you hear that? We're at war!" Mickey and Fay sat silently listening to their excited son. They expected the worse now. He's almost fifteen, but he looks much older. Mickey must have thought to himself. It won't be easy to stop him now. "Now, the Japs are killing Americans, while the Nazis are killing the rest of the world!" Isaac was angry as he continued reading:
The War Department reported that 104 soldiers died and 300 were wounded as a result of the attack on Hickam Field, Hawaii. The National Broadcasting Company reported from Honolulu that the battleship Oklahoma was afire. . .

"Mama! Papa! If we wait any longer, they'll come and burn Manhattan!" Isaac exclaimed. "There's just one way to stop them, that's to fight them!"

On December 7, 1941, Japan unleashed its attack on the United States, and we were to learn about this important event from Commandant Förster. We had sensed the importance of the day's roll call from the festive atmosphere, the starched uniforms and polished boots of the SS mercenaries.

We stood at attention, whipped by a bruising frigid December wind, laboring to breathe, waiting for Förster to ascend the platform. A brazen smile on his face, he stood silent for some time, measuring our mood. When he was satisfied that we were sufficiently defeated, he spoke:

"Our allies, the Japanese, struck a death blow to the entire sea and air power of the United States. The land forces of the imperial armies are preparing an invasion of the American mainland."

"Poor American relatives." I whispered to Roman. "They wouldn't believe. Now look what's happening." Roman chuckled mischievously.

"I can't feel compassion for them." He hissed. "And I don't really want to. They've had it coming."

"You can't be serious, Roman." I said. "If the Axis wins, it won't be just our relatives that'll suffer. It'll be the end of us all, heaven help us."

"Heaven hasn't paid much attention to us either, little brother."

"Attention, you miserable vermin!" I shrank unto myself, hoping he wasn't yelling at us. Förster went on:

"With the imminent defeat of the United States, your uncle Roosevelt will be soon joining you in one of the labor camps, the damned Jew!" Förster's face was all red with excitement; our faces were blue with frost. "When we conquer America, we'll do away once and for all with the Jewish conspiracy!" He stopped, looked us over carefully. He liked what he saw. Suddenly Förster shouted the familiar slogan: "*Jude verrecke!* Death to the Jew!" He was about to descend the platform, when an idea seemed to have struck him. He turned in our direction and gave an order:

"Shout at the top of your voices, swine! Let your American brothers hear you! Death to the Jews! *Jude verrecke!*"

"*Jude verrecke!*" We responded. "Death to the Jews!"

"Louder! Swine! Louder!"

"*Jude verrecke!* Death to the Jews!"

We shouted, and Förster looked pleased. I felt as if my lungs were going to burst. They must have heard the yell in America. I thought. Just like Förster wanted. Even after he left the platform, his mercenaries kept on drilling us for another half hour to their own delight and amusement.

"I surely hope the Japanese succeed." Roman seethed the words between his teeth. "I hate the Americans almost as much as I do our enemy!" He had a wild look in his eyes and I was afraid he'd cause us trouble.

"Be quiet, they'll hear," I pleaded with him, but he went on unabated.

"Look at us, little brother!" He whispered. "The misery you see, is as much the fault of our American relatives as it is the enemy's. At least the Nazis don't pretend to love us. They're doing exactly what they promised to do: exterminate us, as our friends and relatives give tacit approval."

"Roman, please." My brother couldn't be stopped. He looked around slyly. Cousin Menasha's eyes pleaded with him, but he continued.

"What have they done until now? Absolutely nothing! Now they'll go to war because a few bombs fell into their own backyard!"

Förster observed the troubled faces of the assembled. He derived pleasure from their anguish. He grabbed the microphone once more: "There's panic in Washington, and there's confusion all over the United States. The capitalistic swine are demoralized! Wall Street Jews are committing suicides by the tens and hundreds! Soon, there'll be no one left for us to exterminate when we occupy America!" He laughed derisively. "Good joke, eh?" He stopped to note the effect of his humor. He was pleased.

We were utterly dismayed. Förster turned to go, satisfied. He saluted his comrades, raising his arm:

"*Heil* Hitler!"

"*Heil* Hitler!" The mercenaries responded.

"Get on with it!" He barked the order which signified the beginning of our working day. As he turned to go, we followed him with our eyes, burning with a deep, vindictive hatred; the only strength left us.

Fortunately, events did not take the course outlined to us by our commandant. The radio which Felix had hidden in his tool-shed, became our main source of hope and sustenance. It was the only contact with the outside world left us in the Hortensia camp. Only a few days ago, several radios have been found by the ever-present Gestapo informers. Their owners had been publicly executed as an example for those of us who might defy the Nazis' decree against radio ownership.

Now, we were glued to the clandestine programs. The bits of information we heard over the B.B.C. told us that the United States was quickly able to recover from the initial shock sustained by the surprise attack on Pearl Harbor.

A few days later, on December 11, the United States declared war on Germany and Italy as well. There was rejoicing in the ghetto.

"The United States declares war on the Axis!" The B.B.C. announcer shouted joyfully. Our comments followed:

"Blessings on President Franklin Roosevelt! May the Almighty grant him strength and wisdom!" The Hasidim prayed.

"Hitler's days are numbered!"

"Praised be the Lord, God of Israel!"

"Amen."

We prayed with renewed faith. And while the Japanese soon overran the Asiatic continent, the Nazis were beginning to suffer serious reverses on te Russian front. For the first time, we allowed ourselves hope, that with his invasion of Russia, Hitler had signed his own death warrant.

Spring came sooner than usual toward the latter part of February, and the melting of the snow with the warm air brought another typhus epidemic. The death rate was greater than anyone had expected. Once again, we stacked the dead on the sidewalks to be collected by lorries that made regular runs throughout the ghetto.

On my way to work, I looked at the ematiated bodies thrown together in a heap, and I made no comment. It was a matter of great concern to me, as I saw myself grow calloused to the terrible toll in human lives.

"Once the touch of death was upon you," my grandmother said, "and you've wrestled for your life, it won't challenge you again."

"But what about yourself, grandma?" I asked concerned. "You haven't been sick yet."

"Whatever the good Lord wills." She said with resignation. We did what we could to keep the plague away from our doorstep. We kept much to ourselves, drank only boiled water, and washed ourselves as many times as our supply of water would permit. The Hasidim prayed for all of us.

On the sixth day of the epidemic, Max Mandel came down with the dread disease. He had not altogether recovered from the beating he sustained at the hands of the Hitler Youths. What food we had, a major portion had been set aside for Max. Clean, fresh linen, and small scraps of soap, we put to use in trying to restore his health. The four women alternated their perpetual watch at his bedside, and all of us endured his mad ravings.

All to no avail. Max Mandel died quietly in his sleep one week into his illness. "He died like he lived, peacefully." My grandfather said. "Blessed be the Lord for making it this easy for him. Max was a saint."

Amid sobs and lamentations, services were held. The sad melody of the kaddish resounded. "He should have a funeral befitting a wise and just man, a *tsadik*." My grandfather said.

"You know they'll hang you in the middle of the public square if they catch you," my grandmother warned. "The curfew, the sentries." She lamented. Grandfather Srulko knew the consequences of this enterprise, but he was adamant.

"Max must have a proper burial." He said stubbornly. "I can't just leave him lying on the sidewalk for the dogs to sniff and bark at. He lived with dignity and he'll go to his eternal rest the same way, as behooves a Hasid." My grandmother threw up her hands resignedly. Grandfather Srulko would have his way.

It was three o'clock in the morning when the burial party ventured into the empty ghetto streets. There were ten men to form the necessary minyan; I was the eleventh, spearheading the procession as a lookout. Several women, Mandel's closest relatives and friends, had joined the procession. They wept silently. Nora stayed home with the other women of our household at my grandfather's insistence.

The men took turns carrying the body, wrapped in sackcloth in Hasidic tradition, two at a time. Weak from fatigue, hunger and tension, it was a superhuman effort. The procession moved ahead\ slowly and with great caution. The mournful bearers were near exhaustion when they finally arrived at the old cemetery on the edge of the ghetto. It was an eerie procession, and the moonlit night lent sinister dimensions. I shuddered, carrying the two plain boards which were intended by ancient law to become the resting place of the deceased Jew.

My grandfather officiated at the burial. He came from a long line of *Cohanim*—priests—. As a titular priest he held the authority to perform sacred tasks, but he did not quite know how to address the last farewell to someone so close. Nothing disturbed the somber proceedings except the distant occasional rattle of automatic weapons and the regularly revolving searchlights. But as we stood around the gravesight praying, we were constantly alert, sensitive even to the slightest, innocent noise.

His body was lowered into the grave and the last shovel of ground was padded down firmly during continuous prayer. Max Mandel had finally found his resting place.

Suddenly out of the surrounding darkness two Lithuanian sentries appeared brandishing sten guns and filling the air with a deafening sound.

I began to tremble like a leaf. Although I had tried to control my fear, I suddenly discovered that I could not suppress this fearful shaking of my entire body.

"Grandpa! We'll all be killed!" I tried to shout above the pandemonium. The sentries yelled, too.

"*Halt!*"

"*Jude!*"

"*Schwein!*" They cursed endlessly. The women wept hysterically and the men raised their voices in prayer.

"Don't you know the law? Swine!" One of the sentries shouted.

"You goddamned yids! You'll croak for this!"

"We've done nothing wrong," my grandfather pleaded. Please let us go. We meant no harm." A rifle butt into his mid-section quickly silenced him. Praying, he cowered near the ground, now shielding his head with both his hands from further blows. I threw myself on top of the old man, expecting the worse.

"What have you hidden in the ground?!" The second sentry yelled.

"Dig, you abominable vermin! You've buried all your gold and diamonds, Jew, and you think you can fool us!"

It was useless trying to persuade the drunk sentries. The men picked up their shovels. As they dug into the still loose ground, thoughts of resistance must have occurred to some of them.

"We are ten against two." I whispered into my grandfather's ear. "We can take them, *zaydenyu*" I pleaded. "Let's spread the word."

He didn't respond to my urging. His lips kept moving very rapidly, but no sound came out of his mouth. He was deepened in prayer, and so were all the other Hasidim, each praying for his own salvation—or a miracle perhaps of the highest order—as they continued to dig.

The moon faintly illumined the area and the sentries slowly became aware of the women huddled together on the ground nearby. They whispered to one another, then one of them ordered the women to line up. He selected two out of the group and led them to the guardhouse. Now, it was ten against one! As though reading our minds, the remaining sentry backed away a few yards, his gun at the ready.

Suddenly, wielding his shovel like a primeval weapon, Moshe Ehrenmann, the burly droshky driver, lunged at the armed sentry. Hershel Barnblatt followed his friend's example. The surprise was only momentary. It took the Lithuanian only a few seconds to recover control.

"You want to fight?! Eh?!" He shouted with incredulity. "You filthy Jewish scum! That's fine with me! You asked for it!" Once again the air was filled with the deafening noise of the gun rattle, as fire spewed from the end of the weapon's barrel. The two men lay on the ground, but the sentry continued firing at random. We ran in all directions. Some did not run fast enough. My grandfather staggered and fell. He moaned helplessly as I tried to help him up.

"Go Velvele. . . run. . . I won't last very long. . . there's nothing you can do here. . . run. . . Velvele. . . run. . . " He coughed blood. He spoke in a whisper: "You must have strength to fight the enemy, Velvele." Srulko breathed heavily. "And for that, you need hatred. Go on, my boy, hate the enemy as long as you fight him." My grandfather coughed again, more violently than before, and blood spilled from the side of his mouth. Then he fell silent.

"Please, *zaydenyu*," I cried feeling his blood on my hands, "I'll get you home, please don't die, zaydenyu." I addressed my grandfather by the endearing Yiddish word which he loved so much. He didn't move. I tried to lift him up, but I ended up cradling his head in my arms. He didn't move. "*Zaydenyu*, please say something, *zaydenyu*," I begged him. His body seemed to grow rigid in my arms. It became heavier and I could no longer handle it. "It's really nothing unusual," I thought to myself, "I'm getting tired, that's all."

I was exhausted, frightened and confused. Things were happening too fast for me to understand. I shook my grandfather several times, for he seemed to have fallen into a deep sleep. He didn't respond. I put my face to his breath. There was none. Panic gripped all mysenses. "What will I tell grandmother?" I kept thinking. I shook the old man again. It was no use.

My grandfather Srulko Malpo died in my arms on that night in the Piotrkow cemetery. Part of me died there too. It was the first death in our family caused by the war. The one death I was to remember always. I tried again to revive him.

"Grandpa, speak to me! Dear *zaydenyu*, I love you very much. I'll always love you." I said solemnly. But my grandfather was silent. Refusing to accept what I knew had happened, I held my ear to his chest. I heard nothing. I felt no movement. The heart of this kind old man had stopped beating. Then,

I let his body rest on the ground, and I ran as fast as I could, weeping loudly and carelessly into the night.

Two of the minyan survivors, Yosele Friedman and Jacob Weintraub, had returned to the ghetto ahead of me. The task of explaining fell to them. My appearance momentarily disrupted the lamentations. My clothing was in shreds; my face and hands bore my grandfather's blood. Grandmother embraced me and asked her inevitable question. "What has happened? Where's your grandfather?"

I was silent. I couldn't cry. My lips moved, but no sound came out.

"What have they done to you? Are you hurt?" My mother embraced me. "What is it, Vilusiek?" She addressed me by the endearing Polish name she liked so much.

"Hurt? No, I'm not hurt, mama." I hesitated. What good would it do to relate the events? I spoke in fragmentary sentences, trying to capture only the highlights. "The cemetery. . . it was terrible. . . the noise made by the guns. . . Grandfather fell down. . . I tried but couldn't lift him up, mama, I really tried but he was too heavy, I swear he was too heavy." I lapsed into momentary thought, as though trying to recapture some more details. The others waited patiently for me to resume my narrative. I told them all I was able to remember. Srulko Malpo died on the battlefield, and he always wanted to die in his own bed.

There were no more Hasidic sessions from that day on. But they continued the prayer sessions in peaceful defiance of the Nazi orders. Their spirit remained unbroken. Their comments on the Torah had been my only source of learning. I would miss them sorely. Many questions would now go unanswered. I puzzled over so many things; did my grandfather get a decent burial? Did the other victims? Purim and Passover holidays approached, and it somehow did not seem right to observe the festivities with grandfather gone.

We were bedded down for the night on the living room floor, as usual. I was about to fall asleep, when I heard Felusia's voice.

"Are you asleep, mama?"

"No, my dear, not yet." My mother replied, sensitive to the the urgency in Felusia's voice. "Is something keeping you from sleep?"

"Yes, mama." Felusia seemed wide awake. "We're people, mama, aren't we?" The little one asked. "But why aren't we like other people, mama?"

"What makes you ask such a silly question, Felusia?" My mother tried to make light of it. "Of course, we are people."

"Then why are we locked up like this, mama? And why does everyone hate us?" Felusia sat up now and faced my mother.

"No child, we're not hated by everybody." My mother replied patiently.

"Then we won't be locked up much longer? And we won't sleep on the floor any more?"

"We're only sleeping like this because we have guests, Felusia."

My mother's patience sustained her. "Wouldn't you want your guests to be comfortable?"

"When will the guests leave, so we can sleep in our beds?"

"Soon, my dear. They'll leave soon."

"Isn't there anybody outside who cares?" The little one persisted.

"Surely, there is." My mother said. "You must believe it."

"Then will somebody who cares come and let us out of here?" Felusia continued her inquisitiveness. I saw tears welling up in my mother's eyes, and I decided to come to her rescue. Placing myself between my mother and my little sister, I spoke to her gently but firmly: "You must let mama sleep now, Felusia. You, too, must go to sleep and dream the most beautiful dreams."

"What if those bad people come into my dreams, Vilusiek?" The little one asked.

"That's one place we must keep them out of, my little darling. They mustn't enter our imagination. There, we are stronger than they are, and we are free." I explained, but she had already fallen asleep. It didn't matter whether she'd heard me or not. I needed to hear myself.

The Jews kept on praying for a miracle. They prayed, trusting in God's intervention. It was an age old tradition, this reciprocal trust. Hadn't He, blessed be His Name, performed His mercies for His people throughout millenia? The Jews reasoned. He would not abandon them now. They prayed. But God was taking His time.

"We humans deal in hours and days," my grandmother explained patiently. "The Almighty, blessed be His Name, disregards time altogether. He is timeless, my boy, he is timeless." She repeated for emphasis.

"Meanwhile, what are we to do, grandma?" I asked, searching her eyes, but she looked away.

"We must pray, my child."

"Did you hear? Shlomo Zaplocki was shot by a guard in the leg." Nora announced.

"They've been shooting at everyone in sight lately." My mother said. "Let's not give them the opportunity. If they don't see you, they can't hurt you." She added wisely.

"They rounded up some women on Garncarska Street and took them to Gestapo Headquarters." Nora continued her report. "As usual. . ."

"Hush!" My grandmother interrupted. "The children!"

Last night on the roof of our house, Devorah had already told me the sad story. Mania, the nineteen year old daughter of our dear friends the Pinkuseviczes on Garncarska Street, had been forced to dance in the nude for the SS officers' party the night before. She was forced to perform sexual acts, and this morning, her parents found the daughter hanging by the neck in their bathroom. She had used the silk belt of her summer dress which she wore for this last act. The news was all over Hortensia when the woman failed to show up for her regular shift. They said the drunk men continued to violate Mania until she had become completely oblivious to their abuses. They left her lying on the floor as she was, naked, with her legs spread wide apart, in complete stupor.

"I will never let them take me like they did Mania." Devorah said with determination in her eyes. "I'll kill myself before and not after the act." I had reason to believe this was not an empty promise.

Several days went by before I saw Tadzik Bosiacki again. He was silent and looked away. I knew not to pressure my friend with questions. The answers would come, without solicitation. Finally, he gave a slight movement of the shoulders and a long sad sigh.

"Bad news again, eh?" I smiled.

"No, not really, I don't like to be the bearer of bad news all the time, Vilek." He said.

"No one does." I said reassuringly.

"Too bad about Mania, eh?" He whispered.

"Yes, too bad." I repeated.

"There's really no way of knowing what it'll all mean, Vilek. But I'd rather you hear it from me than from them." Them, meant the enemy, I knew. "You understand," he quickly added, "before it's too late."

"I want to hear it from you, Tadziu. I know you mean well with us."

"They're bringing in a high-ranking officer of the Seventh Bureau soon, a *Sturmbannführer* Walter Doerings. He's going to take over the cultural wing of the Gestapo. *Kulturverwalter*, they call him. He's supposed to take over the administration of the ghetto. I smell a rat."

I knew Tadzik was concerned. I nodded approvingly. "Thanks, Tadziu." I touched his shoulder slightly. I'll tell the others.

His first official act on settling down at the Headquarters of the Gestapo at Adolf Hitler Street was to summon the Jewish Council. The meeting was public, a sort of get acquainted session with his ghetto subjects. The people filled the Council auditorium to capacity.

We examined the slightly built man, trying to guess his human traits of character, if there were any. He wore thick, metal-rimmed lenses, which further magnified his large grey eyes. They traveled from person to person, but did not rest on any one for more than a brief moment. I took it that he, too, was intent on probing the character of the people before him. We searched for a formula to deal with our new master, whereas he wished to ascertain his absolute power over us.

His outward appearance showed him to be of humble origin. There were rumors (not entirely without a degree of malice), that Walter was the son of a village priest's daughter. This explained his reluctance to socialize with his fellow officers at the Bureau. He was an "outsider;" a zealot, dedicated to his sacred mission of extracting wealth from the Jews in behalf of the Third Reich.

Doerings exuded the self-assurance of a man totally dedicated to the office he held; that of a superior official of the dreaded Ministry of Culture. He served his Reich by whatever means necessary; imprisonment, the gallows, torture of women and children, all with equal zeal. He was respected by his superiors at the ministry, regarded as an altogether trustworthy man.

"We're in for some trouble." I whispered to Roman.

"Careful, little brother, he might hear." Roman warned.

Doerings wore the simple black uniform of the Gestapo, the insignia of his rank sewn onto the left sleeve. With a face resembling the form of a pumpkin, insipid, bespectacled eyes and the Iron Cross Second Class that hung beneath the skinny throat with a prominent Adam's apple, Walter Doerings seemed the right man for his job; a man to be feared as well as hated.

"*Meine Herren*,—Gentlemen—," Doerings began, "I summoned you here to discuss certain pressing issues."

We were impressed. To Förster and Seemann we were no more than "pigs" and "swine," but Doerings addressed the Jews as "gentlemen." We had almost forgotten the sound of that word, and we were amazed at the tone and polish.

"Gentlemen, as the representative of the Third Reich, I am the *Führer's* personal emissary to this entire province." Doerings turned toward the huge, life like, portrait of the Führer hanging on the wall behind him, and saluted with a crisp "*Heil* Hitler!" We looked on astonished. The "little schoolmaster," as he was respectfully to be called, was not one to be trifled with.

"Precisely," he announced, "and I like doing things the open way," he chuckled while rubbing his palms together, "I've been dispatched here to look into the sudden lag in tax moneys. It is felt in Berlin, at the Ministry of Culture, gentlemen, that altogether too much time has elapsed since the last contingent of ghetto dues had arrived. We must be more vigilant in the future, we must correct this irregularity."

I listened to the bureaucrat, and I couldn't quite decide whether he used the omniscient "we" to impress the Council or simply to convey his unlimited power over his subjects.

"What has happened to the goods delivered regularly to the Bureau by this council?" Haskel Warszawski asked plaintively without elaborating. He seemed beside himself with anger, but he knew to control his emotions in the presence of his formidable adversary. Warszawski was no fool. He knew that the local branch of the Bureau skimmed a good portion of the ghetto "tax" paid to the Reich. But he wasn't going to press his luck. It would serve no practical purpose to point a finger at one master in front of another. He thought for a moment while studying Doerings' inscrutable expression, then, as if in afterthought, he concluded: "I am absolutely certain that the situation can be corrected, *Herr Sturmbannführer!*"

"Not only can it be corrected, but it *must* be done quickly and efficiently." Doerings paused, and no one dared to interrupt. "If I'm not in error, gentlemen, your Passover Holidays are approaching. Taxes are to be delivered to this office before a permit for worship is obtained! Understood?!"

"Perfectly, *Herr Sturmbannführer!*" Warszawski replied readily. He had learned to address the enemy in a formal way during formal occasions. He had almost raised his right arm in a spirited "Heil Hitler!" but he feared it might have been awkward for a bearded Hasid to praise the *Führer*.

I saw a faint smile on Warszawski's face and a twinkle in those wise eyes, and I understood how it might have entered his mind to wish the *Führer* a healthy future. After all, the Jews had cursed his name with every breath and in each of their daily prayers, only to see him grow stronger each day.

But Warszawski was one of those rare practical persons who, though living in times of political unrest, try to keep an instinctive hold on normal everyday life. He more than understood the emotional tension of his time; he responded to it the best way he knew how, for he was concerned with his own and his family's future. This special instinct had kept him alive thus far, and his "juggling" ability had earned him the respect and trust of the community.

"You will deliver two hundred thousand zlotys by noon Thursday if you are to use the synagogue on Friday!"

"Two hundred thousand zlotys?!" Warszawski repeated with incredulity. "It might as well be millions!" He whispered in Yiddish for those nearest him to hear. His shoulders stooped with the awareness of the newest burden.

"Two hundred thousand zlotys is only fifty thousand reichsmark." Doerings drove his point relentlessly home. "Previous quotas were somewhat smaller, but after all, you have missed a good many installments. We feel justified in our desire to retire the debt as promptly as possible. Is that clear?" Doerings' eyes studied his audience. "Think about your children's welfare!"

The motive behind the absurd demand was understood by everyone present. In fact, the Jews harbored no illusions in regard to the enemy's request. Refusal was out of the question. Could they bargain with their children's lives?

Doerings was consumed with ambition. His success would matter to no one but himself. He felt no particular hatred toward these people. As an expert in extortion, he had made a point of studying the habits of the Jews even prior to learning about his new assignment. In all he had learned, he was most impressed by their natural inclination to meekness and an almost fanatical love of their children. But he was also aware of their great bargaining skills. He would make his demands high; so high, in fact, that whatever the counteroffer, he would still be at an advantage. The success of his transaction would surely make his bosses in Berlin sit up and take note of his superior ability. He chuckled inwardly, scrutinizing his adversaried. There was a hush in the auditorium.

I thought of my grandfather Srulko. He was rid of all these worries once and for all. Pictures started passing before my eyes: my grandfather playing the fiddle at one of the weddings; making the guests laugh with his jokes; reciting the prayers or quoting some important tenet of the Torah and interpreting it from memory; holding me in his embrace so close I could feel the tickle of his beard and the great mustache. All that was finished now. Never again would he hold me in his arms and make me smile.

Why, dear God, why must it be that way? I asked silently.

I could not bring myself to envy my grandfather. I wanted to go on, to live, to hate the enemy, to fight.

"We'll do our very best," Warszawski said resignedly. There was surprise written on Doerings' face.

"Only two hundred thousand zlotys will be acceptable!" He pressed on, satisfied. "You may go now!"

The astronomical figure still ringing in their ears, the Jews left the hall. In their worry, they had forgotten to inquire about the two women abducted on the night of Max Mandel's burial.

"Why the silence, Haskel?! Why didn't you bargain?" Shlomo Popiavski addressed the leader of the Council.

"Bargain? What kind of a bargain did you want me to strike up with that monster?" Warszawski reproached his old friend. "Did you want me to offer him half of that? Twenty-five percent? No, maybe only ten thousand zlotys? Tell me?" He was angry. "Where could we get even the ten thousand?"

"Friends, friends, please, let's not quarrel amongst ourselves." Moshe Naiberg pleaded. "This would be their greatest triumph yet." His point of reference was unmistakeable.

Warszawski suppressed a cry of dismay. The purpose of his present existence being utterly ruined by this contact with as formidable an enemy as Doerings, he was only capable of uttering a loud sigh of resignation and a sort of half-derisive exclamation, "All the bargaining in the world would have been useless!" His friends understood and acknowledged the old man's anguish with their own silence.

On his part, Doerings watched the Jews from the window as they slowly walked away from the Gestapo premises. I turned, catching his pumpkin head and small figure framed by the huge window of his office. I wondered about the effects the meeting was going to have on our immediate future. What I could not really know was that when the last one of the Jews had disappeared from his view, the *Sturmbannführer* joyfully slapped his thigh, proud of the manner in which he had dealt a shrewd blow at the cunning Jews. The bargain went beyond his wildest dreams. Two hundred thousand zlotys!, he must have thought to himself. They *will* be impressed in Berlin. They damned better be!

Indeed, his work in the Piotrkow ghetto had begun in a most conscientious and efficient manner. He would take no nonsense from the ghetto rabble, and his merits would soon attract a promotion. How proud and happy his lovely wife Loretta would be! Her own "little" Walter a *Standartenführer*! And the twins, Richard (named for that great composer Wagner!), and Rudolf (named for his godfather Hoess), would play with their father's new uniform insignia! Things would be different for all of them once he "solved" this ghetto problem.

Walter Doerings was exceedingly fond of his family. He couldn't wait to visit with them in Christmas time. They would sing carols in front of the *Tannenbaum*,—the Christmas tree—and he would narrate stories. Tears always came to his eyes during this festive season; the Christ-child in the manger, Mary and Josef, and the three Wise Men . . .

But first, he must attend to these ghetto animals. He mustn't let them get the better of him. Much depended on his success here. After all, he was doing all this for his beloved family the Reich and his Führer, more so than for himself. That much was certain.

Passover 1942 was one Uncle Mickey and Aunt Fay would not forget easily. When Isaac didn't show up at the breakfast table, Fay knocked at his bedroom door and found the bed hadn't been slept in all night. On his dresser, Isaac left a note for his parents:

"I'm going to join up to fight the Nazis. Don't look for me, and don't worry. I'll be okay. Soon as I get settled, I'll be in touch. Love you both. Your son, Isaac."

Fay nearly threw a fit. "You see what you've done, Mickey?" She yelled at her husband. "It's all your fault! If you had kept a tighter reign on him, he wouldn't have done what he did! You've got yourself to blame!" She carried on all day long.

"But, Fay, dear."

"Don't you talk to me!" She was adamant. "Do something! Get him back! I want him back at home! He's only a boy! A little boy!"

"Let's sit down and have a peaceful seder, Fay. Let's not ruin our holiday." He pleaded. "Isaac's no longer a boy. He's a man now."

"How can you sit down to the seder when your younger son's gone to join the army?" She cried. "You don't care. He might be killed. My poor boy."

"You're carrying on about nothing, Fay." He consoled her. "First, they have to take him, and he'll have to prove he's of age. Then, it'll take months before he's trained. By then the war will be over."

"There you go making predictions again, Mickey." She reproached him. "Just like those you made before. Have you forgotten? If it were up to you, there wouldn't have been any war to start with."

They had finally sat down to the dinner table, but Mickey didn't have his heart in the Seder. It was the shortest Passover meal he had ever conducted. And no one asked the four traditional questions; it was the task carried out by the youngest son, but he was gone.

At ten o'clock, on the morning preceding Passover, the phone rang in Warszawski's office at the ghetto Council. He was the only ghetto Jew with the privilege of a telephone. The reward for this "convenience" were the countless hours of worry and a burdened soul of a man responsible for the lives of others.

The effect of the ringing must have been immediate. Two hundred thousand zlotys! Warszawski must have thought, trembling and unable to pick up the receiver. The ringing wouldn't stop. He looked at the reports from the latest results of the ghetto militia's collection. The sum total was nowhere near the amount demanded by the enemy. The Council president sighed heavily. He cleared his throat before reaching for the receiver.

"Warszawski here." He made an effort to speak calmly.

"You will report to my office at two o'clock sharp this afternoon. You will bring the money. All of it! Understood?" The voice at the other end was that of *Sturmbannführer* Doerings.

"I understand, sir." Warszawski spoke with deliberate slowness. His brain seethed with arguments. "I shall be there at the designated time, but I cannot bring the requested amount." He hoped that the other did not detect the tone of anger.

"What?" Doerings shouted. "You cannot what?!" He paused in his perplexity. "You realize, of course, the consequences."

"Without a doubt, sir." By then, Warszawski must have wondered why he had not cut short the talk and put down the receiver. Talk was futile under the circumstances. Instead, he listened patiently, his mind straining for answers and excuses. But there were none, and the voice at the other end was now shouting.

"Yes, sir. . . yes, sir." Warszawski kept on repeating mechanically.

"How much have you collected?" Came the final question.

"We. . . we. . . have. . ." Warszawski stammered.

"Speak up, Jew!" Doerings shouted.

"Twenty thousand. . . approximately." There was a brief, calculated pause at the other end.

"Be here at two, punctually." Came the order. "Call first!"

"Yes, sir!" Warszawski shuddered. Suddenly a peace of bitter calmness came over him. It was best to keep this man humored. The holidays are upon us, he must have thought. What can I tell the Council? What can we do? They had to deal with this man from Berlin, till he could be gotten rid of with some chance of escaping the wrath of the Bureau. Yes, that was the best that could be done right now.

The president of the Council called a meeting. I went along with Felix and Roman. "We are facing a grave problem," Warszawski confessed to the assembled. "The news I had given the messenger from Berlin was not to his liking. It could turn against us, especially during this festive season." He was calm. He appeared rational and almost indestructible.

The assembled had shown a face of harmony—in contrast with the terrifying discord of the enemy's threatening presence. They hated the enemy, and they looked to Warszawski for leadership and reassurance.

"I will go to meet him at the appointed time." Warszawski continued. "You must give me precise directions, as for the rest—depend on me." He fell silent, and I saw his weariness. In my imagination, I compared him to a knight readying to face an evil dragon who preyed upon the people with an insatiable appetite.

"You have our prayers, Haskel." Shlomo Zaplocki said.

"We're behind you." They repeated.

"May the Almighty give you strength."

"Amen." They prayed in unison.

Distrustful of the Nazi's intentions, many Jews stayed away from the Passover services. As he had promised during his meeting with Warszawski, Doerings kept his henchmen on a leash. There were no incidents.

We had left Felusia at home in Nora's care and went to the Synagogue.

This was to be our first worship without my grandfather's presence. My grandmother cried before we left home, but her eyes were dry by the time we had reached the services.

For many years, from the time I was able to walk, I accompanied my father, and later on my paternal or maternal grandfather to the synagogue for the holidays. Passover had always had a special significance, but presently it lent authenticity to our struggle. The events of another age which resembled our own were very much on everybody's mind. Who would be our Moses? Who would lead us to the Promised Land? I never remember the elders celebrating by attending parties or indulging in excessive drinking of alcohol. These eight days had a sobering effect on everyone. The synagogue was resplendent with candle light, adult men wore their *tallitim*—prayer shawls—and the women covered their heads with festive scarves. The children, too, were dressed in their finest.

My grandfather was gone, and I missed him terribly. His place was up there, among the Hasidim, reading from the Torah, his well-modulated voice should resound into every corner of the Great Synagogue.

There was much to pray for. We had been hearing persistent rumors about liquidation activities in communities nearby. Would they soon come our way? When? The question was on every worshipper's lips.

"Have we sinned this much, oh God in Heaven?"

"Let not our sins visit upon our children, merciful Father."

"Has not Abraham asked that You forgive his children for generations to come? It was then You had made a covenant to forgive them and deliver them from their suffering. Have You not made this promise, God? Have You forgotten, oh Merciful One? Even as the ram was substituted for Isaac as a sacrifice, dear God, here, too, we beseech You, forgive us our sins and save our children as you have saved them from the bondage of Egypt."

They cried unto the heavens, but there was no answer.

"Dear God, lead Your people out of this morass," they pleaded. "And give us strength to cope with our lot."

"Hear, oh Israel, the Lord our God, the Lord is One!"

On the second day of Passover, the president of the Council was again summoned to appear at the Bureau Headquarters. Shlomo Popiawski accompanied Warszawski on that occasion, and it was from him that we had later learned the details.

Doerings sat behind his massive desk, his hands folded piously in front of him. He was flanked by two burly Gestapo guards, automatic weapons at the ready.

"I have summoned you today in a most urgent and delicate matter,"

Doerings began unceremoniously. "I want to share this with you in all confidence. May I count on your absolute discretion?"

The two Jews were silent.

He did not wait long for their response. Patience was not one of Doerings' virtues. "As you know," he continued, "we have in Piotrkow a large garrison of young, healthy men." He paused to observe their reaction. There was none. They looked intensely at the enemy and he was forced to lower his eyes and look at his folded hands on the desk-top. He continued. "These young, healthy men, unfortunately suffer from lack of sexual gratification." Doerings hesitated again. "Occasionally, they find relief with women of the street. The result is an unfortunate rise of venereal cases. This situation cannot be tolerated. If we permit it to continue, our war effort in this entire area will suffer a setback."

The two Jews had begun to anticipate the purpose of their visit. Why else would this messenger from Berlin share such intimate knowledge with them? Doerings went on.

"By order of the territorial Director, you are to submit a list of young women from your community suitable to form the beginnings of what someday might become a home for convalescent soldiers."

"What you want, *Herr Sturmbannführer*," Warszawski dared interject, "put in our own language, is that I should become a common pimp. You're assigning me the responsibility for the establishment of a whore house."

"I have not used that word," Doerings emphasized with visible annoyance, "the interpretation is entirely your own."

"Are you serious or do you intend to amuse yourself at my expense?" Warszawski asked, hoping the enemy might see the absurdity of his demand.

"Our task allows us no time for joking." Doerings continued formally. "You will report to this office on Saturday. . ."

"*Herr Sturmbannführer*, please, not on Sabbath."

"Very well, then, on Monday at one o'clock sharp. You will have the list with you. You must not be concerned. The persons in question will be well taken care of. The home will be arranged quite comfortably and in keeping with strict sanitary procedures." He might have continued in his enthusiasm, but Warszawski dared to interrupt once again. A sudden burst of courage had become apparent as he dared to shout at the enemy:

"You believe in God, Doerings?" The omission of the official title was sufficient cause for punishment, but it was miraculously overlooked by the demi-god, perhaps because a Higher Being had been mentioned now.

"There you go catching at words, Jew."

"I asked you a question, sir."

"I. . . I believe. . . well. . . there is a divine soul in things. . ."

"Then don't you forget what there is in the soul of the Jew that is also divine—and that's resignation. Respect that in your arrogant nature and know that you can't press a man too far with a rope around his neck. What do you think we are?"

"You are taking it altogether too tragically, my good man," Doerings condescended to cordial familiarity. "After all, you are a man yourself and you can understand the needs of other men. Can't you?"

"You have imposed monetary taxation on us, and we have complied with your orders. You have blackmailed, robbed, humiliated and even killed some of us in the worst manner, and we have tried to adjust to our suffering. . ."

"Please, *Rav* Haskel. . ." Shlomo pleaded. "Don't give him a pretext. . ."

"Let him talk," Doerings said with a cynical smile. "It might be his final oration."

"Whatever the consequences," Warszawski went on, "I am resigned. It is God's will, not yours, *Herr Sturmbannführer*! You ask of us now that we offer our wives and daughters to you, so that you can use them as common whores! I can tell you, your order will not be carried out! You can destroy us all, but we will not become accomplices to this shameful act!" He threw himself full length in front of the desk, his forehead touching the floor, his eyes shut close and he lay there perfectly motionless and silent. Not even the sound of his breathing could be heard. The dead silence in the room remained undisturbed until Doerings' voice spoke gloomily:

"Look at your own Bible, it is filled with brothels."

"We have come a long way since the biblical days, *Herr Sturmbannführer*." Warszawski responded, still prostrate.

"Come now, Jew, be realistic," Doerings continued, "this is war, and in situations such as these all principles and theories die. Well?"

"May I tell you something?" Shlomo inquired.

"By all means." Doerings nodded toward the old man on the floor. "But get this man off the floor." Warszawski stirred. He got up slowly and spoke very calmly, ignoring Shlomo's signs begging his silence:

"Now let me first tell you, *Herr Sturmbannführer*, we will not be here on Monday with the list you have requested. Not on Monday or any other time!" He concluded completely out of breath.

"How dare you?! You impudent Semitic swine! Do you realize what is going to happen to all of you? You have a responsibility! Carry it out, Jew!" Doerings shouted at the top of his voice. He paused. Somewhat calmer, he continued, "Think of your people, if you're incapable to think of your own welfare, your children!"

"May I have my say, *Herr Sturmbannführer*?" Shlomo asked again.

"Go on, Jew, and I hope you'll make more sense than your Council president!" Doerings yelled.

"I am not going to speak for anyone but myself, Herr Sturmbannführer" Shlomo spoke slowly, placing emphasis on each word. "How can you order us to deliver our women to your soldiers? And how can we speak for the women? It is one thing when your troops rape and ravage them each day, and an altogether different issue when you tell us that they must become willing partners in comforting your sex-hungry 'healthy young men,' as you put it."

"Then, you refuse?" Doerings paused. "You. . . you dare to disobey me?! A representative of the Reich? You. . . you. . . filthy vermin?" He was beside himself with rage, but did well to control it. The two men stood before their enemy, at his mercy, and they expected the worst.

Doerings rose abruptly. It was evident he had made up his mind. "Be here on Monday at one o'clock with the list, swine! No more discussion!"

The two ghetto emissaries left Doerings' office with mixed feelings. They knew that theirs was a moral victory. They had reduced the Nazi from "gentleman" to "swine" in a matter of one brief session. But they were not certain that this victory would last. One does not trifle with the likes of the Sturmbannführer. They were painfully aware of that fact.

Monday came and went. There was no special list for the Gestapo. But even though Doerings' order was ignored by the Council, there were no immediate reprisals. It was exasperating trying to outguess the Gestapo. The final day of Passover had come.

The Great Synagogue which stood only a few blocks away from our home was filled to capacity. Roman and I had worked the nightshift, and my mother persuaded both of us to remain at home to rest and catch up on our sleep. We would have to work the following night as well. We felt dishonest, still, we were tired and needed the rest. In fact, only my grandmother insisted on attending the services. The rest of us stayed home.

"You mustn't tire yourself, mama." My mother admonished our grandmother.

"You worry too much, Bela." My grandmother was in a somber mood, determined to join her lifelong friends at worship. "After all, it isn't as though I have no practice in this manner of thing. You stay, children, I must join your grandfather."

We failed to understand her last remark, but she hasn't been herself since grandfather's death, and we didn't ask questions. Besides, the Great Synagogue was only a few blocks away, and my mother was going to look in on her sometime during the services.

An aura of peace and holiness suffused the ghetto. The evening services were well on their way. One could feel all that was good and sacred—love, affection, mercy, and worship—on this holy day. As on all holidays, His children's supplications are said to be dear and acceptable to the Almighty, blessed be He. And through the silentm prayer, one could hear the trilling voice of the great cantor, which was meant to please the congregation and find favor with their Father in Heaven.

A rumbling noise had awakened us. I looked at the clock. It was almost six, and the services were coming to a close. I went into the living room where everyone was assembled near the window. Below, a long column of personnel trucks and armored cars with the SS insignia boldly displayed, advanced along Zamkowa Street in the direction of the Great Synagogue. There were machine-guns mounted and manned by Lithuanian mercenaries on top of each personnel carrier and truck.

Merciful God! I thought. Doerings' revenge!

"Grandmother!" My mother exclaimed. "The Synagogue must be warned!"

"It's too late, mama!" I cried. "The street is full of them!"

The words and events of that evening had been burned as if with a white hot steel in the deepest recesses of my memory. I was to remember them and talk about their recurrence in my nightmares with fullness and precision for many years afterwards.

The record of the thoughts which assailed me was full of minute details, embellished by sight and sound; cries of anguish and fear, hopelessness, and supplication.

Ma-ariv, the evening service, was ending; that most joyous of songs "It is enough" would be resounding about now. I thought. Another half hour, and the services would let out; the worshippers would return to their homes.

That was not meant to happen, and it was too late for warnings. The rumbling had stopped. *Sturmbannführer* Schröder was in charge now. He barked a few short orders. The SS spread out, surrounding the house of worship in a matter of minutes. Still, the Jews inside the Great Synagogue were unaware. Heavy barricades were put up to block all of the exits from the building.

Mortar fire was followed by incendiary grenades which exploded inside the synagogue. I tried to imagine what was happening to the people inside, but I was unable to extend my imagination to the limits of their anguish.

Frightened and confused, over three hundred people must have pressed against the rigid doors, seeking escape from the flaming inferno. Through our open window we could hear women and children scream hysterically; men cursed attempting to aid those in need. Billowing dark smoke rose to the sky, and the fire was in full bloom. The sun was setting, and the night would be soon upon us.

Suddenly, some of the worshippers appeared in the upper floor windows. The enemy guns spewed fire. We could hear bursts of machine-gun fire at various intervals: ra-ta-ta-ta, ra-ta-ta . . . As I can still hear them after so many years, days on end, even now their sound is still resounding in my ears. Men fell to the ground out of the windows, still enveloped in their sacred prayer shawls; some had managed to toss their children onto the pavement in an attempt to save them from the flames within. The SS marksmen found their targets before they would reach the ground; ra-ta-ta-ta, ra-ta-ta. The little humans fell and remained motionless on the ground.

And then, as if fashioned by some bizarre inventor, a group of Hitler Youths, attired in festive regalia and accompanied by the regimental band, appeared in front of the Great Synagogue and joyfully sang the Horst-Wessel song.

At that moment, Warszawski, dressed in his prayer shawl, appeared in one of the shattered windows. In one arm, he held a small boy, his only grandchild, in the other he held the Torah. His eyes were closed tightly, but his lips were moving in worship.

There was a sudden lull in the SS activity as their attention was drawn to the window apparition. Then there was raucous laughter.

"Hey, Moses! This isn't Mount Sinai!" A voice yelled at the old man.

"The Lord thy God is a consuming fire!" Warszawski recited.

More laughter and derision.

The fire was devouring everything beneath, the priests, the Levites, and the laity who kept on singing and meditating with prayer, while above them Warszawski stood in the shattered window, raising the scroll up high in his arm, merging into a unity with the flaming universe, as his resonant voice was heard pronounce the blessing: "ye, even while cleaving to the Lord your God, are alive everyone of you this day!"

A shot rang out. The old Jew swayed, almost falling as he leaned heavily against the window frame, refusing to come down. He proceeded to wrap his grandchild in his prayer shawl.

Warszawski looked down at Schröder and Doerings—the latter had arrived in his staff car moments after the operation began.—The flames seemed to reach out at the old man's feet and lick them greedily. Now, with the greatest of efforts, he heaved the child onto the ground below as a challenge for the marksmen. The crumpled body lay motionless where it fell. In an instant, the wall collapsed and the old man was swallowed into the flaming structure.

We wept until there were no more tears.

Morning came, and a feeling of horrible sickness had come over me. I must be courageous, I exhorted myself mentally, else I will have no strength left to cope with tomorrow.

The destruction of the Great Piotrkow Synagogue was complete. It had become the sacrificial pyre for all those worshippers, my grandmother among them. The surviving families came to pick up the recognizable remains, placed them in burlap sacks, and carried them to a common burial place among lamentations and cries of anguish. The Synagogue had become a monumental abode of misery. The ghetto was plunged into unspeakable grief.

Why is the enemy intent on destroying the very substance of our spirit? I thought to myself. Then, it was the Great Temple of Jerusalem; now, our Great Piotrkow Synagogue lies in shambles.

I wandered, dazed, through the destruction, and only the shattered walls of the holy place witnessed my agony. The *Aharon Hakodesh* as well as the *Baal Emeth*, though still recognizable, had been horribly desecrated. The Torahs were gone, but worst of all, those many lives, vibrant with their sanctifications of the Almighty, they, too, were all gone. Now, this had become the last resting place for my grandmother, for we had not been able to recover her remains, much to our complete despair.

"God wanted her near Him," my mother signed heavily. "His will be done."

We accepted my mother's explanation for want of a more logical one. For now it will have to do. I thought to myself. But. . . oh. . . the Torahs. . . where could they have gone? I could not bring myself to ask. There was no trace of them left.

Visions of the old man Warszawski filling the frame of the window of the Great Synagogue, engulfed by smoke and fire, the little grandson and the sacred scroll in his arms appeared to me once again. I heard the last audible words he had uttered: "The Lord thy God is a consuming fire!" And now, I thought I understood. . . the Torah. . . the fire. . . the love of righteousness . . . Though Warszawski and the Hasidim had vanished, and so did the Great Synagogue, what they stood for remained in the hearts and souls of the survivors.

So be it.

Passover had become *Yom Hadin*, "the day of Final Judgment." Some of the SS who turned away from the spectacle were ordered to witness the carnage as a trial of their courage and devotion. Others took pictures.

And when the trucks had gone and the ghetto returned to its mournful quiet, we wept no more. I had made a solemn promise to myself; I must never forget those cries. Even if I were destined to meet the fate of those who had perished in the Great Piotrkow Synagogue, I must etch the story in the minds of others before I am gone. In that way, the truth will not be forgotten, the victims will not have died in vain. They will not be pushed into the abyss of history but remain alive in the present. That is my task, and I shall fulfill it.

7

Haskel Warszawski was dead and so were most of the Council members. "There will no longer be a ghetto Council!" Doerings proclaimed. "You shall have only the Militia."

At the head of the ghetto Militia, the Gestapo placed Joel Katzmann, a newcomer from the West, a German refugee. Joel was a World War I veteran of the Kaiser's army, a life long civil servant. He was made of that special fiber essential in the profile of a Gestapo lackey; indefatigable in the pursuit of duty. He had what it would take to safeguard his own interests; the instinct of a loyal servant and a gross lack of scruples, ready to sacrifice anyone for his personal good.

Orders reaching Katzmann were considered sacred and he was never one to question their logic or their validity. In fact, he would often "improve" on the original intent of the order to earn the Gestapo's praise.

Katzmann appeared in his late fifties, balding and with a large aquiline nose. The latter must have caused him much anguish, knowing how his masters despised that particular Jewish feature. For that reason, he wore his eye glasses on the very tip of his nose in his attempt to cover its Semitic features. Early on, we had decided we wouldn't count on that aspect of Katzmann's identity, for we knew from experience that, once given authority over others, he would exercise it with an umcompromising zeal.

Like his superiors, Katzmann wore a pair of shiny boots and carried a swagger stick. When preoccupied with an assignment, he would nervously whip the side of his boots in the fashion of those whom he had emulated.

Roman and I continued as the family's providers and Nora would soon begin work at the factory. Forced labor had become a way of life for the ghetto inhabitants. The special *Meldekarte*, a report card, which was in fact a work identity pass, provided temporary security for its holder and was difficult to come by. We were anxious to have one issued for our mother, but there was no way to convince her. She refused to abandon Felusia, for fear of losing her to one of the frequent ghetto raids.

"It's final," my mother responded to everyone's urging. "I'm not going to leave my little one to the Lithuanians." She paused. "Nor, for that matter, to Katzmann and his Militia." She added forcefully. At the far end of the Hortensia compound, barracks were erected by special workmen brought in from out of town. Work went on at a fast pace, on a twenty-four hour schedule. Night shifts made use of special high-density light, and the activity was interrupted only by shift changes.

These preparations became a source of intensified rumors. In the space of two weeks the new facility, modestly furnished, was ready for occupation. Miles of barbed wire had been wound around the factory area; a small dispensary and disinfection center became part of the compound.

"We must face the future more realistically," Felix spoke, "we must not be deceived by the temporary tranquility after the Passover carnage." He was calm; our new leader. A meeting was arranged in the ruins of the old military headquarters on Polna Street. As an unprecedented gesture of solidarity among the Jews, the Hashomer Hatzair (a leftist organization) met with the Mizrahi (Hasidic youth), even the Maccabeans, an athletic youth movement, joined to devise a plan of action. Felix Rabinowicz led the militant Hatzair; Yulek, the mild-mannered son of Isaac the Gabbah, headed the Mizrahi. He was moved to violence by his consuming hatred toward his father's murderers.

A mere handful of young men and women had gathered in the modern catacombs. At a glance, I estimated no more than a hundred.

"No death without a fight!" Was going to be our slogan. We were going to sell our lives dearly.

"I have made a decision for myself." Felix faced the others without emotion. "I had decided that I can't go on living in constant fear of death; my life cannot be dependent upon the whim of a mercenary guard, a Nazi lackey or a paid informer. And I'll try not to let the enemy catch me by surprise."

"A point well taken, Felix." Yulek said. "Our situation is more serious than many of us want to believe. The Nazis aren't playing games any longer. Their intentions should be obvious to the most optimistic among us." He paused. "It's all clear now. We mustn't allow the enemy to take us piecemeal."

"What if we should make them angry by resisting?" One of the Hasids asked cautiously.

"You're free to leave right now." Felix emphasized each word. "We won't hold it against you if you leave us." He paused, and his intense eyes penetrated those of the inquiring Hasid. "We ask only that you breathe nothing of these proceedings to anyone."

"Maybe he's right," Yulek defended the Hasid, "maybe if we don't challenge the enemy, they'll leave us be."

I looked at Felix, and I could see his rising anger. The others must have noticed too. By now, he was well known for his quick temper. He controlled himself, though, and addressed the few doubters softly, almost with a degree of kindness: "You may go on deceiving yourselves, but I prefer to face death head on. I don't mean to play a hero. I'm as frightened as any of you. Just let me ask you one question: haven't you reached the very lowest point of your existence? Have you no dignity left?"

"We might be worse off if we challenged the Nazis." One of the present suggested hesitantly. "We might be dead."

"Yulek's father should serve as the best answer to your question." Felix addressed the man who, at the mention of the murdered gabbah, lowered his eyes. "There's not a gentler soul among us than Shlomo Zaplocki was, may he rest in peace. He would have never thought of resisting the enemy."

"But. . . you know. . ."

"If we hesitate, we're doomed." Felix was adamant. "The time for playing ostrich is over. We have to take a stand; better now while we're still on our feet."

A few left. The rest stayed on to plan and forge a bond that only death could sever. Yulek was among the latter. Felix nodded and Yulek came forward to his side.

"We have made contact with the Home Army during the past three weeks," Yulek began, "and they had promised to lend us as much support as they can. A shipment of light arms and ammunition arrived only a few hours ago. We'll distribute it among you shortly. For the last time," Yulek paused, his eyes touched those of the assembled, slowly, searchingly, "those of you who wish to leave, now's the time. There'll be no turning back."

They looked at one another, no one moved, though fear was on many faces. Some of the boys could not have been barmitzvah as yet, but the presence of death reached into them and made them mature beyond the logic of all natural laws.

"So be it," Felix said, "you'll be contacted soon. Go back to your homes, and don't draw the enemy's attention. We don't want any of you to get caught now. The Gestapo has its informers everywhere." We left the catacombs, one at a time, fusing our gray images into the moonless darkness of the night.

In the days that followed our meeting, I noticed, among other unusual preparations, the arrival of several units of the SS, predomimantly mercenaries from some of the Baltic states, Estonia, Lithuania and Latvia; young German officers had been placed in charge of the operations. What I didn't know then was that these men were the first units of the *Einsatzkommandos* (Nazi euphemism for "killing units").

We looked at each other helplessly. Once again, we were outmaneuvered by the great organizational skill and speed of the Nazi bureacracy. All we could hope to do from now on was to be vigilant and expect some favorable turn of events.

The first week of October, Katzmann was summoned to the office of *Sturmbannführer* Schröder .

"We shall install high density lights on the market square by the coming weekend. I want sentries on all streets leading to the place at exactly three o'clock on Saturday morning. Understood?"

Katzmann clicked the heels of his shiny boots together. "*Jawohl, Herr Sturmbannführer!* He did not raise his right arm in a salute. He knew where to draw the line. He cleared his throat discretely so as not to disturb his superior but to catch his attention.

"Yes? Katzmann, what is it?" Schröder seemed annoyed.

"A matter of planned rebellion, sir." Katzmann was careful in phrasing his information.

"Yes? Go on!"

"One of my trusted men informs me of a recent gathering. . .well. . .it could result in some trouble."

"What kind of trouble?" The German showed an interest.

"Disruption of order, sir."

"In that case, what do you suggest we do?"

"Take out the leaders, sir." The expression "take out" was Katzmann's way of suggesting arrest. The Nazi thought for a while, then, with a miscievous chuckle, he remarked: "Come Saturday, it won't matter one way or another."

"How's that, sir?" Katzmann was curious.

"You shall see for yourself, Joel. Have patience."

"Anything else, sir?"

"You may go now, Joel. Instruct your informer to remain vigilant."

"Yes, sir." Katzmann turned and was gone instantly.

Saturday's early morning hours were filled with repeated small arms fire, authoritative shouts, cries and lamentations. We got up frightened shortly before dusk. It was that bewitching period of transition when the moon claims the universe from the sun, scarcely leaving sufficient time for man to surmise that he stands alone. Loudspeakers blared for all to hear: "Abandon your homes! Everybody out! Assemble on the street! *Schnell!*"

The Militia carried out the Gestapo orders to the letter, and with utmost discretion. But despite all the secrecy, word had leaked about the mysterious preparations. We harbored no illusions about the approaching events. Deep inside, each of us was preparing for the worst.

As people lined the streets, truckloads of mercenaries arrived supplemented by the Militia. They took charge of the disorderly crowds, shoving and beating them into submission and a semblance of order.

Mothers anxiously clutched their small children as the multitides were herded toward the market square, now as bright as daytime. The newly installed lights worked well. Searching for their families or friends, people shouted names and ran in all directions, only to be beaten back.

"Leave your belongings in your homes!" The voice in the bullhorn sounded almost cheerful. "You shall return to them soon!" In a desperate attempt to comply with orders, people ran back into their homes to leave their bundles, but there, too, they ran into rifle butts.

My mother carried an overnight bag in one hand and held on to Felusia with the other. A guard abruptly tore the bag from her hand, throwing its contents onto the pavement. Some cosmetic articles hit the ground and broke into small fragments. My mother's face looked anguished, but she did not voice her pain. More important things were on her mind. The mercenary laughed derisively: "You won't need these where you're going, Jewish bitch!" He shouted vulgarities, but my mother silently hurried us on. "Good bye and good riddance." The Lithuanian shouted cynically after us.

A search was going on for those who remained in their homes. Men, women and children were hunted down in cellars and attics; shouts of pain mingled with curses and entreaties resounded everywhere. The shooting went on. The entire world seemed terribly confusing and confused.

Only after our arrival on the Adolf Hitler Platz had the magnitude of the enemy's enterprise become clear. On this unprecedented occasion, the combined SS and Gestapo high Commands, the two competing service branches of the *Führer*'s elite fighting units, worked in harmony. Schröder and Doerings shouted commands, whipping people into a semblance of disciplined ranks. Wherever an older person faltered or stopped or a woman cradling her children looked around desperately seeking aid, blow upon blow followed. It was stricktly forbidden to offer assistance of any kind, and those who tried were punished alongside those whom they attempted to help. Once again the bullhorn:

"No one is to interfere in the proceedings! Everyone must follow orders! The penalty for any violation of this order will be death!"

We listened and obeyed.

What we learned much later was that the Poles, encouraged by the SS, started plundering the entire ghetto soon after we had left the premises.

The looters went up and down the stairs of the apartment houses and in and out of Jewish homes, all under the pretext of "looking for stragglers." They soon came out with bags stuffed full of things, their greed showing on their faces. "They didn't have the common decency to let the body cool." Someone remarked.

Obersturmbannführer Helmut Schirmeck was brought in from the *Gauleiter's* office in Krakow. He stood apart from the crowd, barking terse orders at his aides, when necessary.

The market square had been cordoned off tightly by the Lithuanian SS. Toward early afternoon, nearly all of the ghetto Jews had been herded into that small cobble-stoned area facing the city hall on the right and the town church on the left. Behind us was the railroad depot. I looked at my mother anxiously, but her face did not betray her emotions. "Don't let go of your belongings," she urged. Each one of us carried a small bundle. I embraced my violin case.

Felusia was on her exemplary behavior. She followed my mother and did not complain or cry. Nora looked brave, and so did Hayim and Roman. I promised myself, come what may, I wasn't going to break down and cry. I wasn't going to let my mother down. After all, men don't cry, I thought to myself.

By early evening, only small groups of people were still being herded into the square. By dawn, the Gestapo had rounded up the Piotrkow Jews, and the "selection" was about to begin. We sat around in the open and waited through the night. I don't know of anyone that rested, except the small children who slept in the arms of their parents with unconcerned innocence.

"What's going to happen, mama?" I whispered.

"We're embarking on a journey, Vilusiek, you mustn't worry. We'll be all right." She tried to reassure me, but I sensed anxiety even though her eyes were hidden by darkness.

"Where will they take us, mama?" I asked, trying desperately to force my mother to talk. Sensing that this might be the last chance I'll have to hear her lovely voice, to squeeze her precious hand. She, too, sensed the urgency of the moment, and we kept on talking until sunrise; my mother, Roman and I.

We welcomed dawn with mixed emotions. Nature was going to provide us with a lovely day. Will people do the same?

Obersturmbannführer Schirmeck appeared exactly at six o'clock in the morning, as though the time had been predetermined. He observed the multitude, a benign smile on his face. A few orders to his aides and the masses were set in motion.

Once more the bullhorn:

"All able-bodied Jews from the age of thirteen to fifty-five will line up on the right. All others, on the left." Thus the "selection" had begun.

No one paid heed to the announcement. Families clutched onto each other. Blows followed. An old woman was shot by an impatient sentry. She was the first casualty.

As the people passed in front of the Gestapo chief, he motioned with his index finger to the left or to the right. He no longer smiled. This was serious work.

It wasn't long before the masses had fully grasped the nature of the exercise. The young were being separated from the old; the weak from the strong. The pattern was all too obvious. "Look at them to our left." Someone whispered close by. "Do you think they're fit for work?"—"And they're trying to tell us we're all going to labor camps, and we'll return home soon." Another voice spoke. "Fat chance, we'll return!"

"We mustn't follow to the left!" Someone shouted suddenly. "The left means death!" Pandemonium broke out. A wave of humanity swayed powerfully toward the right side of the market square. Women dragged their small children along. Men carried their elderly and disabled parents or supported those who were still able to walk. Those who fell to the ground, were trampled underfoot. Cries for help resounded, but they touched on deaf ears; suddenly, it was everyone for himself.

It took only a moment for the Gestapo and the SS to estimate the gravity of the situation. Crisp orders resounded, and shots were fired into the moving mass of humanity. I saw people falling next to me, then getting up and trying to run again, falling to the ground again, to remain there motionless. The sight of blood became nauseating, and I felt I would retch any moment. People kept on running, desperately trying to escape the vigilant guards. I asked myself where are they running to, but I could not answer my own question.

There was nowhere to go. Like a stampeding herd of cattle, the Jews turned round and came to a halt. The shooting subsided. Loud lamentations were evidence of the many lives lost. The plaintive sounds now mingled with the cold cadence of the eerie ritual. . . Helmut Schirmeck's voice carried on: "*rechts. . . rechts. . . links. . . links. . .*"

It was almost our turn. We approached the area where the Gestapo had set up their "measuring stations." Not until we had come close to one of the guards holding the measuring rod did I notice signs of desperate worry in my mother's eyes. They placed a rod 1.20 meters in height in front of Schirmeck. Children who would pass under the rod were taken away to the left. Some parents chose to go with them. Others had made the decision to go to the right. There wasn't time for much deliberation, the overseer's whip finding its mark, discouraging hesitation.

"You must try, my darling." My mother whispered imploringly to my little sister. "Please, Felusia, try to stand tall, like a grand lady, shoulders straight, head high. Be on your toes, dearest." She pleaded with the little one.

As if she understood the urgency of our mother's plea, Felusia seemed to grow to the occasion. She stretched her slender neck gracefully, and holding her head up proudly, she stepped in front of the crude measuring device, on her toes, like a ballerina turning in the most important performance of her lifetime.

I looked at my mother helplessly. Her lips were moving in silent prayer. She prayed for a miracle, but in spite of all her efforts, Felusia did not meet the expected height requisites. By a desperate few centimeters, she was short of joining those who were destined to go to the right.

At that moment, a Jewish Militia approached and pointed at Felusia. "The child must go to the left." My mother wouldn't let go of Felusia's hand. "To the left! Did you hear?" He shouted. "You must go to the right with the others!" Still no response from my mother. "You'll get us all into trouble if you don't follow orders!" My mother stood firm. He turned to Roman and me. "You go on to the right. Have your *Meldekarten* ready for inspection."

We displayed our *Meldekarten*. "How about you, woman?" He addressed my mother again. "Make up your mind!" He was growing impatient. He tried to pull Felusia from my mother's grip, and the little one began to cry. There were large tears rolling down Felusia's cheeks, and I could not understand how anyone could not be moved by her distress. "You'll be better off without the kid, woman." The Militia man tried to sound sympathetic, but his words had a hollow effect. Now, my mother knelt holding Felusia firmly in her embrace. She wiped the tears from Felusia's cheeks with a clean white kerchief.

"What's the matter with you, *Schwein*?!" Doerings yelled at my mother. "Can't you see you're holding up the others?!" He was about to kick her, but something caught his attention and he hesitated. My mother released Felusia long enough to embrace Roman and me.

"Be brave, my darlings. Don't worry. Felusia and I will be fine. And we'll see you soon, when all's well." She wept now, for the first time allowing herself the luxury of tears.

"Don't cry, mama, please don't cry." I kissed her many times.

"We'll take care. Please, dearest mama, don't cry." It was my turn now to wipe the tears from her face.

Suddenly Doerings pointed at my violin case. "What have you got in there, Jew?" He asked, and I understood what had caught his attention moments ago and saved my mother from a beating. I noticed a spark of hope in her eyes now. The miracle she'd been praying for was about to happen. Surely, if I played for them, they'd let us remain together.

"A violin, *Herr Sturmbannführer.*" I replied in German, and he was impressed with my command of his language. I opened the case. The Nazi hesitated as if to change his mind, then came the order:

"*Spiel! Jude! Schnell!* Play Jew! Quickly!" He barked for me to perform. "Play for your miserable life, swine!" He added, and I suddenly thought that my virtuosity might be able to save us all. I looked at the angry faces of the SS and the Gestapo around me, and I realized that I had no time to lose. I took the violin out of the case, and I was transported to another place, another time.

It is now the year 1937, and I am the nine-year-old prodigy performing with the Warsaw Philharmonic, under the direction of my uncle Mihas Stybel. I place the chinboard firmly under my chin and tighten the bow, applying rosin to the horsehair. The conductor raises the baton, my fingers caress the strings as I warm up, there is total silence, and then I hear the violins in the orchestra softly intoning the accompaniment to Schumann's famous piece *Traümerei.*

In the midst of a hapless throng of my family and friends, in the brief moments of reprieve, I played my beloved instrument as I had never played before. First Schumann then Mozart, Brahms and Beethoven followed, and then again Schumann and J.S. Bach. There was complete silence, and for those few moments everyone listened, Nazi and Jew alike, entranced. After all, this young Jew was playing *their* music; all was well with the world. The sound of music granted us all the miracle of harmony. I hadn't noticed, but the Nazis stood around me chanting the melodies they knew from their homes, some wiping a tear from their eyes when I intoned the melody of Brahms' famous lullaby "Good evening, good night. . ."

I felt the violin being ripped from under my chin violently, with a sudden jerk. I was caught by surprise, and the metal clamp dug deep into my skin and produced an ugly gash. I touched my chin. There was blood on my hand. My mother quickly applied the kerchief to stop the bleeding. "Please, oh please, don't destroy it!" She cried, and only then I had noticed that Doerings raised the violin above his head and smashed it against my skull with great force. The instrument exploded into a thousand fragments, flying in every direction. It was as if God had decided to make me mute, though He had given me the gift to sound His praises. I told myself to stay calm, but my heart was filled with such great intensity of hatred, I wished Doerings had taken a bite of it there and then; the venom inside would have surely struck him dead.

"Enough! Get going, pigs!" Doerings shouted an order and landed a powerful kick to my mother's thigh. She let go of my embrace and doubled up with terrible pain. I knew then that for a brief moment I was playing the fool, unable to understand the true nature of man. It was a kind of terrible childishness which I was not willing to renounce. I knew that children, too, have the desire for power, the will to hurt and to destroy. And I longed with all my senses to do just that.

I'll kill him when I'm given the chance. I thought to myself. Him and his likes, I swear, as long as there's blood in my veins! My eyes were full of hatred as I fixed them on *Sturmbannführer* Doerings, my arms trying to protect my mother.

"Get moving, woman!" The Militia man shouted. "You'll get us all in trouble!" Another quick embrace followed for each of us, and she was ready. "Nora, my sweet girl," my mother cried, Felusia in tow—the little one now on her best behavior so as not to antagonize the SS—as she pushed forward and away from us, "be brave, my dear girl, and God bless all of you!" The guards hurried the two of them to the left side of the market place, where they soon disappeared within the moving mass of the aged and the very young.

"We must go now," Nora sobbed, leading us further toward the right perimeter of the market place. From there, we observed the loading of the box-cars, and the sorting of the remaining people. In the great confusion, I spotted Felix and a couple of my friends, sitting dejectedly near their belongings. What will happen to our plans? I had no answer.

Suddenly a woman cradling an infant in her arms broke through and ran toward Doerings. "Please, do anything to me, only save my baby!" She begged. An SS guard raised his whip to punish the impudent woman. Doerings stopped him with a motion of his hand. "You have a choice, woman," he said calmly, "you go to the right and live, or you can go with the others."

"Kind sir, save my baby, my little girl! Have mercy!" The woman was hysterical.

"*Schmeiss doch den Abfall weg!* Throw away this trash, woman!" Doerings shouted. With that, he turned to walk away. The woman ran toward him, a kitchen knife in her free hand. The guard shouted a warning, and Doerings fell as he turned toward the lunging mother. His right hand reached mechanically for his hip holster, but he never needed to use his pistol. One blow of the guard's rifle butt, and the woman was falling awkwardly to the ground. Blow upon blow followed, until the woman's skull resembled a mass of blood and tissue. Through all that, the frightened infant lay next to its mutilated mother weeping loudly. The concerned guard helped his superior to his feet, while carefully dusting the dirt off the officer's once spotless uniform. Regulations explicitly called for clean attire in public.

"What do we do with this bastard?" The guard asked.

"*Links! Das geht links!*" Doerings yelled. "To the left, it goes to the left!" He repeated. The guard picked up the infant by one of its legs and tossed it into the crowd on the left. I was unable to tell whether the baby was caught in flight or whether it fell to the ground. I renewed my vow: I shall never forget!

There was aunt Sabina and the children approaching the measuring station. Devorah was small for her age, and Michael was even smaller than his sister. They won't pass, good Lord, they won't meet the height requirements. Went through my mind. I called out to them. They saw me, too, and they waved. They looked so dismally sad, all of them, especially aunt Sabina.

"Poor aunt Sabina," Nora said, "she has made a tough decision." Remembering uncle Joseph's erstwhile influence, I knew then that there were no privileged among the Jews. Those who were useful were spared only for the duration of their usefulness.

I will miss them all. I thought silently. Most of all, I'll miss my cousin Devorah. She was a gentle creature with a soft little voice. Now they were taking her away. . . my Devorah. . . with her large dark eyes and black hair and such a pale, thin face. Just looking at her, made me want to love and protect her in her implicit helplessness.

The selection continued for many hours. The SS brought especially trained shepherd dogs to help keep the people at bay. They had been trained to sniff and bark, and they punished those who dared to delay the movement by a last embrace or a farewell message called out across the square. Growling furiously, the animals sprang at their victims, to the delight of their masters. The SS photographer recorded their bravery in countless shots, later to be publicized in newspapers and magazines throughout the Third Reich. After all, the dog's performance was a credit to the ingenuity of his master. With the arrival of the animals, we exchanged only silent greetings with friends and relatives.

Some six thousand people between the ages of twelve and forty-five were assembled to the right of the square. The opposite side numbered many thousands more.

The loading of the box-cars began as soon as the selection was finished. I strained to find my mother and Felusia, now in the company of aunt Sabina and her family, but I was unable to identify any of them in the vast mass of people. It seemed an endless procession into the huge freight cars.

"There will be better living conditions and milder treatment in the work-camp of your destination!" The voice over the bullhorn was encouraging the Jews to "Get going! Get going!" as they climbed up into the waiting cattle cars.

As soon as they filled one car to capacity, the sentries drove the Jews to the next empty one. At one point, I counted almost two hundred to a car. I needed a vivid imagination even to picture the interior of the box-cars. I couldn't imagine the conditions under which those hundreds of people could exist even for the shortest time. I asked myself, what must it be like inside those box-cars? From the looks of it, there must have been standing room only. At best, the movement was restricted to stretching one's neck and, perhaps, an occasional raising of the arms.

What were they thinking about? In the face of death, a person becomes fearless, an animal, no longer responding to intelligence, guided by instinct and impulse. Fear expressed itself in grunts and moans. Instinct made them relieve themselves where they stood, like frightened, beaten animals, pretending all along not to feel anything.

There were some who, moments before they stepped into the freight, had experienced a change of heart. They were shot on the spot or clubbed to death.

"You damned ingrates!" Schröder shouted. "Trying to resettle you isn't enough. You ungrateful scum!"

Clouds gathered overhead while the loading continued late into the night. It began to rain torrentially and the earth turned into mud. Thunder sounded through most of the storm, and an occasional lightning illuminated the eerie procession of people. Morning came, and the sun broke through. In the late afternoon, more box-cars had come into a second rail terminal to accommodate the remainder of the people.

I spotted my mother and Felusia following aunt Sabina up the ramp leading to their freight-car. My mother turned before entering, and our eyes met across the square, imploringly. We all waved at them as they did in our direction, my mother with her clean white kerchief, Felusia her small delicate hand of a child.

They entered the box-car and the door was tightly shut and securely locked. In addition, the Militia nailed long boards diagonally crisscrossing the doors. Why was the Gestapo taking all these precautions! I asked myself. Why should anyone want to escape a better future of resettlement?

The loading was now completed. Only the sentries and their dogs remained. We could hear cries of anguish coming through the cracks in the freight-car walls. The din of voices prevented us from recognizing any of the callers, each trying to be louder than the other. Each competing with the staccato sound of Nazi orders and the barking of their shepherd dogs. Through all that chaos, I kept hearing my mother's voice clearly and vividly: "Be brave my darlings, be brave!"

The evening was humid and cold. They said it heralded a severe winter.

I stamped my feet to keep warm. It was the third day outdoors, and weariness was showing on everyone's face. What's next? We kept wondering. There seemed to be no order in the actions of the Nazis. The resettlement preparation had not gone well; there were dead lying on the ground still to be removed. The transport of sealed box-cars had not moved an inch, and people inside were going mad.

As if in answer to my silent inquiry, the long column of freight cars began to move. I strained to follow the white kerchief as it kept appearing through the small, boarded-up window. I prayed silently. Where are you now, merciful Father in Heaven? I was being crushed—and I wasn't able to run away, to move from the spot. I knew that others had a place for themselves somewhere on this earth—some little corner away from it all, where they could rightfully take their troubled lives. Everyone had a refuge, except us.

We had nothing. Not even a moral refuge in this hour of need; a refuge of hope. Everyone had abandoned us. In all this great, great universe, whom could I turn to with my sorrow?

I beseech You, oh Lord God. I continued to pray. This is no time to turn away from your wicked children; to take a rest. This punishment is too severe for our wickedness. A parent is not to punish his children which are already afflicted with pain and suffering. Oh Lord, if You have no time to spare, then how about the world outside? Make them take notice of our plight.

Only the Gestapo was pleased with the results of their daily work. At nightfall, in the bright lamplight, their polished boot-heels clicked together. They raised their arms high in the mysterious salute: "*Heil* Hitler!" "*Sieg Heil!*"

"Let's get going! Column of fours!" Katzmann's voice was bursting with authority. Now that the Germans were gone, he was in full command.

Leaving the market square, we looked back at the row of freight cars lined on the tracks. They had come to a halt again. The shouts were growing fainter as we gradually put distance between us. We heard sporadic automatic weapons fire coming from the ghetto. I understood. The cleaning-up detail was in progress. There must have been some Jews in hiding. Death was everywhere that night, it fed on itself, aided by the SS, and it grew in the reflection of fear among the wretched ghetto inhabitants.

One more glance back, the ghetto stood enveloped in flames and smoke. This was all accomplished in the space of only forty-eight hours. When machine-gun bullets gave out, the Nazis used flame-throwers to smoke out the fugitives. And while all this was happening, spectators hurried to the event from all over town. They lined the periphery of the barbed wire fence;

old men and their companions, smoking pipe and commenting on the action; young couples, bubbling excitedly; mothers holding up their small children better to record the curious events. "Look," they would say, "the Jews are all gone, never to return!"

Piotrkow was *Judenrein*—clean of Jews—. I could not guess what had happened to my grandparents' home on Zamkowa 20; Srulko's favorite mahogany staircase banister which he was forever polishing; was it gone? Would his paper rubles—that worthless Russian currency my grandfather had kept all these years in the attic—be there when. . . when what? When I return?

At the precise moment we arrived at the Hortensia compound, we heard the whistle of the distant locomotive announcing the approaching freight-train. The tracks passed no more than twenty feet from the camp fence. We stood, waiting for the train to pass, in the hope of catching a last glimpse of our loved ones. It was an unusually long hook-up pulled by two powerful locomotives. Still, it rolled by slowly, as if it meant to deliberately prolong our agony. I could see children's faces peering through the cracks, their eyes wild with fear and filled with the agony of puzzlement. Once again, names were called, goodbyes and admonishments. We responded in like, it did not matter to whom. A last farewell was all that mattered. Perhaps one last bright spot in a fortnight. Slender arms reached out through the crevices; sometimes only a single finger for lack of more space. "I think I'm going to vomit, Nora." I said, doubling up in pain.

"You must be strong Vilusiek. Now, more than ever, you'll have to rely on your own strength." She spoke soothingly, caressing my cheeks and wiping the tears away. "We must stand here and look on; your mama and Felusia are in one of those cars. You wouldn't want to miss them, would you?

"They'll never be back. . . I'll never see them again." I kept repeating.

"You mustn't think that way, my dear. You mustn't torment yourself." Nora could not give up. "Let's pray together. Let's pray for a reunion."

"The only reunion we'll experience will be in the beyond, if there is a beyond!" I said defiantly.

"Do not blaspheme, darling, God will punish us," Nora admonished patiently.

"That's nonsense, Nora!" I cried. "If God doesn't hear our prayers, how could He hear our curses?"

"The kerchief!" Roman suddenly exclaimed. "There! Mama's kerchief!" He pointed to one of the cars. There it was, fluttering in the wind, mama's white kerchief. For the moment, Nora and I had forgotten our argument. I strained to see my mother's hand, perhaps only her fingers holding on to the white cloth. The train was too far for me to distinguish anything, but, once again, my imagination had helped me to understand that the crack in the boards was too small, and she was holding on to the white cloth from the inside.

There were so many things I had wanted to tell my mother, things I should have told her often, but I didn't. Did she know, how much I loved her? I asked myself silently as I waved farewell. Could we have saved them if we had tried? Agonizingly, I had to tell myself that whatever happened did so because we had no options.

I lay in troubled sleep that night, when I suddenly found myself in a room full of people. In the midst of them was my grandfather. I didn't see him at first, and when I did catch a glimpse of him, he was no longer there.

I got up before anyone else to use the bathroom, and there they were again in the mirror, in the corners, all around me there were people. From a distance came my grandfather's voice as his figure faded in the center of the mirror: "never mind the others, look at yourself," the voice said clearly.

He knew. I thought. My grandfather knew what I felt. I was glad I hadn't told any person about my deep hatred for the Germans. The only person who knew about it was God; and now my grandfather. Still, I kept this matter between God and myself, but I knew that He was too busy to pay any attention. After all, God was supposed to teach us love and kindness, to be inoffensive and kind-hearted, but at times He strayed to show us what it is like to hate and to kill. I knew; hatred was only effective when it was kept secret between the hater and the hated.

"I'll remember, grampa." I spoke into the mirror.

8

"*Raus! Schnell! Appell!*" I woke to the cry of Katzmann's Militia. I tried to recall the meaning of last night's dream, but all it had told me was that I must look out for myself from then on, as I heard my grandfather's voice urging: "never mind the others, look at yourself."

With the ghetto now dissolved and Piotrkow *Judenrein*, the Gestapo's Seventh Bureau returned to its Headquarters in Lodz. *Herr* Förster had finally become the supreme law in the Hortensia camp. We had long suspected Herr Förster of being a Gestapo agent. Now, there was no doubt. Only a small detachment of Lithuanian SS remained. Katzmann's Militia became the primary authority over the Hortensia inmates.

It was a fine summer day. Roman opened one of the windows and leaned to look at the passing sentries. Several weeks had passed since the liquidation of the ghetto. Things have become routine; we worked the usual three shifts; listened on our illegal radio to the news from the Eastern front, desperately hoping for a Nazi defeat. Our friend Edelmann came through for Nora and her brother Hayim as well. They had both been assigned to our work section, and we could show them the "ropes." Some of our Christian co-workers seemed now more sympathetic than in the past. We were glad to see that we could bargain for their loyalty.

But still the nights lay black over our heads, and we were unable to accept the routine of suffering, for we bore suffering in a manner we had never imagined it possible to bear

We made our weekly trips to the delousing quarters. The Nazis were stingy on food, but they manufactured an abundance of chemicals in which to submerge their hard-working inmates for delousing purposes.

Despite all precautionary measures taken by our jailers, we were spending most of our free time searching for vermin (we called it 'lice hunting') in the seams of our clothing and in our armpits and body hair. At first, we had tried to conduct the delousing activity in privacy, embarrassed at being observed by an unannounced comrade. As time went on, this activity had become as commonplace as our scavenging for food in the guard's kitchen garbage cans.

"They've got plenty of eggs," I remarked, reaching deep into the garbage can and stuffing my mouth with the foul-smelling mixture. I felt an unpleasant friction between my teeth, and I wanted to spit it all out, but the need for nourishment prevailed over the deep feeling of repugnance.

"Eat hardy, Vilek!" Roman urged between his own mouthfulls.

"Don't look at it, and don't smell it, just keep on eating. As long as it fills you up, there's no difference what goes into your belly."

It was never more than an hour from the time I filled my bloated stomach, and I was hungry again. I concluded that garbage was not the most ideal nourishment.

Hortensia got a new dispensary. It was a welcome addition, though it didn't amount to more than a twelve feet square area in one of the barracks. People whispered to one another that the Nazis want to keep us alive, they need us. Our hopes surged. Things must be going badly on the Eastern front. I thought of Ernst Boost. I could only guess what had become of him.

Whatever the reason, it was good to know that we would have a place to report to when sick or injured. The most common injuries were burns from the molten glass and cuts when the finished product shattered. Until now, we were forced to use what primitive means we had to heal our wounds. Rumors had it that the dispensary was to be well supplied with medications for emergencies. We were also getting several physicians. Resettlement from the West had brought them to us. Piotrkow Jews always traveled many kilometers for good medical treatment in Radomsko. Now, the labor camp was going to have more physicians than the city of Radomsko had even in time of peace.

Förster had selected three finalists from whom to fill the position of Chief Physician for the clinic. Franz Gomberg, M.D., a German Jew from Berlin, was one of them. The two others were Marek Jablonski, M.D., a Warsaw educated physician, and Josef Spiker, M.D., also a Polish Jew. He had received his degree at the Jagiello University in Cracow.

Our twice removed cousin Menasha Ehrenman, the son of Moshe, who did custodial work at the camp offices, told us about the process of selection. Each of the candidates appeared at a designated hour in Förster's office. If married, the spouse was to accompany the applicant. The "interview" was brief. Förster explained the doctor's duties and solicited "contributions" for the dispensary's fund.

Förster was pleased with his own cleverness. Doerings had warned him of the Jew's ability to conceal his wealth. He would show them that his Aryan shrewdness was superior to the Jew's cunning.

Dr. Jablonski was the last of the three candidates. He came with his wife Masha, as ordered. During their conversation, Förster was unable to take his eyes off Masha. She was breathtakingly beautiful, and Förster had almost committed the unforgivable error of rising before a Jewess. As a consequence, the youngest and professionally least experienced of the three,

Jablonski was selected Chief Physician of the Hortensia Dispensary. Drs. Gomberg and Spiker were appointed Jablonski's aides. Dr. Gomberg felt strongly about his own superior professional qualifications, his status as *Mischling ersten Grades,* and became embittered and resentful toward his colleagues. He stormed out of Förster's office, and Menasha heard him mutter something that sounded like "we'll see about it," and "don't worry, you'll get your chance!" Dr. Franz Gomberg was not one to be trifled with. That much was certain.

It had rained that entire day, and it continued into the night. The outdoors were muddy and the camp looked more depressing than usual. During the break no one left the factory premises. We sat around and talked when suddenly we heard loud screams coming from behind the great furnace.

It was bound to happen sooner or later, and it couldn't have happened at a more inconspicuous time; the night shift break period. I ran with the crowd in the direction of the screams. There, in the flickering light of the great furnace, stood Bronia Kotek, vainly attempting to conceal her nudity. A dead silence fell. I could hear her whimpering as she stood alone with lowered head, almost solemn.

It passed through my mind that there was no one in the crowd who pitied Bronia nor cared what sort of fate she met. I was unable to rejoice in Bronia's misery. Why did I think of the cold and the mud covering the ground outside? She stood before us, Förster's mistress, naked, grotesque, with her head shaven clean. Gone was the arrogance of youth, as was the once beautiful hair which she had always put up in long braids. I suddenly recalled my grandmother, the wig-maker, and her own head clean shaven for Hasidic and sanitary reasons. This was not the case.

A fist-sized swastika clearly tatooed above her abdomen branded her as a traitor to Poland.

The men whispered derisively as they formed a circle around the naked woman. She didn't seem to notice anyone. These men who only yesterday might have paid more than their weekly ration to gain her favor, to touch her breast, to possess that most elusive price of all, now stood round the grotesque figure heaping insults on her deaf ears.

"Whore!"

"Bitch!"

"Slut! You had it coming!"

One of the workers threw his coat over Bronia's bare shoulders, and I suddenly wished I had had similar courage. There were whispers.

"It's the work of the Home Army."

"Why did they do it? Poor woman."

"Why pity her? She's a traitor, isn't she?"

"Leave her. You'd do the same in her place, wouldn't you? If only you were as pretty!"

"Well, she isn't pretty any more! Serves her right!"

I wondered what Bronia was doing in the factory at that hour—she was exempted from work by Förster's orders—Was she lured there to meet her secret lover?

The reveille was sounded earlier than usual on the following morning. In a place where any unusual occurrence was cause for concern, this was enough to send chills up everybody's spine.

"Out! Everybody, *Appelplatz!* Get out! Hurry up, you swine!" Förster's voice held that special threatening quality. Katzmann struck at his polished boots with his swagger stick. The Militia corps stood by awaiting their orders.

"A grave crime has been committed during the night!" Förster bellowed. "A woman was violated. The guilty must be found and punished. You must help me bring the criminals to justice, and I promise you, you shall live to see your families!" The Commandant spoke of crime and of justice, and he demanded that the guilty be punished; strange words.

None of the assembled was coming forward to denounce the "criminals." For once, we faced the *golem* with mute defiance, relishing our temporary victory.

"The *golem* will lose his composure at any moment now," I whispered to Roman, "mark my words."

"Let's hope he won't be close to us when he does," Roman responded.

Herr Förster exploded. He jumped up and down in place, shouting incoherently. He lashed out at those within reach with the fury of a wounded god, and the men tried desperately to fend off his blows. Soon, he was spent, and he turned abruptly toward Katzmann who stood at attention throughout his superior's tirade. The exchange was brief. Katzmann clicked his heels together and answered one obedient "*jawohl!*" The *golem* and his staff left the scene, and Katzmann took the center of the podium.

"I promised *Herr Sturmbannführer* to settle this matter," Katzmann began. "We must all share the responsibility together. There's no time to waste. Sooner or later I'll find out who was behind this barbaric deed.

I ask you to come forward with information about the diabolical fiends capable of such cruelty." He paused to catch his breath and to survey the impression his appeal had on the assembled. There was silence.

"You will be rewarded. Your name will not be revealed. You may choose to remain silent and defiant, but think about your families, wherever they are." He whipped his boots with his swagger stick.

"They're even going to punish the dead!" Someone said loud enough for all to hear. Katzmann chose to ignore that remark.

No one crossed the line. The silence continued.

"I am through playing games!" Katzmann shouted. "Do you hear? I'm going to get the swine responsible for this attrocious act, if I have to hold you here forever!" He had gotten accustomed to using the language of the enemy and seemed to enjoy it. "No wonder the Germans hate you! You are nothing but vermin! You're going to stay in place until you fall from exhaustion!" His swagger stick found no rest as he paraded for a few brief moments before us, spitting contemptuously in our direction. He was suddenly leaving the platform in an indignant huff "Keep those damned Jews here till they drop!" He ordered his men. "Do you hear me?! They'll stand here till they fall!"

Three days and three nights we stood in formation. Only the shifts carried on with their work, to be returned to formation when their work ended. During those days, the factory whistle became a symbol of relief. Those who faltered were clubbed into unconsciousness then dragged to the stockade at the far end of the camp on makeshift lorries.

During the second night of our vigil, Katzmann reappeared. He shouted words nobody understood, then seized the wooden club from one of his men and rushed forward unleashing a barrage of blows. Those who ducked or shielded their skulls with their elbows, only received additional blows. Yulek tripped over his own foot, trying to escape the clubbing, and lay helplessly in front of the enraged Katzmann.

Katzmann rushed forward toward our friend striking at Yulek's prostrate body with the full force of his rage. The blows ceased only when the commandant's energy saw its end. We could hear our injured friend as he lay moaning in the stillness of the night.

Katzmann gasped for breath doubling over and the militia personnel looked at their leader with great concern. Such an exercise of violence might prove fatal to a fifty-eight year old.

"Get this trash to the stockade!" He ordered pointing at Yulek.

"Those in the stockade, will rot there until the guilty are brought to justice." He announced calmly. "If the bastards are not delivered to me within the next twenty-four hours, your friends are going to be shot, one every hour."

"He wouldn't do that, would he?" I whispered to Roman.

"Yes." Roman cautioned. "He's desperate."

"Furthermore!" Katzmann grimaced angrily. "From now on you'll stand at attention!" He yelled. "Anyone who steps out of line . . ." Here, he made an expressive sign bringing his swagger stick across his throat.

The four of us were getting off the nightshift when we heard Katzmann shouting from a distance and saw the militia removing several limp bodies to the stockade.

"I can't go on," Hayim moaned plaintively.

"You must," Nora urged her brother with the tone of finality.

"Look, there's Edelmann." Roman pointed. "The Guard is waving us on to come forward."

"There's a truck at Gate #2 waiting to be loaded with half-liter jars. Hurry up, you four! I want it done right now!" Edelmann addressed us, trying to sound indifferent and authoritative for fear that circumstances would betray him. Still, it looked awkward to have been selected out of so many far better suited for a job of such magnitude. We hesitated, and Edelmann shouted, feigning exasperation:

"Get going Jews! I want it done right now!"

We ran toward the rail depot and Edelmann walked off saluting the guard nonchalantly.

That night we learned that of the thirty men and women tortured in the stockade, eighteen "admitted" complicity with the outlawed *Armia Krajowa* (Home Army). Although each of them had told a conflicting story, they were quickly "tried" and sentenced to twenty days in solitary confinement, and that meant certain death. Katzmann had finally won.

Rosh Hashana was not very cheerful for Mickey and Fay. Word had come from Isaac: "We're finishing up with basic training. Looking forward to being shipped overseas. Rumors have it, Africa, to fight the Nazis. I had my choice, and I took this instead of the Pacific. The guys are excited, so am I. Don't worry, things are okay. Love, your son, Isaac." There was no forwarding address, only the postal seal indicated it came from Louisville, KY.

"Aren't you going to get in touch with the authorities, Mickey?" Fay asked. "Can't you see, they're going to send him over to fight in the desert of Africa? You can still do something."

"I'll do nothing, Fay." Mickey was resolute for the first time. "He's made up his mind, and I'm not going to stand in his way, even if I could."

"He might get killed, Mickey." She wailed. "Your son might get killed."

"Worse fate awaits him here."

"What's worse than death, Mickey?" She asked challengingly.

"A dead spirit, Fay." He said with sadness in his voice. "Let's go to the services and pray for all of us. It's time."

She looked at Mickey resignedly. He hasn't been himself lately, she knew. She picked up her coat and followed him out.

An urgent call went out, and the A.K. met with us. We were now determined to fight.

"You called the meeting, Felix. Talk." Piotr Sonik, the local underground leader was his usual laconic self.

"We've got to reach a decision about Katzmann." Felix said quietly.

"We've heard." Piotr said. "Yulek's in solitary."

"Along with some seventeen others."

"Katzmann's only one man." Piotr expressed his skepticism. "One insignificant grain of sand."

"A mountain is made up of just such grains." Felix said softly. He continued to speak with an extraordinary abundance and facility. Phrases came to him rapidly, with great passion, as if some superior power had inspired him. "The death of this man is in itself an insignificant thing," he continued, "but he is a part of a cancer that must be dealt with appropriately."

We listened in silence.

"There might be reprisals." Piotr cautioned.

"We'll have to take that chance." Felix was adamant. "The Nazi is a wild beast. He's drawn his taste of raw blood, and it has only whet his appetite."

"It will be murder." Someone suggested shyly.

Felix looked at us as an austere believer looks at a frivolous crowd. Would we ever awaken to the realities of the day? The question was written on his face. He must have recalled his earlier arguments with the shtetl elders, their scorn, their skepticism. They had paid for it too dearly, he must have thought to himself.

He looked at us again. His eyes seemed to be selecting those who could accomplish the execution of Katzmann. It would be done with dignity, as an act of conscience.

"It must be done!" He stated simply. "Our conscience demands it!"

Piotr stood at Felix' elbow. It was impossible to determine any sign of emotion on his face. His pale blue eyes fastened on the assembled. "It will be done." He said. The statement fell upon the grave-like silence of the room like the thud of the executioner's ax. No one in the room doubted Piotr's pledge.

That night seven armed men broke into Katzmann's quarters adjoining the stockade compound. My brother Roman was among them. It is hardly credible that Katzmann took no precautions for his safety. Only two of his Militia men were on guard at the door. They were quickly tied, gagged, and left lying on the floor.

Quietly, the insurgents faced the commandant of the Militia. Piotr awakened him from his sleep with a tap of his pistol on the shoulder. Katzmann sat up in his bed and opened his eyes to face the barrel of a submachine gun in the light of a kerosene lamp. In a daze, he slowly managed to put together the seriousness of the situation. He pleaded with the men.

His eyes traveled from one intruder to the other. He said in a trembling voice. "I'm a Jew like yourselves. I'm not a Nazi."

"You don't have to be German to be a fucking Nazi." Felix couldn't refrain from responding.

"Please, my family, my children." He pleaded.

"Silence, bastard!" Piotr interjected. "Don't you see? You're *kaputt*, finished right now!" He attached a silencer onto the barrel of his luger.

"Vermin like you doesn't deserve a family!" Felix hissed.

The commandant's hands trembled, he knelt before his judges as he said: "But, I've never even killed a fly in all my life."

No one dignified him with an answer. Events followed rapidly. The commandant was gagged and forcibly led into the solitary. The prisoners were released and led away by two of the insurgents.

"Face the wall, Nazi!" An order was given.

White as a sheet, Katzmann turned. It took only one well-placed shot, which had the sound of a champagne bottle being popped open, and Katzmann fell, bleeding from the side of the neck.

His men found him the following morning. He was hanging from his ankle, tied to a high ceiling lamp. Attached to his back was a note written in bold black letters. It read:

"DEATH TO THE TYRANT! THE A.K."

9

September was unusually cold. There were already flurries of snow, though it melted as soon as it hit the ground and created a terrible mess difficult to wade through. Winter's going to be long. There was a small creek running this side of the barbed wire fence surrounding the camp, barely a trickling of water year round, but it always swelled up with the thawing of the snow. I often sat on the small wooden bridge crossing the water, to find solitude and to watch the stream wind its way into the unknown and wishing I, myself, were a drop of water.

In the spring, the water under the bridge would run violent and deep. Its surge would be capable of forging out a channel for itself even through the most resistant circumstances. How I wished to share that unique power!

I observed the current longingly. What is the meaning of all this? I asked myself, unable to answer. No amount of water could wash away the hatred and bitterness deposited in my breast during my short life. That much was certain. My body quivered against my will as I conducted a dialogue with myself. Even then, in that unique privacy, I looked over my shoulder frequently, afraid the enemy was there, ever-vigilant, relentless.

I recalled asking Roman about the killing of Katzmann. "Was it necessary? Couldn't they just have frightened him a bit?"

"You can't frighten a mad dog." Roman said.

"He had children." I said. "And a wife."

"What good is a man who loves his children and honors his wife but murders other children and violates their mothers?" Roman asked. I was silent.

It's done. And now back to work. Katzmann was dead and everyone let out a sigh of relief. But our view was not shared by the Gestapo.

The execution of Joel Katzmann was as ill-timed as it was brilliant. Not only had it caught Förster and the entire Militia unawares, but it also indicated the overseer's inability to cope with problems of camp discipline. It had also come on the heels of serious Nazi reverses on the Eastern front.

Schröder was recalled from Lodz. He arrived with a strong SS detachment, approximately forty men and several dogs. We braced ourselves for the worst.

Förster was to become the first victim of the purge. Schröder pursued his case with tenacity. Before the week was over, our erstwhile commandant faced a panel of his peers, headed by Schröder himself.—A large contingent of *Volksdeutsche*. Hitler Youths had been ordered to witness this spectacle of Nazi justice, and it was from Tadzik who was also in attendance that I have learned the details about its bizarre outcome.—Although we suspected that we would be the next on Schröder's list, it was a time of rejoicing in the camp. Schröder leafed through some papers with deliberate slowness.

"You are well aware of the reasons for which you had been summoned to appear before us, *Herr* Förster." He began, casually glancing at his former colleague. "The Bureau does not tolerate incompetence, *Herr* Heinrich Förster."

"But. . . for God's sake, Schröder, tell me. . ." Förster stammered. He was interrupted by his superior.

"You will address this tribunal with the proper respect and detachment, *Herr* Förster!"

"*Jawohl!*" Förster replied curtly.

"You shall speak only when spoken to. *Verstanden?*"

"*Jawohl, Herr Sturmbannführer!*"

"We have called you before us to respond to two charges. One, you are accused of the crime of fraternization with the enemy of the Third Reich."

Förster seemed confused. Surely, Bronia would not have gone to the Gestapo to denounce him. He had repaid her handsomely for her favors. Yet he could not be sure. He was standing at attention listening to the charges against him.

"The second charge is a more serious one," Schröder went on, "it is incompetence in the line of duty. How do you plead, *Herr* Förster?" In his desperation, Förster decided to defy his superiors. "You can't be serious, Schröder." He chuckled nervously.

"The accused will limit his remarks to the matter at hand!"

Schröder showed anger. "I repeat the question: how does the accused plead?"

"Not guilty, of course!" Förster replied arrogantly.

Schröder remained unperturbed. That must have worried Förster. What's more, there was that cynical smile on his adversary's lips which puzzled him. Could it be that the Bureau knew something he didn't know? "The bureau always did suspect your sanity, Förster. You have been all too pretentious for your means and position," Schröder went on. "After your latest exploits, however, your lunacy is no longer doubted.

Förster listened in disbelief.

"Not only have you been incompetent, *Herr* Förster," Schröder continued relentlessly, "you have also shown a deliberate disregard concerning the Nuremberg Laws!" Hatred and contempt were evident in Schröder's utterance.

"But. . . I. . . never. . ." Förster stammered meekly. "You never went to bed with a Jewess?" Schröder's smile broadened. "You're either a blatant liar or a complete imbecile, *Herr* Förster!"

Bronia a Jewess? No, it couldn't be! I'd have known! Förster's expression of surprise delighted his tormentor.

Reading Förster's thoughts, Schröder snapped his fingers together. The side door opened.

"Bronia Kotek. . ."

Had Schröder not announced the name of his former mistress, Förster might not have recognized the woman before him. Her swollen eyelids created two narrow slits, hardly large enough to allow full vision. She moved forward with extreme difficulty, stepping awkwardly sideways and only one foot at a time. Her lips were shredded, still bleeding, and there were no traces of nails left on her raw fingertips.

"Bronia Kotek," Schröder repeated, "do you know this man?" He pointed at Förster. "If your answer is yes, nod your head once. Do not make a sign otherwise."

Bronia opened her mouth instinctively, but only uttered inarticulate grunts. Förster realized then that her tongue had been removed or mutilated beyond use. She nodded once.

"This man, he was your lover?" Schröder pressed on.

Another nod.

"Now, listen carefully, Bronia, and reply as best you can." Schröder spoke once again with deliberate slowness. "Was your name originally Bayla Kotzelbaum? Can you hear me? Kotzelbaum!"

Bronia nodded again without visible emotion. The *Sturmbannführer* was elated. He was ready to ask the crucial question.

"*Bist du Jude*?!" He shouted at the tormented woman.

There was no reaction at first. Schröder repeated, now more softly. "*Bist du Jude*? Are you Jewish?" After some hesitation, she nodded again. Schröder indicated a silent order, and two of the guards dragged the limp body of the wretched woman out of the room. As soon as they reached the courtyard, the Gestapo performed one of its rare acts of mercy. One of them approached the prisoner, and the guards let go of her arms. Bronia slumped to the cobble-stoned pavement onto her knees, an expression of complete stupor on her face. The executioner aimed his Luger at Bronia's neck, and the impact of the bullet propelled her forward. She fell several feet away, half the contents of her skull scattering in the opposite direction.

As the shot rang out, Förster knew that Bronia was the more fortunate one. He looked down to the floor as though he wanted to find a hiding place. From the corner of his eye, he observed Schröder. There was a grotesque smile of his former friend's face, a terrible grimace.

"I can see what you have in your mind, Schröder." Förster said finally. "But I don't know why."

"I have nothing in my mind," murmured Schröder as if to himself, with gentle surprise.

Now, I know I am his prey, his quarry, and he's toying with me. Förster must have thought regarding the cool manner of his tormentor. Once again, it reawakened his hate for Schröder , not only for the cruelty he had experienced, but also for his own ineptness.

Förster seemed beside himself, but his mind was lucid. If he was going to hang, he would not play into Schröder 's hands. He would be cautious.

"This tribunal shall reconvene tomorrow at exactly ten o'clock in the morning," Schröder announced curtly. The junior officers present quickly rose to their feet. As if by a secret signal, they all faced the large portrait on the wall. Each raised his right arm in a salute and shouted a formal "*Heil* Hitler!" Förster might have stood staring at the floor, had it not been for the brisk salute of his former comrades. Startled, he murmured an almost imperceptible "*heil*" and slowly walked out of the room flanked by two SS guards.

Instead of convening as planned, the Gestapo took its time. Förster stood before his peers a week late. That was precisely the way of the Seventh Bureau; there was no better way to soften up a victim than through tedious waiting. By degrees, they would break his resistance. It was also then that Schröder had introduced the "third factor." In addition to the charges of fraternization and incompetence, Förster was accused of no less than being of mixed blood.

"Heinrich Förster, *du bist Mischling zweiten Grades*! You're a second degree half-breed!" Schröder said unceremoniously at the very opening of the session.

Schröder 's terse statement shocked the defendant. It also drove home the terrible injustice of his trial. His face ashen, Förster sat silently immobile. Why was he being humiliated? He must have thought to himself. He was neither the first nor the last Gestapo officer to commit an error in judgment. Didn't Schröder himself, and even their superior Doerings, have an appreciative eye for the slender ankle of a beautiful Jewess? Hadn't the three of them wenched together on many occasions? Laughed about their conquests and the dismal end of their Jewish victims?

Förster was also willing to share the blame for the Gestapo's inefficiencies. After all, he had no reason to call himself a paragon of virtue, but neither did any of his comrades. Why, then, this sinister conspiracy to defame his and his family's honor? He was the descendant of a proud *Junker* tradition, and would never admit to the preposterous allegations making him a member of an inferior bloodline.

Was it really Schröder who had thought up this clever scheme? He suspected his subordinate Hans Seemann of being overly ambitious. No, not Seemann. He was neither intelligent enough nor did he possess the cunning to have structured this intricate plot.

Could it have been the Jew-loving Edelmann? It was common knowledge that Edelmann had aided many of the Jewish slaves. Yet each time Förster had accumulated enough evidence, he lacked the necessary witnesses. Even the informers would not come forth to testify against the foreman.

Förster could think of many of his Gestapo comrades who should presently stand in his place. Their own sins against the Reich encompassed a far wider breach of duty than his insignificant involvement with a Polish whore. His was a minor misdemeanor compared to the outrages of his colleagues. He had never beaten an inmate to unconsciousness or inflicted serious injury knowing that production would suffer. The Reich always came first. Hard as he must have thought, none of his associates came to mind as suspects of this insidious plot against him.

Förster looked around the room, his mind pondering his present fate. Suddenly, his eyes caught those of Dr. Franz Gomberg; defiant, challenging eyes. Förster tried in vain to guess why that abominable quarter-breed Jew was there. He did not have to wait too long.

Dr. Gomberg was called to the stand. Förster gave a sigh of relief. The doctor would surely remember how much he owed him. Things would take a turn for the better now.

"State your name!" Schröder demanded.

"*Herr Doktor* Franz Gomberg."

"Do you know the accused?"

"Yes, Sir. I do."

"What was the extent of your involvement with this man?" Gomberg hesitated. He wasn't sure he understood the implications of the question.

"Come, come, *Herr Doktor,* speak up!" Schröder urged. "It isn't all that difficult to make up one's mind about a simple question, is it?"

"The accused was my superior." Dr. Gomberg looked out into the distant courtyard to avoid Förster's hateful grin.

"In what capacity are you employed here at the camp?" Schröder asked.

"I'm a physician."

"In what manner were you selected for your position?"

Hot and cold sweat trickled down Förster's athletic neck. He was finally aware of Schröder's strategy. The doctor hesitated before replying.

"I had to pay for this privilege, *Herr Sturmbannführer!*"

"Why didn't you report it to the Bureau?"

"I was afraid." Gomberg looked directly at Förster. He was telling the truth. "I was afraid of the consequences."

"Had the accused threatened you?"

"Not directly. . . but. . . "

"But what? Speak up, doctor, speak louder!"

"Well. . . now. . ." Gomberg kept hedging for a moment, repeating the expression "well. . .now. . ." several times, but noticing an impatient gesture of his interrogator, he admitted. "I feared for my life. *Herr* Förster was unscrupulous in his dealings with the inmates."

"How many physicians are there in the camp dispensary?" Schröder asked.

"Three, Sir."

"Are you the physician in charge?"

"No, Sir."

"Who's the chief physician?" Schröder detected a note of bitterness in Gomberg's last response and was determined to exploit it.

"Dr. Jablonski had been placed in charge by the accused." Gomberg responded.

"Do you approve of *Herr* Förster's choice?"

"It is not my right to question the decisions of my superior, but my duty is to carry out his orders." Dr. Gomberg emphasized the words right and duty typical of a bureaucrat, and Schröder was alert to take advantage of the age-old patriarchal tradition.

"I order you to speak your mind, *Herr Doktor* Gomberg!" He emphasized the cherished title. "This is a court of law!"

"Förster acted with great bias in his choice," Gomberg blurted out quickly, daring to delete his superior's official title—a most unGerman occurrence and contrary to regulations—Schröder was only too glad to overlook the irregularity.

Förster's hope was shattered. For the first time since his trial had begun, he was clearly aware what it was that Schröder was leading up to. It was Masha, Dr. Jablonski's beautiful wife who was to be his undoing. For her, he had broken all precedents. In addition to the choice position for the young and inexperienced doctor, Förster had assigned the couple special quarters, a privacy never before afforded a Jew. During weeks preceding his trial, Förster recklessly abandoned his routine factory inspections in favor of pursuing his passion for the beautiful Jewess. All that was surely known to the Gestapo.

There had been a great deal of talk concerning Förster's frequent visits with the doctor's wife. Dr. Jablonski knew but he dared not interfere. It was a way of life; a price paid for the right to a day-to-day existence. Dr. Jablonski suffered inmeasurable pain on occasions when he would return home only to find his wife in the commandant's arms. But he remained silent. The young couple knew that their temporary safety depended on their discretion as much as on the commandant's passion.

Now, all this must have been going through Förster's mind. He searched frantically, trying to find a loophole in the law, a precedent in the intricate jurisprudence of the Third Reich, which might exonerate him. His memory must have worked overtime recalling regulations on camp administration. He found it! He found the rule that would save him! The testimony of Jews and hybrids was used against him! All Schröder 's evidence was presented by the scum of the earth. They were not worthy to share the room with him! He must have thought with great indignation. Förster rose to his feet and shouted with the pride of a *Junker*:

"You have no legal right to try a *Junker*! Ancient Germanic blood flows through my veins! You have no jurisdiction over our kind! I must be tried by a tribunal of my peers!"

Schröder observed the hysterical Förster calmly. He took time to jot down some notes, and then he spoke:

"Wolfgang Förster, your impudence is appaling but typical of your kind." Schröder walked back and forth without looking at the accused. "You are quite correct, this tribunal could not try a true *Junker*."

There was a marked emphasis on the word true when Schröder addressed the accused, and that stirred a certain foreboding in the pit of Förster's stomach.

"The *Junkers* are the pride of the Third Reich, but you, Wolfgang Förster, are not a *Junker*. Your shameful behavior has brought dishonor to the Third Reich, and your incompetence is comparable to that of an inferior race!" Here Schröder raised his voice to a shriek.

"Wolfgang Förster, you're not tried here as a misguided son of our glorious Reich! You are tried as a *Mischling zweiten Grades!*"

"What?" Förster attempted to overplay his arrogance. "You won't get away with that! I'll see to it, Schröder! This is an absurd accusaion!"

"Why else would one have such preference for associating with Jews? Can you tell me?" Schröder paused for effect. "Unless, indeed, impure blood runs through one's own veins!" Schröder was so extremely pleased with his own cleverness that he could not refrain from chuckling out loud. He had done what so many failed to achieve before him; he destroyed the proud bastard of a *Junker* who would never let them forget his noble ancestry.

And even during the last moments of his life, as he goosestepped toward the gallows in the middle of the *Appelplatz,* flanked by his former comrades, Förster was unable to comprehend. The noose tightened round his powerful neck, and his grotesquely limp body was left to hang on display for a total of seventy-two hours. Large signs were attached to his chest and back. They read in bold black letters:

ICH BIN MISCHLING ZWEITEN GRADES—I'M A SECOND DEGREE HALF-BREED.

The inmates rejoiced at the sight of Förster's lifeless body at the end of the rope, though his end was in no way reminiscent of Haman's; deliverance was a long way coming.

10

We joked and chuckled secretely about Katzmann's and Förster's fate, but we braced ourselves expecting reprisals; the Nazi way. Conditions at the Hortensia camp did not improve with the elimination of the two principal camp villains. On the contrary, their successors would make a far greater effort to please their superiors in Berlin at our expense.

Schröder was promoted to *Obersturmbannführer*, and *Herr* Hans Seemann became the new *Lagerkommandant.* No one was appointed to take Katzmann's place, and none volunteered. With the typical zeal of a newly promoted bureaucrat, Seemann took immediate steps to restore discipline and order in the camp: stricter curfews, doubling of the Militia guards, severe punishment for the slightest digressions, and a tightening of food rations.

The latter made us increasingly dependent on help from the outside. Our dependence increased each day and so did our vulnerability. The enemy knew the only way to control us: hunger.

"We've got to talk with Nora." I looked at Roman meaningfully, trying not to arouse Hayim's suspicion.

"What's going on?" Roman whispered.

"Things are developing quickly." I sighed, continuing in a tired voice. "The Gestapo's recalling Schirmeck from Krakow. Something big's coming up. Maybe even resettlement."

"Schirmeck? The resettlement specialist, eh?" Roman asked.

"Yes, we must be alert." I paused, "Spread the word. Saturday. . . midnight . . . Block 4."

To offset the anticipated Gestapo action, the Home Army acted swiftly. Our primary target was *Obersturmbannführer* Schröder .

It was late in October and the countryside was frost-covered. The cold had brought a new freedom of movement for the Home Army and increased the Nazi's vulnerability. We would take full advantage of nature's cooperation.

Minutes after midnight, our small group met at the assigned block. Yulek had recovered from his ordeal by then. He, along with Felix and Piotr Sonik, had taken the initiative. By now, the three of them were sure to be on the Gestapo's most wanted list. Their courage and presence of mind served us all as an inspiration. Nora insisted, and we brought her along to the meeting.

Nora had been meeting Felix off and on during the night shift. He had left the camp along with Yulek following Katzmann's execution. I feared that the two lovers might constitute a danger to our operation. Felix tried to keep her out of the partisan activity, but Nora appeared repeatedly at my work station, and I gave in, mainly because our arguing might have aroused suspicion.

"There's Edelmann!" I whispered to Roman. We were both startled to see our foreman at the meeting. We had suspected all along that his sympathies lay on our side, but never dreamed that he was one of us. He smiled. There were no questions. Piotr opened the meeting.

"We have received information that the enemy's preparing another blood-bath." Inadvertently he glanced in Edelmann's direction, and we understood. "We've got to strike first. It's as simple as that."

"What have you got in mind?" Yulek asked wearily. "We're listening.

"Schröder's visits to Mme. Wiasnowa's bordello on *Himmlerstrasse* 13 might be a godsend."

"Explain, please," Felix interrupted gently.

"We've got to capture Schröder to insure the success of our operation. He arrives at Mme. Wiasnowa's each Sunday afternoon and remains there till almost midnight. He is driven to and from the place by his bodyguard. . ."

". . . we know, Hugo 'the ape.'" Yulek sighed.

"That's right. The Mercedes is bulletproof, and the powerful Hugo is fiercely loyal to his master. He must be killed first." There was no apparent emotion in Piotr's voice, nor was there a trace of hesitation in the manner in which Felix and Yulek discussed the taking of a life. I was astonished at their attitude. Have we come this far already? I thought silently. How can we forgive the enemy for remaking us in his image?

There was a long silence. I felt that I had to speak my mind. Springing to my feet, I said aloud: "I am terribly afraid about what will happen to those left behind when we make our move against Schröder." My voice trembled and Felix placed his hand lightly on my shoulder. It was reassuring to feel his support. "I mean, the Gestapo isn't going to take that lying down." I added softly.

"Why worry about that, Vilek?" Felix asked. "Do you really believe the enemy would be kind to us if we were to treat him with mercy?"

"Well. . . I. . ." I was hesitant. "To tell the truth, I'm not sure."

"Think of your mother and your little sister, Vilek." Yulek urged.

"At moments like these, it would help to think of all those dear souls that behaved so bravely and went to their deaths quietly, without causing the enemy grief."

"We really don't know for sure!" I almost shouted. "Nobody can say that they've been put to death." I fought the idea of giving up, though an inner voice kept telling me the contrary.

"Getting back to the business at hand," Piotr interrupted, "we ought to decide one way or another. . ."

". . . there's no doubt in my mind, my friend," Felix hastened to assure Piotr, "that our intention of executing Schröder is to be carried out." He looked questioningly at our Christian comrade whose expressionless face told him almost nothing. It was obvious, Felix had no intention of alienating the only ally we had made on the other side of the barbed wire fence.

Piotr looked at his watch and noticed that there was still a little time left till the next shift-change. He took the watch off his wrist and handed it to Felix. "Keep it, my friend, you'll need it, to synchronize our timetable." Felix put the watch in his pocket.

"Thanks. I'll return it when we're done with the bastard."

"No need to, Felix." Piotr nodded in approbation. "Just keep it out of sight of the goons. I wouldn't want to make it a gift for one of them."

Felix nodded his head dejectedly twice. "Of course. Of course," he murmured. "I appreciate. . ."

Just then we heard the night shift whistle. Piotr seemed uneasy. "They'll be changing the guards now, we've got to decide."

Felix looked at the dials of his watch. "What in hell. . . it isn't time for the shift to change. . ." he luxuriated in having a time piece.

"They're fifteen minutes early."

"You'd better see it their way." Piotr said. "It's Schröder 's time too."

I shuddered, thinking of the task ahead of us. It was close to dawn when we finalized our plans. We had selected three men to execute Schröder. Josef Gabnik, a glassblower, Jan Kublon, called the "giant," a former Olympic weight-lifter and a man of immense physical strength, and Zbyszek Zawada, a machinist. All three were experienced insurgents. The time selected for the abduction was Sunday, an important Nazi Party holiday.

"We all know how the Nazis love festivities," Piotr concluded, "and we hope that they'll observe the day with more enthusiasm than ever. The more they'll enjoy themselves, the better our chances of success."

An "all clear" was given by our men on the lookout and silently Block 4 returned to normal.

We were about to pass through the storage area on our way to the barrack, when we heard voices, followed by a scuffle.

"Dammit! Stop! Stop or I'll shoot! Guards!" The voice unmistakeably belonged to Hans Seemann.

"What in hell is the *mamzer* doing up at this time of night?" Roman seethed, as we both ducked for cover. We heard a female voice pleading, and a man's urging, "run, darling, run!"

"Felix and Nora." I whispered.

We came closer. Now, we were able to distinguish the silhouettes of our two friends as well as the others. It wasn't Seemann after all. Felix and Nora must have stumbled upon an off-duty Lithuanian SS and his female companion. Now, the two women ran away, but Felix, his hands above his head, stood still facing the sight of the guard's pistol.

"Damn! Not now!" Roman hissed.

"We've got to do something, brother!" I urged.

"Do. . . what?" Roman asked.

"Send word to Piotr. It could jeopardize our operation!"

We left silently while Felix was led to the guardhouse.

When I got to Kublon with the news, he put his huge hand on my shoulder. "Felix must take care of himself. There's nothing we can do right now. The plan comes first, Vilek. Remember the plan and get back to work!"

I had no great affection for Felix, but I feared for his safety. What happened if he cracked under pressure? The success of our plan depended on Felix' endurance. I wished him luck, for I knew how persuasive the Gestapo could be.

The following week was a busy one for the Home Army. There were sounds of explosions everywhere and bright crimson flames emerged in the darkness of the night against the Piotrkow skyline. The Bureau called in reinforcements from Lodz. Once again, Doerings arrived in Piotrkow, heading a special SS force, called the Einsatzkommando; it's specialty was terror and resettlement.

As Piotr had forseen, the Nazis were helpless against the hit-and-run tactics of the A.K. For the first time since the Nazi occupation, the Gestapo was on the receiving end.

Our source at the *Kommandantur* informed us that Schröder was raving with anger from dusk to dawn. He took hostages, and they were beaten and interrogated. Still no one talked. The *Obersturmbannführer* was furious, and the fear of forfeiting favor of his superiors took away his sleep. His most trusted informers were silent, and from their evasive replies he was able to guess that something "big" was in the making.

"He paces through his rooms into all hours of the night, and howls like a mad dog." Our trusted informant told us. "And in the morning, when I serve his meal, he takes his rage out on me." Here he pulled up the back of his shirt to show us the bruises; evidence of Schröder 's helplessness.

Schröder's residence was a large house, surrounded by a high fence, well guarded by Lithuanian mercenaries and their dogs. The three men assigned to his abduction kept the house under constant surveillance, studying the commandant's timetable and daily habits. When that special Sunday arrived, we were ready. The Hortensia Partisan Organization was prepared for the eventuality of armed resistance. In Felix' absence, Yulek was in charge. We had planned to carry out diversionary measures and, if necessary, we would establish a common front with the A.K. in the adjacent forest.

As we had expected, marching music blared on Sunday through every radio station. Gestapo communications vans rode through the streets of Piotrkow extolling the virtues of the *Führer* and his Party. Intermittently, they tuned in the happy tempo of marching music. Music was followed by interminable speeches and more music.

The enemy's actions on that festive Sunday were predictable. They had been accurately calculated by the insurgents: late in the afternoon, Wagnerian tunes were broadcast as a prelude to the main event—the *Führer*. When the leader spoke, everyone listened attentively, glued to the master's voice on the radio. And even though the *Führer* delivered his message in the usual hysterical, inarticulate manner, shouts of "*Sieg Heil!*" and "*Heil dem Führer!*" resounded for the longest periods of time.

A state of general euphoria and merriment, culminating in orgiastic celebrations, followed the leader's speeches.

With a fatal punctuality, Schröder's Mercedes arrived at Mme. Wiasnowa's on *Himmlerstrasse* 13. He gave his trusted aid Hugo his last instructions. In good spirits and whistling a complicated Wagnerian tune, the *Obersturmbannführer* entered the whore-house. A block away, I beckoned our men to advance. I had a good feeling inside; for the first time since the War began, I felt part of a common effort with our Christian compatriots, shouldering equal responsibility without fear of rejection. For the first time, I was a Polish Jew and not a Jew without a country.

Josef and Zbyszek, dressed in SS uniforms which they had obtained in one of the Home Army's recent raids, and singing a merry military song, rounded the corner without arousing Hugo's suspicion. At a yard's distance, however, and looking point blank into their guns, Schröder's bodyguard realized his error. He opened his mouth to let out a cry of warning, but he choked and no sound came. The "Ape's" left hand reached for his luger, but Josef had fired his sten gun, and Hugo fell to the pavement with a loud thump.

Schröder had meanwhile entered the bedroom of Mme. Wiasnowa's when the shots resounded, but he had no time to react. Before he could draw his pistol from the dresser, Jan Kublon burst inside through the demolished door, his weapon pointed at Schröder 's belly. Josef and Zbyszek were now at their comrade's side. Before Schröder 's outraged eyes, the insurgents gagged and bound Mme. Wiasnowa to her bedpost. She was left there to the mercy of the inevitable Gestapo investigation. There was no reason to believe that the madam would escape the unique Gestapo justice, for they were sure to reason her into the conspiracy of Schröder's abduction, and Zbyszek's orders were not to waste costly ammunition on the only whore who refused to cooperate with the underground.

Schröder was stunned. Only when they had left Mme. Wiasnowa's premises and Zbyszek took the wheel of the commandant's Mercedes did he regain the capacity to measure the magnitude of what has happened. Then, too, he had seen Hugo's immense body, in a puddle of blood, sprawled grotesquely on the pavement near the car.

Schröder was forced into the back seat of the staff car and seated next to Jan the "giant" Kublon. He studied his three abductors in SS uniforms, and his Gestapo mind must have conceived all sorts of rival conspiracies against his branch of the Führer's service. "The envious bastards!" He must have thought to himself before receiving a karate chop to his neck that sent him slumping unconscious to the floor of the car.

The enemy was enraged by Hugo's death and the daring abduction of their number one man, *Obersturmbannführer* Schröder. Forty thousand Reichsmarks had been offered for information leading to the apprehension of the perpetrators and their conviction. The reward was more than anyone in Piotrkow had ever dreamed of, but no one came forward with the required information. The insurgents derived their strength from the people; silence was their pledge of loyalty, and loyalty was the endorsement of partisan activities.

The Gestapo took hostages at random from the town proper, and a large number of Jews had been selected from the camp. For the most part, the Christian hostages comprised elderly men and women. Youth had gone into hiding, anticipating the ensuing struggle. Prison walls resounded with shouts of pain, anguish and fear all day and late into the night. German bulldozers dug an immense trench on the outskirts of town where horse-drawn lorries transported the bodies of those who were fortunate to die quickly during "interrogation." There were reports that hostages were being executed with relatives looking on. The living carried their deep sorrow in silence.

We expected it to happen, but when Nora was taken in a raid, it shocked and surprised us. We looked at one another, unbelieving, tears in our eyes, trembling with rage and impotence.

"We've got to act, Roman," I said, "you know what happens to young girls at the Gestapo 'persuasion' sessions."

"I know, Vilek, I know it well." Roman said wearily. "But we can't endanger the overall plan."

"To hell with the plan!" I cried. "Can't you see, the A.K. wanted it that way? Those damn Jew-haters will boast the elimination of the most important Nazi in the district and get rid of some Jews in the process. Clever, if we let it happen!"

"There's absolutely nothing we can do." Roman tried to calm my anger. "You know what happens to squealers." He made a sign with his index finger to his throat.

The following morning, a small group of women was marched across the compound toward the gate. Among them was Nora, and we watched helplessly. Suddenly, from one of the small stockade windows, came a shattering animal-like cry calling Nora's name, ending in a desperate wail. It stopped, and moments later it resounded again:

"Norrraaa!"

The monotonous shuffle of the prisoner's feet continued, but the persistent caller drew the attention of the guards. That was enough to seal his fate. Within the hour, Nora and Felix had become objects of intense curiosity for the investigating Gestapo.

"The dumb shit! Now he'll make her suffer for his own goddamned sins as well!"

"Get up, you fucking swine!" A sudden splash of cold water splattered on Schröder's face. He almost choked, but without the slightest protest got to his feet and stood at attention. The A.K. was quick to come to the point.

"The Bureau holds many innocent hostages, Herr Schröder, and all that for your worthless carcass." Yulek spat into the prisoner's face. "We want them released!"

"Let me go, and they shall go free, I promise!" Schröder exclaimed without hesitation.

"Not so fast, *mein Herr*, not so fast." Piotr interrupted. "Your promises mean little to us. Besides, you must be tried for your countless crimes. You've committed many, you know." Piotr spoke with an emphasis calculated to break Schröder's spirit. "Now, you'll listen, and you'll obey!" Schröder stood meekly before his former victims. Desperate thoughts must have traveled through his mind. The years of patriarchal upbringing had had their effect. "Order, discipline, and work," had become household words in Hitler's Third Reich. He had failed as of this moment. Defeat was only to be inflicted, never suffered. The victor is never brought to trial, only the vanquished, the Führer told his subjects.

The partisans were quick to reach their decision. In one voice, the men responded to their leader's question: "Guilty!"

"You have been found guilty of crimes against people, heinous crimes, *Herr* Schröder." Piotr declared. "Have you anything to say for yourself before we pronounce the sentence?" Schröder turned ashen. He trembled with fear, and he spoke in a whisper.

"I'm a soldier, performing the duties of a soldier. No man could do less for his country." He was as meek in defeat as he had been arrogant in victory. "No soldier can question the orders of his superior. Let me live, I beg you. I have a wife and three children in Mannheim. Please, let me live." His body shook in convulsive sobbing.

Piotr smiled contemptuously and spat through his teeth. "We know all too well that you've always done a little more than you have been ordered to do, *mein Herr*, and we shall not delete that from your good record. We must give due recognition to all your dutiful performances, merciful or otherwise." Piotr chuckled derisively.

It was then Schröder must have finally realized that his fate had been sealed. His formal upbringing did not permit him to understand how to act mercifully. And even now, he could not comprehend how these men who held him at their mercy, could find fault in the many acts of selfless dedication to his country and to his people; his Reich and his *Führer*. Of all the puzzling things that had happened to him in the past fortnight, this must have been the most puzzling.

"Surely," he repeated feebly, "you're not going to condemn a man for doing his duty, are you?" He looked at the determined faces of his captors. "Mine is an unblemished record." He boasted.

"You shall live," Piotr declared, "but only if your miserable life will guarantee the safety of the hostages."

"I'm glad to see that you act prudently, gentlemen." Schröder 's eyes lit up with hope at the promise of survival. He was elated that his life was staked against the heap of rubble held captive by his comrades at the Bureau. The useless trash. He must have thought to himself. Just wait till I'm free, I'll show you how appreciative I can be!

Little did Schröder realize the lack of esteem his own peers had held for him. And when he ultimately did, it was too late.

A note was dispatched to the Bureau Headquarters on the following morning. Over Schröder 's signature was an order to release the hostages. The Home Army waited the indicated twelve hours for Doerings' reaction. His response came the following day at sunrise. Fifteen hostages had been hung and publicly displayed in the market place.

Piotr himself delivered the news to the insurgents. "So be it! This is how the Gestapo bargains for the life of one of its own!" "It can't be!" Schröder pleaded. "It's all a mistake! Please, I'm sure this can be corrected!"

"I'm sure it can." Piotr's face became once again an inscrutable mask. "Proceed!" He ordered.

Not far from the A.K. hideout there was a clearing in the forest. We took

Schröder there and he was told to dig a sizeable trench. He went down on his knees weeping and pleading for his life. "Dig!" Yulek ordered. Schröder was digging his grave and his tools were his own bleeding fingers. He had finished his task by sundown when two of his abductors approached.

"Go on, run, Nazi swine!" Kublon spat at the prostrate man. "Run for your life!"

Schröder got up and started in the direction of the forest. His bare feet were cut to shreds and his face was bruised by low-hanging branches. He didn't get very far when he was cut down by a burst from Kublon's automatic. Now he lay still, and the A.K. had a change of plans.

Gunfire and shouted commands pierced Piotrkow's early morning quiet. The sun had not yet broken through, and the pandemonium caught everyone unawares, even the Gestapo. The guards ran out-doors in their underwear, guns cocked at the ready, but they retreated hastily to their quarters at the first grenade explosion. The insurgents disappeared as suddenly as they had arrived. Only the squeal of tires betrayed momentarily the fleeting presence of the black Gestapo staff car which sped into the dark of night like a phantom leaving a cloud of dust in its wake.

Schröder 's cadaver was tossed from the speeding Mercedes onto the pavement in front of the Gestapo Headquarters. The guards approached their leader's body cautiously. Within moments, Doerings and his staff appeared on the scene.

"After them, you idiots! After them!" Doerings shouted at the confused guards. He was beside himself with rage at the audacity of the partisans. But things happened with incredible speed, and the insurgents were gone long before the SS set out in pursuit. Hours later, the SS detachment of mercenaries returned, Schröder 's Mercedes in tow. They had found the abandoned vehicle on the country road; its gas tank empty.

He died like a coward, but the Gestapo was determined to give Schröder a Viking's burial. "The *Obersturmbannführer* was slain in the line of duty," the public announcement read, "he died like a soldier, defending the honor of his country!"

Goose-stepping ranks of his comrades, accompanied by the senseless but penetrating rhythm of the Hitler Youth drums, paraded ahead of the coffin. Fellow officers and civilian dignitaries followed, making it a solemn procession with all the pomp and fanfare of their Teutonic tradition. The entire Piotrkow population had been ordered to witness the hero's funeral, which lasted the better part of the day. The public display was Doerings' insurance against another surprise appearance of the Home Army.

A reign of Nazi terror followed Schröder 's execution. Two hundred and eighty hostages awaited a miracle. But the Home Army was silent. Just as we had suspected; the purpose was to draw large contingents of elite SS troops away from the Russian front; the operation was considered a success.

While the terror lasted, the SS hierarchy had decided to give the mercenaries free reign over the hostages.—Menasha Ehrenmann continued at his post at the SS kitchen. From him we received details about the events taking place in the camp stockade.—Felix's desperate cry from his cell window gave the SS a novel idea. The young women were separated from the other hostages, ordered to undress and forced to perform to Wagnerian music in the stockade yard; the assembled officers, their wives and assorted concubines enjoyed the spectacle.

The bizarre performance was soon enlivened by the appearance of the Lithuanian mercenaries. They, too, had been ordered to disrobe and join the "dance," each selecting his "partner" at random. As the evening wore on, the mercenaries carried off their victims to the SS barracks, and the women that resisted, were beaten brutally, while the "spectators" laughed and threw encouraging comments. Those mutilated by the beating were herded into the far corner of the yard where they were drowned in the stockade well. Their screams could be heard even above the noise of the music, to the great delight of the spectators.

Then, a desperate howling came once again from the stockade window: "Murderers! Stop it! I'm the one you want! I'll talk!" All merriment ceased. The women were led away to the general prison hall. No single cells were available. There was silence among the hostages now; the silence of defeat. Their courage and suffering had been in vain because one of them yielded. Their silence turned into a wake.

Felix returned to his cell. Eyes full of hatred welcomed him. He talked, and he got a brief reprieve from the Gestapo. They had permitted him to spend his final hours with Nora. The lovers embraced silently, and no one dared rebuke the two tormented souls for claiming this last breath of life. No one dared assume the harsh prerogative of judgment.

"You'll see, darling." Nora whispered. "They won't let us down. The A.K. will come to our aid." She caressed Felix' head. "They'll free us, you'll see."

"No, my darling." Felix sobbed. "I don't really want it now. I won't ever be free again."

"Are you trying to fool God, Felix?"

"What God? Your God or mine? I have no God."

"Don't blaspheme, darling." She pleaded. "Everything follows a higher order. What must be, must be, it's fate, my darling. We must have faith, now more than ever."

"Faith is the evidence not seen. It is overshadowed by a ruthless reality from which there is no escape." Felix spoke sobbingly, without the courage to meet her eyes.

Nora prayed. He regarded her tenderly. He held her lovely face in the palms of his hands.

"Whatever happens, dearest, don't allow them to rob you of your faith. It's the fortress of your existence," he said, and he kissed her on both her eyes.

Aided by Felix' hapless confession, the efficient Gestapo machine went into frantic activity to crush the Home Army. But none of the identified insurgents could be found. The infuriated enemy reacted by taking more hostages, increasing the total of prisoners to three hundred and forty. Doerings issued an ultimatum. Bulletins were posted throughout the area:

THE INSURGENTS MUST LAY DOWN THEIR ARMS AND PUT A STOP TO ALL RESISTANCE. THEY MUST PLACE THEMSELVES AT THE MERCY OF THE OCCUPATION FORCES WITHIN SEVENTY-TWO HOURS. IF THIS DIRECTIVE IS NOT CARRIED OUT, THE HOSTAGES WILL BE SHOT BY ORDER OF THE MILITARY GOVERNOR. OBERSTURMBANNFÜHRER DOERINGS.

During the following two days I worked mechanically, hoping and daydreaming about a timely rescue. I found no refuge in my sleep; nightmares about smashed-in heads and severed limbs persecuted me, and I woke frightened and shaken. Everyone was tense and ready. So was the enemy. And deep down, we still hoped that if we did not challenge him, he might spare our lives.

The time approached. The hostages were herded into the awaiting armored vans, and the motorcade moved slowly through the empty streets of Piotrkow. Only an occasional movement of a curtain betrayed the presence of onlookers. There were no incidents; no protests. There was no attempt at rescue. Inside the grey steel of the vans, there was constant prayer.

The convoy came to a halt at a clearing several kilometers beyond the outskirts of the town where an immense ditch had been bulldozed into the landscape of the countryside on the previous day. Five machine gun emplacements were in position. Doerings barked the order to unload the vans. Men, women, and children stood obediently in silence regarding the preparations with disbelief. Only a handful of SS mercenaries faced three hundred and forty condemned. Doerings spoke:

"This is your last chance to save yourselves! Step forward and live!

Help us find the A.K. assassins and go free! Can't you see, they don't care what happens to you? Do you think I wish to have you shot? Step forward and live!"

His entreaties fell on deaf ears. Against all odds, the hope remained that a miracle would happen.

Suddenly, a woman carrying an infant ran toward the Gestapo officer. "Take my boy, my handsome baby, please, take him for your own! I don't care what happens to me, only spare my little son!" She pleaded.

"Speak, woman!" Doerings shouted. "Talk, and both of you go free!"

"There's nothing I can tell you, Sir. I know nothing about the A.K." She spoke the truth. It was common knowledge, the Home Army did not keep a single hideout. Their movements were sporadic and sudden. "See how beautiful my boy is? He is Aryan, he will follow your leader, I'm sure. Take him." The woman wept bitterly.

Doerings gave a sign. A husky guard took the child from the woman's arms and pushed her back into the ranks. With a powerful heave, the SS man tossed the infant into the air in the direction of the ditch. One short burp of the machine gun followed at the nod of Doerings' head. The child fell lifeless into the excavation. Berserk and yelling with unspeakable pain, the hysterical woman threw herself at the Gestapo officer. The SS guard aimed his automatic pistol at her, and she fell limp to the ground riddled with bullets.

"My men are not assassins! They will do their duty, if they must!" Doerings shouted. "This is your last chance to come forward!" He waited. No one moved. "All right. You're forcing me to do it." He turned to his men. "Guns at the ready!" He shouted an order. The mercenaries drove the first group of forty toward the ravine.

The hostages prayed in unison; Christian and Jew, each to his own God. They worshipped as if it were Passover and Easter bound into one. They asked redemption and forgiveness. The prayer continued even as they were driven near the edge of the ditch and ordered to undress and place their clothing on neat stacks by the graveside. Disrobed, they lined up at the very edge of their common grave, embracing loved ones, whispering their last farewells, hugging and kissing for the last time. Then they stood holding hands, their backs turned to the guns. Prayers became faster, more desperate, and totally incoherent. But there were no miracles.

"*FEUER!!*" Doerings' command came suddenly, even though it had been expected. Felix managed to place himself in back of Nora, serving as a protective shield. With the first volley, they fell to the ground, his bullet-ridden body covering hers. When the firing finally subsided, only a few groans came from the moving mass of flesh. These were silenced with skillful pistol shots administered by the merciful *Obersturmbannführer* and his aides. New rows of naked hostages were lined up and volley after volley of machine-gun fire mingled with the cries of pain and prayer. Until there was complete silence. The last of the hostages lay in the ravine, motionless.

Doerings was pleased with himself and the day's work. Another victorious mission added to his record. In the morning, he would report his "counter-insurgency operation" to his superiors in Berlin, substantiating it with photographs taken by his propaganda detachment. They had been very busy indeed. One more look at the mangled flesh below, and he shouted his final order: "Bury the rubble!" The humming of the colossal earth-movers was heard into the night.

The armored vehicles made a triumphant return to the SS headquarters. A special detachment of inmates had been left behind to strip the belongings of all valuables. No resource was to be wasted in the war effort of the Third Reich.

The men of the special detail worked speedily and superficially. They despised their task and they wanted to leave the place as quickly as possible. When they had finally left, only a shallow layer of earth covered the dead. Those still alive found a way to breathe beneath the loose earth though their lungs were bursting with debris and sand.

Nora got to her feet slowly and emerged dazed from her grave. She was creased by a bullet, with a superficial wound on her left arm above the elbow. She stood and in shock recognized Felix' dead body. She heard some moaning nearby but was unable to react.

The night was freezing, and it was that penetrating cold which brought her to her senses. In her daze, she climbed over the edge of the grave, put on some clothing she had found nearby, and walked as quickly as she was able toward the forest. She stumbled over hedges and wild growths, fell down and rose to her feet again, continuing stubbornly to the safety of the wood, feeling protected against the betrayal of men, completely alone and abandoned, she shuddered and collapsed to the ground. Her heavy eyelids closed over the glazed eyes and she fell soundly asleep.

Yurek Brama, the young forester, rose at dawn on that fateful day to get ready for his customary inspection of the district. His dogs were restless, and their barking and howling had caught Yurek's attention. "All right, all right," he called out to them, "I'm coming!" He hurried out of the cabin and released the animals.

For ten minutes, Yurek had followed the sound of his dogs' barking. Suddenly it stopped. He called out, but they didn't respond. He waited, but they didn't return. "Wait till I get hold of you, I'll teach you a lesson, you miserable hounds!" He muttered to himself. Reaching the clearing, he saw the dogs sniffing at Nora's body, while they emitted soft whining sounds. The woman was still, and Yurek was quick to put the events together; the distant salvos of machine guns which had awakened him during the night, his dogs' peculiar behavior, and now, the woman's blood-spattered body before him. He knelt beside her to examine her wound. The blood was congealed due to the severe cold weather. "Lucky lady." He whispered, smiling.

Yurek threw his coat over Nora's half nude body, not without admiring her natural beauty. He carried the feverish woman to his lodge and placed her gently on his bed. Carefully, he proceeded to wash her entire body with a warm damp cloth, inadvertently or on purpose caressing the most intimate parts.

Yurek Brama was a heavy-set, balding man in his early forties. He took the lonely job of a forester because of the facial deformity he had suffered in a ski accident in his early youth which shattered his left jaw into fragments. Men made fun of his twisted face, and women shunned his company in revulsion. He spoke with a slur, and when excited he stammered. Yurek found happiness when he was alone, surrounded by nature, in the company of his faithful dogs.

Three days and three nights Nora lay delirious, and Yurek had not left her bedside for one moment. He knew the common symptoms of pneumonia, and he attended to his patient as best he could. He sat for hours listening to her delirious gibberish, wiping the sweat from her body, and learning a great many details about the events of the past hours, as she relived them countless times in her delirium.

On the fourth day, the fever broke. Nora opened her eyes. She saw the distorted face of the stranger peering down at her, but she was not frightened. "Where am I? Who are you?" She asked in a faint whisper.

Yurek was silent. Mechanically, her hands clutched the cover over her breasts. She tried to raise her head up from the pillow, but it dropped back helplessly. Her strength had not returned.

"You. . . m-m-m-ust. . . l-l-l-ie. . . s-s-s-till. . . N-n-n-ora. . .," Yurek stammered, and Nora wondered how it was that this stranger had called her by her name. She did not recall having ever seen him before.

"You. . . mustn't. . . worry." He tried to speak slowly, unexcitedly without the stammer. "I. . . know. . . about. . . you; you have been very ill, with high fever." He explained patiently. "You're safe here. I'm the forester in this area. No one will look for you in my cabin. If they do, my dogs will warn us." He then introduced himself, almost too formally for the prevailing circumstances. He smiled, and his face seemed almost normal. He noticed her embarrassment and the protective gesture she had assumed.

"There were things I had to do. You were very sick," he said apologetically, "I hope you understand. You were quite a sight when my dogs found you, unconscious in the woods." Nora gave silent thanks to the Almighty. She realized that fate had put her at the mercy of a total stranger, but once again she reached for strength in her unwavering trust in God.

Nora's youth and an unbounded desire to live combined to bring about a quick recovery. In only a few days, though still weak, she was able to leave her bed and perform limited chores. She wore the loose-fitting clothes provided from Yurek's wardrobe. He went about his work in daylight, and when night came they would sit by the fireplace and chat about the War and related things.

"It's time for me to go into town for supplies," Yurek announced on the morning which had marked the end of Nora's second week in the cabin. "Usually, I wouldn't have had to go in until next week, but there are two mouths to feed now. We'd be out of provisions soon if I don't."

Nora became accustomed to this man, to the constant grin on his distorted face, to his slow speech and to his gentle ways. She knew he had saved her from an unknown fate and she was grateful, and yet there was a strange feeling inside her each time she'd noticed the manner in which he regarded her. She was aware of it, but did not let on. Her instinct warned her not to trust him. When he was gone to town, she might take a chance and steal away, she decided.

"How long will you be gone?" She asked.

"Not very long. Half a day, perhaps." He replied. "Be back before sundown, surely."

"What. . . if. . ."

"Nothing to worry about. You'll be fine; I'll leave the dogs. They're sure to keep all strangers out. If the dogs should warn you, run north. There's a cave nearby where you can hide." He pointed north, toward the hills. "I'll look for you there if you're gone on my return."

He left with a short "bye," and the fear of the persecuted had returned to her soul. The dogs. They would lead him to her, wherever she went. She quickly abandoned her plans of escape. She waited, and every innocent noise coming from the forest alarmed her. The whistling of the wind in the trees announced danger; each crackle of a dried-out branch announced enemy footsteps.

She sighed with relief at the friendly barking of the dogs late that afternoon and went outside to greet the returned forester.

"What's going on in town? Have you heard about the people in the factory?" She pressed for answers.

"The camp's still there." He replied slowly. "Not much going on now, but there's a lot of talk about resettlement, soon."

"How soon?" She trembled. "I've got to get back!" He saw her anxiety.

"There's no way you can do that. You'd get caught, no doubt about that." He looked at her "that way" again. She thought.

"I've got to see my cousin." She insisted. "He's only a boy. Hayim's just a baby. I've got to take care of him."

"The Gestapo's on the alert. They're looking for an escaped foreman . . . a German, I believe. Someone by the name of. . ." he thought for a short while, "yes, Edelmann's the name. I remember, because the people in town are laughing about him being a Jew and fooling the Gestapo into believing he was a German and a member of the Party."

"Have they taken any more hostages?"

"Not that I know of. But there's also a price on Piotr Sonik's head. The Home Army leader, you know?"

"I remember him well." Nora would not say more than that, for fear of revealing that part of her past which she could not afford to make known. He looked at her again in that sheepish way, and she sensed that he was getting excited.

"And there's a-a-a re-wa-ward. . . a-a-a b-b-b-ig one," he calmed down and continued less agitatedly, "posted for all fugitives." He concluded without looking directly at her.

Nora wept bitterly. She was worried about Hayim, and felt guilty because he was still in captivity, hungry, perhaps beaten, and she was free. Hayim was her only remaining blood relation. Even now, her own life in jeopardy, she was concerned about her cousin's welfare.

She tried to be helpful placing the provisions in the cupboard. On the very bottom of one of the boxes she had discovered a half-liter bottle of vodka. She was about to place it on the shelf, when Yurek jerked it out of her hand and walked out of the cabin. She was startled by his reaction to her discovery, but she was too preoccupied with Hayim's fate to dwell on Yurek's peculiar behavior.

That night, even as he approached the cabin from a distance, she could hear his cursing the dogs and stumbling over objects. Yurek was drunk, and she tried to hide in the farthest corner of the cabin, hoping and praying that he might fall asleep before he'd look for her.

"Gotyenu, mayn tayrer Gotyenu." She implored in Yiddish, the language her God understood best. "My dearest, darling God, help me now, please, dear Lord, help me!"

"C-c-c-ome h-h-here J-j-jewess. . ." Yurek stammered excitedly.

"Come here, this instant!" He took the last swig of vodka and tossed the empty bottle into the fireplace. It shattered into small fragments with a sound reminiscent of air-raids and bombings. Frightened, Nora lay in the corner cowering and trembling. Her strength was gone from her sinews. She knew it would be impossible to fight him off.

"You're not that kind of man, Yurek." She pleaded meekly. "Must you do this?" She asked, pointing at the shattered bits of glass which had burst into every corner of the room. "And just after I had tidied it up a bit. It's not like you to behave this way, Yurek."

Suddenly, he was calm. "There are many things you don't know about me, Jewess," he replied mockingly, "but you'll learn sooner than you think." He approached the cowering woman.

"You'd better sleep it off, Yurek." She begged in desperation. "You are tired now, and you can't think straight. Tomorrow you won't be able to get up for work, and you'll regret it all." She tried to sound firm and concerned at the same time. She remembered from somewhere that firmness was the right attitude toward drunks.

"Come here, right now!" He ordered and moved in her direction with great effort. "You and I belong together, Jewess. I liberated you, didn't I?" He grabbed her by both arms and pulled her to himself. —Here, I had to extend my imagination to its limits in order to picture the events which followed.—

Nora pushed Yurek away with a force strengthened with fear, and he lost his balance and fell back against the wall. Infuriated, he lunged forward more rapidly than could be expected of one in his condition. Nora fell to the floor and he hovered over the trembling woman menacingly.

"You f-f-filthy slut! You J-J-Jewish swine! How da-da-dare you st-st-strike me?!" He was out of breath with rage. She tried to evade the blows, but some of them landed on her face and shoulders. "F-f-for so-so-some f-f-fancy SS-SS o-o-officer you wo-wo-would un-un-undress, wo-wo-wouldn't you? B-b-but I'm n-n-not good enough f-f-for you, am I?" He yelled.

"Please, Yurek, have mercy." Nora pleaded vainly. "I'm still weak from the sickness. You know what I've gone through. I'm still not up to what you're asking of me." She appealed to his reason. "Maybe, later on. When I'm feeling better. You and I could be very good friends, you know. Please . . ." She saw him grapple with his trouser belt, not responding to reason. "Oh, God, dear God, help me, help me, now." She prayed.

"Di-di-didn't I li-li-liberate you, Je-je-jewess? Di-di-didn't I ri-ri- risk m-m-my li-li-life and my-my-my jo-jo-job to-to-to nu-nu-nurse yo-yo-you ba-ba-back to-to-to health? Wh-wh-where's yo-yo-your gra-gra-gratitude?!" He yelled at the top of his voice, proceeding to rip the clothing from her body.

For a few brief moments, Nora was able to fight him off, as she kicked, twisted and scratched. She sunk her teeth into Yurek's neck, but her resistance only made her more desirable to him.

"You should have left me where you had found me." She wept. "You can never force me to love you. Please, Yurek, let me go now." She sobbed. "Perhaps later, when it is all over, I'll come to you of my own will. Not out of gratitude, you hear? But because I like you a lot. Please, Yurek, stop!" She beseeched the forester.

Her efforts fell on deaf ears. Yurek was a driven man. Nora's own strength was waning. She remembered, before she lost consciousness, Yurek's terribly distorted face very close to hers, his foul breath hitting her nostrils. While she lay under his weight helplessly, he came into her violently, time and time again.

When she had awakened, it was morning. Naked, she lay on the cabin floor next to the overturned table. The havoc around her brought back some vague recollections. Then, there was also the pain; not altogether physical. It was more the result of a gradual awareness that the long years of maternal tradition had now been snuffed out; that she was no longer pure. Even if she were to survive this dreadful ordeal, she would be unable to envision a normal life. Now she was like all others.

"God, oh my dear God, why this punishment?" She inquired softly. "What have I done to displease You so? Gotyenu, why have you turned from all of us?" She held her face in both her hands and sobbed bitterly.

Her first resolve was vengeance. Yurek was gone. She dressed quickly. Instinct dictated escape, but where would she go? Yurek Brama's cabin was still the safest refuge for the present.

Hours later, the forester returned. He looked disheveled and remorseful. Nora went about her chores as though nothing had happened, and Yurek seemed astonished at her attitude. He muttered something under his breath, and Nora didn't respond. He addressed her, but the woman ignored his presence, and he left the hut to busy himself with the dogs. As he walked out, she heard him mumble something about an impending snowstorm.

White, blinding snow kept falling for days. Soon it blanketed the horizon. It was a typical Polish winter which once again imposed itself upon the countryside and forced all life into hibernation. Days became shorter, and Yurek spent most of his time indoors. Twice in one week, in spite of the snow, he went to town, allegedly to pick up provisions. Nora sensed a change in Yurek's behavior on his last return from Piotrkow, but it was only out of concern for Hayim that she had broken her silence.

There was something wrong, Nora knew, but she feared that questioning might arouse Yurek's violent temper. He was beating her daily, often after making love to her. He was drunk most of the time and seemed infuriated about her presence. He derived an eerie satisfaction from his violent behavior toward her. Alcohol had become the catalyst which lent him courage to force her into submission.

"There's talk, your cousin Hayim escaped from the camp," Yurek lied on entering the cabin. He knew how to hold her captive.

"How did it happen? Where is he?" She had forgotten her own fate momentarily. Hayim had been entrusted to her care, and now she realized how miserably she had failed the boy.

"Nobody knows." Yurek avoided her eyes. "All I know is that his name was on the list at the *Kommandantur* along with those of other fugitives."

"Is there anything else?"

"There's even a bigger price now posted for information leading to the capture of escaped Jews." He spoke very slowly to avoid stuttering. Now, he let out a short chuckle. "I was tempted."

Nora's heart beat violently. "You wouldn't! Would you?" She looked at him anxiously, and he kept silent, avoiding her eyes. "Am I not worth more to you alive than the price offered by the Gestapo?" She tried to sound as alluring as the circumstances permitted. He glanced at her from the corner of his eye.

"Come, let's not try to fool one another." He grimaced. "We've had our good moments, but we both know that you hate me as much as you do the Gestapo." The grotesque grin disappeared.

Nora was puzzled and alarmed at Yurek's attitude. Could he know she was pregnant? Was he indifferent as a result of her pregnancy? No, he didn't have any way of knowing that she had missed her last menstruation.

"You mustn't betray me, Yurek." She pleaded. "I'm living up to my bargain, aren't I?" She wept bitterly.

"I made no bargains with you, Jewess. Besides, I've become a *Volksdeutscher* now." He showed her his new I.D. card. "I've got to think of my own future. You wouldn't care about that, would you? All you can think of is yourself and your cousin." He turned to go.

"What are you going to do?" Nora cried, though she tried to keep her composure. "You're not going to report me to the Gestapo! Are you?" She was breathless. "You know how they treat women, Yurek. I've been like a wife to you. I'm. . ." She intended to tell him about his child she carried in her womb, but he looked at her and laughed contemptuously. It took all her willpower to remain silent, mute with grief. He laughed and tossed his new identity card on the table. "Here, read it yourself."

She now realized why he was making those frequent visits to town. She read the document with incredulity. His name had been changed to Johannes Tor, that much she understood, and he was raised to the rank of an officer of the *Heimwehr*—Home Front.

A sudden calm came over her. "You must do your duty now," she said, returning the document. She felt a wave of relief. It was over now. "They'll call you Hans for short, you know?" She added with a faint smile.

"You don't understand, Nora, you'll never understand." He was suddenly overcome by sentimentality. "You're a good woman, but you're a Jewess. There's no place for you in the Third Reich. I'm truly sorry, but there's nothing else I can do."

"You can have mercy and kill me right here." She said without looking at him. "And spare me the Gestapo. You'd do that much for an animal. After all, you're a forester."

He was startled by her honest request. "I couldn't do that, Nora, I couldn't kill you in cold blood."

Two days later, Johannes Tor delivered the captive woman whom he had initiated into womanhood to the Gestapo. The Bureau rewarded him generousl: a five pound sausage and one quart of vodka plus a *Volksdeutscher* bonus, twenty-five reichsmarks.

"A true *Volksdeutscher* performs his duty without seeking rewards." He was told, inquiring about the promised reward of a thousand marks. "You have proven your loyalty to the Reich, Hans." The clerk patted him on the shoulder, while the guards dragged Nora along the hall to her cell. Yurek pocketed the rewards, turned silently, and left the premises. He hurried to the town tavern, where he treated his friends to drinks and gave a detailed account of his strange tale. In the end, that's how the story came to me.

Nora was being violated repeatedly by her interrogators. Soon she was exhausted to the point of indifference. In her unique way, she reasoned that Hayim was safe because she was paying for his freedom with her own ordeal. Nevertheless, she did not permit herself to think that her God was as demanding as it seemed. Throughout her painful experience, she accepted her fate; it was bashaert, she told herself.

The Gestapo suspected Nora of Home Army connections. They were relentless in their pursuit of the "truth." She prayed for strength and the courage to face the end. "Don't let me suffer much longer, dear Lord." She begged her invisible Master. "*Gotyenu*, please hear my supplication and grant me rest."

It was one week from Christmas. "You will look your best today. The inspector is coming." Her guards told her.

There was food and drink on the table when she entered the hall; the place was festively decorated with branches of greenery.

"Eat and drink and groom yourself a bit," she was ordered by the officer in charge. "Tonight, there will be no interrogation. Tonight, you celebrate the week of Christmas with all of us." He was almost jovial.

How appropriate. She must have thought to herself. Christmas, my last meal. Why one week early? She had given up trying to figure out the reasons for the Nazis' activities. Four young women sat around the table. They were joined by festively uniformed SS. A fifth SS man took his place next to Nora's. She understood. Quietly, Nora made up her mind to make them pay the price.

As the evening progressed, the SS was becoming increasingly sentimental. They lit candles and sang carols to the accompaniment of an upright piano. The soldiers drank *Schnaps* and vodka till, at the nearing of dawn, the holiday spirit became thoroughly obscured. Their voices sounded louder and shriller, and their behavior was unrestrained.

"This one's for the long road East!" They kept toasting each other, and Nora understood. They weren't looking forward to spending their holidays in the cold trenches on the Russian front. She understood them; as one condemnned understands another.

The women lost count of the repeated violations. They resisted at first, but after a while they seemed no longer capable of hearing or feeling. They simply remained in their prone positions, their legs spread wide apart, motionless and unfeeling, mumbling inarticulately what sounded like unending prayer.

Nora maintained an awareness throughout by remembering the names of her beloved ones and through continuous prayer. There was no reprieve. As soon as some of the revelers tired, they yielded their victims to those who had been waiting their turn at the door.

Our cousin Menasha witnessed the orgy in his capacity as the commandant's orderly. Weepingly, he gave us a detailed account of the final moments.

In a sudden and violent manner, Nora broke away from her tormentor who stood aghast at the woman's unexpected courage. He was still holding on to his loose trousers. Half-mad and weeping hysterically, Nora ran toward him. In all her fury, she took hold of a kitchen knife and with a wild yell plunged the sharp weapon into the SS man's belly.

"In his drunk stupor, the mercenary stood for a moment grinning awkwardly, puzzlement on his face. His body shook violently, he let go of his trousers and fell to the floor." Menasha paused.

"Nora knelt over her victim," Menasha went on, "soiled with his blood, completely spent and unable to move. Guards entered quickly and dragged the muttering woman into the courtyard. Their repeated blows and the barking of the dogs mingled with the sounds of festive music. I looked out into the yard. One of the SS sent a bullet through the back of Nora's neck."

Menasha paused and we wept bitterly. "I guess, she herself didn't know what was happening to her then. She fell lifeless to the pavement, but moments before I could swear I heard her humming an age-old lullaby to her unborn child; her still beautiful face in complete harmony with the universe."

Menasha finished his account. We sobbed in quiet desperation. Then, someone intoned the melody, and we joined in:

"Where, oh, where can I go. . . ?"

11

Two winters of the war had come and gone. Gone, too, was my family, save my brother Roman; my only blood relation left me. I missed my dear people, and I could no longer sleep soundly for the terrible guilt which welled up in my heart; I have survived thus far, but I didn't dare guess the fate of all the others.

We were all in tears when Menasha concluded his account of Nora's last moments. I pressed his hand and gave him a huge bear hug. He was the only intimate friend Roman and I were able to maintain in the camp. One does not easily forge trust in confinement where "everyone is for himself." But our distant cousin Menasha was different. He was kind with us, our elder by seven years, we shared every morsel of food between us and looked to him for moral and spiritual support. Now, that Edelmann was gone, it would be increasingly difficult to sustain ourselves. But we had no doubt it would be easier if we stuck together. For what would soon be two years, Menasha had equally suffered and hated as we have.

"I've no doubt that immesurable suffering is coming, and that we won't be able to avoid it." Menasha said. "But I also have no doubt about the thing that sustains me. I know it will likewise sustain us all in the darkest hours of our lives; a consuming hatred for the enemy, and the certainty that the great monster must falter."

"I've hated the Nazis every waking hour." Roman said. "But, I guess, I don't hate enough to forfeit my life killing them." I was silent, still afraid to reveal my feelings.

"I understand what you mean," Menasha smiled sadly, "when I let this hate loose, I am almost overcome by it. I cannot change now and be different, but I, too, don't want to die. Let no person mistake this hatred for a vice, nor slight its power. Hate drives me onward, else I would give up in body and spirit. The only way I might hope to love someday is to search my way out of this abysmal darkness."

I listened to Menasha, and I knew that we were of like mind. Menasha was someone for me to look up to. He had cut his earlocks now, but I still recalled him as the Yeshiva *bokcher*, a student of the Torah, running around our neighborhood with the fringed garments loose and attracting the ire of our Christian countrymen.

It was of no use to warn him in those days. He'd respond with some appropriate dictum from the Tanach, for he was able to quote it at will as he was also intimately familiar with all of the prayers and knew them all by memory. "They can only strike at my body but never at my soul," he would say, "and in the end I end up the victor."

With his frequently bloodied nose and torn clothing, Menasha looked nothing like a victor to those who knew him, but I had always held him in high esteem for his learning, and now I envied him for the knowledge he had stored in his mind; the only item of personal worth the enemy would never be able to take from him.

The knowledge I possessed was that of a sixth grader; hardly anything to boast of. And my studies of Judaism had scarcely commenced at my grandfather's home when his untimely death had put a stop to the limited aspirations I had harbored to follow in his scholarly path.

Surely, somewhere in this world there is a place, where people like us live "normal" lives without fear and the dread of tomorrow. As time passed, I found my thoughts drifting to those imaginary corners of existence, wishing for things that seemed more distant than the stars.

I felt a terrible void, and I started to walk with a shuffle, my shoulders stooped and the back bent like a bow; that heavy gait characteristic of enslaved and burdened humanity. I had begun to regard myself an "inmate," something I had been able to hold back until then. At first, without knowing the reason, I would shrink inward whenever I perceived a strange noise, a voice raised in anger or with authority. My eyes would constantly scan the immediate surroundings for anything threatening. I was becoming increasingly aware that each inmate was for himself and survival was uppermost on everyone's mind.

A gradual transformation of my way of thinking was taking place. Although I did not favor these changes, I was unable to halt their relentless progress. Is this how man matures? I asked myself. Is this the path leading to adult life? If it were so, then I wished to reject it all, without the slightest hesitation, for I disliked the man I saw myself becoming.

Hatred had now become the singular preoccupation of my daily existence. I lived in a world filled with the terror of unanswerable riddles; a world in which madness had become the rule and evil so commonplace that human kindness was regarded as a source of great wonder and admiration.

I was haunted by the overwhelming burden of a mad humanity where well-being was as unattainable as was the mere thought of freedom. Dreas evolved into a series of recurring nightmares, and I was obsessed by imagined faces of demons grimacing at me from everywhere.

I envied Menasha's knowledge, and I felt inadequate whenever I attempted to compare myself to any of my comrades. They were all years older than I, past their barmitzvah, ahead of me in matters concerning growing up and education. Though not altogether ignorant, I knew I was going to die the death of an illiterate. Either a boy of twelve or slightly older, depending on how long I was destined to endure this perpetual nightmare.

The year 1943 was rapidly approaching. I would be thirteen then. I knew I would want to become barmitzvah when the time came. "For my grandfather." I told Menasha.

"You mustn't despair," Menasha encouraged, "we'll manage somehow."

I regarded my friend with incredulity. "I fear I'll die without being consecrated." I was fighting tears. I looked away to avoid his searching eyes.

"Bar mitzvah can wait, you know? A Jew can be consecrated at any age." He smiled faintly. "And I'm sure the Almighty will not hold it against you," Menasha hesitated, "under the circumstances."

"I've been praying for it, you know?" I said softly. "I've been told that God hears our prayers. Does He, Menasha?" I asked and my friend didn't respond immediately.

Does God really answer prayer? I agonized inwardly. I was young in my faith, and too many unexplained things had happened for me not to question Him. Was there any use in praying? Did God really care what happened to us?

"There's a reason for everything," Menasha assured me with Hasidic logic, as if reading my thoughts. "God is the Creator. We are some of His creations." He paused. "Probably His most troublesome." He added with a sad expression.

"As a child, I was told so many fairy tales," I confessed almost in a whisper. "Was God one of them?"

Menasha looked at me, full of compassion and understanding. Tears welled up in his eyes. He shook his head meaningfully and said nothing. We shared some of the bread crumbs he had been able to "organize" from Seemann's kitchen. As usual, before we ate, he blessed those stale crumbs: "We give thanks to the Almighty for allowing us to partake. Amen." Menasha concluded, and we said "amen" after him in unison.

I slept most of that night, as though I had been consoling myself about the good things that were about to happen, the way Menasha would anticipate them. His own faith had lent me the much needed courage.

"After the midnight shift! Behind the great furnace!" Menasha whispered under the watchful eye of our new foreman Franz Müller, who had replaced our friend Edelmann. I nodded in silence. We were forbidden to communicate during working hours. Franz wouldn't like that.

I remembered our new foreman from the days when he was still a Pole and went by the name Franek Mlynarz. Even during the ghetto days he was an informer for the Gestapo. He specialized in hunting down fugitives, especially those taken into shelter by their Christian friends. Noted by his superiors for his dedicated service, Franek soon became *Volksdeutscher*. That's how he transformed into a Franz Mueller.

In his new role, Franz had occasion to make many speeches to the inmates. One such talk was especially curious because it reflected the views of his masters: "We know what we're doing." He started. "Work is a virtue, and we hate lazy people. You Jews get what you've earned, because you're lazy. We Germans are honest. If you want to learn, we'll teach you to work, but we won't waste our time on nonsense. You want to work, we'll give you work, otherwise we'll send you straight to hell. *Verstanden?*" His vocabulary included some key German words and he made sure he used them at every opportunity.

Franz Mueller marked my mother and Felusia for deportation when they were about to find shelter with the Bosiackis. As a courtesy of one *Volksdeutscher* to another, he warned the Bosiackis not to go through with their plans; they would be no exception in his pursuit of duty.

We met shortly after midnight. We were all there: Moshe Lasker, Yossele Barnblatt, Menasha Ehrenmann, Saul Friedman, Moniek Weintraub, and others assembled behind the great furnace, each man wore his tallit, the prayer shawl. They swayed back and forth, quickly reciting their liturgy, their eyes turned heavenward; children and survivors of the Great Piotrkow Synagogue Passover inferno.

I had often wondered why it was the Jew recited his prayers from memory and with such great haste. That night, I finally understood. As I watched the men worship, their eyelids tightly shut, and only their lips moving, the reason suddenly overwhelmed me. Through generations of persecutions, the Jew practiced his craft of clandestine worship often on the run. How else was he to communicate with the Almighty, if not in haste? I asked myself.

Menasha conducted the services. With closed eyes, caressing the prayerbook like the true Hasid he was.—Beads of perspiration pearled from his forehead on down behind the collar of his shirt. With my brother Roman at my side, I approached the eerie assembly, awed by the spectacle. We came to stand close to our dear friend. It seemed he hadn't seen us yet, for he continued, engrossed in his pious activity. Suddenly, the prayer had stopped as if at a given signal.

The men gathered around me. Menasha placed a prayer shawl round my shoulders and handed me the prayer book—the *siddur*. The men began to chant the prayers.

I responded, transfixed, chanting along with the others, reaching into deep recesses of my memory to rekindle the limited knowledge of lithurgy I owed to the infinite patience of my grandfather Srulko.

For those few moments, I led the minyan in the recitation of the kaddish. When the last "amen" was sounded, Menasha spoke, and I listened astonished. "I want to call on the barmitzvah, Velvele, son of Henryk, to lead us in reciting the current Torah portion. By chronology, it isn't time as yet for him to take on responsibility. But circumstances have made him into a man before his time." He paused, briefly glancing at the assembled. There was an expression of approbation on their joyful faces, and he continued. "We are certain, the Almighty will not begrudge us this premature act of faith. We're here together now, and only the Lord knows where we shall be come September. Let us commence."

With a gentle smile on his face, he handed me a silver pointer. To my great amazement, a miniature Torah was "unwrapped" before me, and placed on a makeshift pulpit; a wooden crate covered with a prayer shawl.

I pointed at the sacred words chanting the prayer preceding the reading of the Holy Scriptures in the manner of the Hasidim: "*Barchu et Adonai Hamvorah, Baruch Adonai Hamvorach leolam vaed. . .*"

The great furnace spewed fire, the Hasidim chanted, and I became barmitzvah. To offer the kiddush, Menasha uncorked a bottle of choice vintage wine from Seemann's cellar. "He won't miss it," he said with a twinkle in his eye. "A toast to our barmitzvah!" He raised his glass. "*Mazal tov!* Good luck!"

"I shall never forget this occasion, Menasha," I said with tearful eyes.

"And neither shall the Almighty, blessed be He." Menasha responded quietly. "You don't know how lucky you are, Velvele." Menasha smiled. "You're the youngest of us all, and you've put your barmitzvah behind you at twelve, all proper and according to the Law. In short, you have a wonderful life ahead of you."

Each new report of German setbacks in the East had brought us renewed hardship. And every bold new venture of the resistance movement caused severe reprisals. Townspeople were arrested at random, interrogated and tortured, only to be shot in the end to discourage those who would think of aiding the partisan movement.

A small SS detachment was left in Piotrkow; Ukranian SS replaced the Germans who were dispatched to the Eastern front. The factory overseers received orders to cover up preparations for an impending camp evacuation, but with all their bureaucratic secrecy, we were able to draw our own conclusions. Menasha kept us informed about the frequent couriers arriving at

Seemann's headquarters, pouches full of secret orders, SS and Gestapo brass attending meetings planning the "great move."

"They're getting ready to 'resettle' the Hortensia camp." Menasha said. "If we want to make a break for it, the time is now."

"You're right." Roman agreed. "We'll have to move before they do."

"The sooner, the better." Menasha nodded.

"We aren't ready to go over the fence as yet." Roman spoke for the two of us. "I'd sure as hell like to see Hayim safe with one of our Christian friends before we go." With Nora gone, we were Hayim's only family. We didn't want to separate from him, but an old friend, Jerzy Skowron, offered one of us sanctuary. We discussed the offer with him.

"We have no way of knowing whether we would be doing you a favor, Hayim." Roman suggested.

"I understand." Hayim nodded. "I'm too tired to run."

"God willing, we'll meet after all this is over, and we'll look back and have a good laugh." Roman said.

"I don't think I'll ever be able to laugh again." Hayim said.

"Nothing will ever be like it was. Not for me; not for any of us." He fell silent. There was no need for further discussion. We understood.

That night, I lay awake longer than usual, and it wasn't because of hunger or worry. Countless memories and questions crowded into my mind. Not long ago, we were all together: my father and my dear mama, and little Felusia. A family like any other, we carried on a normal existence. We had a small but comfortable apartment on Modrzejowska 3 in Sosnowiec. My mother's beautiful voice resounded from one end of the dwelling to the other, and we all shared great dreams and ambitions. Ours was a happy family.

Then, my mother developed asthma and suffered prolonged coughing spells and dizziness. She wasn't a picture of health, but she managed to conceal her affliction from my father. It would only be an added worry for him, she knew. With our means, a sanatorium was out of the question. Besides, my violin lessons came first.

Every summer, we vacationed in the country for several weeks. We looked forward to those summers with great anticipation; the fresh country air did my mother a world of good, and we enjoyed the farm animals as well as the wholesome life. My father joined us for the entire last week, and we returned to the city together ready for another year.

My whole life was filled with music. If anyone had told me I'd ever have to live without music, without my violin, I would have found it hard to believe. Now, all of that was true.

I lay awake on a wooden, five-tier bunk, wondering where the next meal would come from and utterly astonished at my own acquiescence. I observed the sleeping faces of my comrades; talking and tossing in their sleep, crying out names, tormented, each by the hell of his private nightmares.

I was a twelve-year old, with the mind of an old man. The only profit of my brief existence was the time given me to know and love them all; and now they were gone, and I wasn't sure I'd ever see them again. I lay there, anguished by a thousand questions; a child who carried the burdens of a man ripe for his grave. How easy, I thought to myself, would it be to end all this once and for all.

Thoughts of loved ones kept me going. Some of them had been resettled by the Nazis, and some have been killed. I made a solemn pledge to myself not to love too readily and not to give of myself freely. I feared being left behind, abandoned. I also promised myself not to show tears to this indifferent world. Instead, I had learned to weep inside myself. I knew it would be hard to keep it all within, but tears signified weakness, and I would not be weak, not now, not ever.

In the days that followed, even the guards abandoned their usual secrecy. "They obviously don't care," Roman observed. "From the looks of it, I'd say we'll be going soon."

"We've got to act fast." Menasha said. We agreed.

"They're bringing in a new transport of coal." I said, refering to the monthly fuel delivery. "Can you get us on that detail, Menasha?"

"You and Roman?"

"Yes. And you've got to be sure to put Hayim on with us." Roman insisted.

"Hayim? You're sure?" Menasha asked, concerned.

"It's a must. We've got to be on that unloading detail together." Roman said. "This is it. Hayim goes over the fence. We might not have another opportunity like that soon."

"Hayim?"

"Yes, he agreed." Menasha shook his head. He understood.

"Can you trust your contacts?" Menasha asked.

"It's not a question of trust, Menasha." I said softly. "I don't know what that word means anymore. It's now or never."

"So be it." Menasha said matter-of-factly. "I'll arrange it."

On the following Sunday, Menasha had placed our names on the coal unloading detail. We got word to Jerzy, and by noon that day we were on our way to the rail spur at the far end of the camp. It had been snowing uninterruptedly the last hours, which favored our plans. The blizzard continued as we started unloading the freight cars. There were tons of the black substance, and carting it away on small wheelbarrows seemed an endless process.

By nightfall, all of us resembled miners. The fine black powder penetrated our clothing and skin; our lungs were filled to capacity, and the annoying tickle caused outbursts of violent coughing. We piled the coal onto a pyramid-like structure, a fair distance from the revolving light on top of the guard tower. The falling snow combined with the moonless night to make us virtually indistinguishable. The sentry swung his arms and stomped his feet to keep warm. We could hear the sound of his steps from afar, but we were unable to see him.

"Hope Jerzy's on time." I whispered.

"Don't worry, he'll come." Roman said, nervously glancing at Hayim, who kept throwing large pieces of coal onto our wheelbarrow with his bleeding bare hands.

"Remember, we mustn't cough when the time comes or we'll give away our position." I warned them both.

"This is the last one!" Roman said, firmly grasping the handles of the wheelbarrow. "Now, take some snow in your mouth! It'll melt and prevent coughing!" He suggested. "You know what to do when we get to the clearing, Hayim?" The boy nodded. Roman lifted the load, and we pushed on each side.

At approximately thirty paces from the freight car, we came to the designated spot.

"Jerzy waits beyond the clearing to the left! Hurry, Hayim! God be with you!" We hugged. There was an eerie pressure at the pit of my stomach. Hayim said nothing. By now, we had learned to say good-bye in silence. Why speak? Words betray emotions. We listened to the sound of his quickly departing steps, muffled by the soft blanket of snow.

"Did we do the right thing?" I asked.

"There wasn't much else we could do." Roman repeated several times as though trying to convince himself while Hayim's shadow disappeared beyond the ravine.

The days since Hayim's escape were punctuated by feverish preparations for the impending camp evacuation. A team of "experts," an SS *Einsatzkommando*, had arrived from Lodz to oversee and partake in the action. The snow had stopped falling. On a cold December day, the staff car pulled into the Militia headquarters. The brass stepped onto the yard wearing warm leather greatcoats and ear-muffs. It was bitter cold when it didn't snow, and they came prepared.

It happened in the middle of the night. We were jarred from our uneasy sleep by a terrible explosion. The earth shook violently, and I thought it was the end of the world. Everybody rushed to the window, and what we saw was awesome and unbelievable.

"The goddamned Cossacks have blown the glass factory to smithereens!" Someone exclaimed. "What's next?"

The night was lit up by what seemed the most fantastic display of fireworks. Brilliant fountains of screaming glass lava exploded time and again in all directions and gave the impression of a raging volcano spewing magma from the angry entrails of mother earth.

We watched fascinated and fearful, knowing the significance of the eerie spectacle. "The bastards have killed everyone on the night shift!" Menasha said, gritting his teeth together. "They've destroyed Hortensia; we're next!" He concluded.

Soon, we heard the barking of the dogs and shouts in the languages we had learned to despise equally with German: Ukrainian and Lithuanian.

"It's too late now." Roman remarked sadly. "The beasts are here." It was obvious, he meant the animals as well as their keepers.

"We should have made it for the forest when there was still a chance." I said, shaking with helpless rage.

"*Alle raus! Schnell!*" They shouted for everyone to get out. The order didn't surprise us, for such action in the middle of the night was predictable. But even though we were able to see through the Nazi's game plan, we were helpless for the moment.

This time, "resettlement" was much simpler than before; we had no luggage to carry onto the awaiting box-cars; no bedding or extra clothing and no toilet articles. Only the proverbial shirts on our backs and, if fortunate, a few mementos to remind us of our loved ones tucked away between the shirt and the skin.

By dawn, we marched down to the loading ramps on the market place. Word of our departure got out, because nearly the entire Piotrkow population came out to bid us farewell or to shout hostile, derisive remarks:

"It's about time! Off with you, vermin!" They yelled.

"Get on, filthy Jews!"

"To the soap factory with you, Yids!" There was raucous laughter.

I tried not to listen, to block out the sound, to leave my hometown only with the memory of the Bosiackis, Edelmanns and Boosts and my many friendly compatriots. Once again, I was reminded of the virulent anti-Semitism always present in the souls of our Christian countrypeople.

The three of us were the first to climb into the freight-car. Instinctively, we hurried toward the far corner. Six feet above the floor, there was a narrow window—one of the four in the entire car—boarded from the outside with not too heavy boards. Human stench filled the inside of the box-car, and there were traces of excrement and straw on the floor; evidence of their recent use in the transport. The car had been loaded to capacity—there were in all ten cars for some 2,500 Hortensia inmates—about 220 men to a car—the sliding doors were sealed tightly behind us, and we heard the clicking of the padlock being secured into the locking mechanism. There was standing room only.

It was dark inside the car, but it paled in comparison with the abysmal obscurity in my soul.

"I don't know how long we can last," Menasha whispered, "but we'll last longer near the window." He pressed his hands against the boards; they gave a little. "They must have economized on the nails," he chuckled, "steel's getting scarce in Nazi Germany," he thought for a moment, "the better for us."

"What do you mean?" Roman asked.

"When the time comes, I'll explain." Menasha smiled mysteriously. We knew, there was no way we could pry information out of Menasha. He'd tell us when he was ready.

Suddenly, we heard shots and shouts of pursuit. The view from our narrow window revealed nothing. Soon more shouts were heard.

"Do you think? Can it be? They're doing it right here?"

"Goodness, you talk a lot of foolishness." Menasha reassured us.

"They need us alive more than dead. No, they're not ready to kill us yet." He tried to convince himself as well, while we huddled close to the wall.

"Probably some poor devil tried to escape." Roman guessed.

"Why would anyone, under the very noses of the SS guards?"

"Instinct, little brother, instinct." Roman emphasized. "Some people can't stand the thought of being caged like animals."

"Why not wait for a better opportunity?"

"Patience is running out," Menasha joined in, "they won't wait, no matter what happens to them."

"What if we all ran at once?" I asked. "They couldn't shoot all of us! Could they? Some would get away. Maybe we'd even get some of them in the process. Eh?"

"To succeed, we'd all have to act without fear and selfishness." Menasha said softly. "Without trying to guess which one would get hit first. Each of us wants to live, and this keeps us from acting with courage. The Nazis know that. They count on it."

"But we've got to take our chances. Chance is all we have left!" I was getting excited.

"Quiet, brother." Roman warned. "This kind of talk'll get us all in trouble."

"Your brother's right, Vilek." Menasha calmed me down. "There's still hope." He motioned up at the window. "At the right moment. . ."

". . . you mean? We'd. . . ?" Menasha placed his palm to my mouth quickly, a bit too forcefully, hurting my lips.

"Hush! Walls have ears. This is no time for discussions." Menasha stretched his neck, trying to penetrate the darkness. "No telling what a man would do for a slice of bread or some fresh air. There have been betrayals for less." He whispered.

"But. . . we shouldn't. . . if it might hurt the others?"

"Think *only of yourself*—*only* of yourself? No one else will do it for you!" Roman whispered close to my ear, placing emphasis on each word. I tried to understand.

We were interrupted by the characteristic sound of metal hitting against metal as the train began to move. Soon, it gained momentum, and we could no longer hear one another. In the terrible congestion, each of us was supported by our neighbor. Our bodies were pressed tightly together, shielding us from the bitter cold outside.

It wasn't until the third continuous night of travel that we had begun to worry about our destination. For the first time since my separation from my mother and Felusia last October, I was able to understand the conditions in which those two dear persons had made their journey to. . . wherever.

The stench was becoming intolerable. People were relieving themselves where they stood. Some squatted in their own excretion, praying to die. Some did. The dead bodies were moved to one end of the car, which provided more room for the living. We tried to control conditions at first by designating another corner of the car as a kind of latrine; we covered the faces with ragged clothing taken off the dead.

On the third night of our voyage, enforcement of sanitary regulations had become impossible. Diahrrea had afflicted most of the men. They were so weakened by the illness that moving from the spot was an effort they didn't wish to undertake. They had finished their food rations on the first day of travel, and now they looked enviously at those of us who had rationed their crumbs prudently.

My thoughts traveled again to my mother and Felusia; how could they have managed through all this? I asked myself silently. How much longer before we'll fight one another for those remaining crumbs?

Late into that night, only a few insomniac wretches kept their worried vigil. Exhaustion set in. Aided by the monotony of the metallic music generated by the friction of steel and the violent swaying of the freight car, I fell into a restless sleep. . .

. . . I saw myself at a little railway station, somewhere in Upper Silesia. I knew where I was because of the many tall smokestacks, characteristic of the coal mines and steel mills, and the distant Tatra Mountains. There were few people present at the station.

To one side, not far from where I was, standing on a spur, I saw a freight train. There was no indication how long the train had been standing there. There were no guards near it; no sound came from within the boarded up box-cars.

Against my will and reason, I felt inexorably drawn toward the eerie sight. Suddenly, a thought occurred to me: I was looking at the first trainload of Jews on their way to. . .somewhere. . .and then, I realized that I really didn't see them. I smelled them!

It was a freezing winter morning, and the foul stench of human urine and excrement was carried from the cars on toward me by the chilly wind. I came closer, and I could now see the excrement and urine seeping through the floorboards and cracks of the wagon. I heard the viscous substance drip down onto the tracks and fill the gravel between the rails.

Dear God almighty! I heard myself say. They're packed in there like cattle. They'll never make it to their destination.

All of that happened rather quickly, yet I remembered being deeply disturbed about the unfair treatment of those poor defenseless people. "Perhaps, they'll be better off dead." I heard someone say, though no one was nearby. "They'll be spared whatever destiny awaits them where they're going. . ."

A sudden jolt woke me. Now, I had become even more aware of the stench of urine and excrement in my immediate surroundings, penetrating the clothing, into my skin. Instinctively, my hand reached out and brushed against the soiled pants, but at first contact I withdrew it rapidly in revulsion. How long will it take before my own senses grow callous? I thought. When will I accept these circumstances without feelings of revulsion and disgust?

Were it not for Roman's pocket knife, we might have lost count of time. Each day, he carved a notch in the board above our "bedding," at first only to break the monotony of travel; after a while, it had become a necessary activity.

During the four days, the train had stopped once for approximately one hour. "*Raus! Alle raus!*"—"Out! All of you, out!"—The guards yelled at us. We slid wearily to the gravel siding, and no more than three inmates had been allowed to leave the box-car at a time. The guard led us to a spot in the woods: "You have three minutes, *schnell*! Do it, Jew!"

It was bitter cold and we squatted over the snow, the three of us. The guard hovered nearby, his sten gun at the ready. I looked at Menasha and Roman, and we shared thoughts silently. "Don't even try." Menasha's eyes begged. I wondered what would have happened if all three of us jumped the guard. Our time was up, and I never had a chance to find out.

A crisp cold wind was blowing, and I trembled above the frozen soil. We walked slowly toward the box-car, to the squalor and stench, where others were waiting their turn. "There'll be another chance, Vilek." Menasha whispered. "Have patience."

I didn't tell him, but my patience had expired with the last crumb of bread.

On the fifth day, the interior of the car began to show signs of deterioration. The stench of urine, excrement and human sweat mixed into a foul concatenation that attacked even the most insensitive of nostrils. At first, we had tried to cope by appointing sanitary crews which disposed of the impurities as they occurred. But as Roman carved the seventh notch on the wall, conditions had deteriorated beyond imagination.

Most of the inmates had become weak and indifferent, able only to stare apathetically into nothingness. Lice infestation became a source of great concern to us, for we were not able to bathe since the transport had begun.

"I fear an epidemic, Menasha." I whispered, remembering the not too distant events of the Piotrkow ghetto.

"It may have already started." Menasha responded.

"What are we going to do?" My voice trembled with fear. "It'll finish us off." I pointed toward some of our sick comrades. The dead were also with us.

"Have faith, my friend." Menasha urged.

"Faith. . . in what?" I asked faintly. "Why didn't we dump the dead on our last stop?"

"The guards wouldn't let us, remember?" Roman said.

"Have faith in the Lord." Menasha interrupted.

"Don't you think it's a little too much to ask?" I asked the Hasid.

"God never asks too much of His servants." He responded.

"Then, He's amusing Himself at our expense." Roman suggested. "Our God seems to have a poor sense of humor."

"Hush! Don't blaspheme!"

"He can't punish me much more than I'm already punished?" Roman exercised the defiance of apathy.

"We'll have to make a move," Menasha changed the topic of our conversation, "or we're done for."

"Let's talk to the corporal at the next stop," Moshe Lasker suggested, "he's got to listen or he won't have any laborers left by the time we'll get to our destination."

"How do we know he wants us there alive?" Yossele Barnblatt remarked.

"Why would they go into this much trouble anyhow?" Moshe asked. "They could certainly use the freight train for their war effort. We must be important to them or they'd have buried us in Piotrkow."

"So be it! Let's talk to the corporal tomorrow!" The corporal was the one in charge of the transport.

"If only Uncle Mickey and Aunt Fay could see us now!" Roman mused. "They'd surely be glad they hadn't sent that affidavid we asked for. After all, they don't want a herd of stinking cattle in America!" He chuckled cynically. "They must be celebrating Hanukkah right about now, don't you think, Menasha?"

"If my calculations are right, we're in the middle of our freedom holiday." Menasha answered.

"How very appropriate!" Roman said bitterly.

"Don't be too hard on our American relatives, Roman" I cautioned. "Maybe they did try to help."

"You don't really mean that, little brother," Roman grinned, "they didn't even take time to reply to papa's last letter. They were so worried about all that money we'd scoop up in the streets of Brooklyn."

"Forget it for now." I suggested. "There's not much you can do about it."

"I can continue to hate!" Roman replied.

I was glad it was dark, and I was unable to see my brother's eyes, though I could sense the intensity of his hatred. I wasn't pleased with what I saw happening to my brother. I wondered how much longer it would be before I, too, would hate our American relatives and friends. For now, all I could think about was my will to survive. I'll make it! I thought silently. Just how, I don't know, but I've got to go on!

The train kept on moving faster with only occasional brief stops on out of the way rail spurs during which, we reasoned, trains with higher priority had been allowed to move ahead of ours. On one such stop-over—and they were now seldom made at daylight—our transport guards exchanged amenities with the passing troops. Through the cracks in the wall boards, I saw artillery pieces and heavy military equipment on the slow-moving platforms.

"They're on the run." Menasha remarked. "Did you hear them?" He alluded to the few remarks we had heard in passing, "the front's moving westward!" Menasha trembled with excitement.

"A lot of good it does us," I remarked, "we're moving in the same direction."

"Not much longer, Vilek. Not much longer." Menasha repeated, and it sounded like a promise.

We kept moving southwest, and Roman carved the eighth notch into the wall board. I suspected that some more of the sick must have died by then, but the doors were kept shut, and the stench had become unbearable. The occasional complaints and mournful groans of the sick had by now completely subsided. It had become painfully clear to me now that we had become a transport of the dead.

I was suddenly reminded of a curious song my mother used to sing during childhood days reminiscent of the czarist rule in Russia and its dominions: *Czar lee splugatsya veedal manifest, mertvych osvobodya, rzyvychpod ahrest. . .* The czar had given orders, you must free the dead ones, the living you'll arrest . . . It didn't take the Nazis very long to follow the czar's counsel.

Great hopes and longing stirred in me, my mind racing back to those days of a happy childhood. With all my might, I had tried to escape this world of abysmal horror, to a world full of love and beauty, of pleasant surprises, where the only hurt was caused by an inadvertent thoughtlessness of a loved one. But the freight train raced in the opposite direction, and I knew that my only refuge for now was my great desire to see the enemy in defeat.

Night had come, and it was the end of the eighth day of our journey into the unknown.

12

On the battlefield of Borodino, where Napoleon had fought the bloodiest of his battles on September 7, 1812, the invading Nazi armies began the attack on Moscow in the middle of October, 1941. As they had done 129 years earlier, the Russians attempted to block the way to their "Holy Moscow" and, as then, took up the battle with great tenacity. But the elite SS troops gradually pushed the Russians back out of their fortified positions of Mozhaysk.

It was now almost Christmas 1942 and the battle for Moscow was still raging. It was as important as the one fought in the year , but it was tougher, mightier, and longer lasting. Its cruelty and disregard for dignity and life would be inscribed in the never-ending history of human conflict.

People fled in panic, and general chaos resulted. The occupation of Moscow seemed imminent. And then, again, as it had done more than a century before, a powerful ally joined the demoralized Soviet forces. The weather god succeeded where the Russians failed despite their display of power, despite the sacrifice of millions of citizens. It rained and snowed uninterruptedly. The earth sucked up the dampness like a sponge, and the German attack got stuck in the kneedeep mud and melting snow.

Even God took a day off from labor on the seventh day. For us, it wasn't meant to be that way. By our own calculations, we must have come near Kielce, a town which boasted 18,000 Jews before the war. Just before dawn, we were jolted awake by the violent screeching of steel as the train came to a complete halt.

Although badly shaken in the resulting pile up, I let out a sigh of relief. Now, we'll be able to unload the dead. I thought. But nothing happened. We waited and no one came to open the shutters. It seemed odd that the train would abruptly stop in the middle of nowhere for no reason. In desperation, the inmates began to shout and bang at the walls of the cars.

"Open up! Let us out!"

"We need to shit! Open the door!"

"Let us bury the dead!"

Suddenly a loud explosion shook the air. It was followed by a series of smaller ones on all sides of the train, then a fussilade of automatic weapons. Cars were catching fire, and the whole place turned into a howling inferno.

Through a crack, I saw a tall bearded man leading and directing a band of attackers. They must have shot and killed the guards in sight, because there was no longer resistance from the train itself. The attackers continued to shoot, now into the cars, tearing some of the inmates' flesh into bloody bits.

"Dear Lord! Our friends have come to free us!" Went quickly through my mind.

"Menasha!" I yelled through the din of explosions. "The partisans! They've come to help!"

"Don't count on the Poles, Vilek!" Menasha yelled back. "Get down on the floor! Flat on your bellies!" We lay prostrate, and Menasha continued. "They'll hand us over to the Nazis for a pound of sausage and a pint of vodka!"

I remembered the forester's betrayal of Nora! By and large, our countrymen collaborated with the enemy, and loyalty was an exception not a rule.

"The Russians are here!" Someone shouted.

"*Tovarisch! Syuda!* Over here! Comrade!" Another voice called out.

We pleaded at the top of our voices—first in Polish, then in Russian. Menasha pushed against the boards obstructing the small window above us. They were more obstinate than he had suspected at first examination days ago. "Give! Damn you! You've got to give!" He kept muttering under his breath.

By now, all the guards had been killed, but the shooting continued. Suddenly, the door was slung open and a barrage of automatic-rifle fire was sprayed into the interior of our car. Shouts of pain and anguish resounded in Polish and Yiddish. I knew then that these men were no friends.

"It's the A.K.!" Menasha yelled. "Stay down!" The bullets ricocheted in every direction, sowing death in their bizarre flight.

As if that were not enough, flames were beginning to lick the floor and smoke was filling the car.

"Shut the door!" We heard an order given in Polish, and the sliding door had been shut and bolted again.

"Hurry up, Menasha!" I urged. The smoke was biting our eyes to tears.

"We've got to get out of here!" Roman shouted. We piled some of the dead against the wall to give Roman and Menasha the needed height. They both hammered against the narrow boards now weakened by the fire, till their fists were covered with blood.

"It's giving! We did it! Let's go!" They both yelled triumphantly.

We piled out of the narrow window, and those still able to move joined us. To reach the window, we stacked some more of the dead on top of the others and climbed over them. I hesitated at first, but Menasha pushed me toward the motionless heap of our comrades, yelling through the commotion: "It's all right, Vilek! The dead are helping the living! This way their death is not in vain!" He urged. "Now, climb!"

I didn't know what it was that made me jump finally, whether it was the intensity of the heat or Menasha's urging. I joined Roman on the ground. Menasha was next. "Hurry up! Let's go!" The excitement of the moment made me tremble all over. My legs shook terribly, and I could hardly walk, but the excitement had lent me the needed strength and I joined my comrades in their flight.

The first deep breath of fresh air had an exhilarating effect. It was a misty moonless night, but in the flicker of the burning box cars we were able to see the movement of the armed men—there must have been close to one hundred—and the dead SS sprawled here and there in our path.

"Hold it! Wait!" Roman held back suddenly, pointing at a group of men who had just opened another box-car. "Let's see what they're up to." We squatted on the ground inside a narrow ravine.

"All right now, everybody out!" One of the men shouted an order. He spoke in Polish. Only a few inmates complied, jumping to the ground, they stood before the box-car shouting thanks to their liberators. The armed men stood silent, their weapons at the ready, waiting for the last to vacate the car.

It took only a slight nod of the leader's head — we saw the glow of his cigarette move vertically—and the men opened fire. Before we were able to overcome our astonishment, some thirty of our comrades lay motionless near the tracks. One of the armed men jumped onto the car, spraying the inside with bullets. He jumped off, and from the ground tossed a grenade. The explosion was amplified by flames that enveloped the structure.

"The assassins!" Menasha hissed. "I won't forget! I won't forgive!" He ground his teeth and clenched his blood-covered fists. "Have you ever seen anything like that?"

I wanted to come out of my hiding and shout at the top of my voice. Instead, I remained rooted to the spot, terrified.

Systematically, our countrymen repeated the activity, putting those box-cars aflame where they suspected survivors. Soon, there remained only a grotesque skeleton of heat-twisted steel. The insurgents then placed some weapons near the bodies of their victims.

"That's fine!" The leader spoke. "The Jews killed the Nazis, the Nazis killed the Jews!" All laughed uproariously. They boarded the train's locomotive, after having gathered some of the SS weapons and disappeared in the distance singing a patriotic Polish tune.

"Damn the anti-Semitic bastards! Damn them to hell!" I cried bitterly. "Jan Kublon wasn't like that! He wouldn't have killed unarmed men!"

"Why would the A.K. do a thing like that?" Roman whispered sadly. He, too, was stunned by their action.

"What's the difference now?" Menasha brought us back to reality.

"Makes no difference who's the killer of Jews; they or the Nazis." In silent anguish, unbelieving, we lay for almost an hour in the gully. Altogether there were seventeen of us. I was happy to see some of our childhood Piotrkow friends among them. We were now determined to fight in much broader terms than we had ever imagined. Our hatred extended to those whom we had hoped to befriend as our comrades-at-arms.

"If it's a fight they want, a fight they'll get." Menasha was the first to break the solemn silence. "Let's salvage what's left and get going!"

We climbed cautiously out of our hiding. Left behind were some automatic rifles, and all sorts of sidearms, grenades and enough ammunition to wage a small scale war. There was food, too, in one of the half-charred cars which had served as the guard's kitchen. We all feasted.

"Roman! Come here, quickly!" I called to my brother, who was busy going through the pockets of an SS guard.

"Look." I handed him a photograph I had found in the breast pocket of the dead man. Sitting on a sofa in a modest living-room, was the SS guard in uniform, surrounded by his family: two small sons and a lovely young woman. Neither of the boys could have been over seven years old. The woman's face beamed with pride as she regarded the SS insignia on the man's uniform.

"Look on the reverse side," I said. There, barely visible, was an address: "Lindenallee 442, Berlin, S.W."

"Well, here's one Nazi that won't be coming home to his Frau this Christmas all covered with glory," Roman said. He was about to tear up the photo, but I stopped him with a motion of my hand.

"Why not send it to the woman? She'd appreciate knowing. . ."

"What in hell is the matter with you?" Roman yelled at the top of his voice, abandoning all caution. "Has anyone of these bastards sent a photo of our mother and Felusia back to us right after they gassed them?"

"Can't you see? That's just it, Roman, that's the point."

Disregarding my argument, he tore the photo into small fragments and spat after it as the pieces scattered into the snow.

"What do you think we are, little brother? The Swiss Red Cross? Pick up your gear and let's get going!" Roman was calmer now. As he looked at me, he said quietly: "This is war, Vilek. Now, you must forget everything else." He went on without looking me in the eye. "There's no place for feelings in war. No compassion."

"I don't think you understand, Roman."

"I understand what you'd wanted us to do. Let that be enough for now." He picked up his bundle from the ground. "Now, let's go!"

I put the SS man's belt across my left shoulder and filled my pockets full of grenades and ammunition. The belt buckle had the same inscription as all of the others. *Gott mit uns.* The dead man's Luger lent me a sense of security. We were about to depart when I noticed his boots. There was a lot of wear in them. I thought. I sat onthe ground, trying to put them on, when Yossele Barnblatt approached. He was barefoot, rags around his feet.

"I've been looking for just such a pair." He said. "Your shoes are still fine. Let me have those."

At first, I wanted to keep my prize, but I saw that the boots were more Yossele's size than mine. Besides, he was right, my shoes were still in good shape. His face lit up with a broad grin. With the enemy's boots on his feet, Yossele felt ten feet tall.

Within the hour, everyone was ready to move out. We were all armed now, each had found some type of weapon. We looked at ourselves and we saw a formidable band of men; the meakness of defeat had given way to a fresh feeling of courage. Though no one had spoken, I knew they all felt as I did: my self-worth had just risen considerably.

As we hurried toward the distant forest, my fingers caressed the Luger. The touch of the cold steel felt reassuring. What was it in that tool of death that made me think all of a sudden that I was many times the person I really was? I wondered silently. To my count, it must have been Hanukkah now or close to it. How very appropriate. I chuckled inwardly. I wasn't going to lay down my life without a fight. If only our relatives in America saw us now!

"Let's rest for a while!" I heard Menasha's voice, and I sat down, leaning against a fir tree and was soon lost in my thoughts. . .

On the last day of Hanukkah, the Meyerowitz family received a letter from Isaac. They hadn't heard from him since basic training, and they welcomed the news with great relief.

"You go on and read it this time, Mickey." Fay insisted. She was in tears and her hand trembled when she handed the letter to her husband.

He read: "Dear mom and dad, I'm with the 159th Engineer Combat Battalion, and we're on our way to finish off what's left of Rommel, the 'Desert Fox,' in North Africa. I figure, the sooner we get that situation under control, the better chance I've got to fight the Nazis in Germany.

"It's all very secret, so don't go telling all your friends, okay? I hope you all have a nice Holiday season and you don't have to suffer too many shortages. I'm okay. Will write soon again. Love, your son, Isaac."

Fay wept and Mickey consoled her. "He's okay, mother. You have no reason to cry."

"If he only knew what we have to put up with." She wiped her tears. "What with the butter and sugar being rationed, and it's getting so you can't get a Hershey bar or a pack of chewing gum." She carried on, and Mickey listened patiently. . .

Unteroffizier Ernst Boost had been promoted to sergeant, *Feldwebel* "in the field of battle," as his orders indicated. The men of the Supply Company he commanded dragged themselves silently through the ice-cold snow. The snow melted into their boots, their feet were soaking wet, and their legs felt terribly cold. Claysmeared overcoats hung heavily under the wet shelter halves. Only the glowing cigarette butts in the corners of the soldiers' mouths were dry and warm. Sergeant Boost's unit was a part of the eastward movement. It was an altogether different invasion; the invasion of Russia, a mass of land known to have swallowed many an intruder.

The road was too narrow to form a proper march column, and the infantry trod along in long rows on both sides of the knee deep snow. No proud goose step. No songs. During their occasional rest periods, the soldiers consumed their food rations hastily in the road ditch. At night, they lay somewhere, man on man, to store up a little warmth before standing guard.

No one rode. The horses had to be spared. For a long time, there had been no oats. Hay was occasionally found, but most villages were left in heaps of ashes by the retreating Russians.

Approaching the front lines, the infantry was repeatedly engaged in heavy fighting with the fresh Siberian troops and numerous Soviet armored brigades.

"For a defeated people, the Russians are fighting quite well!" Boost's second in command remarked. After all, the *Führer* himself announced Nazi victory on the Eastern front a long time ago. No one was able to comprehend why the Russians continued to resist so obstinately.

"It must be, they didn't take the *Führer* seriously. He should talk to them in Russian, and they might comply." Boost remarked jok ingly.

As it was, the stubborn "Russky," as the Germans called their enemy, persisted in the defense of his "Holy City." It puzzled the aggressor that the people continued such a seemingly hopeless struggle. The *Führer* had promised his armies a quick victory. Here it was almost Christmas again, and the fighting hasn't let up one bit. Victories on the Western front made the Nazis seem invincible. Everyone knew this. Goebbels boasted about it in his frequent propaganda broadcasts, and the entire Third Reich believed it.

"But do the Russians know it?" Boost allowed himself to think out loud.

As time passed, the soldiers had begun to joke about their fate, secretely at first, increasing in boldness with the knowledge that the few spies among them were too busy drying their own socks to be overly concerned with a few "innocent" remarks made here and there.

For six days, we traveled northeast, mainly on foot, aided by peasants who risked their lives harboring fugitives in spite of the ever-present Gestapo informers. We were working our way to the province of Volhynia, a thickly wooded area of eastern Poland near her new borders with Russia. We headed toward the city of Lublin, having been told that partisan units of the Polish Socialist Party (P.P.S.) were operating there.

In our search for friendly partisan units, we were driven by one desire: a chance to get near Treblinka. We've been assured by eye witnesses of mass exterminations there, but we kept hoping that our loved ones might still be alive and in need of our help.

"Hold on, little brother," Roman said, his teeth chattering as we huddled together in the bitter cold. "We'll see the day when our enemy will wear the mark of a prisoner on his uniform. It'll come! For our mother and Felusia, for our grandparents, it's got to happen! We must survive or there'll be no one left to say kaddish. No one left to bear witness."

"If we only make it through this goddamned cold?" My jaws chattered as I blew my breath into the palms of my hands.

"Think about the future!" Roman said. "Remember our loved ones, and hate the enemy." He paused. We listened, and suddenly there was a thundering sound. "Can you hear that, Vilek?" Roman asked as the earth shook mightily. "Those are our guns! The Russians are on the move!"

Roman woke me during the night, and we both listened to the distant rumbling of the heavy artillery. "I can hear them," I said, "but how do we know whose they are?" I listened for a moment and I couldn't refrain from asking: "And what if they are? If they hit us here we'd be dead for sure. What's the difference whose bullet kills you?"

"Don't talk such foolishness, little brother." Roman smiled. "Our guns won't aim at us." It was simple for him but far from a logical consequence for me.

"Our," was a strange sounding word. During the last couple of years, nothing seemed to be "ours" any longer, and we belonged nowhere. What did it matter where the guns were aimed? I thought to myself. They were aimed at us first and foremost, for we had been the real victims while the gods did battle!

In the Lublin forest, we came to an abandoned log cabin. It was a godsend. We set up camp, sheltered from the howling blizzard. Yossele's fingers were frostbitten, and Moniek complained of numbness in his toes. I could't wait to set foot inside, anticipating its warmth. "I hope it'll keep out the wind." Saul said.

"There'll be no fire!" Menasha took command. "Do you understand? No fire. Smoke will attract attention." There were no objections, although it did seem a pity not to use the fireplace. "On a clear day, they could spot the smoke for miles." We understood. We had learned to suppress disappointment, and each one of us was grateful for the little comfort the walls would provide. The wooden floor was a far cry from the icy bedding of the countryside.

"We'll have to stand guard, starting tonight." Menasha said. "Two at a time. Choose your partners."

We weren't strangers to shifts. The setting was different now, but the routine was familiar. I was excited at the mere thought of standing guard with a rifle in my hands. It made me forget fatigue.

"And remember, there'll be no sleeping on guard." Menasha admonished. "It could cost us our lives." He was right. Roman and I stood the first shift. The openness of the forest and the howling wind made us shrink into ourselves.

"Roman, is this real, you know, is it our war now?" I whispered anxiously.

"Yes, little brother, it's the real thing." Roman replied. "We're soldiers now."

"What. . . if. . . someone. . ."

". . .suddenly appeared . . . uninvited. . .?" He finished my question.

"Yes. . . what. . . if. . .?" "Stay calm and alert. If necessary. . ." Roman pointed at the trigger mechanism.

"Just like that? You mean, shoot? How do we know friend from foe?"

"Friends announce themselves, foes don't." With that piece of advice, we separated. Roman walked to the northern periphery of our hut; I the southern. We kept circling the area, meeting every now and then to exchange words and continue on our way. Our first watch was lonely, cold, and uneventful.

Two days later, our food supplies nearly gone, we decided to slip into the nearest village, Lubartow, to "requisition" some food. Menasha chose four Piotrkow lads to accompany him: Tuviah Moshkovitz, the eighteen year old son of the town smith and strong as an ox; Zeviah Zaplocki, seventeen, the son of Shlomo Ganev the elder of the Great Synagogue; Yacov Teitelbaum, a twenty-year-old "adolescent" who giggled every time he was embarrassed, and our old friend Yossele Barnblatt, nineteen and a hot tempered giant who would have fits of stuttering when provoked by the least bit of excitement.

"I don't have to tell you how important this mission is for all of us."

Menasha addressed the small band. "The villagers are a closely knit com-

192 WILLIAM SAMELSON

munity. They look at strangers with suspicion." He paused. "Hide your weapons. We'll only make use of them when it's absolutely necessary and only when I give the sign. Agreed?"

They nodded silently.

Menasha went on. "We'll have to be on the lookout for elements who don't want any Jews around these parts. They're on the run, too, and they don't want the Nazis coming after us. These people can be treacherous."

"How do we stay out of their way?" Zeviah asked.

"We'll move under the cover of night."

"What if we stumble on them anyway?" Yossele asked, playing the devil's advocate.

"We'll do what has to be done." Menasha's eyes had a determined look. Both his hands caressed the automatic gun. This is the mild-mannered Hasid I've known all these years? I thought to myself. My discovery of Menasha's new character had a sombering effect on me, but I was unable to tell exactly why.

"I'm frightened." I whispered.

"There's nothing wrong with that, little brother." Roman responded. "So am I."

There were last moment instructions for those of us who remained behind at the camp site, handshakes, bearhugs and well-wishes.

Rumors had it that partisans were active in our area. Most of them were leftovers of Red Army units who stayed behind German lines after their encirclement by the Nazi invasion. There were also left-wing and Communist Ukrainians and Poles who fled into the forests to escape persecution at the hands of Ukrainian Nazi collaborators. There were only scattered Jewish partisan groups, who lacked in armaments and experience in guerilla warfare.

It was almost dawn. We were sound asleep, when, suddenly, shots resounded and we found ourselves surrounded by some fifty rugged- looking, well-armed fighters. Their guns were cocked. Our own sentries walked slightly ahead of the intruders, their arms raised high above their heads. "Good Lord." I prayed under my breath. "Let them be friendly! What would Menasha do, if he were here?" I thought to myself. "Where have we gone wrong to be caught off guard like that? Menasha will be very angry," I worried.

"Everybody down! Belly up!" The order was given tersely in Polish and we quickly complied. "If they're A.K. we're dead." I thought silently. My luger was only a foot away. I glanced at Roman. He nodded.

"Stay down, and don't argue with the barrel of a sten-gun." Roman whispered.

"What an absurd way to die." I thought to myself. "Out here, without knowing why. It's like dying someone else's death. I'm really terrified!" I whispered to Roman.

"Silence! Who's the leader of this miserable looking bunch of amateurs?" No one made a sound. "Come! Speak up!" Startled, I glanced at the speaker from the corner of my eye. It was a woman! She could not have been over eighteen; a brunette dressed in men's khakis, sten-gun over her narrow shoulder, a beautiful face with pronounced cheekbones and penetrating dark eyes that defied the stern sound of her voice.

"Come on! You! Talk!" She pointed the sten-gun at me. I was unable to give a reply. We hadn't formally selected a leader amongst us, although Menasha assumed some of the responsibilities of leadership. Then again, Menasha was gone.

From the far corner of the cabin, I heard the sound of Moshe Lasker's tenor intoning the melody of our ghetto song: "*Voo ah-heen zol eekh gayn, az yede teer eez farmakht. . .? Where, oh where can I go, when every door is tightly shut. . .?*"

Our captors looked at one another puzzled. The woman turned to a huge, bearded man.

"What do you think, Anton? They couldn't be!"

"What if they are, Pola?"

"Let's make sure. . ."

"All right! On your feet, everybody!" Anton ordered.

"You!" The young woman pointed at me. "Come here!" I approached. "Are you Jews?"

"Yes." I replied.

"Where do you come from?"

"Who are you? What do you want with us?" I suddenly blurted out.

"You were right," the woman turned to the one called Anton. She smiled. "They're Jews. No one else would answer a question with a question!" Everyone laughed. Ours was a laughter of relief and thanksgiving. Our "captors" relaxed their weapons. One of them, a boy no older than I, placed some wood on the fireplace. Soon, we were sitting near the fire, eating, drinking and exchanging stories.

"We were sure you were the A.K." Anton said, pouring a second bowl of hot pea soup into an aluminium container which I held out to him. "If we hadn't heard that Yiddish song. . ." He made an impressive sign with his index finger.

"And we thought you were the A.K." I said laughingly. "We were already saying our last prayers." I told him about our recent experience with the Home Army. He shook his head in sympathy.

"The A.K. has orders to kill everyone that would oppose its future takeover

of the country," Anton went on. "They kill the Jews, because they say you're
Communists. They'd be happy to let the Gestapo and the SS do their dirty
work, but they often do the job themselves."

"Aren't we all fighting the same enemy?" I asked.

Anton shrugged his powerful shoulders. "The A.K. fights two enemies,
the Nazis and us. We fight the Nazis and the A.K." He paused. "Confusing,
isn't it?" He asked, getting ready to leave. "It's my turn to stand guard." He
extended his powerful, calloused hand. "My name's Anton Niedola."

"Vilek's mine." I introduced myself. "Before you go . . ." I hesitated. "Will
you tell me. . . how is it that. . . this girl. . . woman . . . so young. . ."

"Oh? You mean Pola?" He chuckled. "Quite a woman!" He smacked his
lips together. Then, he suddenly became serious. "That one," he shook his
head, "she's our leader. Not afraid of the devil himself!"

"Isn't she a bit young to be the leader of the whole unit?"

"Age has nothing to do with it, my young friend!" He said. "It's what
you've got in here!" He pointed at his stomach. "It's guts that counts!" Anton
became pensive. "Almost two years ago," he continued, "when Pola was fifteen . . .or was it fourteen? Oh well, it doesn't matter. . . there was an
Einsatzkommando activity in her village. Ukrainian SS. They took hostages
to avenge the killing of their local informer by the partisans." His voice
saddened and came almost to a whisper. "Her whole family went that day.
The Nazis killed them all except for Pola and her thirty-seven-year-old mother.
The two women escaped the carnage, but only after being raped by the
bastards." Misty eyed, Anton continued after pausing for a moment to reflect. "From that day on, together, mother and daughter hunted the Nazis
and their local helpers. On one occasion, they killed fourteen Germans traveling in two personnel cars and came back to their partisan unit with all of
the captured weapons. Another time, they ambushed a convoy and killed
twenty-four Germans with mines and grenades." Anton fell silent again, and
I thought that the tale had come to an end.

"That sounds almost like a legend, Anton." I said, awe struck.

"And a legend it may well be, my young friend." His smile bore a semblance of pain now, as he continued. "A day came when Pola and her mama
fell into a Nazi trap. Mama used up all her rounds of ammunition and five
grenades before being herself killed by an enemy bullet. Pola sprang at her
mother's killer and smashed his skull with the butt of her sten-gun from
which she had never parted. She was wounded, but she swam the Bug,
crossed the *pushtcha*, the great forest, and fell unconscious close to our camp
where we found her the following morning. She's been with us ever since."
Anton walked toward the door, opened it and stood in the doorway for a
moment. A smile on his face, waving at me before he disappeared into the

darkness, I heard him mutter to himself, "She's quite a woman. . . yes. . . a lot of woman, our Polusia."

That night I slept more securely than I had slept in a long time.

Menasha returned the following morning in the company of our friends plus two men from the village. I ran toward them. "Menasha! Yossele!" I called out joyfully. "How wonderful to have you back!" They were looking around.

"What's. . .going on?" Menasha motioned toward the new faces.

"We are now partisans, Menasha." I went on to explain, and my friends were pleased. "You'll want to talk to Pola, our leader."

"Pola? Our leader? A woman?" Zeviah winked, smiling.

"She's a tigress!" I said enthusiastically, remembering Anton's words. "Don't underestimate her."

They talked, and Menasha instantly liked our new leader. "Lubartow has a small Ukrainian garrison," Menasha briefed Pola. "It's an easy pick, whenever we're ready." She was pleased.

"When the time comes, we'll take it." She looked at Anton with a smile on her face. He nodded approvingly. "First, we must whip all of you into shape, though." Pola smiled. "Anton will take care of that in as little time as possible."

Anton taught us guerilla tactics and the use of weapons and high explosives. "Derailment of troop trains will be our main activity." He said. He was a patient instructor, and when we failed to understand, he continued until he was sure we all grasped the meaning.

We took instruction in horseback riding and shooting, and soon we were able to ride while drawing the rein with our teeth, leaving the hands free to do the shooting.

On the sixth day of instruction, Pola addressed us: "You have worked hard, and Anton tells me that you're ready to be tested." She paused. "We can't afford to waste live ammunition, so the test will come in action. I hope that you've learned enough to function as a disciplined unit. Each of us has a job to do, and we depend on each other. This is the most important principle of our effectiveness." She nodded at Anton, who proceeded to explain our mission.

"The territory of our operation runs along the Wieprz river in the wooded area north of the towns of Pulawy and Lubartow. There will be an armored SS convoy passing through Pulawy the day after tomorrow. The German encirclement of Moscow has been broken. These are reinforcements. They must not reach their destination." Anton paused to allow for questions. There were none.

I looked at Pola and I could not help thinking: So much beauty to be wasted on destruction. The Nazis are monsters, and they make monsters of all of us. This is their most sinister crime, their deepest shame.

Within the hour, we were on our way in full force. No one was left behind. Pola rode ahead, accompanied by her two lieutenants, Anton Niedola and Zbyszek Podrozny. I understood they were more than merely her associates in war. My suspicions were confirmed the same evening when we had reached the farm not far from Pulawy.

"What did I tell you?" Menasha remarked to Roman, with a meaningful wink. It was then I noticed my friend Anton leaving the loft.

"They must have pulled straws," Roman chuckled, "and it looks like Anton got the short end."

The farm belonged to a collaborator peasant. We were safe there because their homesteads were seldom searched by the police.

"As long as they're useful to us, we tolerate them." I heard Anton say. "When they betray us . . ." He made a short sign to his throat. "They're dead!"

Our unit numbered sixty-seven men and women fighters. We now had two light machine-guns, one sub-machine-gun, assorted rifles, sten-guns and pistols, and plenty of grenades. Besides, Menasha's group had stolen enough explosives from the Ukrainian garrison in Lubartow to blow up trains for the remainder of the war.

At dawn, Pola was at an observation post high up in the hay loft. Zbyszek took notes, while Pola and Anton scanned the countryside through field glasses. We could hear the rumbling of tanks and the sound of heavy motor vehicles.

"Maybe this is more than we can handle, eh, Pola?" Anton remarked lowering his binoculars.

"Don't be silly," Pola replied, "the stronger they are, the more confident and arrogant they become." She smiled. "It works in our favor. They won't expect us and . . ."

". . .but there must be at least a whole SS Panzer batallion, and look at the foot soldiers! They're swarming into the village!" Anton argued vainly.

"They're not expecting us, are they?" Pola asked.

"Well. . . no. . . not exactly."

"That's our superiority! Let's get things ready as planned!"

The three leaders left the loft. They now had an entire day to plan the operation. Munitions were rationed out. We cleaned and oiled our weapons. I recalled Anton's admonition: "Prevent jamming! Oil them well! You'll never get a second chance!"

Under the cover of darkness, we moved out as silently as we came in. The peasant and his wife watched us leave. "May the blessed Virgin Mary be with you!" The woman cried making the sign of the cross. He echoed. "Amen!" He, too, crossed his chest.

It was nearly midnight when we reached the SS concentration. Silently, we separated into small groups; each of us fulfilling their special task. I was terrified. My first military action. What will it be like to kill someone? In my mind, I ran through the instructions over and over again. "Place the plastic inside the tank turrets! Secure it well! Set the fuses at half an hour!" I could almost hear Anton's voice.

"You must hate this guy's guts, my friend," Anton advised, "it'll be easier this way to spill them." Would I be able to pull the trigger when that moment came? I prayed that things would go well. I didn't have to look into my enemy's eyes while setting the explosives. There was a kind of anonymity in this type of killing. "Was that also the way the Nazis killed the Jews?" I thought silently. "Each one of them sheltered by anonymity? No, I mustn't allow for such comparisons." I quickly proceeded to dispel my doubts. After all, ours was a just anger, aimed against a murderous aggressor; the merciless killer of our families.

It had taken well over an hour by the time we finished. The tanks were ready to blow. I set the mechanism carefully at half an hour. Now, all that was left was to retreat, wait and watch. The unsuspecting sentries passed within arm's length of the charges. God, I prayed silently, don't let them hear the ticking.

With only six minutes to go, shots and shouting came from the far end of the camp. SS sentries were dragging one of our men toward the guard-house almost fifty yards from where we hid, yelling abuses and striking him with their rifle butts.

"Anton! Now! A diversion!" Pola hissed. "They've caught a novice!" The "novice" was our own Yacov.

"Ready?! Let's get going!" Anton yelled, aiming at the nearest sentry. We ran, spraying automatic rifle fire at the astonished SS. At that moment of surprise, the two SS men dropped Yacov's arms, and he ran as if possessed by demons. It took the disciplined SS only moments to regroup and return our fire.

"Anton!" I yelled and ran toward my friend who lay bleeding in the snow.

"Go on! Never mind me! Get the bastards!" Anton shouted through the din of explosions. "Someone betrayed us!"

I ran and I killed, hoping all along that the charges would soon go off. The steel grip of my sten-gun was getting unbearably hot, and I had long since stopped counting my victims. The War was mine now, and I was part of it. "I am now one of them." My soul wept while the barrel of my weapon continued to spit its fires of hell at the enemy.

The explosions went off with a mighty quake. The SS was momentarily stunned, as evidenced by a temporary lull in their activity as they retreated to take cover. Anton was severely hurt. Quickly, we collected our wounded and made an orderly retreat.

We would count our losses back in the safety of the forest.

We made our way back toward the farm through the dense woods. Anton and Yossele lay on the makeshift stretchers. Zbyszek carried the third man piggy-back. There was no time to prepare another stretcher. The triumph of our mission might have been complete were it not for the casualties; nothing short of surgery was going to save Anton. Yossele's leg wound was less serious.

We stopped for a brief rest and reconnaissance not far from the farm. I joined Yacov and Zbyszek, and we moved cautiously toward the farm yard. We found nothing unusual, but the farmer did not respond to the sound of our three short whistles.

"Over there!" Zbyszek pointed up toward the cable lift to the hay loft. The two limp bodies of the peasant couple hung grotesquely. We stood rooted to the ground.

"We had guests." Zbyszek whispered.

"You think any of them stayed?" I asked.

"We'd better find out right now."

We came toward the barn. Zbyszek in front, while Yacov and I stayed back, our weapons at the ready. The couple's bodies were riddled with bullets. On their backs was the usual inscription: OUR PAYMENT TO SABOTEURS!

I knew then with the cold certainty of fear that we were betrayed. I recalled Anton's warning. The question was: by whom?

"We've got to get a decent bed for Anton or he won't make it." Zbyszek said.

"What if the SS returns?" I asked.

"We'll have to take that risk." Zbyszek replied softly. "Anyway," he continued, "they won't be back soon; they've got what they came for." He nodded toward the two peasants. "I'd like to get my hands on the swine who informed!" He spat through his teeth and turned to go.

Pola listened intently to Zbyszek's report. Intuitively, she argued that it was a trap. She looked at the delirious Anton. He was feverish, perspiring and repeating incoherent expressions in his delirium. It was a hard decision, but she had reached it in a moment of weakness. We inched forward toward the farm.

No sooner had we arrived into the barnyard, when the huge gates opened wide and we faced the barrel of a 88 mm. tank cannon.

"Run for cover!" Pola screamed, kneeling in front of the two wounded.

We opened fire and tossed a few pineapple grenades which bounced off the tank as it moved toward us, all of its guns spewing fire. Like a terrible monster, the huge steel structure was almost on top of us.

Pola jumped out of the way. By some mysterious force, Anton rolled from his stretcher facing the belly of the steel vehicle. Seconds later, a powerful explosion shook the tank, setting its fuel on fire. Infuriated, we ran screaming toward the burning structure. Menasha, possessed by madness, jumped onto the turret and used the barrel of his gun to pry open the manhole. He hurled a stick hand grenade inside, closing the manhole. None of the crew members escaped.

The man Zbyszek was carrying on his back was dead. Four freshly dug graves marked the farmyard as we readied to leave. The lives of our two comrades were too high a price to pay for our small victory. Anton's death created a particularly deep void in our ranks. Someone would have to carry the news to his father. Anton was the last of the four Niedola sons who had given their lives fighting the Nazis.

That night, Pola talked to headquarters. None of us knew where our instructions originated, and we preferred it that way.

"We're moving on to the Istra region," Pola addressed the unit for the first time since the skirmish. She was her resolute self once again.

"That's along the Molodilnaya, Polusia." Zbyszek remarked. "It's inside Russia, isn't it?" Zbyszek smiled mysteriously. "So they need us, after all, to fight their war, eh?"

"Prepare the men to move out." Pola gave the order. She was in no mood for jokes.

"Isn't anyone going to say kaddish for the dead?" I asked Menasha.

"You don't say kaddish for a goy." Menasha replied.

"I don't see why not!" I was adamant.

"Menasha's right," Roman said. "You don't."

"I'm going to recite it just the same." I said stubbornly. "You're forgetting, I was barmitzvah."

"You'll still need a minyan." Menasha reminded me.

"Minyan or not, if you refuse me, I'll do it by myself!" They could see that I meant what I said.

"And how are you going to separate the Jew from the Gentile?" Menasha asked.

"I don't intend to separate anyone." I looked at my Hasidic friend pleadingly, and his resistance yielded to compassion.

The prayer shawl over his shoulders, Menasha prayed. This was the same person who only a short while ago tossed grenades into the flaming entrails of a German tank. I listened enraptured while he intoned the solemn chant of the age old supplication, and those present countered with the customary "amen."

When we finished the services, Menasha addressed me. "I didn't pray for the dead alone. My words were for all of us, just in case there'll be no one left to say it after we're gone."

"You don't know what you're saying, Menasha, my friend." Roman admonished the Hasid.

"On the contrary, Roman. I know very well what I'm doing." Menasha reflected for a moment. "Let me explain: we have now become like them. This is our enemy's greatest triumph. First they took away our homes and our families. They made us forget laughter and robbed us of our dignity. Now, they've made us forget the most precious trait of all Jews, mercy. We kill just like they do, without mercy, without compassion."

"Not quite, Menasha, not quite like them. We have not killed the unarmed, the feeble, and the children."

"Give it time, my friend. That'll come too." Menasha shook his head in utter helplessness.

Ironically, the enemy's reverses had also become ours. Turnip soup had replaced our favorite peas, and even that was thinner each day. We tried in vain to find a morsel of horse meat in our daily ration. The booty from our frequent raids on enemy provisions confirmed our suspicions of severe shortages within the Third Reich.

Now, the resourceful Nazis invented various types of *Ersatz* or substitute; margarine was extracted from coal, and bread tasted more like sawdust each passing day. Even the occasional handouts from friendly peasants had begun to dwindle; a baked potato was truly thought of as a meal "fit for a king."

One of the many Soviet defense sections in the Istra region stretched out along the Molodilnaya. The Russians were quartered in large earthen emplacements which were heated by huge metal ovens. In comparison, the Nazis occupied trenches which they called "ice cellars." Behind the German line, there were large virgin forests, the so called *pushtcha*; for the moment, that was where we would stay to continue our activities, Pola explained. Treblinka will have to wait. I thought to myself. Be patient, mama.

The Nazi units were once part of the powerful Fifth Panzer Division. Decimated and badly in need of relief, they held onto their positions as ordered. A few days had gone by since their last engagement on the Volokolamsk-Istra road. Twenty-three Russian tanks, two of which were fifty-two ton units, had been knocked out but with heavy German casualties. Our orders called for much harassment of the weakened remains of the Panzer Division.

The remainder of the Soviet armored brigade retreated to the surrounding villages behind the Molodilnaya. They fought bravely trying to defend Novo-Petrovskoye, but it fell to the crack SS 46th Panzer Corps on December 21.

At the same time, the Eleventh Panzer Division crossed the Istra Dam at Lopatova after removing some eleven hundred mines and two tons of explosives. The Nazis were jubilant when they received the news of the successes of the Fifth Corps at Klin and Ssolnetschnogorsk. During the stillness of the night, we could hear them celebrating into the early morning hours.

The combat conditions resembled those of the fighting days in the first "big War" of the twentieth century. Rest and heat were denied the aggressor. The Soviets burned their villages, installed liquid explosives with ingenious time fuses in the chimneys and stoves of the largest buildings. The invader was furious but helpless against these tactics. After having taken Novo-Petrovskoye, the Nazis settled down for a few days of an uneasy rest.

In our first three weeks in the region, though we were short of arms, we were able to derail four East-bound trains. We killed Nazis, blew up two bridges and destroyed a mercenary garrison in a fortified village. From our frequent raids, we had confiscated machine guns, sten-guns and explosives. Pola beamed with pride.

"Anton would be very pleased with the work you're doing!" Our commander had told us on one occasion. We remembered our friend and hero and secretly called ourselves "Anton's Brigade."

Sensing an opportunity, the Soviet command ordered a counter-offensive in the Istra sector. The initial reconnaissance was carried out by a relatively small combat team; riflemen, tanks, and supporting weapons rolled at dusk through the forest toward the bridgehead in German-held territory. The soldiers were dressed in white and could not be seen by the Germans. The thick layers of snow camouflaged motor noises.

From my lookout point, on elevated terrain near the village of Stepankovo, I was able to observe the drama below. Our unit was waiting for an opportunity to present itself. Now, a Russian spearhead tank neared the lonely village. The Soviet first lieutenant, the tank commander, stood in the turret warming himself in the hot air rising from the motor cowl. He communicated with the crew in a subdued voice.

Suddenly, a figure appeared from the shadow of a hut. Trampling to warm his cold feet, the Nazi trooper neared the tank. "Halt! Wer kommt da! Stop! Who goes there!?" His voice must have droned lazily.

Silently humming, the tank turret swung around, until the muzzle of the cannon pointed directly at the first building. Radio communication from tank to tank must have followed. "Fire!" The overwhelming noise drowned out the sound of the lieutenant's side-arm as it felled the inquisitive sentry.

Flames roared through the wooden structures. Confused soldiers dressed in shirts and socks tumbled over one another as they ran through the snow to reach the safety of the forest, only to run straight into our position and be mowed down by our relentless machine gun fire. They cried for mercy, their hands high in the air, but our orders were explicit: "Take no prisoners!"

An entire division staff had been taken by surprise. The Russians unleashed everything they had; even antiaircraft took part in the assault. Huts which had served as munition dumps exploded with devastating noise. "What a waste!" I heard Pola say. "We could have certainly found better use for all that ammunition!"

Only a quarter of an hour later, as suddenly as the destruction had begun, silence set in. The tank commander must have radioed the news of the breakthrough to his superiors. The Soviets were on the move.

13

Although the Nazi supply and engineering units spent every short wintry daylight hour repairing the roads, the heavily loaded supply columns were hopelessly rooted in knee-deep snow, sleet and mud. The Nazi front line units suffered their first lack of provisions in the course of a campaign. Potatoes were served three times daily. Many a commander and general ate millet day after day, while the fully loaded supply columns were unable to move forward or backward. Air supply was out of the question because the airfields resembled the roads.

I had known now for some time that *Feldwebel* Boost's supply unit was part of the Armored and Infantry troops whose lines we had orders to infiltrate and sabotage. Would it be too much of a coincidence for us to meet in combat? I shuddered at the thought, and I prayed we wouldn't. It had gotten so that I began to imagine Boost's fate, and each passing day I could feel his presence ever nearer.

Boost and his companions must have dug in underground and in caves at the forest edges. Only a small blue smoke spiral between the pine tops betrayed to us the nest of twelve to fifteen men, tightly pressed together around an improvised tin stove, freezing in semi-darkness. Had not Boost's feet been previously dried, they would have hung from his body like two ice blocks.

I knew him well, my friend Ernst Boost. How he must have agonized over the fresh supplies of ammunition, fuel, the daily food rations, and winter clothing which were stored in the wagons, ready for distribution, but he dared not guess when the roads would be passable again.

Besides, it had become increasingly more difficult to deliver supplies. Though they labored indefatigably, the ranks of the Supply Company had been decimated in their effort to bring provisions to their embattled comrades. The foxholes were difficult to spot because of the incessantly falling snow. Moreover, the moving supply men were easily picked off by Siberian marksmen up front and our own men in the rear.

I knew the kind of person he was, anguishing over the loss of his best men without evidence that the lines had been supplied, I imagined Boost to have been desperate. All that was left him now, was a detachment of replacements, boys in their late teens at most. It seemed like only yesterday, I heard him say to me me that this was "no war for children." And when I had asked whether this was how grown-ups were supposed to act, to serve as role models for children, he smiled, shook his head sadly, and replied: "Grown-ups lacking in maturity are much more dangerous than children."

I was beginning to understand. The citizens of an invaded country took up arms to defend their native land; theirs was the strength of a people pushed to the limit. And in their strong resolve, they were aided by the perfect whiteness of nature, which rendered the enemy impotent.

Driven by my great concern, I shuddered with an eerie foreboding that, his patience exhausted, Boost swung a large sack of provisions over his shoulder, shouted some last-minute orders to his second in command, Cpl. Walter Nagel, and ran. For some time, I followed the dark spot, as he moved swiftly from one fox-hole to another.

"The fool, Boost." I whispered to Roman trembling. "It must be him." I spied the moving target through my field glasses, and actually hoped that he might succeed.

"Give me those glasses." Roman strained his eyes into the vastness of the white horizon. "Can't really tell." He avoided my searching eyes, and I knew he lied.

"It must be him." I insisted. "Who else would care enough or be this foolhardy?"

Roman did not argue my logic, and I knew he agreed.

"Every German you pick off will break the morale of at least ten others," I heard Sgt. Ivan Schepiloff instruct his Siberian sniper unit which had joined us earlier in the task of disrupting the invader's communications. His men were well trained and well equipped. They wore white snowsuits, impregnable fur-lined boots, and spread destruction with high-powered deer rifles.

From behind a fir tree, Schepiloff slowly raised his rifle to his shoulder. "Now, aim right," he murmured to himself, "and squeeze off slowly. We've both got our duty to perform." He repeated stubbornly as he squeezed the trigger mechanism. The shot resounded and echoed through the vast white fields. I looked at the distant spot, as he hesitated, took a few more steps, then stumbled slowly through the snow where he lay still.

"Good Lord! I thought silently. Boost is dead. Goodbye, my dear friend!" I whispered under my breath. There were no tears left me to cry, though I was deeply affected by what I saw.

It was bitter cold outside; there was a howling wind blowing, but I didn't feel the freeze. My eyes remained peeled on that distant spot of a dead or dying man, who would soon become part of the frozen landscape.

To Sgt. Schepiloff, the dark spot signified another dead invader. Only I knew to mourn my friend Ernst Boost. "Some day," I murmured to myself,

"I must carry your message to your wife and children and tell them how good a man you were." I made a solemn promise.

Hours had gone by. I knew that Boost's men must have strained their eyes into the immense whiteness, hoping to see his familiar silhouette returning as he did so many times before. This time, he would not return.

Cpl. Nagel was one of the many who stood, weapons ready to fire, guarding the precious corduroy road leading to the village of Mussino. Around them there was nothing except loneliness and cold. The visibility was less than ten meters and except for the sporadic firing, everything was quiet. Nagel must have thought about Boost. His feet began to freeze, and he walked in place to keep them warm. Occasionally a branch broke. He listened. The dark forest was silent and Nagel must have had the feeling he was being watched by a thousand eyes. Should he have given the alarm? One signal would have called the relief men who sat in the earth hole warming themselves around a small fire. But an experienced soldier gives the alarm only when there is a definite cause. Two hours of guard duty passed in constant tension. He looked forward to warming up a little by the fire and dozing off in a light slumber before his turn came up again.

On the following morning, the fog lifted at hours after a misty dawn and permitted a clear view of the frosty winter scenery. A group of SS officers stood on a ridge nearby at the observation post of their battery. The edge of a wood ran along a distance of three thousand meters, vanishing into the horizon. Plain fields, kilometers in width, stretched between the ridges and the forest, with a few dark brown bushes here and there. Grain stubble and some sharp furrows shone through the light snow ceiling. The sun gradually climbed higher. One of the Nazi regiments was to push toward the north and situate itself behind the main line ready for the attack.

Young Nagel joined the SS officers at the observation point and must have felt proud and important. Eager to impress his fierce companions, the youthful noncom was especially watchful.

The enemy's movement was easy to follow. Our unit was situated no more than a few hundred meters from the SS observation post. Suddenly, I saw sixty to seventy horsemen appear in the direction of the intended attack. The Nazis fired a few artillery shots at them, and they disappeared into the woods. The SS had apparently expected the riders, and no special significance would be attributed to their movement north. The village of Porfinikovo was on the right of the observing officers. It had already been the showplace of heavy infantry battles and was once again under Soviet fire.

As if from nowhere, four Russian tanks appeared. They drove directly at their target. Only once did they stop short to form a small circle. The SS observers on the ridge must have asked themselves why their concealed tank howitzers and antitank guns on the edge of the village held their fire.

Indeed, no infantry followed the rolling and continually firing steel giants, but penetration seemed imminent. However, behind the guns and cannons stood battle-proven SS who had previously destroyed several tanks at point blank range. Their steel ruins nearby served as weird reminders of the encounter. With sudden fury, the lead tank exploded into black smoke. Then, the three remaining steel boxes were hit. Slowly they burned out. I could see none of the crew leaving the flaming structures.

There was total silence. While all attention was still directed at the quick skirmish, I heard a sudden command to the north not far from where I was. I spotted a considerably large number of horsemen, who soon disappeared behind the frost-covered trees. Orders must have been given. Salvos exploded. Soon, the Siberian riders reappeared three thousand meters in front of the village line. First, there were a few, then fifty, one hundred, three hundred horsemen. New masses broke from right and left, from east to west.

"Damn!" Zbyszek exclaimed gritting his teeth. "I don't believe it! The idiots are going to attack on this wide open parade ground!"

Nevertheless, with unbelievable speed, the horsemen formed skirmish lines one after another and then a third rank from the rear. The last file set far off from the woods, broke off to the left, and galloped southward.

I rubbed my eyes in disbelief. It was an indescribably beautiful picture, the bright winter landscape and a cavalry regiment in a full charge; stirrup on stirrup, the horsemen bent deep in the saddle wielding glittering sabers.

The Mongol storms seemed to have returned. The small, black, shaggy animals with the saddle-grown Asiatics impetuously streamed into the Occident. "The poor devils," Zbyszek murmured once again, "at least then they had an even chance. Those were the days!" His contemplation was suddenly interrupted by Pola's voice: "The fools are begging for it! They'll be smashed to bits!"

Indeed, the German batteries fired from open firing positions. We stood by helpless, watching, as their projectiles blended with the red fire-trailing shells of antitank weapons. From the village south of the advance SS position, all barrels were blasting. A single cloud barrier of exploding shells hovered over the oncoming cavalry squadrons. The charge did not falter. In that mass of fire an inexplicable right turn was completed, and the spearhead of the regiment stormed into the open side of the horse-shoe shaped village.

At the head of the advancing horsemen was Sgt. Schepiloff. His squad was headed straight at the embankment position under Feldwebel Nagel's command. The horsemen were no further than fifty meters from the embankment when the terrified sergeant shouted "*Feuer!*"

This was no mirage of the past. The small black creatures stained the · snow. Animal guts spilled on dying riders.

"My God!" I exclaimed. "They've gone stark mad." I looked on at the unspeakable spectacle, and my soul wept while my eyes were dry. "It wasn't enough for man to kill his own species," I thought to myself, "now he was taking out his rage on innocent animals as well."

I experienced a vivid recollection of my grandmother's teachings; in my early youth, she had told me a curious story about the redemption of the earth and all of its inhabitants. It was to come about at that moment when sworn enemies mix their blood in mortal combat and give up their souls for the well-being of all.

"At the very center of this tale lies the idea that a spiritual and universal Being rules and permeates the world," my grandmother said, "and that man's finite spirit is capable of being flooded with His light and goodness. The world of nature and man is His temple as well as His handiwork. . ."

My grandmother's tale was developing before me, as I watched the carnage from my observation post, I thought: is this to be a sign of God's great wisdom?

The earth had already soaked up the blood of the adversaries Anton Niedola and Ernst Boost, as they lay somewhere, fixed into the frozen horizon. The next victim of that sacrificial ritual was about to forfeit his life, as I watched him lead the cavalry charge against the fortified SS battery. There he was, Sgt. Schepiloff, atop his small Siberian charger, up front, wielding his saber wildly at the entrenched enemy ahead.

I heard the staccatto sound of the air-cooled machine-gun, rat-ta- ta-ta, rat-ta-ta-ta, and I knew that Nagel must have squeezed the trigger. There must have been a strange fascination for the Feldwebel to command so much power, as his forefinger kept on pressing the hot metal more fiercely than he had probably wished to. He must have felt an ineffable joy deep in his proud heart. He was doing all this for his *Vaterland*.

The rapid fire of Nagel's men unseated many, but the momentum of the attack carried the remainder into their midst. "Death to the dogs!" Schepiloff s saber cut a startled Nagel's neck from one shoulder to the other. There was no time for the German to shout with pain. Only the eyes carried the mark of terror as the head rolled into the snow. Instantly, Schepiloff was caught by an enemy bullet. His shaggy little horse ran a little while longer, without direction.

The German artillery organized into an effective cross fire. Horses flew through the air and fell to the ground torn to shreds. Horsemen whirled one on another. The leadership was lost. The animals, wild in the exploding hell, galloped in all directions, crowding together in their terror, trampling everything living, dying and already dead under their hoofs. The few riders who had managed to stay in the saddle, disappeared in the concentrated mass. Artillery kept on hitting mercilessly into the havoc, and with the added devastation of antitank shells, the last vestige of an attack crumbled to bits.

Into this terror a second cavalry regiment charged bravely from the same point of the forest. It seemed weird and incredible that the same spectacle would be repeated after the bloody defeat of an entire regiment. The distance and the direction of the attack was well known from the previous encounter and full annihilation proceeded even faster. Thirty riders, led by an officer with a high-raised saber on a beautiful fast horse, almost reached the village as the only survivors of the nearly thousand men. They fell attempting a valiant leap over the gun emplacements.

The white, snow-covered plains, empty and calm an hour ago, were a red-spotted winding sheet on which numerous dark dots lay moving jerkingly; others lay still, very still. The exhausted little Cossack horses came toward the edge of the wood into the village and near the machine-gun ridge. The high saddles were empty. Here and there, I saw a few cavalry men crawl strenuously to seek cover, and a few in shock wandered about the area aimlessly until picked off by the SS sharpshooters.

That which thirty minutes earlier had come roaring up in a thunderous charge, lay shattered in the hail of shells. A deep stillness had come over the battlefield. Silently, we observed the destruction. As if compelled by a secret impulse, we raised our hands in a final salute to valiant men. Through the silence, we were able to hear the sound of sharp orders as the SS regiment began the attack.

The last of the three adversaries lay dead, yet there was no peace in sight. Was my grandmother's story another falsehood or a fantasy? Was I to go on believing any of the tales of my childhood days or were they all a delusion, a figment of my laboring imaginagion?

Inconspicuous as it may have seemed, the skirmish at Mussino had marked a new turn in the battle for the Soviet capital. We received orders to intensify insurgence activity in the area. As a consequence, the attack of the Fourth and Third Panzergruppen had been halted and the Germans took up defensive action. The offensive of the two Panzergruppen northwest of Moscow had drawn all available Soviet forces from the west front to the defense of Moscow. The Russians added to these new forces all the seemingly inexhaustible reserves of manpower of their giant land.

I remembered well the promise the *Führer* had made to his troops each time Christmas neared. And like in the past, our radio picked up the characteristic broadcast on the eve of the holy day, introduced by all the fanfare of Wagnerian music and visited by all of the national glory of the Thousand Year Reich:

"*Nächste Weihnachten sind wir zu Hause!*" The *Führer* shouted into the frozen landscape: "We'll be home, come next Christmas!" And the background music was drowned out by the shouting, hysterical tribute of the faithful: "*Sieg Heil! Sieg Heil!*" While the orchestras continued to play their happy marching tunes. . .

14

Hayim vaguely remembered Roman's admonition as he climbed over the compound fence. The next thing he heard was Jerzyk's hushed voice coming at him from the dark.

"Hayim? Is that you, Hayim?"

"It's me," the boy replied, still trembling.

"Over here! Quickly! Over here!" Jerzyk urged the hesitant boy. "Come on! Don't be afraid, Hayim!"

"I'm not afraid." Hayim quickly approached Jerzyk's shadow.

Jerzyk sought reassurance in Hayim's composure. They ran, catching their breaths only after every fifth leap.

The Skowrons received the fugitive with open arms. They were decent people and they tried to make him feel at home. Jerzyk—Hayim's senior by two years—had become his constant companion, playing games, talking seriously like grownups. Hayim had a hard time adjusting to the life of a fugitive. He was permitted outdoors only briefly at night. His days had all been marked by fear, vigilance, and confinement.

"Soon, my son, soon you'll be free." Mrs. Skowron had often tried to encourage the boy. She called him "son," for she treated him no different than her own. "The Nazis are retreating, and we ought to see the Russians here any day now. All this will pass like a dark cloud."

"What about my family?" Hayim asked. "What about my father? Who'll liberate him? And what about the rest of my people?"

"Nothing we can do about your daddy, son." Mrs. Skowron said, holding back her tears. "Rest his soul, he's with the Almighty now."

"My father would rather be here with me." The boy said stubbornly. "But they killed him. I'll never forgive them!"

"Don't ever forget what they've done!" Mr. Skowron said. "Don't you forgive either!"

"For as long as I'll live! I swear!" The boy pledged.

"Anyway, you're the lucky one," Jerzyk interjected, "you got out sooner than the others."

"Even a day in prison is a day too long." Hayim suddenly whispered as if to himself. They marveled about the teenager's uncommon wisdom. Skowron gave his wife a meaningful look with a nod of his head. Hayim wanted to go on and tell them exactly how he felt, but he didn't speak for fear he would hurt the Skowron's feelings. He knew how difficult life had been for them since his arrival. He would not make trouble for them.

There were spying, inquisitive eyes everywhere; eyes created and nurtured by wars alone. Hayim would wait. He had learned to wait. He would not jeopardize the safety of his benefactors. And in his solitude, he wondered about the world.

He remembered vividly his early childhood, the sights and sounds of Piotrkow, especially the *Yidn Gass,* the Jewish Street, where he was born to an honorable family of the town's *khozon,* thecantor. How he had loved to listen to his father's resonant voice during religious services! He sat up front, in the seat especially reserved for the *khozon's* family, and even as a small boy he would hum the liturgy along with his father's delivery.

The family gatherings at their Sabbath dinner, the relatives' get-together on high holidays, those were the moments etched in Hayim's memory, now a boy of thirteen, contemplating the end of his world. Too, there were memories of the tenement houses where everyone knew the other, friend or foe; where the elderly would congregate in the large yard for an evening of chess or dominoes to the incessant kibitzing of a gathering of "experts." Hayim's was an orthodox upbringing, and his life was tranquil and full of colorful simplicity.

It was intoxicating, inhaling the picant fragrances emanating from the grocery store of Zalman Fusslavski on *Yidn Gass.* The most exotic spices hung there from the ceiling; garlic garlands, dried mushrooms and prunes. There were open sacks of beans, barley, salt and sugar, and many items he no longer remembered, but for the fact that they had made his mouth water each time he would pass.

He closed his eyes and visualized all those things and places. He could almost feel their presence. His very favorite was Pinhas Slatnik's bakery. What he would give for one whiff of the sweet aroma of freshly baked bread! Eagerly, each day he would wait to run the errand and fetch the bread from Slatnik's bakery. Mr. Slatnik, a kind old man, would reward him with a freshly baked roll, still steaming in his tender hand as he eagerly devoured it before returning home.

Oftentimes, he had accompanied his mother Malke on her frequent grocery trips. He carried the basket and listened to his mother's bargaining with the store owner, regardless of the price. Bargaining was a way of life; part of being thrifty. He was proud of his mother's ability to economize. After all, whatever change she had saved from her grocery moneys would become his allowance for the week, a kind of reward for his good work. Truly, his mother was a "queen" in her own rights; that was the meaning of the Hebrew word *malke.* Each time he remembered, he felt a profound guilt, for when the Gestapo had taken her on that freight train with all of the others, he had no time to tell her how much he loved doing all the things they had done together.

The many distant voices of the vendors extolling their wares along the walkway resounded in Hayim's imagination. There were all kinds of men and women cruising the streets. Vendors, junk dealers, fish mongers, the ever-present street musicians and, to be sure, charlatans and thieves.

Hayim was surrounded by love, learning early to be content with the things he had been given, never asking for more, and always remembering to be charitable.

There was the colorful figure of the water carrier. A man whose back had been bent with the weight of two pails of water attached to each end of the yoke, as he regularly delivered the precious liquid to households. For they had no other source of water but for the distant well on the outskirts of the shtetl.

Misty-eyed, Hayim looked back to his happy childhood to find solace and strength as he was preparing for the worst. They were all gone. Dearly loved ones, friends and all that once signified a community of people bound by ancient ties of tradition and customs that had endured for millenia. He looked back, and his only regret was that he was left all by himself, with no one to accompany him on this difficult journey. "I should have gone with them," he whispered sadly, "I shouldn't have tried the impossible. No one can hide from these monsters for very long." He knew what was coming, and he readied himself with formidable resolve.

Even though precautions had been taken, Hayim's presence in the Skowron household could not remain a secret forever. Out for a walk, Jerzyk was often confronted by some of his friends: "Why can't we come by to see you at your place anymore?" They asked. "You find excuses to keep us away nowadays. What's the matter, Jerzyk?"

"Maybe the Skowrons are hiding some Jews? Eh, Jerzyk? Maybe you're getting good money for keeping a Jew?"

When his friends talked like that, Jerzyk would swing wildly. They respected his fists and ran, but at a safe distance, they stopped and yelled: "Jew-lover! Jew-protector!" They mimicked the walk of a Hasid, laughing and pushing each other in the middle of the street as if attacking a Jew. "Say, Jerzyk! Maybe you're one of them?!" He made a gesture as if he were to pursue them, and they ran off, yelling back: "*Jude! Jude!*"

Jerzyk turned from them, hiding his face in his hands, nearing tears. None of the accusations had stung him more painfully than that of being paid for providing Hayim's sanctuary. He would keep the encounter to himself. He saw the great fear in Hayim's eyes every waking day, and he would not add anxiety to his friend's labored existence.

Hayim's world became a make-believe. Whenever guests came calling on the Skowrons, he hid in the confinement of the tiny shelter built for him behind a false cupboard wall. There, he would eavesdrop on the mysterious discussions. The visitors spoke about politics and the world situation; some of it he was unable to understand, some was all too obvious. Sunday's visit of the Pogodnys was no different.

"Another execution this morning in the market place, eh?" Mr. Pogodny said.

"Do we know the poor devil?" Mr. Skowron asked.

"Moshkowitz, the tailor. You remember, the one from *Ulica Zielna*. They finally found his hiding place near the old ritual bath."

"Poor man! Didn't have a chance!" Mr. Pogodny said. "With the prize on every Jew's head, they haven't got a prayer!" Hayim understood all too well the reference to the "prize," and he wondered how much longer it would be before they found him too.

"We had no idea old Mr. Moshkowitz was in hiding!" Mrs. Skowron's voice was full of sadness. "He was last seen being loaded onto the freight train along with his family. You know, the train that went East!" She added with a meaningful nod.

"He must have gotten off somewhere along the route."

"But why would he return here? It was a clear giveaway."

"He came home. This is the only familiar place. It was his home, where all his friends were."

"His friends. . . and enemies." Mrs. Skowron remarked.

"Seems like the Gestapo gets their Jews sooner or later," Mrs. Pogodny continued. "They say, the tailor's contact failed to deliver for six days, and when the Jew's food ran out, he took the risk. He was caught before turning the corner."

"By one of *ours* at that!"

"If only Tuviah were here," Hayim thought in his hideout. "His father's dead, and there's no one left to say kaddish for the old tailor."

"Hah! We always had a better nose for detecting the Jew than the Gestapo." Mr. Pogodny added with a sense of pride. The others were silent. He chuckled embarrassed while getting up to leave.

It was early spring, and Hayim had been languishing in the confinement of the cupboard for over two months. Soon, it would be Passover, the first he would spend away from all of his loved ones. Even last year, they had managed to observe the holiday in the ghetto. A deep sense of grief and great loss pervaded his whole being. . .

. . .the family was seated around the seder table: his father, the *khozon*, made certain all of the objects prescribed by tradition, which symbolize the spirit of the festival, were in their proper place. His mother, Malke, as always, was the very soul of the seder. She had made all the preparations, at great personal sacrifice. No one would know how she had come by the roasted egg or the *kharoses*, the parsley or the lettuce. Hayim alone knew why his mother had pinned up her raven hair in a neat bun at the nave of her neck. It was to conceal the missing gold earrings which she had bartered away for the food they were about to consume. He knew, because he witnessed the curious transaction.

"We are about to begin the recitation of the ancient story of Israel's redemption from bondage in Egypt." The *khozon* recited in his resonant voice. "And thou shalt tell thy son in that day, saying: It is because of that which the Lord did for me when I came forth out of Egypt." Then, the seder leader went on to explain the symbols of Passover, and when Hayim's turn had come, as the youngest of those present, he asked the four questions.

"*Mah neesh-ta-noh ha-lai-loh ha-zeh mee-kol ha-lay-lot?*—Why is this night of Passover different from all other nights of the year?" He now recalled that it had taken his father, the *khozon*, the whole night to explain the wonder of the exodus from Egypt and the defeat of Pharaoh, smitten by the mighty hand of the Lord our God. Following that, they ate the traditional foods, symbols of the struggle for human freedom, and they retold the ancient story of Israel's liberation from oppression in Egypt. And they sang "it is enough. . . *dayenu*. . ."

As he sat in the darkness of his hideaway, Hayim was gripped with uncontrollable sobs, trying to come to terms with a situation similar to that which he had only known through the annually retold story of Passover; a situation beyond his control. This very moment, in Jewish homes everywhere they said: "It is enough. . . *dayenu*. . ."

"Why have I been left alone in this dismal hole to perish by myself?" He asked himself. "Abandoned by God and men? And if I am to perish, so must mankind, and so will God as well!" Hayim's very soul shouted the challenge. He knew he blasphemed, but he couldn't help the flow of his thoughts. They had entered his mind like a forceful flood whose tide he was unable to stem no matter how hard he tried fighting the blasphemy of his rage.

He tried in vain to reason with himself, but the grief for all that which could not be undone was far greater than his capacity to reason. "If You are there, dear God," he murmured to himself, "then You must know that I am so dismally ignorant about those precious things all youth experiences in the course of time. Am I to be denied the daily walks to school? The joys of learning, sharing, and remembering? The excitement of a soccer game with my schoolmates? The mystery of first love, its ecstasy and pain? The joys and misery of life's circumstances?" Hayim sobbed bitterly, and his small body shook helplessly. "Why won't You let me learn about life itself, dear Lord? Am I not too young to die?" He asked.

"What is it, Hayim, my son?" He heard the concern in Mrs. Skowron's voice. He was startled and momentarily incapable of replying. "Come now, dear boy, take a hold of yourself! You mustn't carry on this way," she continued, "someone might hear. We must be careful!" She cautioned. He took hold of himself. He dried his eyes and cheeks with his shirt sleeve, and now he was composed.

"It's nothing, mama Skowron," he assured her. "Only, it's so dark and lonely in here. I wish I could come out into the fresh air for a while, play in the yard and look at the skies and the sun." He pleaded with the woman and she was unable to resist the small plaintive voice of the frail prisoner. Jerzyk interceded in behalf of his friend, and Mrs. Skowron yielded, allowing the boy to play in the nearby yard. "All right," she admonished, "but only for a little while. We can't be too careful!" She knew it was against her better judgment, but she couldn't help herself, "blessed Madonna, Mother of God of *Ostra Brama*, protect us all." She prayed under her breath, and made three times the sign of the cross.

The yard was around the corner, and ran directly into the deadend alley, terminating at the old deserted brewery. Hayim was fascinated by the mysterious, abandoned location. He had a glimpse of it once from the window of the Skowron's living room, and he had felt that it was waiting there for him to be be explored and conquered. If only he could conquer his own fear first.

The day seemed ideal for an exploratory excursion. The sun was shining brightly. There was that certain tentative warmth in theair; a sign of renewal. As he strolled through the yard, he spied a solitary wildflower, growing, as it seemed out of the hardness of a rock. "It's astonishing," he thought to himself, "how so many lovely things survive even in the midst of a catastrophe."

As he walked through the yard, Hayim felt at peace. He had made up his mind to leave the Skowrons that night. There was no reason for him to jeopardize their safety. He knew he had overstayed his welcome.

"There he is! There is the Jew!" Someone suddenly shouted in Polish, and the boy heard booted footsteps all around.

"Oh, my Lord! Merciful God! They've come for me!" He exclaimed in Yiddish, gripped with fear.

Across the yard, he recognized Jerzyk's schoolmate ahead of two Gestapo men and and group of Lithuanian mercenaries. A crowd of onlookers gathered. Some were delighted with the spectacle, others protested: "Let them finish with the lot of them! Filthy Jews! Serves them right!"

"But he's only a boy! Look at him, how frightened he is!"

"He'd only grow up to be a lousy thief! To steal us blind!"

"I still say it's wrong to kill helpless children."

"Jew-lover!"

That last remark silenced the protestors.

One of the Gestapo agents was interrogating a pedestrian, while the other ran after the fleeing Hayim in the far corner of the yard. At first, the boy turned calmly to go, but now frightened by the shouting mercenaries, he panicked and ran.

"*Jude! Jude! Halt!*"

"*Verflucht nochmal! Bleib stehen!*"

"Damn you! Stop or I'll shoot!" Shots resounded through the hollow space of the yard. Voices shouted curiously. "A Jew! A Jew! There he goes!"

Hayim ran straight into the dead end of the merciless wall of the old brewery. There, panting and urinating down his legs, he tried to pray but no words came. A small crowd gathered to observe the ritual. Those who looked on, saw one of the Lithuanian SS reach the diminutive boy. It had become breathtakingly quiet. Hayim tripped and fell awkwardly. The guard pulled him up by the crop of his hair, then looked toward his superior at the far end. There was a scarcely perceptible nod. The mercenary put the barrel of his Luger to Hayim's head and pulled the trigger.

Hayim is the Hebrew word for "life."

Piotrków, Poland, ca. 1914.
A family portrait of Vilek's paternal
roots. *Standing, from left to right:*
Uncle (by marriage) Haskiel,
Aunt Rachel (his wife), Aunt Yita,
and Aunt Rifka. *Seated, from left
to right:* Henryk (Vilek's father),
grandmother Faygel, grandfather
Hayim, and great-grandfather
Velvel.

Sosnowiec, Poland, ca. 1939.
From left to right: Roman, Felusia,
and Vilek.

Vilek's father, Henryk (seated), September or October 1939, leaving for the Eastern front.

Survivors of Kolditz Concentration Camp. Borna Municipal Hospital, June, 1945.

Six months after liberation, with nurse Trude, Borna Municipal Hospital, October, 1945.
The German physicians were astonished. Hair appeared and grew on our once clean-shaven skulls. Gone were the protruding bony features of our palid faces.

15

When the weather improved enough to travel, our partisan unit had received orders to move into the region of Biala Podlaska. On our way there, we begged Pola's permission to digress into the Piotrkow area. We wished to pay a quick visit to the Skowrons, hoping Hayim would join our unit in the woods.

Yossele and Roman came along for the ride. We left our horses in the thick of the forest, and traveled on foot. On our arrival there, we were met by Mrs. Skowron, who tearfully recounted the sad events of the past few days.

"You ask who could have denounced him?" she sobbed. "Nowadays there are so many informers in these parts, it's difficult to tell." She wiped her cheeks and blew her nose loudly. "Besides, the reward they pay for a Jew's life is more tempting each day, what with the shortage of food supplies and the Nazis confiscating the yield of our farms and our hard labor." She broke out into more sobs.

We left the Skowrons at nightfall with promises to return. Jerzyk hitched up the only carriage left them to take us into the countryside without attracting attention. From there, we were on our own.

"Go with God," he whispered as we hugged, "I can't tell you how sorry I am about Hayim. And they didn't even let us bury him!" His eyes filled with tears, and we left quickly, not to allow him to carry on any further.

"We know, Jerzyk." I said, pressing him to myself. "We know." Jerzyk let us off at the edge of the great Piotrkow forest. I looked back, till Jerzyk disappeared in the distance.

"Let's get the horses!" I said. "We've got some unfinished business here!" We mounted up. The others followed me without question.

"I remember the days when the forest laughed and the trees were singing." Yossele said.

"Ah, but that was so long ago." Roman remarked with sadness. "In another time; another life."

"The berries we gathered here." I reminisced.

"And the mushrooms! Basketfuls of them!" Yossele exclaimed.

We rode without fear, and we talked without looking over our shoulders. Only the trees whispered to us tales of sadness and terror; revealing human anguish beyond compare.

I put my hand into the left coat pocket. I touched the rough metallic surface of the two pineapple grenades. I cocked the trigger mechanism of my Luger. "We're ready." I thought to myself, and none too soon, because there stood Yurek Brama's cabin in a clearing no further than fifteen yards.

We dismounted. Roman covered the east side of the cabin; Yossele went around the back. I walked toward the front entrance. There was no sound of dogs.

The cabin was in great disarray, but there was evidence of recent habitation. "He must be making his rounds." I thought. I called the others inside.

"He's gone for now." I said.

"We'll wait." Roman said. There was a look of steel in his eyes. I sat at the wooden table in the middle of the room. "Nora was sitting here not so long ago." I thought. Roman and Yossele crouched against the wall behind the entrance door.

We heard the dogs from the distance. "He's coming." I said in a hushed voice.

Yossele chuckled. "Very obliging, he didn't let us wait too long." At first sight of a stranger facing him with a luger pointed at his belly, Yurek turned to run. Yossele shut the door behind him with the flat of his foot, leaving the dog outside. The animal barked loudly, sensing danger.

"Tell the monster to shut up!" Roman ordered. Yurek complied stuttering, and the animal walked off to the doghouse.

"Well, well, what have we got here?" I pointed at Yurek's black uniform. "A regular Hitler's militia."

"And a nice swastika on the sleeve." Yossele cut the armband off Yurek's sleeve and held it up for us to see.

"We've come to see Nora." I said. "You remember Nora, the Jewess?"

"We've heard she lived here a while back." Roman said. "Did you know her, Yurek?" The forester's face turned ashen.

"I. . . I. . . d-d-didn't know a-a-any one b-b-by that n-n-name." Yurek stuttered incredibly.

"Hey, relax." I said. "No reason to get excited. Here, come, sit down." I pointed to a chair across the table. Yurek obeyed. He seemed calmer.

"So you didn't know any Jewess by that name, eh?" Yossele played with his pistol. "You know what we do with liars?" he smiled cynically. "We do even worse to traitors." At the mention of that word, blood seemed to have left Yurek's face completely. He sat speechless, terrified, breathing with great difficulty. He spoke calmly now, catching his breath in intervals.

"They killed her," he looked down to the floor. "They came, took her away and killed her."

"Who's 'they,' Yurek?" Roman asked.

"You know, the Nazis. They took and killed her."

"And you had nothing to do with her death?" I asked.

"Nothing, no nothing. They did it." He repeated.

"You're a lying bastard!" Roman shouted.

"And a fucking collaborator!" Yossele added.

"We all know about you, Yurek." I said calmly. "They said in town, you couldn't keep it a secret; how you betrayed her and then bought everybody drinks at the pub."

"How much did they give you for the Jewess, Yurek?" Yossele asked, his knife at the forester's throat.

"I-I d-d-don't re-re-remember." Yurek lost his composure.

"Well then, I'll refresh your memory." Yossele ran the blade across the forester's face, drawing blood. At the feel of his own blood, Yurek got down on his knees, weeping like a child, begging for mercy. The sight of this grown man begging for his life brought on a feeling of pity somewhere deep inside me. Yurek suddenly lay on the floor in terrible convulsions emitting inarticulate sounds and shaking like a leaf.

"Let me put an end to his miserable life!" Yossele suggested. I was trying to think what Nora would have wanted us to do. I could not imagine she'd want us to carry the memory of this animal on our conscience. Roman approached the prostrate Yurek. The latter was now completely motionless.

"I think he's dead." Roman put his fingers to the forester's throat.

"I can feel no pulse." My brother got up. "Let's go."

"Thank you, Nora." I whispered under my breath as we put some distance between us and the forester's cabin.

"The bastard died of fright!" Yossele laughed. "And just when I was looking forward to putting a bullet through his dumb head!" We rode the rest of the way in silence.

We joined our comrades at the new headquarters in an abandoned hut not far from Terespol—a small village on the new Russian border. This was the end of the line as far as the Polish narrow railway gauge would go. On the other side of the border, the wider Russian gauge began.

Our daily reconnaissance revealed that twice weekly, at the Terespol railway depot, freight was transferred from arriving trains to one side of the border or the other. Transports of wounded arrived from the Eastern front, transferred onto an empty train that was waiting on the Polish side to receive them. Transfers were made quickly during the night, not to reveal the Nazi casualties to the watching Poles. From the West, trainloads of fresh supplies of personnel and equipment were arriving. Their transfer would be made in broad daylight, for all to see the might of the Third Reich.

Train arrivals and departures were exceedingly punctual; the pride and joy of Nazi bureaucracy. The transfer was quick and efficient, and the train was on its way within a few hours. An *Einsatzkommando* of the elite SS, under the able command of *Obersturmbannführer* Kurt Willhaus, was head-quartered in nearby Biala Podlaska and charged with station and operations security in the area.

Willhaus was a former assistant master of a secondary school. He was honest, pedantic, painstakingly punctual, and unfailingly loyal to his supe-riors. He demanded the same qualities from his subordinates.

Customarily, a strong detachment of SS was dispatched to the depot moments before the arrival of the trains. The timing was perfect. No sooner did we hear the whistle of the incoming train, than the SS trotted in at double-time into the depot, sten-guns at the ready, taking full charge of the operations.

"We'll keep the SS busy, while you plant the explosives!" Pola instructed the four volunteers. "Lay them along the tracks on both sides. Give it fifteen minutes to blow after the switchover."

To think that four of the most dilligent former Yeshiva scholars, Tuviah, Yacov, Yussuf and Pinkhas, comprised the commando, whose task it was to blow up the enemy transport, was almost like believing in miracles. It was true.

"There's strength in small numbers," Zbyszek remarked. He was now Pola's chief aid, the one in charge of special task forces. "Remember," he instructed the departing four, "the inconspicuous will survive this war, because the enemy pursues the obvious." He paused. "Lay your charges carefully. Pres-sure mines are a delicate business. There's no margin for error!"

"Menasha was right, after all," I whispered to Roman, "the enemy destroys what we had built. Now, we destroy it as well. We are indeed like them!"

"We must fight fire with fire, Vilek," Roman replied, "we do it the best way we know how."

"It's not that simple," I insisted. "Seems like the world has gone mad and we are right at the very center of its madness."

"Trouble with you is that you're taking things too seriously, little brother. You're becoming a regular philosopher." Roman smiled.

"There's hope as long as we're alive and well."

"But. . ."

"There are no 'buts' when you really get down to it." Roman didn't let me go on. "We'll fight the bastards on our terms. We're not strong enough to fight on theirs."

"We're now assassins, too, Roman." I said sadly. "We kill grownups."

"What do you mean?" He was startled by my statement.

"After all, killing is supposed to be the concern of grownups, not of children." I explained, but my explanation only added to his perplexity.

"The Nazis have sworn to kill us all, one after another, if we let them." Roman argued.

"We don't even know who it is we kill any more. . ." I pondered. . ."is there a friend among them?"

"In war there are no friends on the other side, Vilek!" I didn't have to look at Roman's face to see the intensity of hatred burning in his eyes. I knew it was there.

"Yes there are!" I almost shouted, and he knew I meant the likes of Edelmann and Boost.

"Okay. . . okay. . . you don't have to get mad." Roman sounded apologetic. "There aren't too many Edelmanns and Boosts among those bastards."

"If there's only one, that's one more chance for us to survive." I insisted. What really gnawed deep inside me was my awareness that our actions were a contradition to all of our ancestral principles; the ethics of our fathers. It was as though we were peeling off the vestiges of a solid, decent past, one by one, and all that was going to be left us was the crude nucleus of man's primitive nature. . . "honor thy father and thy mother. . ." echoed in the deep recesses of my mind. They, too, were grownups, weren't they?

The commando was leaving. We embraced our friends. "Good bye, Tuviah! Take care, all of you!"

We saw them waving goodbye even as they disappeared in the thick of the woods. If they were frightened, they didn't show it.

When the word came for us to move out, we were ready. The unit split into four groups. To create a diversion, we were to attack the garrison of Lithuanian SS on the outskirts of Biala Podlaska. Shortly after midnight, we approached the compound. All hell broke loose. We attacked with everything at our disposal. We tossed grenades at will, and the shrapnell created havoc among the surprised mercenaries who had come out of their barracks in complete disaray; sleep still clouding their minds. With each explosion, I saw bodies fly through the air, yells of pain mingled with the desperate orders of their superiors.

"Kill them! Kill them!" I kept repeating to myself as I sprayed sub-machine gun fire indiscriminately into the approaching SS. Shouts, curses, pleadings for help, resounded into the din of battle. The enemy must have grasped the hopelessness of his situation, retreating into the safety of the barracks and leaving wounded and dead behind.

Quietly, as we had arrived, we withdrew. Our four comrade ssuccessfully accomplished their mission in Terespol. By that timethe Germans would have called for reinforcements. *Obersturmbannführer* Willhaus' *Einsatzkommando*, aided by a battalion of the 40th SS Panzer Corps, set out in pursuit of our unit at Biala Podlaska. The Nazi railway link between East and West lay destroyed; it would take weeks to make it operable again. Even at a great distance, we could feel the powerful temblor as we eluded the SS.

We had soon realized that it was easier to attract the *Führer*'s elite guard than to get rid of it. Willhaus on our heels, we retreated back to the forest. A large meadow stretched out before us, beyond which lay our camp.

"Look at it, Roman," I whispered, "just like a soccer field, eh?" He seemed worried.

"Be still now, this is no time to have soccer on your mind."

"It's like old times," I tried to humor him, "all that's missing are the two goals."

"If you don't shut your mouth, you might be put to rest on this beautiful meadow." Roman was tense, so were our companions. We crouched in the tall grass, listening. The silence of the meadow and the uncertainty of the forest were frightening. It was too silent, and there was no trace of the enemy, as if the earth had swallowed them up, armor and all.

"Polusia," Zbyszek addressed our leader, "I smell a rat. Let me take a couple of men across the meadow. If they're there, this will smoke them out. If we make it, you'll follow."

Pola nodded. Without further discussion, Zbyszek motioned two men to join him. Cautiously, they stalked through the clearing and without an incident, reached the distant line of the trees. Zbyszek looked back, signaling us to move on.

A few yards into the clearing, we came under cross-fire. "It's an ambush!" Pola yelled. Machine gun rattle came from the direction of the forest line as well as from our flanks. We hit the ground, returning fire at the invisible enemy. Suddenly, all was still again. I felt my stomach turn violently, and fear gripped my mind; a sensation I had experienced on many previous occasions, but none that intense. Two huge Tiger tanks rolled out in front of us.

Many thoughts went through my mind. They've killed Zbyszek and his party. That's it. We haven't got a prayer.

"Let's get out of here!" Pola shouted, but no sooner did we begin to retreat than we heard Willhaus' voice through a megaphone across the clearing:

"Lay down your arms! Come out with your hands above your heads! You are surrounded! You don't have a chance!"

A sustained machine-gun salvo was sprayed above our heads! We lay still, breathing heavily. Menasha's lips kept moving in prayer. I looked around at the others. Fear was in everyone's eyes.

"They want us alive," Roman whispered. "They won't shoot, because we're worth more to them alive than dead."

"We can't win this stinking war all by ourselves," Menasha sudenly said, "but I'd surely like to see the swastika on the run."

"What are we going to do?" I asked.

"Stay here till nightfall. Maybe then. . . under the cover of darkness. . .we'll somehow be able to. . . "

Menasha didn't finish his sentence. Pola suddenly ran toward the invisible enemy, shooting wildly and shouting barely audible abuse. It took only one barrage to fell her. Her fingers convulsively squeezed off the final rounds, and the noise died down while she must have breathed her last breath of life.

A falcon flew overhead, spiraling gracefully in its flight. It seemed an awesome sign to perceive that noble bird at this particular moment. Ancient legend had it that a heroic soul finds a noble body to enter when it leaves its troubled mortal shell. "Could this have been the new home for our departed leader?" I prayed. I was reminded of King David's words which were as appropriate for the present as they had been in the Biblical times: "But now she is dead, wherefore should I fast? Can I bring her back again? I shall go to her, but she will not return to me."

None of us wept. And no one was reciting kaddish. After all, one does not say kaddish for a *shikse*.

Our hands high over our heads, we walked toward the edge of the meadow as directed, expecting the worst. Once there, we were quickly surrounded by the Ukrainian SS who came at us from everywhere, weapons at the ready.

"They don't take any chances, do they?" I whispered to Roman.

"You will be silent, swine!" I felt the butt of the SS man's rifle, and I caved in. "When we've done with you, you'll be sorry we didn't kill you here!" Were it not for Menasha and Roman coming to my aid and dragging me along with them, I might have joined Pola there and then.

We were herded into two large open Wehrmacht trucks, and the convoy was on its way toward Biala Podlaska.

"I envy Hayim and Pola." I whispered knowing that there was no way the enemy could hear. "They're free at last."

"At what prize, Vilek?" Menasha asked. "They're dead, too."

"You call this life?"

"You mustn't talk this way, Vilek. You must have faith." Menasha admonished.

"Faith, in what?"

"In the Almighty, blessed be He." Menasha said.

"I don't know that I can, Menasha." I said softly. "I have compromised more than my share, it's God's turn now."

16

The basement of the Gestapo headquarters in Biala Podlaska became our home. Alternating soft and brutal treatment, the Bureau interrogated us endlessly about our partisan activities, things we had little or no knowledge about. Each day gone by was marked by a hanging of one of our comrades. The people of the little town witnessed each of them. Their deaths only made the rest of us more determined to keep our silence.

Another week went by, and we were on the verge of breaking down. Then came the electrifying news of the Warsaw uprising, injecting renewed vigor and hope into our resistance. Three whole weeks, the Jews fought off several brigades of *Waffen* SS before the ghetto succumbed to hunger, pestilence and the superior fire power of the Nazis.

We had learned about the last days of the Warsaw ghetto from the few survivors who had been brought to the Biala Podlaska camp following the liquidation action. We listened anxiously, eager to hear about our relatives, Uncle Mihas and Aunt Lola, who may have been part of the insurgence.

"No, I don't recall the Stybels." The sad-faced man muttered, annoyed. "Never heard the name Stybel." He sat down in the far corner of the room, steeped in thought. We respected his silence and his great losses.

"See that old man over there?" Roman pointed toward a newly arrived Jew squatting on the floor. His clothes were torn to shreds and his head was covered with dirt. "He's only twenty-nine years old."

"It isn't possible." Menasha shook his head. "He looks more like sixty-five."

"That's what I thought," Roman whispered, "until they told me who he is. You're looking at the celebrated pianist Robert Kadetzki. Remember, he was soloist under Uncle Mihas' baton at the Lazienki Park the day you also performed?"

How could I forget those happy days? Of course, I remembered. Each time Uncle Mihas turned our way, we would wave at him, to the amusement of the first row guests, and Aunt Lola blushed up to her earlobes. "But this can't be the same man, can it?"

"Indeed, little brother," Roman shook his head. "The very same man. Suddenly Kadetzki began to mumble, at first incoherently, then phrases that connected and made sense. We sat around him and listened.

He went on to tell us about the last days of his beloved Warsaw and the extermination camp called Treblinka. "They took her from me, they took my Tania, my dearest, my very own life. I shall never see her again. Why did they leave me to mourn eternally?" He asked, swaying back and forth. There was so much grief.

He paused. His eyes expressed his sadness. Though they were tearless, I could see them weep. He continued, his voice breaking with anguish: "We fought bravely, oh how we fought. In the end, we were overcome by superior forces. But even then, we can say that our hopeless struggle in the Warsaw ghetto will be remembered as far more significant than all of the great battles of this despicable war. While the battlefields influenced its outcome, our Warsaw uprising was a reaffirmation of individual dignity; a turning point in the evolution of mankind."

Kadetzki slumped forward in silence, and I didn't expect him to go on. Just as we turned to leave, his wailing voice called us back.

"I was separated from my wife Tania," he recounted, pronouncing her name with much love and tenderness, "and we never saw each other after the clean-up action started." Kadetzki spoke into the void, as though we didn't exist at all, for he gave no indication that he was aware of our presence. The pain of his experience carried him back, and he pressed his fists tightly to his temples as though to force out the voices of despair. Through circumstances, he had become a "time-capsule," his only purpose was to keep alive the loving memory of his wife Tania.

"Shortly before the final evacuation, all the sick were taken from their homes as well as the hospitals. The elderly had been put in one compound with the children of the orphanage. Almost five hundred people in all. . . five hundred innocent people," he repeated in his monotone voice, ". . . some were shot, others killed by phenol injections." He hesitated, straining. "I wish I were with them, but now I must mourn all of them, I will mourn the whole world which has gone mad!" He stopped, and we waited patiently.

"We were ordered to bury the dead in a mass grave at Okrzej Street. We threw the bodies into the great ditch, while the assassins stood by and took from us what we had found in the victim's belongings. In the end, the survivors were assembled in the old synagogue.

"We prayed all night. At dawn, the Gestapo ordered some of us to be transported to Treblinka. As for those remaining behind, I can only despair."

Menasha's lips were moving rapidly, and we knew he was praying. We recognized the kaddish when we caught the last veimru, and we said "amen" in unison.

"The train transport was dreadful," the man continued, "for those days and nights, we were crammed into the box-cars; children cried and women went insane with grief and worry. It was dawning, when we arrived. There was a glimmer of hope; we saw an inscription at the rail depot printed in bold letters: ARBEITSLAGER TREBLINKA, and we hoped to work for our lives.

"The train pulled onto a spur and then further into the forest, a distance of about three to five kilometers. And there . . ."

The piano virtuoso choked as he continued to sway back and forth, now emitting inarticulate sounds. I had hoped he would go on, as I was anxious for a glimpse into the final hours of our loved ones, but seeing what suffering it had caused the man, I found myself hoping that he would stop tormenting himself. He continued:

"Hundreds of corpses lay in a clearing. Luggage, clothing, and other personal belongings were strewn around among them. Everything was in a state of chaos. The SS used clubs to drive us out of the cars, and while we ran, Lithuanian mercenaries had climbed onto the rooftops and shot volleys of machine gun fire into the frantic crowd. Men, women and children wallowed in their own blood. Desperate, wild screaming filled the air.

"The shooting subsided, and those of us who were still alive were herded through an open gate into a barbed wire area. They assigned us the detail of cleaning the box-cars. When we finished, we lined up the corpses in an orderly file of twos within the enclosed area. The bodies were doused with some strong-smelling substance and set afire. And all along, the SS forced us to work quickly, while they held a bottle of Schnapps in one hand and a club in the other.

"The memory of children held by their feet and slung against tree trunks will haunt me as long as I shall live; I pray not much longer. They beat us time and again, with no apparent reason, except for the pleasure of the SS Commandant and his staff photographers.

"On little food, we were forced to do the most demanding and demeaning work. Each day, several transports arrived, repeating the routine of the previous day. We kept alive on what food we found in the confiscated bundles of the condemned.

"Some transports arrived with corpses ready to be cremated. There were no wounds on their bodies, twisted onto one another, their skin was an icy blue. As if through a miracle, a few three to five-year-old children survived the gassing. Totally deaf, only their eyes expressed terror, for they were unable to speak. We could not hide them from the SS for very long. They took these children to that open area where they had to wait until a transport of the old and the very young would arrive to share their fate.

"From Treblinka, groups of two to five hundred men and women were driven naked through the forest. Row after row, holding hands like children engaged in a macabre dance, they were ordered to the rim of the dredged graves. The SS made a sport of killing those unfortunates by shots to the back of the neck. As the victim fell, the guard applied a hard kick to the body. I heard them argue over who had kicked his victim the farthest.

"There was a small house not far from the forest. On the outside, it looked no different from any other house. Inside, its rooms were laid out with the finest tile. On the trail leading up to that house there was a large sign which read, TO THE BATHS. In the hall, another sign instructed the arrivals to remove all their valuables, such as currency and jewelry, even their eyeglasses, in neat bundles to be collected at the reception window. Persons trying to hide their possessions were beaten half to death. The name of the small house was Barrack X.

"Then, one day, the arrivals were no longer shot. The Nazis had discovered a less costly and more efficient means leading to the Final Solution: gassing.

"I was among those selected to the detail of removing the remains of the cremated. I died each time I saw the new transports arrive, and I died a little more when I helped unload them. I was dead many times over, until there was nothing left of me except what you see before you; an empty shell.

"I keep seeing those hollow, pleading eyes, they won't let me rest, they're all around me. My own eyes have seen too much, and even now, they see the terror. I pray death to come soon, though I am no longer part of this life. And now, let me be, so I may mourn all those I have buried, they command it."

We sat remaining silent for a long time, stunned to the core of our existence. Many had gathered around the narrator, in the hope that he might mention a name of a loved one or an item that would renew their hope. With that last sentence of the narrative, they silently dispersed, each to his own corner. Their eyes were dry; they were unable to weep; they aged as did the narrator.

"It's all gone now, it's all gone," I muttered to myself as I walked away from the "old" man, "there's nothing left for us." It was then, too, that I understood how it was that a young, vibrant person such as the piano virtuoso Robert Kadetzki, could at once be young and aged, sane and insane, alive and yet totally dead.

Unbeknown to us at that time, our lives had been spared because the Nazis were facing a big problem: an acute shortage of laborers in their war industry. Suffering reverses on the Russian front, Hitler was forced to mobilize all able-bodied men and women into the armed forces. That created a void on the assembly lines in the vital production of war material.

"The Nazis must really be desperate." Menasha said. "Else, we wouldn't be alive today."

SS leaders and the executives of I.G. Farben, Krupp, Daimler-Benz, Dynamit Nobel, and some of lesser renown, gathered in the chambers of the *Führer's* personal architect and intimate adviser, Albert von Speer to discuss the labor crisis. On their initiative, slave labor was introduced into the German industry. This cheap labor-producing plan was compatible with the aims of the Final Solution. Soon, the name of the institution for the "liquidation of every real or suspected enemy of the National Socialist State" became a dreaded household word: the K.Z., concentration camp.

Rumor had it that there were three distinct categories of K.Z. We contemplated our chances and hoped to reach an Arbeitslager or work camp, that being the mildest form of punishment. At the worst, we would be willing to settle for the *Straflager*, a punitive, hard-labor camp.

Once again, we were herded into box-cars. This time we traveled west. That much was certain; the way east was to the Russian front. We traveled six days and seven nights. We were permitted out of the boxcars once every twenty-four hours. On those occasions, the train would stop at an isolated place in the darkness of the night where nobody knew or guessed the location. While the train was in motion, the noise in the over-crowded boxcar drowned out all communication. Only when we squatted to relieve ourselves on the occasional stops, we would strike up a conversation. Stammering with the intensity of the freezing temperature, I broke the silence.

"Roman?"

"What is it, little brother?" Roman heard the fear in my voice.

"Where do you think they're taking us?"

"To work, of course, where else?" There was a tremor in Roman's voice.

"You don't sound too sure."

"It's too damned cold to talk, little brother. That's what it is."

"But so many have gone on transports before us, Roman. Where were they taken? No one's ever heard from them again."

"How should I know, Vilek," Roman got up and tied the old worn out piece of rope round his hips to hold up his trousers. "Why don't you quit worrying. Things'll work out somehow. Didn't they till now?" He was anxious to get back to the car. "Besides, we're together, aren't we?" He added as an afterthought.

"Well. . . yes. . . "

"This is not the time to lose faith." Roman was impatient. "Come on. Let's get back or they'll be after us. You heard the whistle."

In the darkness of the box-car, amidst loud, querulous voices, all of our concerns seemed to fade into the background. Not that we had suddenly replenished our confidence. Worry about the future had a hard time surfacing, silenced by more immediate concerns.

There had been a time when going on transport meant almost certain death. I remembered the separation from my mother and Felusia, then my paternal grandparents and most of my aunts and uncles on our mother's side and then on our father's. They, too, were herded into box-cars like these never to be heard from again.

I recalled the ghetto and the almost daily run-ins with the relatives which had been caused by overcrowding rather than by a personal dislike of one sort or another. After all, we were not accustomed to sharing such sparse living quarters which offered neither a measure of privacy nor relief from illness. Soon, this ordeal would end somehow, I thought, it was all a terrible mistake. Then, we would seek a place of our own where life was comfortable and without stress.

Then came the *Stukas* and the Nazi invasion; the minyan for Max Mandel's burial and grandfather Srulko mortally wounded by the Lithuanian sentry. At first, I thought the wound was slight. But he died in my arms; the last of our family to be laid to rest on the old Piotrkow cemetery.

"Thank God, at least we'll know where your grandfather lies buried." My grandmother's words rang in my ears even after considerable lapse of time. But my grandfather's death had taken a heavy toll on the morale of the family.

"Nothing will ever change," my grandmother kept repeating in her subsequent depression.

"Sad as it may be," my mother argued, "unless the change is for the worse." Her words were prophetic, and my grandmother became the second family victim in the Passover destruction of the Great Piotrkow Synagogue. Along with hundreds of worshipers, she went up in flames to join her beloved husband Srulko.

"Mama, where do you think grandma's gone to," I remember asking my mother.

"She's gone, my child," my mother replied, "to pay her last debt to the Lord."

As the days went by, my mother's pronouncements had become prophecies. Things did in fact change for the worse. And they kept on changing. The more the Jews cursed their enemy, the stronger he became.

"Buchenwald! Buchenwald! We're on our way to concentration camp Buchenwald!" Someone close by shouted. The rumor spread throughout the transport. We had heard of those types of K.Z. Grotesquely, the Nazis nick-named them *Knochenmühlen*, bone grinders.

As we were carried nearer our destination, I realized that soon we would be in the company of habitual criminals, incorrigible homosexuals, Gypsies, defiant clergy of all faiths, the feeble-minded, and the political opposition of the Third Reich. The Jew, it was said, possessed the combined qualities of all those "undesirable" social elements, and rumor had it that those who entered a *Knochenmühle* had rarely if ever left it alive. The Nazis were on the run, but they were dragging us along to their doom. Everyone said their days were counted, there were rumors of Nazi defeat in Africa and a disastrous rout of three Armies at Stalingrad. Now, more than ever, the prospect of seeing them as P.O.W.'s looked real. I wanted to live, and my thoughts wandered off to my relatives in America . . .

"What's wrong with you, Victor?" Fay asked her son. "You haven't touched your food."

"Talk to us, son." Mickey implored.

"What's there to talk about?" Victor defied them both.

"Anything's better than your eternal silence." Mickey said.

"Daddy's right, Victor dear. You never talk with us anymore, whatever it is, you're keeping it all inside. It's no good for any of us."

"Things are happening all over, and I've got to do something or else I'll go mad." Victor looked at his plate.

"That's crazy talk, son." Mickey remarked.

"What's so crazy about it? My brother's a year younger and he's with our troops in Sicily, getting ready to march into Germany. Here I am, sitting at the dinner table like nothing's happening, and you expect me to eat." Victor was nearing tears.

"What do you want to do, son?" Fay asked.

"I've got to sign up."

"One sacrifice in the family's enough!" Fay wept. "I won't hear of it."

Victor stood up. "It's got nothing to do with sacrifice, mom." He walked over to his mother and embraced her. "Think of all of our relatives over there. How much have they sacrificed?"

"There's nothing we can do about that now." Mickey said. "Besides, they haven't called you to sign up yet. So why rush things?"

"Mickey! You talk like it's okay for your second son to go off into that miserable war! I'll hear no more of it!" Fay cried.

"I didn't say anything of the sort." Mickey tried to calm his wife. "I just said to wait and see."

"Like you did then?" Victor asked with no intended cynicism. His father looked at him startled, then at his wife who sat quietly weeping. He walked into his room and closed the door behind him.

On the following day, Fay found a note from Victor telling his parents that he, too, had gone off to sign up for overseas duty with the Army.

"Dear God all mighty! What has he done?" Fay's knees buckled down under her, and Mickey helped her to the couch.

"He'll be okay, darling, he's a big boy." He reassured her.

"Why is this happening to us, Mickey?" She asked.

"Maybe it's God's way to redeem us for our failures?" It was more a question than an answer to hers.

"Sure. . . sure. . . our youngest is called Isaac, isn't he?" she wept.

"My baby. And now the other's gone too." She was inconsolable. Mickey held his wife in a silent embrace for a long time. . .

It was late February when we arrived at our destination: K.Z. *Buchenwald!* It began snowing in the early morning hours as the train pulled onto the special spur, and by the time we had stepped outdoors for the march into the compound, the ground was covered under a thick blanket of crisp snow.

The camp was a sprawling compound in the woods of Thuringia, high up in the hills, in the midst of a splendid beech forest whence it had gotten its name. Buchenwald boasted a barbed wire fence which carried a high electrical charge and guard-towers every thirty meters along the camp's perimeter; a machine gun barrel could be seen on the tower platform. The weapon was placed on a turret for better maneuverability. Each tower was equipped with a large spotlight to illuminate the area between the barracks and the fence during all hours of the night.

The sliding doors opened. "*Raus! Schweinehunde!* Out! You dirty dogs!" The literal meaning was "pig-dogs." No other language can claim such double expletives. As I looked around the box-car, I just now realized that some of those who had begun the Odyssey would not be coming out. As I was leaving, I caught sight of Kadetzki, slumped over against the wall. He had received his wish; his worries were over. The SS guards had no trouble persuading the rest of us to form a column of fours. A few shouts, some blows, and we did as ordered.

"Remember! Do all they say!" Menasha whispered under his breath.

"What if. . .?"

"There are no ifs! You understand?" Menasha was adamant. "Do all they order us to do, and let's try to stick together!"

The entrance to the camp was a large fort-like gate flanked by two immense towers. We followed through that gate, and we could see the wrought iron mottos inscribed above it: RECHT ODER UNRECHT MEIN VATERLAND! RIGHT OR WRONG, MY COUNTRY! And ARBEIT MACHT FREI! WORK MAKES YOU FREE!

We ignored the first, but the second dictum lent us renewed hope for survival. "You're right, after all, Menasha," I whispered, "as long as we'll do our job, we might get out of this yet!"

I saw row upon row of dreary-looking barracks that stood at a good distance from the fence. That immense, barren space through which we would march to reach the barracks, was the *Appelplatz*. All white now, because of the recent snow, the red clay beneath it promised to be quite dry and dusty during the summer season. This, and the ghost-like appearance of the barracks that stretched out across the vast distance of the camp, made my heart skip more than one beat.

"I hope they'll let us keep the family photos," I whispered to Roman.

"How can you worry about the photos at a time like this?" Was his hushed response. As we marched into the *Appelplatz*, it was late morning. Our reception committee comprised the SS, Croatian and Ukrainian mercenaries, our own Kapos and, not to be forgotten, fierce-looking shepherd dogs. We entered a long corridor formed by the SS and the mercenaries which was no more than five to six feet across. The SS with their sleeves rolled up, each brandishing a billy-club or a wooden stick, shouted merciless abuses and swung at our ranks as we passed through. The dogs growled and strained on their leashes. Blows kept raining down on those nearest the edge of formation, immediately drawing blood on their heads, backs, arms, and shoulders.

"*Schnell! Schnell!*" The guards laughed happily, amused with their entertainment, each one trying to deliver blows harder than his companion. There was no avoiding it, even though we tried to maneuver ourselves into the very middle of the screaming, desperate mob. The SS kept us in place.

I saw some men falling, and on first impulse I was going to stop; an urgent inner voice compelled me to help, else they might be trampled by the desperate stampede.

"Go on! Vilek!" Menasha pushed on. "Don't stop! Don't look back! Just go on!"

Some managed to pick themselves up, but others remained in the snow while we pressed forward, encouraged by the brutal blows and trampling the bodies deep into the snow.

At last, we saw the open space of the *Appelplatz*. The "initiation" was over, and we joined our comrades in the vast ranks.

"What's a Kapo?" I asked Menasha. I had noticed the insignia sewn to the breast pocket of one of the inmates over the green triangle designating a criminal prisoner.

"Comes from the Italian word il capo, which means 'head' or 'superior.' All I know is that he's an inmate in charge of the barracks, in return for which he gets a little more food and less ill-treatment at the hands of our masters."

"And the bastard takes it all out on the rest of us." Roman remarked.

"Aren't we close to Weimar? It's around here somewhere, isn't it?" Someone asked.

"About seven kilometers down hill." Menasha volunteered the information. "Once the hub of German culture, the home of Goethe, Schiller, even Beethoven lived here for a while."

"Now, it's the K.Z. Buchenwald and the I.G. Farben." Roman sneered.

"Isn't that why we're here?" I asked. "Aren't we supposed to work in their munitions factory?"

"Let's hope so, little brother, let's hope." Roman said, glancing at our fallen comrades we left behind.

"You there! *Schweinehunde!*" An SS guard shouted in our direction. I shrunk into the column of men surrounding me, trying to become as small as possible, almost invisible. It was to no avail. The Kapo rushed over, wielding his billy club, thrashing at us with all his fury, as if to impress his superiors who held on to their sides with laughter. I was struck on the shoulder, but I didn't feel the pain; the fear overshadowed it.

Suddenly an SS guard rushed into the melee, clubbing everyone in his wake. He grabbed Menasha by one earlock which had somehow managed to slip out from under his tight cap, and pulled him out of our ranks. The guard went berserk, hitting Menasha with great force, soon bringing our friend to his knees.

"Undress! Jew!" Menasha complied, taking off his jacket and shirt. He was kneeling now, half-clad, in front of his antagonist. "Pray to your God, Jew!" Menasha's lips moved quickly. "Louder, swine!" Without looking at the SS man, Menasha prayed the maariv or evening services; it was time for it anyhow. His face was now covered with blood; one of the blows punctured the skin on the left temple. Snow clung to his body as he fell, to the delight and amusement of the guards, while they now gathered round him in a small circle.

"Your God isn't listening, Jew!" Maybe He's on vacation, eh, Jude? Or maybe there's no *Judengott* after all?" They laughed uproariously, narrowed their circle around Menasha and proceeded to urinate onto his face, hair, and on that whole picture of piety. Menasha prayed on. "See, Jew? This is what we do to your God! We piss on Him! That's all He's good for, that Jewish God of yours, to piss on!" The guards suffered violent hiccups, they laughed so hard.

I observed the spectacle with horror, and suddenly recalled my friend's prediction, now knowing that Menasha had been right. There would come great suffering to us; sorrow which would make the past events seem trivial by comparison. And I knew then, that there are degrees of evil even as there are degrees of goodness and of life itself.

By the mere caprice of a guard, Menasha might have been dead but for the interference of the Kapo.

"*Herr Sturmbannführer*," the Kapo volunteered, "may I point out that this is a healthy specimen. Leave him to me. I'll teach him the right ways of the Third Reich. We can still get a lot of mileage out of him."

"You're quite right!" the officer slapped his thighs. "Let him go!

"You're very fortunate, Jew! You had better pray to your Kapo from now on! It was he who saved your miserable hide!" The guards roared with laughter while Menasha raised himself to his feet with great effort. He was bruised and bleeding, but he was alive.

"The Kapo certainly wields a lot of power," I whispered to Roman. "He snatched Menasha from certain death."

"Thanks to the Almighty alone, blessed be He," Menasha protested mildly. "We must go on praying and waiting patiently." He added as if to himself.

"Wait and pray for what?" I asked.

"For another miracle."

"A miracle?"

"Yes. Like the one that happened moments ago."

"You might soon wish that it hadn't happened at all."

"Don't ever say that, Vilek." Menasha admonished. "Once they break your will to live, you're through."

"How are we to expect miracles to happen, when our God has abandoned us long ago, Menasha. Even His angels are absent. Only the spirits of the dead come our way, and they, too, are powerless."

"Don't blaspheme! Tonight, you'll recite a hundred shemas!"

"God has forgotten our language, and I have almost forgotten His!" I said defiantly.

"Then, you'll have to try to remember once again, if only to ask forgiveness!" Menasha pleaded.

"It's God who should be asking *our* forgiveness, and this is quite the right place for a *Din Torah,* and may the spirits of all the murdered children be our witnesses in this trial!"

"You're mad! You don't know what you're saying!" Menasha shook with fear and helplessness. He composed himself. "His ways may seem strange to us at times, but they're always just." He said quietly, and I sensed a new surge of strength in his voice.

"My dear Menasha, can't you see there's no plan in all this. . .this miracle as you call it?"

"God's ways are strange and beyond human comprehension." Menasha said.

"The worst of it is, things have been happening to us completely unsolicited," I said suddenly.

"We are Jews, isn't that enough?" Roman argued.

"Is that all the reason they have to drive us to hell?"

"It seems like it, doesn't it?"

"Yes, it does." I concluded.

We might have continued, but Roman pointed to the building we had now approached.

"Look! At last, we'll take a bath!"

There was a large inscription in black letters over white background: BAD UND DESINFEKTION. "My God." I thought, more out of habit than conviction. "It's the same trick they had used in Treblinka. Barrack X." I recalled Kadetzki's story and his own recent death. There it was: the windowless room we had heard so much about. But this one was real; no longer an incredible tale. It was happening to us now. The room without an exit. At the far end of the large room, there was a small door. Where does it lead? We were ordered to undress and arrange all our clothing and personal belongings in a neat bundle. A special crew of inmates was assigned the task of sorting out the valuables into categories of apparel and items such as eye-glasses or pocket knives, etc. Even the snapshots of our loved ones were taken from us. "How was I going to remember my mother's features?" I wondered. They also searched us for gold teeth and bridges which when found were extracted on the spot with common steel pliers. The rectum was then inspected for money and valuables. I was glad I had bartered Boost's bracelet for a loaf of bread long ago.

"The Nazis certainly don't miss a trick, do they?" I whispered to Roman.

I was reciting my prayers as we entered the delousing chamber, and I continued for the duration of the ritual. I had heard about "showers" before. People walked in, but seldom were seen leaving.

All of us stood naked. The mighty men of the shtetl were there: Moshe Davidowicz, the wealthy grain merchant, and Mendel Kazanski, the butcher, both very important and powerful men within the Council of the Elders. They stood now alongside the meek and the lowly. Fear was written in their faces, and I saw that they weren't different from others. I looked at those once mighty men whose word and deed were respected and feared by all. They tried, without much success, to cover their private parts with the palms of their hands, and I was almost tempted to chuckle at their awkwardness.

"Get on! Get on!" There were orders that had to be obeyed. Painfully, all our body hair was removed, first the head, then the armpits, and last the pubic and anal regions. The instruments were blunt from frequent use and nobody cared to sharpen them. The places on our bodies where the hair had been removed remained rough and bleeding. The raw flesh burned, but there were no complaints. After all, as long as there was pain, there was life. As my grandmother used to say: "Little pains don't kill."

"Guess, there's not much of it left." I remarked to my brother, pointing to the many flesh punctures. "Blood should be gushing out, but there's only a trickle here and there." I grimaced awkwardly, and my brother nodded his head resignedly.

They submerged us, one at a time, in a large tank full of formaldehyde which served as disinfectant. It was strong, and it stung at the open wounds. We walked toward the showers, anticipating the flow of warm water, hoping to wash off the effects of the chemical. The water was ice cold. We shivered under the icy flow, still expressing thanks for the unpleasant liquid. "It isn't gas. . .it isn't gas!" I kept repeating silently.

I looked at my striped inmate's clothing, Dutch wooden shoes, and one blanket per person had been sufficient evidence that we were granted life; at least temporarily. I squeezed Roman's arm. There was some hope after all. The number was printed on a tag, sewed on to the left side of the jacket above the breast. I was #116420. The sum total of the numbers amounted to fourteen; the years I had now lived on planet earth. I was not superstitious by nature, still the unusual coincidence made me wonder whether this was some kind of omen. I had decided not to think about it. Besides, I was much too preoccupied already, without engaging myself in silly guessing games. Roman was #107350. We had been given a new identity.

"While you are here, you will be known by your number," the commandant shouted. His voice had an inhuman sound, charged with cruelty. The knowledge that this individual was now responsible for my fate frightened me terribly.

"Remember this number well," he continued. "When it is called, you must respond quickly, obey the orders, and work hard. That may help you survive this terrible war!"

There were several small holes in the back of my jacket. They might have been caused by large caliber bullets. I prayed a little faster as I put my forefinger through one of them. As we were marched toward the distant barracks, I held on to my loose trousers and manipulated the stiff wooden shoes with my toes, trying to keep them from getting stuck in the snow which had quickly accumulated at the bottom. I concentrated every few steps to remember hitting one clopper against the other to shed some of the snow. The bullet holes were quickly forgotten.

Nearly two thousand inmates had been crowded into one barrack, an area which could at best accommodate five hundred men under normal circumstances. There were five boarded tiers of "bunks," the lowest being the floor and the topmost immediately beneath the ceiling. The only furniture in the barrack was a long wooden table along which there were some rough benches. There was no bathroom, nor was there water of any sort to drink or wash your face.

"Hurry! Let's climb to the top!" Menasha urged. As soon as we had reached the top tier, we "claimed" a small portion of the fifteen square feet for ourselves. Twelve more inmates would soon pile in on us, and we would sleep, pressed tightly together, seven at the head of the bunk and eight at its feet. The atmosphere was like an animal's lair.

"No one's going to step on us." Menasha was pleased.

"Nor will they shit and piss in our faces." Roman managed a chuckle.

The Kapo delivered a well-rehearsed speech. He talked about absolute obedience to the camp rules and the consequences of going out of line: "We're going to get along fine, as long as you follow the rules. We obey the law here! I am the law!" He stopped and looked at us probingly. No one dared to breathe loudly. "Any questions?" He asked rhetorically and continued, knowing that we wouldn't dare interrupt him.

"You'll get your food rations in the morning after Appell. Be sure to hold on to some of it, and don't lose any or you're dead! If some bastard steals from you, he might just as well sign your death warrant! You catch anyone stealing, bring him to me. We'll give the asshole a one-way ticket to hell!" He made a motion with his thumb running across his throat. We understood.

I mourned the confiscated family photos. Maybe the mental pictures of our loved ones would become stronger. But I couldn't help wondering how long that would last before their memory fades. "Do you still remember mama?" I asked Roman. "And Felusia?" I looked at him anxiously. "Please, describe them to me in detail, Roman. How did they look the day they had gone on the transport?"

My brother and I invented games, taking turns in describing our mother's and Felusia's features. This was to become a daily ritual; a linkage with the past.

"Let's repeat it each day," I pleaded, "or we might forget altogether."

"We'll do that, little brother," Roman's eyes glazed over, "as long as we'll stay together, we'll talk about them."

We avoided the thought that we might some day be separated, still we knew that this possibility existed every day. Daily we heard of transports leaving Buchenwald for its sub-camps. Their destination was always a mystery to everyone, and we could only guess whether it was for life or death. The SS was particularly keen on separating families or siblings once they learned their identities. And that was why Roman was registered in Buchenwald under our mother's maiden name, Stybel, which so far kept us together.

"Why couldn't we have been born as part of the great Aryan community?" I asked Menasha. He looked at me, and his usually sad eyes expressed a glimmer of a smile.

"Because, my dear Vilek, because the Nazi 'Point Four' program states that 'only members of the Aryan race can be citizens. A member of the race can only be one who is of German blood, without consideration of creed.' I know all this sounds very complicated to you, my young friend, so to make it simple, let me say that no Jew can become a member of the race. Not even a convert, like in the days of the Spanish Inquisition." Menasha swayed as he talked, and I knew that words didn't come easy to him, he was choking and fighting his tears. "You know, Vilek, they drill this theory into every German child's mind. I guess, the Nazis need some kind of a barrier; they feel out of place in the world. Who knows, maybe now they can feel more secure."

"How do we fit into all that?" I needed an explanation, though I knew it wasn't going to help lighten my burden.

"They need us, too, Vilek, " Menasha explained patiently. "They keep us for the contrast we provide. That's why they hold us captive. . ." he paused, as if to find the proper words, "temporarily, at least."

"And. . ." I hesitated. . ."when they no longer find any use for us? What'll happen then?"

"Come, it's time we got some sleep, my friend." Menasha cut the conversation short. I didn't press. "There's surely a lot in store for us, come tomorrow. Let's rest up, if we can."

A small battered container was the only implement handed us for our personal use. Early in the morning, after roll-call, we lined up for our daily food rations. The container was half-full of lukewarm turnip water. I put the edge of the container to my lips trying very hard to imagine that it wasn't what it was. The fluid would not go down. It tasted foul and bitter, and I spat it out as soon as my tongue had touched it.

"You'll soon learn to swallow it, whatever it is," a crusty old inmate addressed me. "This fluid and a slice of bread is all you'll get for the day." He nodded meaningfully. I made a determined effort to drink at least part of it. With a grimace, I asked: "What is this?"

"It's soup." The inmate said.

"Are you sure?" I asked unbelievingly.

"I'm sure," said the man, "and soon you'll be certain too."

It didn't take long. The dirty bowl of luke-warm water was all the man had said, and I had become increasingly less squeamish.

Even before we had been assigned work details, the prolonged lack of nutritious food caused our bodies to gradually lapse into deterioration.

Day after day, I listened to the sound of angry voices of our keepers. My eyes saw only hostile faces, for even the inmates in their quest for survival had become hostile toward one another and fought at the slightest provocation.

As time passed, each new moment in Buchenwald was to become a new experience. So, too, we were to learn the identity of a mysterious timber-built elongated structure that stood, somewhat isolated, to one side of our barracks. We thought it to be a wood-pile, nothing more.

"Over there!" Our Kapo pointed toward the wooden shack. "That's your latrine!" He paused to observe our reaction. Each morning, after roll-call, you'll get a chance to take your daily crap!" he chuckled wickedly. "That's if you'll have anything in your gut to crap with!"

The shack had no walls. We looked at one another, questioning each other with our eyes. The enemy had stripped us of our belongings, our families, what little humor we possessed, and the hope we had harbored evaporated as well. He had gradually chipped away at our native dignity, until there wasn't much left, and I no longer felt like a human being; not even like a beast of burden, but more like an inanimate object.

Though it was not an enclosed area, the foul stench was unbelievably intense. Two six-by-six planks had been placed over a ditch fifteen feet in length and three feet wide. I looked down, but I didn't dare guess its excrement-filled depth. Fat white worms crawled lazily on the discolored surface. I squatted on the now befouled beam, trying to relieve myself, observing the disgusting worms beneath and the swarms of huge green flies buzzing ominously close. I felt nausea coming on, my bowels refusing to move.

"Merciful God in heaven," I thought silently. "What if I were to lose my balance?" My heart pounded heavily and I was afraid those squatting near me could hear. I looked down at the dark mass beneath me with utter disgust, and the fat white worms continued in their never-ending motion within the colorless viscosity on a journey very much like my own.

"Don't look down, little brother!" Roman whispered next to me. "The trick's not to look down!"

I sat there for a long time, and finally nature itself came to my aid when my whole body shook in a violent vomit. Were it not for Menasha on one side, and Roman on the other, I would have surely fallen into the mass beneath, as others had done before me. I was furious at my own weakness, and in order not to despair altogether, I taught myself to think of the punishment I would mete out my enemies when this was all over. I imagined myself their torturer, even executioner.

The Kapo's powers were awesome. At the slightest provocation, he would order a "delinquent" inmate to stand for hours facing the wall after work, else he would have him perform knee-bends till the prisoner dropped from exhaustion, only to be kicked to unconsciousness. Wounds opened, the flesh yielding to the blows of the instrument of punishment, but the injuries drew hardly any blood at all as time and lack of proper nourishment took their toll.

There was an element of predictability in the very instability of our existence; a gradual but inevitable turn for the worse in the monotony of suffering.

"If ever there was a time ripe for the arrival of the Messiah, let Him come now!" I remarked to Menasha during our daily prayer session. No amount of prayer would bring about a miracle. Miracles, it seemed, only happened in those magical stories of sad princesses and their heroic rescuers on great chargers, of evil spirits and benign magicians. Was there ever a man named Moses who had singlehandedly delivered our oppressed people from Pharaoh's bondage? My sacrilegious doubts were growing, however much I searched my conscience for evidence of divine intervention in my behalf.

Infested with lice and immersed in abysmal filth, the Buchenwald inmates were soon caught up in a typhus epidemic. Our own Piotrkow ghetto experience must have given both Roman and me a degree of immunity because we were able to continue with our work at the I.G. Farben. We had been assigned to the section manufacturing incendiary bombs; affectionately called the "jaundice section."

It was Roman's task to hold the shell upright while I filled it with the yellowish phosphorus powder. Working at low temperatures to prevent the volatile substance from igniting, our only safeguard was a neckerchief placed over mouth and nose. We were soon impregnated with the yellow product from eyeballs to the nails of our fingers and toes.

We worked diligently, to impress our foreman, a Saxon from the town of Chemnitz.

"116420!" The foreman shouted. "Come here! *Schnell!*" I approached the foreman's small cubicle of a room from which he supervised our activities. "Here," he handed me a mop, "scrub the floor!" He drew the curtain and left me inside the room by myself. I was thankful for the moment of reprieve from the foul smell of the powdered acid.

The third time I was assigned to mopping detail, I noticed on the corner table a small package wrapped in newspaper. Quickly, I lifted the item to my nose, and I immediately smelled the aroma of cheese. "Dear Lord!" Flashed through my mind." A cheese sandwich! What am I to do?"

After a moment's hesitation, I tucked the small bundle under my shirt and continued my work. As I was finishing my task, the foreman returned. I expected the worst. To my astonishment, he went about his work, and I completed mine within moments.

"Come back tomorrow!" he ordered as I was leaving. "This place get's so goddamned dusty!"

That night, the three of us feasted on the delicious sandwich I "stole" from our foreman. As I went on to contemplate this act of mercy, I was astounded that I have come to regard it to be exceptional and out of commonplace of human behavior.

"Perhaps, you might see this as a sort of signal?" Menasha asked, with a twinkle in his eye.

As time wore on, every morning, before the *Appell*, the barracks were emptied of their dead. We carried out the casualties of the previous night, undressed them, and deposited their skeletal remains unceremoniously on a pile at the front entry. They were later picked up by the crematory detail; soon the wind carried the smell of burning flesh our way as we readied for another day at work. Their uniforms were returned to the receiving area, where they were once again distributed among the newly arrived.

Buchenwald boasted its own anthem! The song was written by an anonymous inmate and put to marching music by an anonymous composer. As we were leaving the camp for work, barely dragging our weary bones, the Kapo shouted an order: "Sing, you damn pigs! Sing, till your putrid lungs burst open!" We sang as best we could. We sang with fear, the fear of those expecting the unexpected. "Louder! Louder!" We sang, while the overseers shouted insults and laughed wickedly.

Wenn der Tag erwacht. . .
When the day awakens,
Before the sun can smile,
Our columns march
To the daily toil
Into the twilight of the dawn.

The forest is black, but the sky is red,
And we carry along scarcely little bread,
And deep in our hearts there's much worry.

Oh, Buchenwald, I cannot forget you,
For you are my destiny!
Only he who has left you, can understand
How wonderful 'tis to be free.
Oh, Buchenwald, we don't bewail or cry,
No matter what our fate may be:
Despite all that, we shall say "yes" to life,
Because the day will come when we'll be free!
We shall say "yes" to life,
Because the day will come when we'll be free!

The night is hot and my girl is far,
And the wind sings softly how much I love her,
If only she remained faithful to me!
The rock is hard, but firm is our step,
And we carry along our picks and spades,
And deep in our hearts there's love.

Oh, Buchenwald. . .(refrain)

Yet the nights are short, and the days are long—
And a song resounds that was sung at home:
No one shall take our courage away!
Fear not, and be in step, my friend,
For we carry the will to live
With what blood there's left in our veins,
And deep in our hearts there's faith!

Oh, Buchenwald. . .(refrain)

In an eerie chorus of discordant voices, breathlessly, we shouted the song as we passed in "review" before the assembled SS. They seemed to derive a kind of weird pleasure out of this bizarre spectacle, shouting insults at the marching ranks of the living dead. In their great zeal to torment us, litle did they know that their sport had become a true source of strength and hope for many of us.

Nothing, however, seemed to lift Menasha's spirits. He never recovered from the beating he had received on the day of our arrival, broken in body though not in spirit. But it seemed that his courage had vanished with the loss of his earlocks. He was aging rapidly before our very eyes.

To overcome the prayer prohibition, the Hasidim had agreed by word of mouth on set times during which to conduct their prayer sessions. It was a mystery to us all, how each man to himself knew when to commence worship; at daybreak, at mid-day, and for the maariv at sundown. Regardless of his activity, isolated or in the company of others, the Hasidim prayed, and each man knew exactly when to sound the final "amen" at the conclusion of the memorial kaddish.

It was late evening. I listened to Menasha's supplications, as I had done so many times before. This time, however, it was the tone of his prayer that made me pay attention.

"I was unable to stand up to recite the kaddish, dear God," Menasha muttered, "forgive me, for I've sinned gravely." He beat himself on the chest repeatedly, the hollow sound was that of an open grave. "Whatever the Almighty wills, I shall accept," he whispered softly, adding, "blessed be He."

I knew then that the evening services had come to an end.

Menasha was living proof that every individual has limits to his tolerance; that critical moment when something within him cries out in terrible pain. He no longer clings to life or is capable of harboring hope. Only the deep hatred toward his tormentors keeps him going. Like lightning, the thought occurs to him that there might never come an answer to his desperation. He conceives an idea which then fathers the deed itself. It precedes it as lightning precedes thunder. Menasha must have decided to end his struggle one day when he refused to accept his share of the daily food portion.

"You must eat, Menasha. Please take it." I begged.

"It's wasted on me, Vilek," he shook his head sadly. "It's a sin to waste food."

"It's more sinful to take a life, Menasha." He attempted a smile which ended in a grimace. The pupil echoed his teacher's words. He knew. "You must hold on, Menasha," I pleaded. "Don't die on us, don't leave us." I held my tears. "We'll be lost without you."

After months of camp existence, it had become clear to us that God intended to relieve the young Hasid of his suffering despite our efforts to keep him alive. He seldom left his bunk, and we did our best to cover for him at the daily roll-call.

On those cold nights, when his whole body trembled without end, Roman and I took turns covering our dearest friend with our own bodies to keep some heat between us. Occasionally, we would let out a faint chuckle at the grotesqueness of our skeletal appearance, "it's like one heap of bones rubbing against another, "Roman remarked.

Lucid moments were rare. When they occurred, Menasha prayed fervently, as if trying to remind the Almighty of his continuous presence. "We have a pact between us, God and I," Menasha said, "the Lord, blessed be He, permits me these rare moments of rationality, so that I might remember to thank Him for His many mercies." He breathed with great difficulty. We were silent, and he continued. "You must think me a fool," he tried to raise his body, but quickly gave up the effort. "He'll let me go, I assure you, my dear friends, just as soon as I've concluded extoling His abounding miracles."

As time went on, our friend lay there, in his stupor, his jaws locked in position, unable to move them to utter a sound, less still to chew his food. At times like these, we chewed for him whatever scraps of refuse we could find, then ease it into his perpetually open mouth in the hope that it would, by some miracle, slide down to his stomach.

In this constant worry about survival, my life, too, had assumed the trappings of loneliness, and I became gradually aware that it must be so. I was lonely among the masses of the doomed, in a land of the dead. An awareness had come over me; a realization that all this was meant for me, it was bashaert, destined, as my grandfather Srulko would have said. I had somehow collaborated with destiny in order to become stronger; through suffering to reach solace, through hate to learn love.

In that isolation, I was given one last chance; the chance to affirm truth by seeking life. I treasured life amidst corpses whose faces bore the marks of their last agonies. I recalled my grandfather's words of admonishment: "Reverence for life and personal dignity, you must never forsake these!" Hence, through this vale of suffering and agony of dying, and only out of my fervent passion for life, the seed was sown for the new day.

I was surprised and awed by the obstinate manner in which I had continued to return to things long past, remembering that which had happened long ago, in its minutest details. And it was then, for the first time in my life, I had come to realize the curse and the blessing of memory. . .

"Dear Mom and Dad,

You've probably heard, Italy surrendered on the 3rd of September, and a good thing it is, too, because it was getting rough in those Italian mountains. But here I am, the booming of the guns is getting closer as we're getting on toward Germany. Can't wait to get my hands on those Nazis. Don't worry, I'm taking good care of myself. Not a scratch so far!

Hey, thanks for the letter and the news about Victor. Maybe we'll hook up somewhere in Krautland? I'll keep you posted. Love, Isaac."

"Well? What did I tell you?" Mickey looked at Fay triumphantly. "There he is, already through a lot of combat, and he's okay."

"Let's pray it continues this way." Fay said.

"We've got two fine boys, Fay." Mickey beamed with pride.

"That they are, Mickey." Fay remarked, shaking her head in a moment of uneasy silence. "But I'd much rather have them home, going to school and planning a future."

He looked at her and started to say something, but he changed his mind and walked toward the door. The door-knob in his hand, he turned to his wife with a smile: "Things don't always happen right, they just don't."

The news of the Allied successes in Africa had reached the camp toward the end of 1943. Despite the ban on listening to the radio, the news spread like wildfire. Names such as Oran, Casablanca and Morocco were on everybody's lips. The reaction was electrifying. I saw people whispering to each other where there was only silence before. Suddenly, they became more tolerant of one another. During the same year, we experienced the first Allied air raids in our area. They continued with greater frequency, and we were comforted by the worried and frightened faces of the SS as they crowded into the camp to seek shelter.

Routinely, the *Blockälteste* shouted his daily, "*Raus, zum Appell!*" The narrow barrack doors vomitted the mass of men onto the yard. We formed columns of eights and marched in an orderly, mechanical manner down to the *Appellplatz*. In the dusk of the morning fog which had scarcely risen from the ground, we were illumined by the ever-rotating searchlights from the sentry towers. Thousands of zebra-clad "Musulmans"—as we called ourselves—trotted sullenly, miserable, not alive and not dead. Some were singing, others were silent, others still were doing the "frog-jump" or the "goose-quack" for the amusement of the guards whose tastes and desires were at a constant variance.

"Who is it going to be this time?"

We stood shivering in the cool morning air, as our overseers took endless headcounts and shouted abrupt work orders.

"Hope they don't call Menasha!"

"What's taking them so long?"

"Must have called a missing number. We're in for a long count!"

Often, it took the *Blockälteste* and the Kapos hours before the missing number was located, at times ill, more often dead, seldom attempting to hide. Hence, in order to prevent those long searches, the inmates themselves saw to it that the sick and the half-dead participated in the *Appell*.

"Look! It's Block 6-A again!" Someone remarked. The missing inmate had been found, dead. The guards were furious, but even they were helpless where death was concerned; the only escape. They tossed him onto a heap of skin-covered bones in front of the barrack.

"I'm frightened, Roman." I whispered softly. "I'm scared because all of this doesn't affect me anymore. I'm no longer nauseous or disgusted."

He nodded. Roman was becoming too weak to talk. The change came about gradually, but we knew it was inevitable, and time was on the enemy's side.

"We've got to do something about Menasha or he'll die, Roman."

"Wish I knew what."

"You think we ought to pray?"

"Maybe."

"Menasha thinks so."

"Menasha's fortunate."

"So? What else?" I was puzzled and concerned.

"We'll think of something, little brother." He took a deep breath. "After all, we've got this far."

Suddenly, I was struck by an idea. It was courage that was now required to go on living, I knew. Courage and a daily summoning-up of one's will. Till now, we've lived on hate and little faith. Courage was needed now, and a belief in that idea struggling so hard to become reality.

"Maybe. . . we could escape?" I suggested hesitantly.

"There's no place we can go from here. . .except. . .there." Roman pointed in the direction of the crematories. "We're surrounded by the enemy. Some have tried to escape. The good citizens of the Reich denounced them, and they were returned. You know how the Kapos like to reward escapees, don't you?"

Occasionally, some had tried to escape, but even that amused the Nazis. Shooting a prisoner attempting to escape earned the SS a furlough and a citation, and some a promotion. Soon, the inmates gave up the idea of escape, and the SS spread rumors through their informers of successful escapes to encourage attempts. The SS had even arranged that at certain hours of the night Kapos delivered victims into the zone between the gate and the wire fence where they were shot "trying" to "escape."

"It's all so unreal, Roman. All of this. You and I, and Menasha lying in his own shit, talking to his God. We're struggling to please the Nazis, or to stay out of their way; refusing to die. It cannot really be happening. Can it?"

"I, too, expect to awaken at any moment, but waking could never be like this." Roman said wearily.

No sooner did we settle at the barracks table to eat than we heard the *Blockälteste* report: "Attention! Block 364, Wing B, 245 inmates eating!" An ambitious SS *Scharführer* had decided that this was a good time to inspect the barrack.

"What? You pigs! Aren't you under the table yet?!"

The bowls were abandoned, the bread crumbs tucked in desperate haste under the shirt, and benches flew to the side as we all scrambled out of the way of the billy club. There were always some stragglers who weren't quick enough to find shelter under the crowded table. They were instantly blood-ied by the indignant inspector, joined by the Kapo and the *Blockälteste*, to serve as examples of how clumsiness and disobedience are treated.

That was one of the many games played by our keepers. They varied with their changing moods. In wintertime, we were ordered out of the barracks to lie flat, our heads buried in the snow. And while we were struggling to breathe, the Kapos raided the barracks, confiscating blankets which we had bought from them at high prices. Some of the inmates dared to protest and were beaten to unconsciousness; their need for the blanket instantly terminated.

When Christmas came, all games ceased. On that holiest of holy days, the camp orchestra entertained with Christmas carrols. The mercenaries and the SS gathered round a large bonfire near a giant fir tree which the inmates had cut down in "our" forest the previous day. They all sang the beautiful "Oh, *Tannenbaum*, and tears welled up in many an SS man's eyes as he thought of his loved ones at home. And as they wept together, they wished each other a very "Merry Christmas, and a return home next year." And the orchestra went on playing all night, while the sweet-scented smoke from the working crematories billowed high into the tranquil countryside.

By the end of 1943, Allied air raids had become a common occurrence in all of the *Führer's* Third Reich. The charming city of Weimar—with its honest burghers and gabled rooftops—only seven kilometers from our "mountain resort" and the site of the I.G. Farben Industry, was not immune to the systematic pounding. At the very outset of these "atrocities perpe-trated on the innocent people of the Third Reich," the Nazi propaganda machinery attempted to minimize the Allied war effort. But the mountains of debris grew by the hour, and the disrupted life of the civilian population spoke louder than all of Goebbels' propaganda organs combined.

Clearing the debris from Weimar streets was a welcome relief from picric acid. The factory lay in shambles. From then on, every morning, hundreds of us were marched downhill to the erstwhile cradle of German culture. At sundown, the march uphill, back to the camp, was lightened with the expec-tation of another bombardment. The planes came regularly, and we rejoiced at the sound of their engines and the tremors they caused.

As days turned into weeks, we had gradually become weary of our daily pilgrimage. The tools we carried seemed heavier. The burden of not know-ing when it would all end weighed heavily on our souls. Each day, the mountain seemed steeper, the distance farther.

"Are we the resurrected Jesus, multiplied a thousandfold?" I asked myself this important question time and again.

Jesus was made to carry his cross up the winding Via Dolorosa but once. Why must we make the ascent indefinitely?

My soul cried silently. There was no answer.

We shuffled through the streets of Weimar. The good citizens gathered to look at the "hardened criminals" who were kept safely under lock and key yonder in the forest by the mountain. They heard rumors. They didn't like having this vermin as their neighbors. Now, what they saw, were gaunt, emaciated, staggering figures; humans with a touch of death written on their skeletal features.

"Serves them right!" some yelled.

"See the rubble?" others asked. "It's all your fault! You must pay for it dearly!"

Grownups jeered and children wielded whips made of tree twigs, with impunity, to the delight of the guards.

"Whip those lazy, no-good criminals!" parents encouraged their small children. "*Jude verrecke!*" they shouted. "Jew croak!"

As we had turned the corner on the Goethe-Schiller Platz, a public square, amidst the rubble stood the larger-than-life monument of the two great spirits out of the German past. The two figures were facing each other, holding each a book in their left, their right hands united in a handshake.

I was compelled by some inner force to look at the two bronze figures, to examine their serene, dignified features, to probe deeper into the signifi-cance of their survival amidst physical and spiritual ruin. And suddenly, it came to me, as I was filled with an overwhelming desire to shout at the top of my voice, to announce to the world, that, after all, we were in good company. I knew then that they and their likes too, had long since been banished from or imprisoned by the new culture of the Third Reich.

Just then, a small rock found its mark as it bounced off with a hollow thud from my shoulderblade. I felt no pain. For that fleeting moment, I felt only exhilaration for the discovery I had just made: Like Sisyphus, I felt the dignity of freedom in my daily descent to hell and the courage of hope at seeing the afflictions heaped upon my enemy.

Soon, the beating and the jeering had stopped altogether. We had ceased being an attraction, and no one came out to see us, save a few children who followed harmlessly, now without the encouragement of their elders to tor-ment us.

"The good citizens of Weimar have tired of beating us," someone sug-gested.

"Don't be a fool," another voice remarked. "We've now become part of the scenery. It's that simple. Take a good look at us. Ruins and all!" There was some faint laughter. It was a strange sound to hear after all that time, still, it was a sign of hope returned. If we could relearn to laugh, perhaps someday we might also know to live and love. My imagination was running amock, and I woke up sweating profusely. I lay awake the rest of the night. I could not hold my thoughts to myself.

"Menasha! Wake up, my friend." I nudged him lightly. There was no need. He was seldom asleep nowadays. "Do you hear, Menasha? The great explosions! You must have courage! We're nearing the end! Your miracle is going to happen after all!"

"The Almighty is merciful, blessed be He!" was all Menasha muttered, as he began his morning worship. He seemed to have partially recovered his strength. We had been able to share some potatoes and other provisions which we have unearthed from under the rubble of some destroyed homes.

I gazed down at him with silent, scrutinizing attention. Menasha's puffy yellow face was wrought with emotion. The yellow of his eyes screwed up at me attentively. Jaundice had set in. I thought desperately.

"I won't be able to take much more of this, Vilek," he said quietly.

"Despite your generous handouts, the poison has yellowed me to the depth of my soul."

"Hold on, just a little while longer, dear Menasha." I put my arm on his shoulder and squeezed slightly. "You saw what our friends have done in Weimar. It's in a shambles. You can't give up now! Not now! When things are taking a turn for the better!" His yellow eyes lit up, I thought, for an instant, at the mention of Weimar. The grimace on his face was a poor substitute for a smile, yet I knew it was meant to be one.

He edged away at once, not even looking up at me, and I saw his gaunt, shabby, famine-stricken figure walk away with lowered head and that characteristic shuffling of the feet.

I watched my friend as one would watch a vision out of a nightmare, then I continued on my way, trying to block it out of my mind completely.

That night, I raided the garbage cans behind the SS kitchen. I grabbed handfulls of egg shells and potato peels and stuffed them behind my jacket. We consumed the "food" in secret, greedily in our bunks before going to sleep. After a while, our teeth had gotten accustomed to the dissonant sound of grinding lime, and our stomachs reconciled themselves to digesting refuse.

"Dear Mom and Dad,

Can you ever forgive me for having caused you so much worry? I know I made you suffer, but it was the only thing I could do under the circumstances or you wouldn't have let me go.

June 27th we boarded ship. We drew a good one, the "West Point," big, fast, and new. It didn't need a convoy for protection, but made the run on its own strength and speed. For most of us it was our first ocean voyage. A few got seasick, but all in all it was a good smooth crossing in spite of the crowded conditions, the abandon ship drill, and the fact that we only got two meals a day.

We're now in Scotland, a town called Greenoch, just below Glasgow. The American Red Cross girls were already on shore to welcome us. It was great to talk to an American girl again after being away from home for a full three months. Hey, you see, this War isn't half as bad as you thought it was?

Don't know what's coming, but something's going to happen soon. Can't tell you what, but the grapevine has it, it's BIG.

Take care now. When I can, I'll write some more. Hope I'll hook up with Isaac's outfit so I'll be able to take care of my kid brother. Stay well and don't worry. Hugs and kisses. Your son, Victor."

Fay cried and Mickey consoled her the whole evening. After several months of silence, Victor finally gave a sign of life. "My two babies, my two babies," was all she could say, pressing the letter to her bosom.

"They'll be okay, dear, they'll be okay." Mickey said. "You see, even our Red Cross is there with them, so it can't be that terrible, can it?

The humiliating defeats on all fronts had spurred our overseers to new "games" with the inmates. Not far from our work party, a group of Jews and Russian P.O.W.'s had been working together under the supervision of SS *Scharführer* Franz Koehler—a civil engineer before the War—clearing a distance essential to city traffic. Koehler was meticulous and demanding. The work was backbreaking even for normal strong men, but for the half-starved . . .only fear kept them going. Koehler singled out a Jew whose strength was quickly waning.

"You there! *Jude*, come over here! Say your last prayers and dig! You're going to die!"

The Jew, Mendel Pototzky from Siedlce, commenced digging resignedly. When the hole was dug, Koehler summoned one of the Russians. "Russky!" The SS man shouted. "Bury the Jew!" The Russian stood hesitant, looking at Mendel, then at the Nazi, then at the Jew again.

"Refuse, will you?! You Communist dog! Now let's see if the Jew will have the same scruples! Get inside! *Schnell!*"

Pototzky was ordered to cover the Russian with earth, which he did, hoping that the Nazi was playing a bad joke on both of them. Moments later only the head of the Russian from his nose up remained out of the grave.

"Stop! Jew!" Pototzky sighed. The Nazi was joking, after all. He thought with great relief. "Get him out!" The Nazi ordered the Jew. Feverishly, the Jew helped the Russian out of the grave.

"Now, you get inside!" Pototzky stepped down into the grave, unbelieving. The Nazi's scheme had gradually dawned on him, but it was too late. "Pray, Jew! Let's see the power of your God!" Koehler laughed. "Now, Russky, it's your turn! The Jew didn't hesitate to bury you alive!"

As he prayed, Pototzky might have recalled with utter bewilderment that practically every corner of the great Siedlce synagogue was filled with the many charities of his ancestors; their honors were imprinted in the stained-glass windows. The glory of his family passed on with the destruction of the venerable walls, but as long as he lived he would remind God of the kovet, the honors and the good deeds. Pototzky wanted to live.

The hole filled slowly, relentlessly, and soon only the slightly moving surface of the debris was the only indication of life stirring within the grave.

"Stump! Russky, stump!" Koehler shouted excitedly, as he jumped up and down alongside the P.O.W. on the fresh grave until all motion ceased within. The Russian turned away, and the rest of us busied ourselves to avoid the eye of Franz Koehler.

"Dig him up!" Koehler ordered two men to unearth Pototzky's body. In his haste, one of them plowed his spade into Pototzky's face. It didn't matter; Mendel Pototzky was dead.

As time wore on, the civilized half of me gradually gave way to my instinctive desire to adjust to my environment. My speech patterns changed, words of courtesy were no longer part of my vocabulary, and I regarded politeness as strange and a sign of weakness. I searched constantly for a purpose to justify my struggle for survival; Nazi hatred and the promise of vengeance now both seemed inadequate reasons.

I had forgotten how to enjoy the sight of a tree or an isolated wild flower. I regarded nature as an adversary; winters had brought frostbite and terrible discomfort; hot mountain summers caused unspeakable weariness and dehydration.

Time and again, we had gathered on the immense *Appellplatz*. Weather meant little to our overseers; whether we would dry up under the summer sun or freeze in the knee-deep snow, the camp orchestra played Wagner and the SS shed tears over the fate of the Walkyries and the struggle of their gods in the Valhalla. The concerts ended, and we would stumble back to the barracks through the snow or mud, frequently losing our shoes and holding on to one another for support.

17

Once I.G. Farben had been rendered useless by the incessant Allied bombing, we were transported swiftly to a sub-camp at the Dynamit-Nobel A.G. in Allendorf. There, in underground bunkers which served as a munitions factory, we labored much in the same capacity as at the I.G. Farben.

As the Allied air-raids increased in number and extent of damage, as "experienced" munitions laborers, we were shuttled from one factory to another. Our work force commuted between Allendorf and Fürstenhagen in Hessisch Lichtenau between repairs of one and the destruction of the other factory.

It was now even more difficult to discern any consistency in our day-to-day existence. To be sure, we felt needed, and as long as there were still factories left, we felt the Nazis would spare the lives of those slaves whose labor was essential in prolonging their war effort. Besides, they knew that, sooner or later, we would drop of exhaustion. The fact still remained that the Jews were to be *verbraucht*, "used up" like you use up a piece of sandpaper.

Once again, we were back in Buchenwald. There was much excitement. We sensed great changes. The B.B.C. broadcast had us all glued to the Kapo's set. The announcer's voice came across clearly, and someone would quickly translate:

ON JUNE 6, 1944, AT 0935 HOURS, A COMMUNIQUE WAS ISSUED BY THE SUPREME HEADQUARTERS, ALLIED EXPEDITIONARY FORCE. IT WENT AS FOLLOWS: UNDER THE COMMAND OF GENERAL EISENHOWER, ALLIED NAVAL FORCES, SUPPORTED BY STRONG AIR FORCE UNITS, BEGAN LANDING ALLIED ARMIES THIS MORNING ON THE NORTHERN COAST OF FRANCE.

Allied warplanes took off from airfields in France. The French were jubilant, and their cry was picked up in every corner of Europe.

Nazi broadcasts on the contrary, were marked by a conspicuous absence of the *Führer*'s hoarse voice. However, it was business as usual within the confines of the barbed wire fence. Would the SS carry out its mandate and destroy the Jews even in their own defeat? We continued to wonder.

"Can you hear the sounds of friendly artillery, Menasha? Do you hear? Feel the earth tremble!" I asked my friend.

In his partial stupor Menasha didn't realize that we had long since ceased our clean-up excursions to Weimar. He had moments of lucidity during which he now often recited from memory the great wisdom of the Midrash. We looked forward to those uplifting moments, especially since they provided the only source of excitement for our faltering friend.

"We've got to keep going, Roman!" I urged. "We must do all we can to survive! Now more than ever! Hitler's end is near!" The earth shook under the impact of the distant explosions.

"We will," Roman responded softly. "Can you hear them, Menasha?" Roman repeated my question. "You must live, you must survive."

Suddenly Menasha turned his head toward us and spoke with the deliberate slowness of a Hasidic scholar. "My dear friends, no one really survives a war. . . we all leave something irretrievable behind. . . something dear. . . indispensable. . . a piece of humanity. . . a part of life. . . part of ourselves . . ." He paused, gasping for breath. "The song of the ghetto ends with the *Maarev, hash-kee-vay- noo*. . . put to rest again. . . we must all pray that we may be put to rest again. . . pray with me. . ."

We prayed together; at first only to humor the Hasid and then to regain our own strength. Uniting in the mystical bond of the condemned, we held on to the last vestige of civilized humanity left us; faith.

"*Gotenyu*, dear God, help us for we have tried and failed." We prayed and we wept without tears. "Love had made us weak and humor made us seem unreal. We hoped that salvation was on its way, and the enemy turned our hope to ashes. All we had left was hate. And now, dear Lord, lift up the curse from us, for we have been punished enough, even for the transgressions of our sinful ancestors. Dear Lord, You have brought us down to our knees, crawling in the dust, show Your trust in us again and let us walk upright; restore in us the dignity of man! Forgive, and be no longer a God of vengeance!" We prayed.

"Hi mom and dad,

Utah Beach was our first actual glimpse of a battlefield. We arrived here on July 19th, a little over a month after "D" Day. I sure wish I'd been here then. Those were the real fireworks.

We could hear the booming of the big guns to the east of us, and once some of the Nazi shells landed down on the beach. The air was real tense before the landing. I guess everybody was nervous.

Soon after, we loaded into L.C.T. boats and finally hit the beach. I felt better facing the enemy than sitting on that tub! The Nazis indirectly drew first blood when two of my buddies from "B" Company were killed while removing mines on the road out of Coutances. Several more were injured.

The booming of the guns got closer. On August first we received the assignment we've been waiting for. We were to be part of a task force whose mission it was to go through the gap at Avranches, drive straight through enemy territory, wiping out small pockets of the Nazis, and bypassing strong points. Our objective was Brest, many miles into the French countryside and far from the Brittany Peninsula.

We've been moving pretty fast since then. By August 4th we moved north toward the village of Miniac. It was in the towns we took that we first realized that we were contributing to the freeing of a people. They cheered us almost hysterically in a joyful demonstration as we rode through the towns. They lined the streets and packed the windows; they cheered and waved and threw flowers. And the girls, you just can't imagine, beautiful dolls would grab you and kiss you right there on the road! I guess that's the most enjoyable thing so far in the campaign.

Don't you worry. I'll be home soon and Isaac too. Love, your son Victor."

"Mickey, I'm so worried." Fay finished reading the letter.

"Dearest, there's no reason to be worried." He assured her.

"Already two of his friends died, can't you see? It's dangerous."

"He'll come through, Fay, you'll see." He managed a smile. "First they got a good reception from the Red Cross; now, there are French girls. Can't be that bad, eh?" Mickey tried to humor his wife but she remained unconvinced.

"And we haven't heard from the younger one in months. Do you think . . . ?"

"Soon as he has a minute, he'll write, you'll see." Mickey paused. "War's a serious business, Fay and not always easy to sit down and write. He's okay, I'm sure." He embraced his wife.

"I just hope they'll come home safe and sound before I worry myself sick." She cleared her throat loudly. "I hope and pray to God."

It was bitter cold on the morning of January 12, 1945 when we heard the familiar voice of our Kapo: "*Raus, zum Appell!*"

We were herded into the *Appellplatz*, where the SS brass were gathered in their finest parade uniforms. Kapos ran back and forth, shouting frenzied orders more diligently than usual, and we had soon become instinctively aware that changes were taking place that would affect us more profoundly than before. We looked at one another silently resigned; only our hollow eyes spoke that special language inmates had learned to understand through the common bond of the oppressed.

"*Achtung!*" The Kapo yelled. The SS officers approached the platform. "The Commandant himself!" A murmur went through the vast ranks. One of the commandant's aids took to the rostrum.

"Silence! Listen carefully! Swine!" We held our breath with great fear. He continued. "The numbers I'll read must step forward and form orderly ranks of fours in front of the rostrum! There will be no talking in the ranks! Act quickly and avoid punishment! Now step lively when you hear your number!"

Endlessly, it had seemed, all of the block numbers had been called. Roman and Menasha were on the mysterious roster. My number had not been called.

"Oh, my God!" I thought desperately. "They're finally going to separate us! Roman! What'll we do? Don't leave me behind by myself! God! Don't let them do this to us! Not now, please!" I pleaded desperately.

At sixteen, I was not yet fully developed. A sensitive, intense youth, my eyes reflected the memory of those days of anguish when I had heard the cries of mothers forced to part with their children—children asking why they could not remain with their parents. I kept hearing little voices, inquiring why these men in black uniforms were so mean. Now, I heard them very clearly, though I had tried to erase those events from my memory, longing instead to recapture the magic of my early youth and the wondrous mysteries of growing up.

Behind me were years of forced labor and ghetto confinement in my native Poland. My sunken cheeks and bent-over frame bore marks of the harrowing past. They had given my already small body an even punier appearance. The clean shaven head had barely sprouted hair, but that was enough to reveal a dark brown hue.

Roman was two years older and only inches taller. He looked at me with his sad eyes, and there was a trace of a dark mustache. He, too, struck a sad figure in the loosely-fitting striped prisoner garb, desperately trying to keep his feet warm while marching in place. It was once again one of those severe winters in the hills of Thuringia and snow covered the ground with a thick blanket, showing nature at its worst.

Roman was silent, helpless and unable to fight back any longer. Suddenly, Menasha exchanged my jacket for his own with a surge of uncommon energy, he ripped my jacket off me and put his own in its place. "Take it, my dear Vilek, and go with God. I haven't much time left, and the two of you belong together!" He whispered forcefully, and there was a mysterious strength in his words.

"No, Menasha, I can't!" I resisted meekly.

"Don't be a fool." He hissed. "I've been spitting blood for the last two weeks."

"May God be with you, too, dearest Menasha! Until we meet again!" I said chokingly, and we hugged. As we walked away, I looked up toward the heavens: "Please, dear Lord, Gotenyu, take note at this moment of Menasha's supreme *tzeddakah*, the greatest of sacrifices one man can offer for another! He's giving his life for mine!"

Our group was driven by the guards and Kapos through the vast assembly yard toward the distant railroad spur, where an empty freight train was waiting. We did not look back; it was like running from Sodom and Gomorrah.

That was the last time I saw my Piotrkover friend Menasha "the Hasid." I would not forget this tall, slim man in his early forties who walked like one unaccustomed to walking. At home, in Piotrkow, he used to drive his own droshky and was a giant of a man. His hollow cheeks were once adorned by a handsome raven beard, and his lifeless hazel eyes once argued the Midrash. They now held the two departing friends in their view, while his lips moved in prayer, though no sound could be heard. That, too, as much as survival itself, was a miracle of faith.

We had traveled four days and five nights, locked in the box-cars. I did not complain. The renewed hardships were not nearly as bad as separation from one another might have been.

On the fifth morning our transport arrived at its destination. The sliding doors came open, and we faced our new masters—men in their sixties and boys in thier teens, with milk fuzz above their upper lip, wearing loosely fitting Wehrmacht uniforms and shouldering somewhat antiquated rifles. They shouted orders, as they attempted to appear more fierce than reality permitted.

"The *Führer*'s desperate. This is not his old team," I remarked as we marched toward the distant barracks.

"You may be right, Vilek, let's hope you're right."

"Look at them! The boys can't be much older than me, and the old men's hands are shaking."

"Give them a little time, and they'll live up to the *Führer*'s expectations. A trembling finger can squeeze off a round just as easily as a steady hand." Roman observed.

"They look harmless enough."

"Don't be fooled by appearances." Roman cautioned.

"I wonder how Menasha's doing. What do you think'll happen to him?" I asked.

"Worry about yourself now, little brother. You can't help our friend. He knew what he was doing, didn't he?" My brother's eyes glazed over though he tried to appear harsh.

"Was I right to accept?"

"Who can tell? Who knows what awaits us here?"

"Am I less selfish because of this uncertainty?"

"Stop blaming yourself. Menasha had faith. He wanted it this way. Stop tormenting yourself." Roman pleaded.

Eventually, I managed to convince myself that all this was meant to be, it was *bashaert*, and nothing could be changed.

"The name of your *Arbeitslager*, is Colditz!" *Scharführer* Emil Tulka shouted. A veteran of the Russian front, he wore the Iron Cross II class round his neck, and a glass eye in the right socket. "As your camp commandant, I am not a man to be trifled with." Tulka went on. "Anyone who gets out of line will be severely punished or shot on the spot!" Tulka looked like a man of his word, and no one felt like challenging him. "We produce the bazooka here. You work dilligently, you live. You don't, you die!" Tulka turned the assembly over to the kapo. He was a man of few words.

Colditz lay thirty kilometers from Borna, in Saxony, on the cross-roads between Leipzig and Dresden. In better days, this had been the center where *Meissner* china was manufactured; a commodity discontinued with the conversion of the factory for war purposes.

"The enemy's doing badly." I said.

"It's bad to be the slave of a crippled master." Roman replied.

"He'll take his infirmity out on you."

"His end is in sight."

"Who knows? Ours may come sooner."

"We are only a few kilometers away from home, Roman, so very close to home." I tried to kindle a spark of optimism in my brother.

"What do you mean?"

"There must be a reason. It must mean something that we had been brought this close to home." I argued. "We're going to live, Roman. We've got to hold out just a while longer."

"I don't know if I can, Vilek. I really don't know."

"We're too close to give up now! You must be brave!" I urged.

"I'll try, Vilek." He reflected. "I can't promise more than that."

"Just think of it, Roman. To outlive the enemy! To see him as a Prisoner of War! To try him as a war criminal! Just think!"

"I'm thinking, but I'm also hungry."

"We'll eat grass, if we have to or we'll live on garbage. Anything to survive, Roman!" I urged. "Think of it, too, Boost didn't make it and we will. We'll visit his widow and the girls."

"You're dreaming, Vilek." Roman was weary. "Hitler won't let us outlive him. Never in a million years."

"We'll do it in spite of him!"

"Dear mom and dad, this is your son, 1st. Lt. Isaac Meyerson. Surprised?

Well, don't be. It's a field commission and there's been a lot of action here lately; that's why the long silence. I'm fine, don't worry, physically, that is. But mentally, that's another story. Our outfit was doing some mop up routine around the German town of Allach in Bavaria. It was a tough German roadblock and the Krauts had it well covered with fire. We couldn't move forward.

We had to take them out, so Lt. Garber called for volunteers. I knew we were close to the concentration camp Dachau, so I joined the small unit. We moved very slowly because the area was mined. Our first casualty was Cpl. Memer; he hit a mine. Then, Lt. Garber heard one of the guys calling for help. As he attempted to reach the man, he was shot through the head. Later on I got my field commission. As the company sergeant, I was in line to take over.

We got through and finally reached the woods. I joined a tank unit that was rolling down toward Dachau. We got there before dawn. Good Lord, mom and dad, I can't describe the things we saw. I stood there like paralyzed, then I started to cry like a baby; everybody else, all the guys, did too.

One of the guys walked over to this railway siding because he saw what looked like some cattle-cars there. There were about forty-five wagons. Then he called everybody, and we ran like mad thinking that there were some Krauts holding out. What we saw was beyond description: the wagons were full of dead, ematiated bodies, piled up like some scrap iron all twisted up and waiting to be melted down. Across the tracks there was the crematory where the Nazis were burning the Jews, only this time they didn't have time to finish their filthy job. The stench was enormous and I was getting sick to my stomach. I wanted to run out of there and kill all of the Krauts, but I just sat there, and cried. Oh, mom, dad, now I know why I came here to fight those damned Nazis. Don't worry, I'll take care. Will write as soon as I can.

Love, your son Isaac"

"Oh, dear Lord, merciful God, forgive us!" Fay whimpered sadly. Mickey held her in his embrace, his eyes turned toward heaven. They prayed.

"Please, dear, don't go on blaming yourself." He pleaded with his wife. "We just didn't know."

"We can't claim ignorance, Mickey." She cried. "Else the whole world will do the same."

"You're right, Fay dear." He agreed. "We should have. . ." She didn't let him finish the sentence. With a loud cry, she ran into the bedroom and he followed her, alarmed. "Fay, darling, don't lock me out, please." He pleaded at the door. "We need one another now more than ever. Please, come out, let's talk about it. Come out, dear."

During the next few months, transports kept coming daily from all parts of Germany. Inmates from Dachau, Belsen, even Auschwitz.

"See? What did I tell you?" I said triumphantly. "This munitions manufacture is important. We're more valuable to the Nazis now alive than dead. They need their own people on the battle fronts. It'll save us in the end."

Roman listened to my logic, shook his head in silence, and went on about his work. To him, I was living in a world of make-believe. Food was rationed out to the new arrivals without an increase in supply while our workload grew. SS reinforcements arrived with each new transport and stayed on as part of the camp guard.

As food became scarcer, Roman talked incessantly about dying.

"I know I'm going to die soon, Vilek." He started. "Remember to bury me. I don't want to die like a wild animal and be thrown to the vultures."

"You're talking nonsense again, Roman." I said. "Why don't you stop it. You only make it worse than it is. Besides, I'm frightened too."

"Wish it would come quickly, without much pain." He ignored my appeals.

"You've never been one to tolerate pain, Roman." I was going to distract him. "Remember the time we got our tetanus shots? It was me who had to go first. You made me prove that it didn't hurt and wouldn't let the nurse touch you."

"You still remember that?" He showed surprise.

"How could I forget? I felt like running away when I saw that hypodermic coming at me, but seeing how frightened you were took some of the fear from me."

"Is that how you feel now?" He reflected.

"In a way." I paused. "I guess, we'll just have to remind each other how important it is not to give up. Not now."

"All I can think of is that I'm dying of hunger. Forgive me, little brother."

"You've got to get a hold of yourself, Roman." I begged. "The end is in sight."

"Yes, I know." Roman whispered sadly. I knew he intentionally misconstrued what I said.

The daily ersatz brew only remotely resembled soup. We connived our turn in queue, to make sure the cook's ladle scraped the bottom of the vat, fishing out the precious residue of bone fragments and turnips.

"They're only rat bones anyhow." Moniek said.

"Good Lord! What I wouldn't give for a decent meal!" Yossele remarked. "Five years of my life. I'd give five years for such a treat!"

"What five years?" Moniek asked.

We looked at one another meaningfully. I was terribly worried about him. Roman's face was drawn, his eyes deeply set in their sockets, circled by dark shadows. It was a familiar sight; we were on intimate terms with death. His face was a reflection of my own.

I tossed restlessly in my waking sleep. I must do something. I thought. Toward dawn, the steaming vats stood ready on the large table. There was no one around. Quickly, I reached deep into the nearest vat, my arm was elbow deep in the steaming substance. Forgotten was the threat of punishment at being caught; ignored the burning, intense heat. I was fascinated by the prospect of running joyfully to my brother with the precious booty of a few bones—perhaps even a particle of meat—tucked safely under my jacket. In our lair, we devoured the booty without guilt or remorse.

Our assignment on the assembly line was to mold the triggering device and the firing-pin for the anti-tank weapon.

"What would happen," I asked Roman, "if we bent the metal just a bit out of shape?"

"The mechanism will not fire," Roman responded in a whisper. There I caught the old fire in his eyes again.

"You know, Vilek, I've been thinking of doing something like that all along." He hesitated. "This way, if we die, we won't die like beasts. The enemy sent us back to our pig's trough. They want us to die without dignity." He muttered absentmindedly. "I'll go mad if this goes on much longer. The most wicked crime is murdering our intelligence and our courage."

"You know what'll happen if we're discovered?" I asked, yet I knew that no threat could keep us from following the dictates of our conscience.

"This'll be for our mother and Felusia. . ."

". . .and for our grandparents . . ."

". . .for Nora and Hayim and Devorah . . ."

". . .and for all the murdered children . . ."

". . .everyone who died *al Kiddush Hashem* . . ."

We repeated to ourselves with every blemished part we punched on our presses. We were uplifted by the singular nature of our conspiracy. We whispered about it in the secrecy of our bunk. We hallucinated visions of the enemy anti-tank crews trying to fire their defective weapons at the Allied tanks; being crushed under the steel giants with a puzzling look in their faces while they screamed with fear at the approaching behemoth. It was good to be part of the resistance again!

Tulka suffered fits of absurd rage, during which the good eye turned into a goggle, threatening to burst out of its socket. At Colditz, Tulka was the embodied power of autocracy, grotesque and terrible. It was so, because he represented the power of the Third Reich, he was its guardian. And it must have become clear even to the *Scharführer* by now, that the vestiges of that power had begun to crack in their fragile foundation.

On the few occasions, when Tulka addressed the inmates, I was able to sense a loathing he felt for all of us. "How is it that he hates us with such intensity," I asked Roman, "when he had never before laid his eyes on any of us?"

"His one eye," Roman corrected me. "He hates us by instinct, little brother. He can't be much over the age of twenty-five; a product of the Third Reich and the *Führer's Mein Kampf*" Roman paused. "Besides," he added, "we must pay for the loss of his eye."

"Dear mom and dad,

I wish I didn't have to be the bearer of such terrible news, but you'll be getting a letter from the State Department right about now (maybe you've got it already?!) and I'd rather you hear it from me: Isaac died a hero's death, and I know how you'll grieve for my dear brother, so let me tell you that he didn't die in vain. I talked to his company Commander and learned from him things I never knew about my kid brother. Just before they got to the big concentration camp Buchenwald, Isaac went ahead of the unit, he volunteered on a mopping-up mission. The Krauts were wicked with their 88's and mortars; the stuff came crushing in on Isaac's platoon all the time, and they were pinned down and couldn't move ahead. It was then, Isaac got up and ran in a moment of blind fury, reaching the Nazi pill-box, he blew it up with a few grenades, killing all inside but not before he got his: shrapnell hit him just as he reached his objective. He was dead on the spot but he took fifteen Nazis along. You can be proud of your son, mom and dad.

I reached Buchenwald yesterday, and I know why Isaac died trying to get there before me. The damned Nazis took almost everybody out of here by freight train days before we arrived. Some poor souls had been left. They just walked around like the living dead. Oh, God, you should see them!

We're moving on East, and I hope I'll be able to find somebody of our families there. There is a ray of hope. We're bombing all the railway tracks now, and the Nazis won't have those trains anymore to transport their slaves.

It's getting close to the end of the line for the Nazis and their Third Reich. Pity we had to lose lives in the process, but I guess that's the way things happen. We killed many Nazis; the odds were way up, but I feel that there could be no ratio that could even up the toll. I'll take care, so please don't worry about me. I'll be seeing you soon at home. I'm now with Gen. Patton's Third Army, and it was because of him that we liberated Buchenwald.

The war had moved deep into central Germany now, but still there are small pockets of the enemy around and there is also the problem of finding and arresting high ranking Nazis taking refuge in civilian clothes. They're hiding out in small towns and villages in droves and the population protects them.

We're screening these towns and throwing out Nazi mayors and putting people in office that we think might be converted to our way of thinking. Oh, they would all protest well enough about how much each of them hated the Nazis and how they were all "good" Germans, but very few of them fooled us, and our catch of Nazi criminals was pretty large. I'm probably boring you with all this, but you'd be proud of me the way I used my Yiddish and the little German I learned in school to talk to these bandits over here!

We also came on vast stores of materials and goods the Nazis had stolen. I saw the roads filled with liberated Russians, Poles, French and people from many other countries who had been held in captivity by the Nazis for years. The stories they told us were not pretty. Buchenwald told me more than words could tell. Barbarians could not have thought up a more gruesome torture than the so-called civilized Germans inflicted on their poor victims. When we got there the bodies were still piled high; bodies of those unfortunates who almost made it. The bodies were merely skin and bones, and their gaunt faces reflected the horrible existence they had been forced to lead. After seeing Buchenwald, I knew I'd kill every bastard SS man I'd find.

So you see, Isaac didn't die for nothing. I know it's not much of a consolation to you, but it'll help you to know all these things to ease your mourning for our dear Isaac.

I love you both.

Your son, Victor"

Fay listened to Mickey's painful, monotone reading of Victor's letter, occasionally interrupting with a heavy sigh. Only her constant sniffling indicated to him that she wept. He finished and put the letter on the table. There was a moment of uneasy silence, and Mickey sat for a long while lost in his thoughts. He was surprised that Fay had taken the news with such uncharacteristic calm.

"It's all finished for me now." She said. "They've killed my baby. There's nothing else for me." Her voice had a hollow sound and her face bore the expression of utter resignation. "I felt it in my bones all along." She added. "It was *bashaert*."

Only then did Mickey realize the reason for Fay's unusual resignation. She was preparing herself all along for the inevitable to happen. Now that it has come, she accepted her fate without spite or rancor.

"Wish you wouldn't talk this way, dearest." Mickey implored his wife. "We're still a family."

"But the baby's gone, Mickey. He's gone forever." She repeated.

"There's Victor." He said.

"Victor'll get along without me." She replied. "He's a man now."

"Don't talk nonsense, dear." He tried to embrace her but she withdrew. "We're still a family. We need each other."

"Isaac, my darling Isaac, he's gone now." She almost hummed to herself. Mickey looked at his wife with deep concern. It was his turn now to weep. His fingers tore into the crop of his hair as Fay was leaving the room. He was weeping loudly now, repeating to himself: "I'm guilty, Lord. Don't be too severe on your humble servant, oh Lord."

Three major powers had met at Yalta to decide the fate of the enemy on February 10–17. The year was 1945. We listened to their joint communique over the clandestine radio:

WE HAVE CONSIDERED AND DETERMINED THE MILITARY PLANS OF THE THREE ALLIED POWERS FOR THE FINAL DEFEAT OF THE COMMON ENEMY. THE MILITARY STAFFS OF THE THREE ALLIED POWERS HAVE MET DAILY THROUGHOUT THE CONFERENCE. THESE MEETINGS HAVE BEEN MOST SATISFACTORY FROM EVERY POINT OF VIEW AND HAVE RESULTED IN CLOSER COORDINATION OF THE MILITARY EFFORTS OF THE THREE ALLIES THAN EVER BEFORE. THE FULLEST INFORMATION HAS BEEN INTERCHANGED. THE TIMING, SCOPE, AND COORDINATION OF NEW AND EVEN MORE POWERFUL BLOWS TO BE LAUNCHED BY OUR ARMIES AND AIR FORCES INTO THE HEART OF GERMANY FROM EAST, WEST, NORTH AND SOUTH HAVE BEEN FULLY AGREED AND PLANNED IN DETAIL. OUR COMBINED MILITARY PLANS WILL BE MADE KNOWN ONLY AS WE EXECUTE THEM, BUT WE BELIEVE THAT THE VERY CLOSE WORKING PARTNERSHIP AMONG THE THREE STAFFS ATTAINED AT THIS CONFERENCE WILL RESULT IN SHORTENING THE WAR. NAZI GERMANY IS DOOMED, THE GERMAN PEOPLE WILL ONLY MAKE THE COST OF THEIR DEFEAT HEAVIER TO THEMSELVES BY ATTEMPTING TO CONTINUE A HOPELESS RESISTANCE.

The Soviet offensive westward through Poland was gaining momentum with the conclusion of the Crimea Conference, and our excitement was beyond measure. Suddenly, our greatest foe was time itself. Each day we listened secretely, our ears glued to the radio, to the Allied broadcasts.

"Dear Lord," I prayed, "sustain us a bit longer, give us strength to endure a few more days. After all, dear God, what's a few days in the course of Your Creation?"

"The Nazis are on the run! The swastika's cracking up, little brother." Roman was joyful for the first time in months.

"Now all of us are fighting for time, the master as well as the slave." I mused.

We began to plan our future.

"Give me a baked potato, and I'll never complain about food again." Roman said.

"We'll put up gravestones for the family at the old Piotrkow cemetery, won't we, Roman?"

"It'll be the first thing we'll do." Roman responded. It was a good sign. "Once this is over," he added.

"But. . ." I hesitated, "I'm afraid, Roman. . .I think I have forgotten what it means to be free."

"Don't worry, little brother," Roman comforted me, "you won't have any trouble with it, when the time comes." He paused, searching for an appropriate example. He found one. "You know, freedom's much like riding a bicycle or learning to swim; once you get the hang of it, it'll come back to you, no matter how long you've stayed away from it."

While we talked about survival, there were renewed rumors about another transport. The rumors became persistent with the increased intensity of air-raids and the rumbling of Allied artillery as the front line got nearer. We listened, and the approaching thunder of the explosions sounded like the music from Beethoven's symphonies; it signified the nearness of a liberating force. But the hushed sound of rumors brought with it the old fear. What if after all we had endured till then, we might be denied to experience the end of our enemy?

We had heard that name mentioned time and again. They said that more than fifteen thousand Jewish children passed through Theresienstadt in northern Bohemia as they were being trucked to the gas chambers of Auschwitz. The camp was intended as a model to be shown to outsiders, where musicians were encouraged to form symphonic orchestras and musical ensembles, and children were active in art classes.

"Theresienstadt!" The camp was on everybody's lips.

"Why would they want to drag six hundred corpses the distance of one hundred and twenty kilometers? Surely, they'd make a faster retreat without us."

"You understand, I have orders!" Tulka began in a hoarse, provoking tone. It was hard to determine the natural sound of his voice for he had surely never used it when addressing us. "I don't like this more than you do!" He continued, while we stood on the assembly place on a misty May morning. "I'm only doing my duty. Orders of the *Reichsführer*! We march tomorrow at dawn!" He paused, as if gathering his thoughts. "Anyway, the Soviets are near! Some day, you'll thank me for saving you from these damned Communists!"

Tulka glanced at his wristwatch. This confounded rabble is taking up much of my precious time. He must have thought. From the looks of it, he must have promised his wife and their two boys to be home for supper.

"The deceitful bastard sounds almost sincere!" Our Vilna friend Abram Bachter hissed under his breath. We welcomed Abram into our Piotrkow group, and we looked up to him, a man in his late forties. He was a Biblical scholar, quickly dubbed "the rabbi." He didn't mind. His voice was deep, almost harsh, and yet caressing in its harshness as he addressed us with much affection.

"What are we going to to, *rebbe*?" I asked. Abram's eyes still held the fire of the faithful within them. His large aquiline nose gave the impression of being larger than it really was because of the total absence of flesh on his cheekbones.

"We're not marching with them." Roman interjected.

"We won't make it, if we march." Abram said.

"It's too close to give up now." I whispered. "Let's think about it."

"What's there to think about? We're not going." Roman said stubbornly.

There wasn't much time for involved planning. That night, listening to the rumble of heavy artillery, we made our bid for freedom. We had no time to lose. Evacuation was only a few hours away. It looked easy. We climbed into one of the large inactive furnaces, up the tall chimney, several flights of small steps had led us into a niche where we settled down on a couple of blankets. Our eyes adjusted to the darkness and our sense of touch detected items we could not see.

"We'll stay put till they leave." Roman said, and I detected a slight tremor in his voice. If he was frightened, my older brother was trying very hard to conceal his fear. I was glad of the darkness, which allowed me to conceal my own fright as well.

I could hear the shots and Tulka's shrill voice giving commands. I dared not breathe, and I prayed the same memorized prayers over and over again. It was the longest night of my life.

"If we both survive, or only one of us," Roman whispered solemnly, "let's make a promise, a covenant, right here and now." He paused, and I didn't dare interrupt. I sensed the importance of the moment. "Let's swear to tell the story of our descent into hell. We have witnessed the destruction of Polish Jews; if we remain alive, we must bear witness. We mustn't ever let the world forget!"

"Will the world believe this unbelievable experience?" I asked.

"Never mind that, Vilek." Roman was adamant. "There'll be those who will deny all of this some day; the Nazis out of guilt; the rest of the world out of embarrassment. But we can't worry about either of them. We have a mission to fulfill, else all of those martyred deaths are going to be meaningless."

"Why wouldn't the world believe?" I asked. "After all, the Christians repeat the Jesus story every year. Are they afraid they'd forget it? And wasn't he one of us?"

"That's different, little brother." Roman's voice betrayed impa tience. "Maybe they want people to think the Jews killed their God?" He paused. "Maybe that's why they hate us so much. Oh well, let's not talk about Jesus at a time like this."

"Just the same," I insisted, "if Jesus were here today, he'd be hiding in this chimney alongside all of us. I can hear our grandfather Srulko's voice: 'You mustn't forget! You mustn't forgive!'" I sobbed quietly.

We embraced. "Please forgive me if I've offended you in the past. I meant no harm." I pleaded.

"And you must try to forgive me for all the pain I had caused you, little brother." We made peace with one another, and though we had tried to alternate sleep, we were vigilant for every small noise coming our way.

Dawn was announced by more shouting and commotion in the factory yard. We recognized Tulka's voice again, shouting, giving orders, threatening. The rat-ta-ta-ta of automatic firearms broke often into the yelling din of humanity; of cries of pain and lamenta tions as we huddled in the dark entrails of the chimney quietly, afraid that our uneven breathing might be overheard on the distant *Appellplatz*.

Time and again, the metal shutter leading up to the chimney had been opened and closed, and the metallic sound reverberated throughout the hollow shell of our hideout. Our silent prayers rose in intensity each time the small gate opened.

We had lost the sense of time, and it seemed late afternoon when all the shouting ceased.

"Thank God, they've gone" I whispered.

"We're safe," Roman responded. "I think we're free."

"Lord only knows," I whispered in return, "be still, it might not be over yet."

"*Scusi, amico!*" Suddenly a voice called out from below. It belonged to one of the Italian P.O.W.'s who were brought to Colditz a few months ago. "We're here, below you!" The voice insisted. "Where are you? Speak to us, *esta bene*, we're friends, *amici*! Don't be afraid!"

"Oh, God," I began whimpering. "The Italians will attract the search party, as sure as we're here!" We couldn't risk responding. The voice continued urgently, "*viene liberta!. . . americani!*"

"We're not the only fugitives!" Roman suddenly whispered. "We'll surely be missed! Tulka's nobody's fool! Damn! This would have to happen right now! They'll hear the lousy Italians yelling below! Why can't they keep their mouths shut?"

"We've got to get out of this rat hole!" I suggested. "If the Italians found it to be a good hiding place, so will Tulka!"

"As soon as it gets dark outside!" Roman agreed. In long silence, we planned our retreat, and suddenly it was too late. We heard the metal shutter open, and it was clearly SS Commandant Tulka's voice shouting into the furnace:

"All of you, up there! Come out at once, you damned pigs! Come out or we'll fire the furnace and fry you alive!"

The fugitives hesitated and the SS forced a straw sack into the opening of the furnace. Tulka was about to put a lighted match to it when the two Italians emerged and went down to their knees before him. "Please, please let us live," one begged, "there are four little ones, bambini, and my wife, Giovanetta, waiting for me in Naples. Please, I meant no harm, I want to live," he pleaded.

"Can you hear the big guns of the *americani*? They're so very near, let us live! We are not fighters! Let us go back to our families," the second Italian begged, weeping.

"Is anyone else up there?" Tulka shouted. "Tell the truth, is anyone hiding there besides you? Speak and go free!"

The promise of life was too tempting for the desperate Italians, and it took only a short moment for them to make up their minds. Once again, Tulka approached the furnace. He placed his head into the opening, and we were able to see the reflection of the glass eye in the narrow streak of light which entered from the outside.

"The bastards!" I seethed angrily.

"Don't judge too severely," Roman cautioned sadly. "You can't be too sure you wouldn't do the same in their place."

"Out, you dogs! Come out! *Schnell!*" Tulka shouted, as smoke began its slow ascent, soon filling out the narrow confines of the chimney. The smell began to irritate our eyes at first, and soon we couldn't breathe. I coughed violently.

"It's no use, Roman!" I pleaded with my brother. "Let's get out or we'll fry in here!"

There was nothing we could do now but accept the blows of the SS as we surrendered. Tulka was enraged, blow upon blow rained down on our bodies. The sounds of battle were approaching rapidly, and we dared to waste his precious time.

"March!" He shouted. The two Italians remained apologetic, the SS cursed, and some of the young recruits laughed as they led us toward the main factory yard. It did not matter anymore. We continued to pray as we were led to the far end of the yard. There we were ordered to line up against the tall caliche wall, our arms raised high.

We were preceded there by the others. There was Yossele, glancing toward us fearfully, unable to sustain our questioning looks. And there was Tuviah, standing between Yossele and Yacov Teitelbaum, Roman's classmate from the Piotrkow *kheder*. And there were the others.

"I can't believe I'm seeing right!" I whispered. "It's Yacov! Standing next to Yossele, isn't it?"

"It's him all right. When did he get here?"

"What does it matter now." I shrugged my shoulders. "We're all in for it anyway."

Abram was next in the lineup, and then there were the two Italians and some thirty-five more fugitives.

"*Gotenyu*, dear Lord! A miracle now. . .give us a miracle, we beseech You. If there ever was a time for miracles, it is now!" I prayed. The world suddenly became more beautiful. It was a splendid May afternoon. The birds were chirping and the sun and the clouds were painfully new to me. "Dear God," I prayed, "I haven't yet begun to live . . . don't take me away yet. . . let me live a little, dear God. . ."

As we approached, I had noticed a man next to the two Italians, his face mutilated, bloodied to a pulp. "Don't you recognize me?" He whispered urgently. I stared aimlessly without response. The man began sobbing quietly, his face grotesquely distorted. "I'm Moshe," he sobbed, "Moshe Lasker, Piotrkover. I was your grandfather's neighbor on Zamkowa Street."

From the corner of my eye, I glanced at the man whose *shtetl* nickname was *Moshe der starke*. He used to be a giant of a man who could lift the side of a droshky with one arm and replace a broken wheel with the other. He was a town legend, the strong man of our shtetl, someone who would take up for the weak, who would protect the Hasid from the town ruffians on the prowl. Now, Moshe faced a crisis of his own, and his features seemed to beg forgiveness, as if apologizing for his impotence.

The Italians prayed weepingly, kneeling on the ground, their hands piously folded, invoking the mercies of the Father, the Son, and the Holy Ghost. Everyone prayed. There wasn't much time left, the machine-gun emplacement stared at all of us, and each had tried, as best he could, to make peace between God and himself.

Tulka came forward. "Pray to me, you dumb pigs!" He shouted. "Your God is busy with more important matters. He has no time to listen to a few miserable swine such as you! I'm your god now! Do you hear? I'm the one you must pray to!"

We ignored the ranting of the "glass-eyed monster," which further enraged him. "Now! Lie down! Face into the dirt!" He ordered, and we obeyed. Tulka unbuttoned his britches and urinated on top of the prostrate worshippers. His young subordinates followed eagerly his example. Still, we continued to pray.

"Hear oh Israel, the Lord our God, the Lord is One!"—In the Name of the Father, the Son, and the Holy Ghost!" Echoed the two Italians.

"I piss on your prayer! I piss on your Gods!" The shrill voice was that of a raving madman. "I'll make you regret it, you stupid shits!" Tulka looked wildly at the men lying before him. He took his luger out of the holster and aimed at them. "Get up now! Over there! Line up against the wall!" Our prayers intensified. He ordered the machine-gun trained on the line-up. "You!" He counted off the first group of five on the extreme right. "Step over there!"

"Fire!!" A brief salvo followed, and the men fell to the ground. Another salvo, and then another. I counted between fifteen to twenty men, as the firing noise drowned out the mourner's prayers. It all took only a few seconds and then the firing ceased.

"Thank the Almighty!"

"Praised be the Lord!"

"We're alive!"

We looked around as if in a daze. The two Italians were still in their kneeling position, praying. Our small group from Piotrkow stood in silence, stunned, unbelieving. We weren't quite able to understand what had happened. We tried not to look at the bodies of the men sprawled in thin puddles of blood, their faces distorted with fear; their souls had found no relief in death.

"Bury the dogs! *Schnell!*" Tulka barked.

He wanted us to bury the dead as quickly as possible to conceal the evidence from the approaching Allies. We reasoned. We went about our work eagerly, still hoping to be spared. It was then 3:40 p.m.

"I'm going to give up. It's no use. I can't go on any longer." Roman whispered. The two of us had placed another limp body of one of the victims onto a narrow board. We attempted to push it up a steep hill where we had previously dug a trench. Each time we shoved the board upward, the body rolled off the flat surface and went down the hill. With a supreme effort, we labored to place the body back on the primitive stretcher, but as we inched upward again, the nightmare repeated itself. The board bit into our bleeding hands. The dead man weighed a ton.

"Go on without me," Roman pleaded. "I can't climb that hill again. It's like a giant mountain. Let them shoot me!" He said, resigned to his fate.

"You've got to go on, Roman," I begged him, "it's not a question of your life alone. They'll kill us both."

Roman glanced back at me. He was not ready to accept the responsibility for my death.

"I'll try, little brother. As God is my witness, I'll try."

"Now, all you have to do is to hold on to the body so it won't fall off. I'll do the pushing." I tried to devise a strategy. "You understand?" I asked anxiously. "When I'll get tired, you'll push. There are only a few steps left. Together, now!"

Holding on, and shoving upward, we inched ahead, while the "glass-eye" watched assiduously. Suddenly Tulka turned his attention to the excavation nearby. A victim's body lay a few steps away, the hollow grave was nearly completed to accept its booty. Leib Glikier, a Hasid we had only recently met, was up to his waist inside the grave, continuing to dig while praying in his melodic, resonant voice. The sing-song of the Hasidic delivery attracted the camp commandant, and he approached the laboring man, submachine-gun hanging from his shoulder.

"Jew, what are you doing?"

There was silence.

"Swine! Pay attention when you're spoken to!"

Still, silence. The digging and the sing-song continued.

Tulka was infuriated. "You shall be taught a lesson, swine!" He yelled. "You must dig much wider! We'll need more space!" He ordered.

Leib put down the shovel and took a few steps toward the lifeless body in his charge. "Stop! Jew! What do you think you're doing?" Tulka yelled.

"I'm done with the digging. Now, the burial." Leib interrupted his prayers for the first time.

"No, you're not done yet! You'll be done when I say you're done! Dig some more, swine!" The SS man shouted, and the cynical smile on his scarred face gave him almost a human appearance. "I ordered you to dig much wider! Can't you follow orders?" He continued to grimace. Patiently, Leib Glikier picked up his shovel and continued to dig. While doing so, he had also begun to hum the kaddish, its words blending into the sound of the crumbling earth as it fell downward, propelled by its own momentum.

"Let's join Leib in reciting the kaddish, Vilek, there'll be no one left to say it for us," Roman suggested.

"You must pray to me now," Tulka spoke and the smile was gone from his glass eye. "You must worship me because your God is weak, but I'm here, and I'm the master. Pray to me and I'll give you life!"

Leib ignored the SS man. We continued our recital of Hebrew lithurgy in silence and hoped the earth would part to swallow the SS man. But nothing unexpected happened, and Leib Glikier had dug to the intended depth and width. Tulka looked on with approbation.

"That's enough, Jew! Now, I ask you once again, will you pray to me for salvation?" Tulka pointed his luger at the praying Hasid. The SS man was furious. Leib turned his closed eyes toward the skies, his hands folded on his groin, he prayed.

"All right, you swine! I gave you a chance!" Tulka seemed hesitant. "Throw the carcass into the hole!" He ordered, and Leib complied, lowering the dead body carefully into the grave. "All of you! Come and see!" We approached as ordered. "You'll all witness this deed!" Tulka shouted. "I gave this swine his choice, and he refused to obey. It is my duty to. . ." He paused, then he went on. "I was just following orders! Remember! You'll bear witness! It is my duty!" He repeated, looking at the silent inmates. "Speak! You damned swine!" He addressed us. "You'll bear witness to this!"

We looked at him unbelieving. "Indeed, we will bear witness," we thought silently, for as long as we shall live.

"We will bear witness!" We said in unison. Tulka turned toward Leib once again.

"Jew! Get inside!"

Leib Glikier stepped down into his own grave at the very moment the luger in Tulka's hand discharged and a deafening noise filled the air. For one brief moment no one heard the distant rumble of artillery. Leib Glikier fell into his shared grave, a narrow streak of blood trickling down the side of his mouth.

"Cover him!" Tulka barked the order and we went to work silently. As we tossed each shovel full of earth into the grave, we knew that we, too, were buried under the unfriendly soil along with our comrade Leib.

"And no more prayers, swine!" Tulka shouted as he walked off.

The burial lasted till 8:00 p.m., the sun had already gone down, and it was dark. We listened to the small arms fire.

"They're terribly close now," I whispered. "This sounds like rifle fire."

"I'd say about five kilometers away." Roman sat on the ground breathing heavily.

"Do you think the SS has gone?"

"Who knows?" Roman whispered. "Let's worry about ourselves now." We waited in the yard, trembling.

"They can't have gone? Can they?"

"Wouldn't it be crazy if they did? Wouldn't it?"

"If they killed us now. . ."

". . . there'd be no one to bury us for them."

We talked back and forth. Finally, we made our way to a lonely spot in the dark barracks. We climbed on top of the roof, carrying some blankets for a night's lodging. The night was clear, as we lay listening to the chorus of small arms fire competing with the more distant rumbling of artillery. We knew how vulnerable our hiding place was, but overcome by exhaustion, we fell into a restless sleep.

The sound of rifle fire coming from a ditch nearby woke us. We heard the sound of voices speaking in a strange language.

"Roman! I can't believe it! I know they're Americans!" I shouted through the din of explosions.

"How can we be sure?" Roman was cautious. "They could be the enemy."

"The enemy doesn't talk the way the cowboys talk!" I insisted. "Try to remember the American movies we saw! That's the language of the cowboys! Let's take a peek!"

Both of us crawled on our bellies toward the edge of the roof. We looked down at the backs of a small patrol of soldiers in olive colored khakis, crouched inbetween a small ravine, firing at will at some invisible target ahead.

"I know they're Americans! I just know it!" I exclaimed. "Here, let me show you." Before Roman was able to respond, I strained my neck over the edge of the roof.

"Americans!" I called out the word I had so often heard before, the word that had become symbolic of all that was good, of a people that were free, of humans that were committed to helping other humans.

"Americans!" I shouted again, but my physical condition only permitted a whimper. I knew they couldn't hear me.

Suddenly, one of the soldiers turned as if to rest. He sat up below the ravine, facing the barrack. His rifle resting next to him on the ground, he reached into his back-pack drawing a small flat can out of one of its pockets. Still, unaware of the four eyes staring down at him from the edge of the roof, the soldier began to eat the contents of the tin can.

"Sardines!" I smacked my lips. "Damn! I can still recognize real food when I see it!"

"I can almost taste it." Roman remarked greedily. At that moment, the soldier looked up, and seeing the two shaven heads above staring down at him, he yelled some inarticulate phrase to his companions. As they all turned, their aim was now directed upward, and bullets whistled mercilessly past us.

"You and your Americans!" Roman said breathlessly as we were making our way below. "I told you they were the enemy! I just knew it," he added, pleased that his lack of faith was borne out.

"I still say you're wrong, Roman." We squeezed beneath one of the bunks. "It's all a mistake, you'll see."

"A bullet's a bullet!" Roman whispered, trembling. "Whether it's a friendly one or not. This mistake could be our last one!" He caught his breath. "The Nazis didn't kill us, the Americans will do it for them." He looked at me, pale, full of unexpressed suffering.

But I was struck and surprised by his sudden obstinacy. It seemed to indicate to me that he was returning to himself in his awakened consciousness which comes as a result of a rebirth of hope.

A lifetime passed before my eyes. It seemed such a long lifetime, yet I haven't lived at all. God! How I wanted to live! Now, more than ever before! I realized how terribly wrong it would be to be felled by the hand that had come to give us life. There was a breathlessness in this very utterance which contrasted so strongly with the hideous years of mockery we had experienced at the hands of the Nazis.

All at once, there was silence. We lay flat on our bellies, praying. Then there were footsteps sounding against the wooden floor of the barrack.

"I feel their presence," I whispered almost inaudibly.

"I can smell them," Roman responded. The scent of the approaching strangers hit our nostrils. It was different from the stench of the inmates, our companions of the past. It was also different from the smell of SS and the mercenaries.

"It's the smell of freedom, little brother," Roman whispered.

"It must be, because it isn't the odor of death," I remarked. Just then, straining to look up, though the tip of my nose was touching the floor, I saw a pair of very different foot wear; those were not the Nazi boots of authority. The wearer of those shoes walked softly, without a whip in his hand for chastising inmates.

"Poor devils," a voice said. "Just look at them. They're skin and bones." I did not understand the meaning of those words. I only perceived a deep, masculine voice, with an exquisite timbre as that of a lyrical baritone. It was soft, but unafraid and full of compassion. Next, I felt myself lifted from the floor, feather-like, into the powerful arms of the strange-talking warrior.

I dared to open my eyes and look up into the face of a black soldier. The impression was very special, beyond the range of commonplace definitions. It was as though I had achieved a weightless state of profound well-being in the arms of the messenger of God. Menasha's miracle was happening after all.

"Everything goin' to be okay now, little feller." My giant said, smiling. "Don't need to be 'fraid no more, you hear?"

I only understood that smile. There was a complete absence of anger in his manner. It had an unequalled force of expression, so far-reaching in its human quality that I refused to believe it pointed out merely the exception to the rule. It was that mysterious force of kindness which accomplished momentarily the destruction of the prevailing evil. It was there unscathed. I stared down from his smiling face at the broad line of his shoulders, his powerful chest and the amazing strength of his limbs.

After all, this was the first act of kindness I had experienced since. . . since . . . I had forgotten that very distant time. All things had become blurry all of a sudden, and as I strained to remember and to comprehend, a strange feeling had come over me, and I fell into a deep slumber. . . unafraid.

PART TWO

18

A hand softly touched my shoulder. I woke, rubbing my eyes with incredulity. The medic had come to feed me. I looked round at the rugged, unshaven faces of the American soldiers. Some wept, others clumsily massaged their eyelids with the bent forefinger as if to remove some foreign particle. They were silent.

The brief excerpts of my life passed before my liberators' eyes. Much more has been left untold. The events that were not revealed in my narrative were easier to guess than to understand.

How did it happen?

Is it possible? It must be. I'm here.

Is that enough? No. But it must be.

Aren't you thankful? Not really. Why should I be?

Thankful to the Almighty, you know. It's customary to show gratitude for a deed of such magnitude.

True, I'm here, but I'm also there, in hell. It follows me wherever I go. I can't hide from it—for it is inside me. I can't kill it—for I'll die with it. You're mad. You're raving mad. It helps, if you want to go on.

"Your name, please." A voice inquired. It was the voice of one of my liberators. A pleasant voice. Strange, they should ask my name. #116420! I answered with deliberate slowness. Was it distrust or force of habit? Both, perhaps.

Name? What's a proper name? Does everyone have a name? Joy! I have my very own name! I'm no longer a number, a cipher devoid of individuality. I am someone after all! There were times I'd have rather been a shepherd dog. The Nazis gave their dogs meaningful identities: "King," "Queen," "Sultan," "Fritz," et cetera. At times, when my jailers were angry at their dogs, they would call them "Jew." The dogs did not like to be called by that name, and they tore many an inmate to shreds. That was their vindication. Thereafter, their masters restored them to their dignity of being a canine by naming them after royalty.

Did I survive?—I don't know.

Now safe among my liberators, an eerie feeling of guilt suddenly came over me; I questioned my right to have survived and I wished I had perished along with those many others.

I kept on asking myself why it was that I survived this harrowing ordeal, and I found the answer in what my grandmother had told me so very long ago: "The memories you'll store within you will make you a memory capsule." I was saved to become a witness. How else will the world ever learn what had happened behind those walls of secrecy that had been guarded by the Third Reich? How were they to know what had occurred in the Nazi occupied territories, which were no more than a huge death factory?

Curiously, they gathered round me asking to tell them about my experiences. I thought for a moment, not knowing where to start. Then I suddenly understood the immensity of the task, I let out a sustained shriek, whereupon I lay down on the ground, barely aware of my audience, breathing heavily and murmuring inarticulate sounds only intelligible to the demons inside me.

No one stirred. They looked on puzzled and they were unable to guess my affliction which held me captive and wouldn't let go. By the time I reached my sixteenth year, I had lived several lifetimes. I was weary and felt very old. I had been put to death and buried by my enemies, only to become resurrected time and time again. Each time, I asked those who knew: "Why all this? Why so much attention for one small person such as I? Does not the Almighty, blessed be He, have better things to do?"

"Hush! Don't blaspheme! I was admonished." In the Creator's universe everything has its reason." The sages swayed their bodies back and forth as they argued. Occasionally they scratched their splendid beards. They spoke in a sing-song manner which they knew was most pleasing to their Maker. "We must be patient," they said.

I was taught to wait. "Wait for the Messiah," the sages told me. "Be patient, and wait, He will come. You must be ready to receive Him when He comes." I was ready many times over, but I wondered if I'd ever be young again.

I knew of no other family survivors except Roman. Yes, there was Haya, a second cousin on my mother's side who was eventually transported to Bergen Belsen. I recalled one night of the last winter in Buchenwald. Tired, we returned from our daily shift, barely able to drag our feet. A friend brought the news of a transport of women having arrived from Birkenau. They were temporarily housed in one of the empty barracks high on the hill in the outer camp perimeter. "Let's go see," Roman pleaded. "Maybe there's family." The prospect of climbing several kilometers up the hill was discouraging. "We'll go the first thing tomorrow." I had offered.

However, the women were evacuated at dawn. Roman learned of their departure from one of the inmates who had stoked the locomotive for the journey.

"The family name must not die!" I kept thinking. Not now! I was given another chance. A chance, for what? To build anew? Of course. To replenish! But what. . . if. . ..? No "ifs" now. This was my destiny, my Covenant. The mysterious Blessing. . . Do not forget. . . do not forgive!

"Do you have a light?" A voice addressed me. It sounded familiar, and I looked up. It was difficult to determine the man's age. Everyone of us looked aged. Chronology played a small role where physical wear and abuse were concerned. We all had that in common.

"Here," I lit his cigarette with the lighter I "confiscated" from one of the Nazi guards, "you look familiar. . . do we know each other?" My eyes met his. Large, intense eyes, a well of sadness and anguish within. "I have a feeling we've met before."

He seemed embarrassed. "Cigarette?" He offered one out of a small slim pack. "British, they're mild." He held them out to me. "Go on, take one." He insisted. "It's getting so, everywhere we look, we see familiar faces. . . perhaps. . . it's that we want to see them. . . need to see them. . ." He placed special emphasis on the word need.

He might have gone on, had I not interrupted him impatiently. "No, I'm not imagining. I've seen your face before. . . was it Piotrkow? Hortensia?"

"Vilek!" He let out a triumphant yell. We hugged. "You're Srulko Malpo's grandson! Of course, how could I have forgotten?"

"And you. . .you must be. . ." I searched my mind for his name, but he came quickly to my aid.

"Moshe Naiberg. . . the Hasidic sessions. . . at your grandfather's, *olom v'sholom*, God rest his soul," he quickly added, his face lifted up toward the heavens. "He was a fine man, your grandfather, a fine man indeed."

The memory of my grandfather brought tears to my eyes. He saw the change and was quick to go on. "I'm on my way to Poland. . . must hurry. . . left our little girl with some Christian friends. God knows what's become of her."

Now I remembered the frail little girl that always accompanied this man to the Hasidic sessions. Tzipora was her name. Mrs. Naiberg had been taken on one of the transports early on, and there was no one in whose care Moshe would leave his daughter.

"Tzipora," I said softly. "That was the name of your little daughter, wasn't it?"

"Yes," he showed surprise, "how well you remember." He grew silent for one brief moment. "She's my future now. I must go to her, my little darling baby."

"I hope you'll reunite in good health, Moshe. If you should meet any of my people, tell them where we are, my brother Roman's here with me."

"Now, that you mention it. . ." he suddenly remembered, ". . . I did see one of your relatives as I passed through Belsen. Haya was her name, I believe, a cousin on your father's side."

Haya's alive. Merciful God. Then, there's hope that others might have survived as well. I must go. . . search for them. . . not now. . . soon. Moshe regarded me with great compassion.

"I'll be going now, Vilek. Got to catch a transport to the border." We embraced. "Stay well, my friend. Don't lose hope. There's a saying "as long as there's life you're bound to meet." He grimaced.

"I'm glad you crossed my path, Moshe. Have a safe journey." I knew what I had to do, and I was impatient with myself from that moment on. Moshe's brief visit was strangely construed as a summons to seek out my next of kin. I kept thinking that Haya urgently needed my presence. I couldn't wait, and Roman understood.

I came as soon as I was able. There were countless miles of barbed wire that stretched endlessly. A meaningful reminder of the past; a monster reaching out into the present. I knew, Haya was taken on the same transport with my mother, Felusia, Aunt Sabina and cousin Devorah. Besides, she was another family survivor, and I was compelled to go to her and ask my many questions; questions survivors asked of each other. Now, we met. We stared at each other; strangers.

Hollow eyes. Ears eager to hear words of encouragement.

"You look fine," I said.

"You too. How you have grown! You're a man now!" She smiled faintly. She notices my concern. I thought to myself.

"Don't worry. My hair will grow back soon." She hastened to assure me.

"I know. It will be as beautiful as it once was," I said softly. "What's become of my mother, Felusia, of. . . Devorah. . .? Aunt Sabina. . .? The others?" I spoke with much hesitation. There was fear in my trembling voice.

"We were separated. Devorah and your aunt Sabina were on a transport to Auschwitz. The rest of the family were taken north, I came to this place." Haya wept, but there were no tears.

"You have no idea. . . where they were taken?" I insisted gently.

"They said. . . oh, I don't really know. To work in the industry. Rumors. Who can tell? You must look for them. Promise me."

"I will. I can't accept their irrevocable absence. I keep waiting for their return. I think of them as having gone out for a long walk or taken a trip to somewhere. I wait for a sign of life, to welcome them and fill the house with laughter and song once again." I spoke as if to myself.

"Do you remember your mother? Can you still vividly see her?" Haya looked into my eyes.

"My mother has become a sort of blur to me, a picture taken out of focus. I often strain to remember, but I can't. Is it this easy to forget the image of our loved ones? Only the memory of her personality endures. Remember how she sang? Everywhere around the house I heard her beautiful voice. Whether it was in the kitchen, or in the shop, when she was helping father with the tailoring. I heard her sweet voice and her radiant laughter. There was seldom a frown on that beautiful face. She was altogether beautiful, I remember that." I exaggerated to embellish my mother's image.

"And, I remember how she would cuddle my head in her breast whenever I was troubled, or hurt," I went on. "She used to say: It's not as bad as all that, is it? Mother loves you, Vilusiek, and your hurt will disappear before you're twenty-one.' The pain disappeared, almost miraculously. When my father's voice called for her to assist him, she would let go of me slowly, tenderly, not to shock. With that beautiful smile on her face, she would speak, carefully choosing her words: In a couple of years from now, you'll think all this very trivial, you'll see!' I knew it was so, because my mother never lied. This is how I remember her," I concluded.

"You must keep this picture of her forever," Haya said with sadness in her eyes.

"I shall. Each day, I'll dedicate a few moments to remembering my mother, else I might be denied even these small fragments of her presence. Until we meet again." I lowered my eyes, unable to meet hers.

There was a brief pause.

"What will you do now?" I resumed.

"I don't know. Haven't had time to think."

"Can I do anything for you? Anything, Haya?"

"A tooth brush. I just wish I had a tooth brush."

"Is that all?"

"Yes, it will do for now. Can you get it for me?"

"If you wish."

I was about to leave when she called out. I returned to her bedside.

The antiseptic surrounding stifled my imagination. I looked around at the others, and it seemed as though the lepers have returned from the abysmal caves. Their fetid shackles smashed, they endured. I thought to myself.

What did the Almighty mean when He said: "Be fruitful, and multiply, and replenish the earth, and subdue it. . . ?" Was it to be done without suffering? How was that possible? Was not suffering a part of life? More questions.

"You may keep these." She handed me a small bundle of papers.

"What is it?"

"You wrote to us then. . .when you were still in Piotrkow, and we were in Warsaw. . ."

"You kept them? All this time? How was it possible?"

"It's easier for a woman to conceal things than for a man. Devorah left them to me. They kept me alive. Now, I no longer need them . . . she would want you to have them . . ."

"I. . . I. . . can't. . ."

"Go on. . .take it. . . and don't forget the tooth brush."

My own scribblings. I couldn't resist. I was compelled once more to view the past.

Each time I finished a page, I struck a match to it. I was alone in the caboose of the slow, east-bound train. The sad pages turned into flames that crackled happily to life. I resented that. They had no right to joy even as they turned to ashes.

The last scrap of paper was gone. I did it. These were the ashes of the past. I trampled them underfoot, until the very last fragment disappeared.

Only hatred remained. It was etched into my heart with the bitterness of memory.

There is a hard road ahead. I would not look back, for fear I might turn into a pillar of grief. . .

19

I t was the spring of life again.

Suddenly, things were different. I stood hesitant, unbelieving, almost numb. Vanished was the presence of the Camp Commandant, though his memory lingered on. Gone, too, were his wretched hirelings, the Orderlies and the Kapos. Only their spectre remained.

"You're free to go now, Vilek," The U.S. Army Captain repeated in Yiddish. There was a certain gentleness in his voice. It was a new sound to my unaccustomed ears, though not at all unpleasant. I kept staring at the wall. I found myself fighting a sudden urge to reject this man's kindness. My thoughts wandered beyond the present. They traveled somewhere into the dark abyss of the years from which I found myself emerging, and I ignored the efforts of the questioning officer. "You'll be sent to a fine hospital," the Captain continued with concern. "With good care, you'll soon regain your health. Then you can begin a new life."

I remained silent, motionless, as if in a mysterious reverie. The Captain hastened to add: "Who knows, you might even go to America."

America. . . a new life. . . that was once a dream also. My father Henryk had once envisioned this dream for all of us. He pleaded in our behalf in all those letters he had written to our American aunts and uncles; letters purified with tears. Yet, they seemed letters without destination, addressees without compassion. Though they were written years ago, when I was only ten years old, I recalled the events vividly.

"You can step aside now, step aside and let the next one in line through," the Captain repeated patiently but with an undertone of authority.

I complied mechanically, immersed in thought, yet responsive to the sound demanding obedience. Six-and-a-half years of regimentation had left their mark. I was used to obeying orders.

The officer spoke without haste. I looked at him stubbornly, despising his patience. "It's easy for you to tell us we're free! How would you know what freedom is! You've never lost it!" I shouted angrily at the unsuspecting American. The Captain looked up from his paperwork startled. My companions worried about the consequences. They tried to asuage our liberator.

"He's only a boy, Captain."

"He's mad!"

"You mustn't pay attention, Captain. His mind is affected!"

"Will you shut up, Vilek! You'll get us all in trouble!"

"Let the boy speak," the Captain interrupted, "let him."

I looked the American in the eyes. They were kind eyes. Understanding eyes. I resented that, too. I was immensely pleased with myself, although I did not understand why.

"You can't fool anyone with your hypocritical kindness! Where were you when we needed you? I hate you! I think, I will hate you as much as I do the assassins of my family. You're as guilty as they are!" I sobbed hysterically. "I can't accept charity from you!" My shoulders stooped, my head bent downward, I was unable to sustain the kindness of the American's eyes. My body shook grotesquely, venting my rage in sporadic sobbing.

"There's no cause to feel this way, Vilek." The Captain tried vainly to reason, to quiet me down. "Everyone accepts a little help now and then. It's not meant as charity. Someday, I might be asking for your help, who knows?"

I turned away and walked slowly and with much effort out onto the yard where others waited their turn. I could not understand the Captain's patience. Why did he not strike me? The others surely would have done so. I thought to myself. Doubt followed on my heels. Confused, I suddenly remembered that I had promised myself to advance a step at a time, cautiously and without haste. I must get the feel of life slowly. Things were happening too fast to make sense.

"Guess you've been in a long time?" Someone addressed me and I looked up in the speaker's direction somewhat startled for the intrusion. With the intuition of the inmate, I was instantly aware that the man was not one of my people. Perhaps it was in the manner of his speaking, perhaps in the cold grey eyes that invited distrust. I could not explain that eerie "inner voice" of the persecuted that cautioned me now, as it had so many times in the past come to my rescue. I hesitated.

A long time? What's a long time? A year, two years, perhaps three or more? Long rows of barracks; interminable barbed wire fences; the unforgettable, suffering faces. . . the barbed wire might be gone someday, but there are invisible walls surrounding me, as they do each of the survivors.

"Four-and-a-half years. I was in four-and-a-half years." I responded mechanically. "Do you think that's a long time? Is four-and- a-half years a long time to spend in prison?"

"Of course it's a long time. But there's no reason now to be angry, is there? won't do any good," the man grinned.

"That's what everybody keeps telling me. They expect, by some magic formula, to bury the past in one swift move!" I cried. "We'll all bathe in the waters of the Danube to cleanse our bodies from the impurities of hell! We'll purge the mind, never to remember again!" I was tense, challenging, and my body trembled with excitement. "After kicking us around for that long a time, they now want to wipe the slate clean; they tell us to resume life as if nothing had happened. But the truth is, a lot has happened; that's the truth!" I repeated. I was on the verge of a breakdown. "Why don't they at least grant me the privilege to remain master of my own memory; to dispense with the last trace of my own sanity as I see fit, without compelling me to humor the guilt-ridden, grovelling world of today?"

"I don't wish to forget the past. But neither do I want to go on suffering. Let the dead be buried. Life must go on." The man hesitated a moment as if to catch his breath. Then, he asked quickly, as if in search of a better topic of conversation: "Say, where was your childhood spent?"

"Childhood? It's more like a dream than a reality—if it weren't for the scars, I wouldn't know there was a childhood," I said, "When I was a young boy, they swaddled me behind barbed wire fences. They called it 'forced' labor, and like a hollow grave, it enveloped me in its cold confines."

"There's nothing left? Just like that?"

"Not exactly. Some vague shadows are there—it helps me to understand things better now. I feel alive." I replied.

"What do you mean alive?" He seemed astonished at my answer.

"Well, can you see me?" I responded with my own question.

"Of course, I can see you." He smiled faintly.

"You see, all this time, I was nothing, a number." I continued excitedly. "It got so I thought that nobody even saw me. Now, I'm alive again—and you can see me. So, there's your answer."

The Russian looked at me quizzically for a long time. Then, as if resigned to the fact that there was something wrong with me, but that he was willing to tolerate and accept, he went on.

"You're fortunate anyway."

"How do you mean that?"

"Well, you're a successful survivor. Why worry?"

"If you call survival success, then I'm successful."

"Don't you believe it? Isn't it what this life's all about?"

"Sure, but there must be more to it than mere survival. There are other things, too."

"Like what?"

"Like where are all the children? Where's their laughter?"

"You mustn't brood about things like that."

"And when I think of the future, I think that my children won't have grandparents like normal children have." I was on the verge of tears again.

"Look at him." The man chuckled. "Skin and bones, hardly able to walk, and he thinks of making babies already." I ignored the man's veiled joke. I remained silent.

"Anyhow, if there's more to this life than what it seems, I hope you'll find it. Say, what's your name? Mine is Misha Dury." He offered a handshake. "I like you. You really gave that American a hard time."

"Despise his guts. And the likes of him!"

I wanted to cry, to laugh, and to shout with joy. The will was there, but my body was incapable of the noble effort. It was only a heap of bones wrapped in a tough layer of yellowish skin, weighing thirty-seven and a half kilos. We waited our turn to see the attending physician. It was as good a time for small talk as any.

"Vilek's my name," I introduced myself, and we shook hands. While Misha talked, I scrutinized his slightly slanted eyes, the narrow lips and wide cheekbones. I wondered about the man's age. He could have been in his mid-thirties, though his parched skin made him appear much older. An emerging crop of blond hair concealed any trace of grayness. He might have been a good six feet tall once, but in his present hunched condition he gave the appearance of average height. It did not seem likely that he weighed much over one hundred pounds.

I deliberated whether to become receptive to the "old man's" attentions. Dormant suspicions returned momentarily. Misha could have been one of "them." I recalled. After all, young boys were used by adult inmates. Most every barrack orderly had his very own boy. Women were not easy to come by. The boys soon learned to acept their fate gratefully; it meant survival. Misha might have been a capo, maybe even higher than that in the camp hierarchy. No one would ever know. That was not a relationship to build one's trust on.

"When you've been engaged in a dialogue of the deaf for so long, words don't come out that easily anymore," I said softly, as if to myself.

For now, Misha had to remain an unknown. It would take a while to prove himself trustworthy. With the rest of the survivors I had a lot in common. Years of shared confinement cemented a bond between us. It was not really what one could call friendship. Friendships are rarely forged in prisons.

It was more like a dependence upon one another; the telling and the retelling of old stories to make the time pass; the unspoken promise not to steal a few crumbs of bread from the other when he slept; that special animal sense that made you risk safety for the other at times of emergencies.

"You are Russian?" I asked a rhetorical question, and I was glad I had found something to say. The prolonged silence was becoming awkward.

"Yes, I was prisoner of the Germans two years, nine months, and fourteen days. Tried to escape twice, was caught both times. See this?" Misha extended his left hand as he spoke. The middle finger was missing. There was only a grotesque stump left in its place.

"What's that?" I was caught off guard by the sight of the half finger. I became self-conscious.

"The finger, it's missing.'

"I . . . can. . . see that, but why?" I stammered.

"When they caught me the second time, snap! They chopped it off," Misha made a downward motion with the open palm of his left hand, "and they promised to chop off an additional one each time I tried it again."

"Did you?"

"Don't be a fool. Look at it! They ruined my hand. I'm, you might say, an invalid. Besides, there was nowhere to go. All this is enemy territory. Everywhere you go, you're surrounded by him and his agents." Misha was out of breath. "How about you, Vilek, did you ever try to break out?"

"No, there was no point to it," I said with a shrug of my shoulders.

"I guess, you must have been a kid when you came here." Misha seemed startled by his own observation. "Hardly out of grammar school."

"Fifth grade completed," I said softly. "I can't read well at all. And I have forgotten how to write altogether." There was deep sadness in my voice, and Misha sensed it.

"Don't worry, friend, it'll come back quickly."

"I doubt that. It seems like there's so much I should know that I don't know. So much I'd like to learn, to understand, and so little time to do it."

"Patience, my friend. The Krauts will make it all up to you. I promise you that," Misha said with a twinkle in his eye indicative of a sense of humor of which I had thought him incapable.

"Fat chance they will. They deny we exist." My voice was edgy, full of hatred.

"But they can't deny you the things they took from you." Misha saw another crisis approaching. "They've got to make it up to you." "They swear they knew nothing about us. They never saw us, nor did they know what was going on in their own killing factories. They shed tears when they look at us, and they are fearful of the few emaciated half humans who defied destiny and dared to survive. How inconvenient for the would-be assassins! The good burghers promise never again to believe another demagogue. 'The Führer was the devil incarnate,' they tell us, 'we Germans are peace-loving people.' And they hasten to make the sign of the cross." I trembled with rage. "Pious like the rest of the world."

"You're getting too excited about it." Misha looked concerned.

"Tell me, what are you going to do now that all this is over?"

"Oh, I don't know. Haven't really given it much thought. How about you, will you go back home?"

"Haven't decided that either. I've been thinking about it off and on." Misha grew pensive. "I keep remembering my family, but I want to stay here and have a look around. Hell, I don't know, the family might not even be alive any more. I'm from the Ukraine, you know. What the Nazis didn't destroy, Stalin will be sure to continue. He'll finish their handy work, you can bet on that."

"Freedom is confusing, isn't it?" I asked quietly. "The more I think about it, the less I understand."

"One thing's clear. We've got to get well before we can start making plans. Just look at us." Here, Misha burst out laughing, but I was unable to join in. He laughed for both of us, at the grotesqueness of our appearance; at the unreal world surrounding us. We saw each the reflection of himself in the grotesque features of the other.

All at once, I was startled and impressed by my own inability to laugh. I suddenly recalled my family's trip to the country. One morning I came to watch the farmer's wife as she milked the cow for our breakfast milk. She saw me standing in the doorway. It was a good distance away from where she sat. Totally unaware of what she was about to do, I stared as she squeezed one of the teats in my direction, squirting the fluid at my face with an uncanny accuracy. We both burst out with a resounding laugh, and some of the milk moistened my lips. The liquid was warm and pleasant, as life itself. It was glorious to be alive. It was good to laugh.

"We're in no shape to plan our future at this moment, my friend," Misha went on, startling me from my reverie. "The way I see it, we've got to get on our feet first, like we once were, before we start planning."

"That's not easy, Misha. It can never be the way it was. Not for our kind."

"You know what I mean, Vilek. We have to get in shape. The scars in our souls are too deep to heal quickly. Who knows, maybe we're stuck with them forever. If we could just get well enough to plan our future like other people, that'll be a good start."

"We are not like other people, Misha. We haven't been like other people for a long time. We've forgotten how other people plan to do things. We've forgotten what it means to be like other people. What makes you think we can change?"

"It'll come with time and patience, my friend. It'll be as it once was. It has to, or all the suffering, the hope, and the pain of survival wouldn't make much sense." Misha said.

"It's going to be difficult to relearn. It'll be harder yet to remember without hatred, and to remain patient." I was surprised at the intensity of my hatred for all things past, and I feared the future more that I would admit to myself. I would never reveal that fear to anyone, for I have learned to cope with it privately.

"Vilek!" The medics called my name, and I responded quickly when it was my turn. I felt no fear when they told me to undress.

"My God in heaven!" The doctor exclaimed. "What have they been feeding you?" I stood against the daylight which streamed in through the open window. "Why, there's almost no need to take x-rays," the doctor said. "How did you ever make it?"

"We always saved half of the daily slice of bread," I answered his first question, "because we were never sure there would be food the next morning." I grinned. "Sometimes, we would steal garbage from the SS kitchen. There were lots of eggshells, you know. The Nazis had no shortage of eggs."

The doctor looked at me incredulously. "I'm sure, this explains the fine set of teeth you've kept, young man."

The hospital in Borna proved to be of greater value than anyone could have imagined. After all, we did not expect much from the Germans. The American military ambulance delivered all nine of us to the impeccably clean institution called Stadtkrankenhaus, which stood for the English Municipal Hospital. Borna lay thirty kilometers south of Leipzig. It was one of those picture post-card towns, no bigger than any other rural settlement.

Captain Phil Weinberg made good on his promise. Painstakingly, he worked out the most minute details involved in our transfer from military to civilian authorities. He secured the best medical care available. Through his stubborn insistence, we were placed in the personal care of the two prettiest nurses, Trude and Inge.

"Now, here's what I call true Nordic stock!" Misha could not contain his enthusiasm. He lacked self-discipline. I thought.

"No telling how many baby Vikings they've produced for their Führer," Abram Bachter remarked caustically, with ill concealed hostility in his piercing eyes.

"Come now, cheer up," Misha pleaded good humoredly. "Where's your sense of fair play? Look at it this way, what they did in the past is their business, what we intend to do with them now is ours."

"I don't find it amusing, but I won't keep you from fraternizing with these despicable blond harlots!" Abram retorted stubbornly. We respected him although we occasionally joked about his nick-name, "rabbi". His profound knowledge of liturgy went unchallenged, so everyone looked to him for answers during times of crisis.

Abram Bachter was no saint. He hated every German man, woman, and child. He was especially mindful of his hatred whenever he felt the pain in his left leg, bent like a bow, a gift of Gestapo brutality.

"I fear the technicians of genocide," I whispered to Misha.

"They're meek in defeat, Vilek my friend," Misha chuckled. "They don't dare remember Himmler's motto 'blessed be that which makes one tough,' they're tame and remorseful now."

I would waste no time on idle talk. "I need to take a crap." I suddenly felt my bowels move. "And I'm sleepy."

I was eager to place my head on the fresh smelling linen of the clean, soft pillow. Before slipping under the white, starched covers, I looked at the comfortable bed with mixed emotions. How often, during the past years, had I dreamed of such luxury. Now, that I had it within easy reach, I was afraid to place my half-starved body upon it.

There was Misha, whose philosophy and appearance were in such savage variance with the terrifying experiences of the past; there were the nurses, Trude and Inge, whose mysterious attractiveness I was still at a loss to comprehend; then, there were the others, companions of many years of slavery.

Briefly, too, I tried to think of my own future—it was urgently present— of my unrestrained hatred; of my immediate and long range plans; of the best way to achieve them.

The two nurses undertook their task with dedication. They cared for the emaciated heaps of bones asiduously, laboring day and night with the eagerness of mother hens. They sponge-bathed us religiously twice each day; they fed us with the food supplied by our American benefactors; they disposed of numberless urinals full of pale urine and innumerable bed-pans of anemic excretion. In short, not only did Trude and Inge work as though they were immersed in penitence for the absolution of their collective guilt, but quite unwittingly they also became a favorite subject for the men's nocturnal "after-lights-out" vocal reverie.

The two beautiful nurses became an added incentive in the rapid physical recovery of the convalescing survivors. The German physicians were astonished. Hair appeared and grew on our once clean-shaven skulls, and some of us had already managed to part it one way or another. Hair was a luxury which we had almost forgotten existed, and now it assumed the role of the first reminder of human vanity. We regarded with incredulity the group photos which were taken at our arrival to the hospital and those we posed for a few weeks later. Gone were the protruding bony features of our palid faces. Gone, too, were the dark sockets which nestled the eyes. In their places there was the wholesome aspect of a rounded cheek, and flesh had covered, at least partially, the once prominent skeleton. Within two month's time, the hospital administration was prepared to discharge us from their care. The officials were delighted. Our prompt recovery would surely earn them coveted praise from the Amis (the abbreviation for *Amerikaner!*).

Formal discharge papers were forwarded to the United States authorities from the desk of Chief M.D. Werner Giescke. The letter read:

With the recommendation of the Chief M.D. and the approval of the entire medical staff, the former K.Z. inmates are herewith released from the care of the Borna Municipal Hospital, having most remarkably recovered their full physical and mental faculties.

Captain Weinberg refused to believe the hospital staff. No human being, he reasoned, could recover this fast from an experience as harrowing as that of the survivors. Besides, the Captain's conscience demanded that the Germans pay, at least in part, for the many years of high living at the expense of the rest of the world. "I'll attend to this matter in time," he snorted at the staff delegate who handed him the impeccably worded statement from the Chief M.D.

Captain Weinberg did not suspect in the slightest that Trude and Inge were the "medicine" that contributed to the quick recovery. On the contrary, he suspected the Germans of trickery. Trying to explain that most unusual medical experience was to no avail. The Captain refused to believe the "outrageous fabrication" purely for religious reasons.

Captain Weinberg was a Jew from Brooklyn, New York. That made him sensitive to our needs. We knew that and we were quick to manipulate the Captain to our advantage. As in the case of other G.I. Jews, each time he spoke to us, we detected strong feelings of guilt. We knew they all wished to make amends, and we weren't going to dissuade them.

Captain Weinberg was engaged to marry a girl from his neighborhood. He kept telling anyone willing to listen about Malke's family. They left Poland before the War erupted because Moshe Lox, the father, was about to be drafted into the Polish army. On his arrival in the United States, Moshe changed the ancestral name Loxowitz to the more American sounding Lox. He was told the Americans liked people with short names. The Americans were not too keen on pronouncing strange sounding names; short names were easier to pronounce.

The Captain was deeply in love with his Malke, which was the Hebrew word for "queen." He carried her snapshot in his wallet, showing it to everyone, unsolicited. He wanted the whole world to rejoice with him.

"See? Isn't she beautiful, my Malke?" He said. "Pure gold, she is pure gold." It implied that Jewish girls in the United States were the epitome of virtue and beauty. "When you come to the United States you'll find girls for yourselves just like my Malke," the Captain added proudly.

We did not want to disillusion Captain Weinberg about our "Jewishness." We exchanged meaningful glances. Saul Friedman, Moniek Weintraub and Zeviah Zaplocki had witnessed the slaughter of their families in the Piotrkow market place. It was there, too, Srulek had seen his bride of three months fall to the ground mortally wounded by SS bullets. We had all lost our Jewishness in Piotrkow. The problem was, how does one explain these feelings to a man whose background boasted only happiness.

Every time Captain Weinberg talked, I understood the sadness in Srulek's eyes. The American's casualness was aggravating. Had it not been for the comfort of the hospital facilities, for which he was solely responsible, his stature might have been of a much lesser significance to us all.

In anger, I almost burst out shouting. But I knew it was more expedient to be silent. How can the American understand the tragedy of war, when he shows such puzzling indifference to his victory? What does all the suffering of mankind mean to an individual whose uniform resembles that of a general? How can he have any feelings about humanity when all he talks about is "his" Malke Lox?

Soon, the hospital yard resounded often with laughter. We tried desperately to recapture our lost years; playing hard, eating well. Accumulating excess energy, we even competed in athletic activities. At first clumsily, but gradually we seemed to regain confidence and agility. The doctors encouraged us to increase the pace of our play. "The harder you play the healthier you are," the chief M.D. repeated.

Months later, and well on our way to complete physical recovery, I was startled from my sleep shortly after midnight. I listened. My eyes strained. They were half-closed, groggy with interrupted sleep. I was not quite sure whether the sights and sounds were real or imagined. They came from the direction of the bed next to mine. With some effort, I was soon able to distinguish two figures, a woman and a man, engaged in a bizarre drama.

The woman straddled the man's midriff, her thighs held him in a loving embrace. As if in a trance, her pliant body followed a ceaseless vertical motion. He lay on his back under her weight, his eyes closed and the head twisted in ecstasy, emitting inarticulate sounds, grunts foreign to my ears. Then, the man's eyes half opened, his fingers tightened around the woman's breasts, while he raised his lips towards them, soon emitting suckling sounds. Then, again, the man's searching fingers pressed the woman's firm buttocks convulsively as she murmured almost inaudibly. . . "dearest. . . Liebchen. . ."

I began to understand. I knew that life's drama itself was here at play.

Suddenly, the heaves became more violent, more intense, the murmurs more audible, increasingly more incomprehensible.

"Oooh. . . Jesus. . . sweet. . . Jesus. . ."

"Dear goood. . . you're killing me. . . "

"Don't mind dying this way. . . do you. . .?"

"Nooo. . . go on. . . go on. . . don't stop. . ."

The voices kept in harmony with the rhythmic motion of their bodies. I felt the very poetry of the encounter stirring in the depth of my soul. I experienced a peculiar tingle at the roots of my hairs, as if an invisible hand caressed them lovingly. Then, there was silence except for the soft murmurs and moans as the woman lay back and all motion ceased.

A similar scene from the distant past appeared before my hallucinating mind's eye. It took place under different circumstances, in different surroundings, I saw a small room in the ghetto. It was dark, and I heard the trembling voice of a small boy:

"Mother? Mother, are you there? It's so dark here, and I am frightened. Can I sleep with you tonight, mother?'

"Mother's here, darling. Go to sleep now."

"But I am frightened, mother. You always let me sleep with you when I am frightened."

"Don't be stubborn, Vilusiek. Hush. Sleep now."

"I told you long ago to get rid of him!" A man's voice interrupted rudely. "He'll be trouble yet."

"Why is he with you, mother? Why is uncle Joseph here?" The boy's voice trembled with anxiety.

"Sleep child—I told you, Joseph, once and for all, the boy stays! He's all I have! The children are all I have now!" She argued with her lover while trying to assuage the child. "And stop this arguing, or you'll wake the others."

"When's papa coming back? I miss my papa." The small boy wept.

"Bela, if he doesn't go, I go!" The male voice threatened.

"Joseph, you give me no choice. Please, be reasonable." She pleaded.

"I've been reasonable long enough. Besides, you'll have the Germans fucking you when I'm not around. You don't really need me?"

"Go back to sleep, Vilusiek, don't be stubborn." His mother addressed the boy endearingly once again, listening to his sobbing.

"I like the German, mama. Corporal Boost brings us food and chocolates." The boy insisted.

"Just listen to the brat. He likes the Nazis," the man exclaimed.

"Bet you anything he'd love me too for a bar of chocolate."

"There's always food for you here, Joseph. Don't mock the child. You'd starve without it like the others."

"Are you trying to tell me something?"

"Only that we're all in it together," the woman said softly. "And that you don't get anything free in this world."

"But you still need me to. . . "

"Stop that now! The boy will hear."

"I wish he'd catch us in the act. It's time he should learn a few lessons of life."

"How can you? Please, not now! I beg you, you'll wake the little one." She pleaded.

The boy approached his mother's bedside somewhat groggily. In the room's darkness, he could distinguish his mother's body under the weight of Uncle Joseph's violent movement, and he could hear her softly moaning, emitting scarcely audible words and sounds.

"Oooh, you're an animal. . ."

"Still?"

"A dear. . . dear monster. . ."

"No more corporals or sergeants?"

"No more. . . I promise. . ."

I stretched. The scene faded as suddenly as it had appeared. I was no longer sure I hadn't dreamed it all.

"Eh, Vilek my friend, are you awake?" It was Misha's voice next to my ear. "You want to try?" Now I saw the Russian's face close to mine. I closed my eyes tightly, pretending to be asleep. "I know you're awake, my little friend. Come, come. No harm will come to you, I promise." Misha insisted. "You've got to start sometime. Now is a good a time as ever." The Russian chuckled.

"Leave me be, Misha." I was angry without knowing why. "Get away from me, I tell you. You'll wake everybody in the room." I hissed at the persistent Russian.

"I'm exhausted, Vilek. You understand, kaputt." Misha whispered while Trude settled into my bed, giggling unceremoniously.

"Tell her to get the hell out of my bed, Misha!" I pleaded, but the Russian turned on one side and went to sleep.

The nurse covered my body with kisses. A totally new sensation took hold of me and I was momentarily breathless though I had tried to resist.

"You're as pure as a virgin, my little lion," the woman murmured, while I remained silent, fascinated and paralyzed with the most painful pleasure, unwilling to put an end to its effects.

"I will go slowly. . . don't be frightened. . . there's nothing to fear." She spoke intermittently, and I wanted to scream when she took hold of my erect penis with one hand while caressing my testicles with the other. I closed my eyes shut and turned my face away, not daring to look, trying to make-believe as if it were in a dream, a fantasy. But her soft sounding voice brought me back to reality: "Has anyone ever told you that you'd make a great lover!" The woman asked.

Slowly, with a deliberate gentleness, she brought her face closer to my penis, and I was now able to feel her breath on its sensitive surface. Then, her moist lips enfolded its throbbing head deep into her willing mouth. It was a feeling of pain and pleasure at once like none I had ever before experienced. My soul screamed insufferable curses while my conscious mind blessed each anguishing moment. And then, I fainted in ecstasy exclaiming to the only woman I had ever loved: "Maammaa. . . oooh. . . sweet maammaa. . .!"

20

As far back as I could recall, I had wanted to own a pair of genuine Nazi boots. They were a symbol of authority; that authority no longer was there, but my peculiar need endured. I wanted a pair of boots exactly like those I had had to shine on so many occasions for my former masters. If for no other reason, but for the satisfaction of grinding them into the dirt. "Then, I'll stand there and piss on them before I toss them into the garbage where they belong." I insisted stubbornly.

"Why don't you take it up with Corporal Blake?" Zeviah suggested.

"It might get him in trouble with the captain," Abram cautioned.

My kinship with Bill Blake, the black G.I. from Tennessee, who had lifted me from the floor on that May "liberty day," went deeper than our mutual hatred of the Nazis. We communicated well despite a language barrier.

"We got to stick together, Vilek," Blake insisted, you and me know what it means to go hungry. The hungry become rebels. You and me, we're rebels."

"Aren't you worried about the captain?"

"Fuck the captain. He's got no business with us doing things on our own time. Besides, he don't have to know, does he?" Blake said with a chuckle and a mischievous gleam in his eyes. Sunday morning Bill Blake entered the hospital ward, a broad smile on his face. He, too, was happy about our miraculous recovery.

"You're okay now, so let's go." His voice was shrill with excitement. "Come on, let's do it!"

"Hey, Zeviah, why don't you come along?" I invited my friend.

In his haste, Blake virtually dragged us both out onto the sidewalk in front of the hospital. "See? That's a motorcycle I just repossessed from a fucking Nazi. Let's ride! I'll give you both guns and you can kill some Krauts! Okay?"

At the curb stood Blake's booty; a German military courier motorcycle with a passenger attachment. Clad in our striped inmate's uniforms, sandals on bare feel, Zeviah seated himself behind the driver, and I climbed into the side-car.

"Here they are," Blake handed us each a submachine gun, "all you have to do is pull the trigger, the bullets will do the rest, simple, eh?"

"I'll think about it," I said, "but, in the meantime, let's go look for a pair of boots," I repeated for fear my American friend had forgotten.

"Let's go! Hold on now!" With that admonishment, Blake shifted into gear, the motor accelerated to a roar, and the vehicle surged forward. Soon, we passed the city limits. In the residential section Blake pulled up to a beautiful villa and stopped the motor.

"This is as good a place as any to look for a pair of good Nazi boots," Blake said with a loud laugh. We came to the massive door of the impressive dwelling. Zeviah looked at me meaningfully.

"You had better take along your gun," Blake warned.

"I'd rather not, it might go off by accident," I said hesitantly.

"Things like that don't happen by accident." Blake assured me.

"If it's all the same to you, I won't take it along."

"Well, I'll carry mine just the same, I have a hunch we might get lucky and shoot ourselves a little Nazi pigeon." Zeviah laughed hysterically. It was a nervous laugh.

"I don't want you to kill anyone for me, do you hear? Not for me!" I shouted angrily as we entered the premises. The massive brass nameplate read: "Ing. Karl Heinz von Seeger."

"A fucking aristocrat!" Blake spat resoundingly, and the saliva slid slowly down the plate lettering.

The front door was unlocked. Blake remained outdoors "to keep an eye on things," he said. I followed Zeviah into the spacious lobby, laid out with rich Italian marble, multicolored and shining like polished glass. There were two wall-size mirrors on both sides of the entrance. They made the hall look much larger than it was. A solid mahogany staircase wound its way to the upper floor, guarded by a heavy banister of impressive workmanship. The stairs were, for the most part, carpeted, as was part of the hall. It was difficult to guess the origin of the carpets; but at first glance they seemed genuine and expensive. We stood in the entrance speechless, only our dazzled eyes moved from one object to another in silent awe.

"I'll be damned!" Zeviah hissed. "Get a load of this! Just like the mayor's mansion in Piotrkow. Surely it's not one of those poor little schmucks who did all the fighting on the front line. It's a big fish, I tell you! He was right where the money was all along, and he's got a lot to show for it. Take a good look, Vilek, some of it might have belonged to our friends and relatives!"

Like a flash, the memory of my grandfather's modest house passed through my mind. How jealously the old man had guarded the shiny, massive staircase that wound its way gracefully to the upper portion of the house! It outlived him in the end, poor soul, and my grandmother, too. They were long dead before their house was partially destroyed by a direct hit from a Russian bomber. Fortunately, the old couple went first. The destruction of their beloved property might have provided more agony than death itself; such was their attachment to their worldly possessions.

"Well, now, don't let's just stand there, Vilek! Let's have a look around! Maybe we'll find what we came for!" Zeviah encouraged me.

We entered through the door to the right of the vestibule. There was a light switch. We were momentarily blinded in the narrow confines of a large closet. "There! Vilek, in the corner! A pair of boots!" Zeviah shouted with joy. "Your boots, Vilek!"

"They are beautiful! What a shine! Touch them, Zeviah, the surface feels like glass! Here, touch!" In my excitement I shouted in Polish, Yiddish, Russian and a smattering of Hungarian; it didn't matter. Even Blake understood, his smiling face curiously peering through the open window.

I stood in the middle of the vestibule, clutching the precious boots under my arm. The power they possessed infused a new kind of excitement into me; the terror of the past years melted into a translucent nightmare that I wished to leave behind me, never to experience again. These clean, shiny boots, how many innocent victims had suffered under their brutal imprint? How many were disemboweled by the force of one well-placed kick, to suffer irreparable damage? I forced myself to brush those thoughts aside while giving way to a novel sensation.

Joy was a simple thing, easily understood.

We were about to leave, when a middle-aged couple appeared at the head of the stairs. The man, graying at the temples, was tall and held himself straight, occasionally leaning slightly onto the rail as he descended. The woman was most likely the younger of the two. Visibly shaken by the presence of the intruders, she remained at the top of the stairs. The man descended, facing the barrel of Zeviah's submachine gun. We stood at the foot of the stairs, hesitantly, not knowing whether to admire the man's courage, or silence him before he voiced his views.

"The boots, those are my boots, young man!" He spoke. "Where are you taking them?" The tone of authority was still there, but it no longer inspired fear.

"They're not yours, Nazi swine, they are mine now." I made an effort to be calm. "You took my shoes and made me walk on my bare feet all through the war. The soles of my feet had blisters inside blisters. Damn you, Nazi, you took everything from us. This is not much for you to give up." My voice seethed with hatred.

"How dare you intrude? This is my house, and you're stealing my property! You were wronged by the Nazis. Go after them. I only fulfilled my duty."

"What kind of duty?" Zeviah grinned. "Why didn't you run away with the rest of the criminals?"

"Why should I run? I was an officer of the Wehrmacht. I did nothing wrong. I only performed my duty." The German repeated slowly with poise and authority. "Besides," he went on, "all that is past history. We must remember the barbaric outrages of the few among us, never to allow the events ever to recur, but don't act as they did. You are not thieves! Where is your decency? We now live among civilized people!"

"Let me burp my gun into his Nazi carcass. Then we can kill his bitch Frau up there!" Zeviah was feverish with the desire to vent his anger. I'll show the Kraut how civilized he's taught me to be!"

"No, Zeviah." I spoke slowly. "You don't have to do any killing for me. They're my boots. What has to be done I'll do myself." I turned toward the German. I didn't really know what I wanted to say. I had nothing to say; nothing of any significance. I took hold of Zeviah's gun and pointed it at the nearest door. "Get in there!" I ordered the German.

He obeyed, and we entered a large, well furnished room. We stopped. "Turn around!" I barked an order. We stood, silently facing each other; the survivors. The gun was now in the hands of the erstwhile victim. It was directed point blank at the hated enemy. "Could I pull the trigger?" I wondered. I also wondered what went through his mind though he feigned courage.

"Turn around."

"No, I'd rather die facing it."

"Turn around, damn you! Do as I say!" Suddenly, I became very angry. Why should I let this fucking Nazi have his way? I thought. He's had it long enough.

The German's face showed that he knew as a certainty what he had suspected all along. This boy was no killer. Merely a child. He could be handled easily. The German's confidence returned promptly.

"All right. If you must. Get on with it, quickly." The German turned slowly. As he turned, a small handgun appeared in his hand. "You . . . goddamned son of a bitch! You. . .!" I shouted while my index finger squeezed the trigger mechanism impulsively, aiming the weapon at random. The impact of the first bullet caught the man squarely in the shoulder and he fell; his massive body lay at my feet. Just then his own gun discharged rapidly, as the dying man's fingers tightened around the trigger convulsively until there seemed no rounds left.

The gun shots mixed with the woman's loud, anguished shriek coming from the top of the stairs. For a brief moment, my hate was almost gone.

"Did you kill the bastard?" Zeviah was joyously curious as I reappeared. "Say it, say you killed him!"

"He pulled a gun on me, the swine," I said. "Let's go! Let's get out of here!" I tossed the boots to the floor, and then the gun. They fell with a loud thud. "The Kraut was right, after all, we're no thieves. Besides, the boots are not my size!" Zeviah picked up the gun on his way out.

Departing, we caught a glimpse of the woman as she reached the room. We heard a loud cry of despair like one obsessed, and immediately following, the sound of a discharging handgun. We boarded the motorcycle and took off without looking back. "I thought there were no more rounds left in his gun," I said, glancing back toward the villa.

I felt as though a heavy burden had been lifted from my shoulders. For the first time, the stigma of defeat was left behind. It lay in the plush vestibule of a defeated enemy no longer envied. Zeviah grinned at my remark. He tried to understand, even though he could not quite reconcile his own thinking with mine. "So what." Zeviah remarked. "Lucky for her, there was a round left. After all, she belongs with her mate. Hope they have a fair flight to Walhalla." He let out a wild chuckle, as his mind's eye once more caught the picture of the frightened German.

"Want to try somewhere else?" Blake yelled through the din of the accelerating motor.

"No, let's call it a day."

"How about a little celebration at the P.X.?"

"That's the best suggestion I've heard today." I yelled back. There was no anger left in me. And there was no anger in Blake's sudden but exultant yell "Deutschland kaputt!" for which the rapid backfire of the engine was a worthy accompaniment.

The Sunday papers carried a headline story. Roman broke the news at the breakfast table. "How do you like that! They're trying to pin the murder of the German couple on us!" he shouted.

"What's all the excitement about?" Yossele asked.

"Here it is, on the front page!" Roman read for everyone to hear:

PROMINENT COUPLE SHOOTING VICTIMS

A dastardly deed has been committed. Gunned down and robbed were Karl Heinz von Seeger and his wife, Helga. The incident occurred at the couple's villa on Gneisenau Strasse 173. Neighbors alerted the authorities when they heard shots coming from the villa shortly after midnight. Witnesses say they saw a Negro G.I. in the company of two men dressed in K.Z. outfits on the premises of the von Seeger villa. They had all been drinking prior to the break in. The Negro was heard shouting

"Deutschland kaputt!" and other obscenities as the suspects drove off on their motorcycle. The vehicle was later found abandoned near the 66th MIS Detachment. The authorities believe one of the suspects to be a member of that unit. The U.S. authorities have pledged full cooperation.

Roman let out a sharp whistle through his teeth. "This looks very serious."

"Wouldn't you know it? The Americans get more worked up about two miserable dead Nazis than they did when the Nazis fired the ovens of all the crematoriums." I seethed. "Besides, we'll swear we didn't come near the damned Krauts!" I added.

"No one will believe your story. It'll be your word against their neighbors'. The Americans are careful nowadays not to strain relations with the Germans," Yacov remarked.

"You mean, we could go on trial?" I whispered in disbelief.

"It could happen. The judges of the new German court are mostly hold-over Nazis. The exiled jurists have not returned to their homeland," Abram explained.

"But. . . how. . . can they. . .?" My spirit sank. I spoke softly, scarcely for my own ears.

"Simple. They invented 'denazification.' A former Nazi fills out a long Fragebogen, a questionnaire. His 'character references' are his comrades in arms. He is cleared by the reviewing board, and becomes eligible for a civil job. Clever, eh?" Abram went on.

"Good God! Things haven't changed much, have they?" Yossele remarked with a chuckle.

"Let's not give up too easily. We've got to do something quickly or we'll be tried in their court of law. Just think about it. Think about the headlines it would make!" Abram concluded.

"We've got to keep quiet and stay vigilant," Zeviah cautioned.

"You're worried, eh, Vilek?" Misha's voice startled me momentarily. "The trouble with you is that you take life much too serious. People like you discover too late the humorous side of life. Worse yet, you might never get to see it."

"I've got a problem" I grinned, although I didn't feel in the mood to reveal my thoughts. "Yes, it was a foolish thing to do." I wondered how Misha knew. I didn't trust the Russian completely.

"That wasn't a smart thing to do. Did anyone see you?"

"It's all so weird. It happened too fast. The bastard was going to shoot me, so I shot him instead. It's weird, I tell you. We didn't kill the woman. Honest, we didn't."

"This is a time to stay calm," Misha said.

I sat silently for a while, somewhat bewildered, still worried. Then I said softly, more to myself than to Misha: "Life's not to be trifled with."

"I know just the right thing for you." Misha smiled. "Trade's sister. Hot little bitch. Give her a try, Vilek. The kid's only fifteen. Bet she hasn't been laid yet, you know what I mean?"

I looked at my companion without expression. "Is that all the Russian can think about? Women and sex?" I thought. The past had a way of flashing through my mind. I wondered if I'd ever be able to say with confidence that I truly survived. "No thanks. Not right now. I know you mean well, Misha." I was tactful, concerned I might hurt the man's feelings. After all, he meant well. I mused.

"I understand."

"I hope so."

"And you mustn't brood. It won't help matters, you know? Let time work things out," Misha added, as he turned to go.

I did not expect serious contemplation on the part of the Russian. He somehow did not fit into that role. There was still much mystery about Misha.

That night, in the exaggerated solitude of my uneasy sleep, I was witness to the most bizarre execution of someone who resembled Yacov; a shouting mob of brown-shirted creatures wielding sharpedged swastikas, hacked away at the defenseless man, who soon lay in a pool of blood. His accusers resembled *Herr* and *Frau* von Seeger dressed in the uniforms of Allied soldiers wearing swastika armbands.

I awoke drenched in sweat. The alarm clock showed half past four. I would be getting up soon anyway. No matter, I wasn't going back to sleep.

"Hey, rebbe, wake up!" I tugged my friend by the sleeve. "Wake up, I've got to talk to you."

"What in h. . ." Abram rubbed his eyes. He glanced at his watch. He didn't curse as a rule. But waking up in the middle of the night was not expected anymore. "Vilek, what in heaven's name is so important that it can't wait for another hour? I ought to. . ."

"I just had the most horrifying dream," I interrupted the bewildered rebbe.

"You wake me because of a nightmare?" Abram was annoyed.

"Who sleeps without nightmares? Tell me!"

"Okay, okay, I know. I'm worried about Yacov. It was him I saw in a pool of blood." Here Abram sobered up completely. He spit to the side three times as superstition dictated for the prevention of bad luck. He sat up on the bed, and I waited patiently for his comment.

"Come, Vilek, sit by me. Let's reason this out together," Abram said. I knew I was in for some skillful Talmudic speculation.

"You have known me for a long time, Vilek, eh?"

"I. . . guess. . ."

"We went through a lot together, yes? We ate together from the same vat, starved together, picked lice from the seams of our clothing together."

I made no attempt to interrupt, though I didn't like being reminded of the past. It came to mind altogether too often.

"Most significant of all," Abram continued, "we experienced pain together. Pain brings forth man's true nature like nothing else. Do you think I'd let you down after all that?" He asked. "So why don't you go back to sleep?" He added quickly, "tomorrow we'll talk."

"I just think the Krauts have a lot of *hutzpah*." I used the Yiddish word for "nerve." "It robs me of my sleep."

"If you don't quit worrying, you will arouse suspicion. Would you like that?" Abram cautioned.

I grinned at Abram without saying a word. The rebbe made a motion with his hand, as if swatting a fly off his nose, then he turned toward the wall and began to snore.

On the following Friday, it was near midnight when we were summoned to Captain Weinberg's quarters.

"Lucky we waited up," Yacov quipped. I trembled with presentiment. Surely, it was the matter with the Germans. I thought.

"I would not call you at this late hour," the Captain began apologetically, "but this could not wait. Within the next few days the United States Military Government will announce the withdrawal of its occupation forces from East German territories." He paced excitedly back and forth. "With the withdrawal of our forces, the Soviets will take over this entire zone of operations. Damn it all! I was hoping we would have more time." It must have been of serious consequence for Captain Weinberg to curse.

"You've got to make up your minds," the Captain went on. "Remain here, and be repatriated to your homeland by the Soviets, or come with us. You'll have a chance to emigrate to the United States of America. Europe is like a tired whore, worn out and past its prime."

I welcomed the news of leaving. It was just in time. The farther away from this place, the better, I thought.

"We are with you, Captain, one hundred percent," Abram said. He looked at me with that certain air of prophecy, as though he wanted to say: "I told you not to worry. Things work out." I understood.

"That's a good decision, men. You won't regret it. Life in the States is much better than here." Weinberg repeated with obvious satisfaction. Just then, the field telephone on his desk rang. He picked up the receiver. "th M.I.S.

Detachment, Captain Weinberg speaking." He listened. "Yes, sir. . .Yes, sir." A short pause followed. "Yes, Colonel—I understand—moved up—zero—seven hundred hours on Monday. Yes, sir!" He replaced the receiver and sat for a few moments silently.

"What is it, Captain?" Abram asked.

"That was Colonel Yancy, the area Military Governor."

"What's wrong, Captain?" Yacov asked.

"We have to move out sooner than expected." The captain looked at a point on the opposite wall as if to avoid our eyes. "In fact, we're moving you out on Monday morning."

"We've only got two days, Captain," I was overjoyed, "but that's no problem. We have very little luggage to pack. The Nazis saw to that." Everyone laughed.

"Where are we going?" Yacov asked.

"I believe, it's Hamburg."

"Hamburg?!"

"Where are we going to stay?" Abram asked. "The city's in ruins."

"The British have special quarters prepared for you." The Captain sounded almost formal.

"The British?!" Roman exclaimed.

"No cause for worry, *kinderlech*." He used the Yiddish word for children for the first time since liberation. "They're better than the Soviets," he concluded, but all of us felt we've been betrayed.

Early Saturday morning during breakfast, Abram was approached by Misha Dury.

"I have a special favor to ask of you, Abram," Misha said.

"Well, let's hear it."

"I want to marry Trude."

"So, why ask me?" Abram looked puzzled. "I'd be the last one to object."

"Because we want you to perform the ceremony."

That was too much even for the rebbe. It was one thing to be called rebbe in jest, but quite another to be asked to administer the holy vows of matrimony.

Abram looked at the Russian in total disbelief. After another moment's hesitation, he could not resist asking once more:

"You want *me* to do *what?*"

"We discussed it, Trude and I, and we agree that we would like very much to be married as Jews, the traditional way. We want you to officiate."

There was no mistake. Abram understood the man's intention. He looked at us and we looked at him. He was visibly embarrassed. We were silent. Abram had to decide for himself. How was the Russian to know, "rebbe" was only a nickname?

"But. . . I'm not. . ." Abram Bachter, the Vilna merchant of "holy water" wanted to confess the truth. But he hesitated long enough to reflect on the opportunity offered him. Was he not one of the few who were spared by the Almighty? — blessed be His name — surely, he was saved for some higher purpose. Abram speculated. He dared not question the Lord's reasons for guiding him out of hell. Why not begin the new life by sanctifying the union of two unbelievers? Can he refuse and allow the two souls to follow the path of damnation? A man is not offered an opportunity such as this twice in a lifetime. Abram reasoned.

"We decided to convert to your faith permanently. Will you do it?" Misha was anxious.

Overjoyed, Abram Bachter accepted Misha's request and his new calling with gratitude. His desire to serve squelched a persistent admonishment of his conscience against proselytizing.

"We'll have to hurry. You know, we're leaving Borna in two days." Abram said. His voice sounded instantly more dignified, indeed, like that of a rabbi. "I'll ask Captain Weinberg to serve as a witness. His presence will make it legal." There was a grin on Misha's square face.

Abram Bachter outdid himself. It took only hours to prepare the two proselytes. Misha and Trude proved exceptional students. All who came to know them admired the couple. Inge was bridesmaid. At Misha's insistence, I was the best man. Captain Weinberg's prayer shawl was spread out above the heads of the newlyweds to serve as the traditional canopy. The entire hospital personnel witnessed the ceremony, and Chief M.D. Giesecke was moved to tears giving away the beautiful bride.

"Her parents died in an air-raid, you know," he said, "and she's like our own child to us." Mrs. Giescke sobbed happily, adding: "*Ja, ja*, like our own little girl, she is."

That, too, brought memories to my mind. Memories of a small, fragile girl of seven, who was denied forever the right to choose between solitary life or matrimony. That fateful morning, almost four years ago, in the market place in a small town in Poland little Felusia—Feigele, "little bird," we called her—shared the destiny of all Jewish children who were too young and frail to work for the Nazis. I tried, but I was unable to put those puzzling events into perspective. And I recalled Abram's stoic pronouncement: "Those are the ways of life, some day you'll understand."

The solemn vows were spoken. Misha and Trude joined the ranks of surviving Jews. "By the authority vested in me," Abram spoke slowly, hesitating at the word *authority*, "I now pronounce you man and wife."

With that sentence a new life began for the newlyweds and a new career for Abraham Bachter, as he would be called from then on. It was inconceivable, but it was true. A double metamorphosis was taking place. The new-lyweds assumed a gradual appearance of Jewishness, and Abraham seemed to thrive on his new rabbinical responsibility. Not only did he sanctify the newlyweds, but his own life underwent a similar sanctification. There was rejoicing.

"There's one debt I've got to pay before leaving," I said quietly.
"Not another one of those visits?" Roman grinned. "Haven't we had enough for now?"
"It's not like that." I was apologetic without knowing why.
"Don't take it so seriously, brother. I was only kidding." Roman laughed. "Come on, tell me."
"Remember Ernst Boost? He made me promise I'd visit his home in Leipzig when the war was over."
"Don't be foolish," Roman smiled. "That was just talk, just empty talk, nothing else."
"No, Roman, it wasn't that at all." I was adamant. "He was good to us. He meant all he said. His family ought to recognize us from the photos he sent home!"
"Okay, okay, don't get excited." Roman tried to defuse an argument.
"I must tell his wife and children how he died." I added softly. "I just know that I have to do it before we go north."
"I'm coming with you," Roman said. "You'll need some help carrying things for the poor Krauts."
"Don't say that, Roman! I know you mean well, but don't call them that. Boost wasn't one of them!" I admonished him, and Roman grew silent. "Boost was a decent human being," I added, as if to justify my intentions.
The city of Leipzig lay in shambles. As far as the eye could reach, there was no housing left intact that could be inhabited by humans. The G.I. driver let us off, after much searching, amidst rubble where once was a street called *Eisenbahnstrasse.*
"That's it, boys!"
"Thanks a lot." We jumped to the ground.
"We'll meet at the old Rathaus before seven p.m.! I'll be waiting!" The truck pulled slowly away.
"This is the street, Roman. Now all we have to do is find number 134."
"How can you be sure it's number 134?"
"I remember it well. Boost made me repeat it over and over again, until I knew it in my sleep."
"Look, there are people moving about in those ruins. Let's ask. Someone's bound to know the Boosts." Roman pointed to an underground passage.

Among the debris was a small marker, an arrow directed downward, with an inscription Bierkeller. "Hey, it's a pub. The bartender ought to know everybody around here."

A man with a handlebar mustache stood behind the bar. A few tables were occupied by quiet customers.

"What'll it be?" The bartender asked.

"We're looking for the Boost family." I turned toward the inquiring man. "Wonder if you could help us find them?"

For a brief moment, there was no reply. We were being scrutinized from head to toe; would they trust our good intentions? I wondered silently. The man turned his back on us. Suddenly, he pivoted back.

"What are you selling?" He motioned at the two large sacks Roman deposited on the ground. "Maybe I buy." The bartender nodded toward a young man at one of the tables who then left the premises discretely. I suspected it was to warn *Frau* Boost.

"It's not for sale, but you can get a can of good American coffee, if you help us find the Boosts," I said eagerly. "You don't have to worry. I'm an old friend."

Just then the young man returned, followed by a woman in her late thirties in the company of two teenaged girls. One of the girls was approximately my age; That's Margot, I thought to myself. The second one was about three years younger, that must be little Helene.

"Willi!" *Frau* Boost cried out. She sobbed unhaltingly. "My poor Ernst," she went on, "how I wish he'd be here to see you. He looked forward to this day. He never stopped telling us about you, Willi, about his adopted son. And mine too," she hastened to add. I felt uneasy in her embrace, feeling the warmth of her tears on my cheeks.

"Margot, Helene, kiss your brother Willi!" She urged the shy girls. That, too, was the legacy Boost left. I was to be their adopted son when the War came to an end.

"My Ernst died at Wyazma, Willi." She volunteered, and I listened, not having the courage to tell her that I was there too, and saw it happen. "His unit was snowed in, nearly frozen, and Ernst was making his usual deliveries. A sniper got him. That's what they told me. He was an easy target against the blanket of snow." She sobbed convulsively. "Just one week before he died he wrote about homecoming. He always mentioned you in his letters." She wiped her tears. "He was coming home for Christmas. It was the third Christmas he had been promised to spend at home. Dear God, Ernst is gone forever, and all I've got left is his Iron Cross First Class." The girls joined their mother, weeping softly. "And we have you, Willi," Frau Boost added anxiously.

"I can't stay, I said sadly. "We're leaving for Hamburg tomorrow morning."

"What's to become of us, Willi?" Frau Boost wept. I looked at her despairing face and her tearful eyes. For a brief moment, I was prepared to compare this weeping woman to my mother. As if she had read my thoughts, she pulled me aside. "I know everything Willi," she whispered out of the earshot of the others, "about your mama, and my Ernst. He never kept things from me. That's how he was. There was nothing between them, nothing to be ashamed of. They just kept company, that's all. I know that for sure, because Ernst told me." She repeated. "Ernst was a good man, a decent man." I felt myself blushing, and I turned my head motioning for Roman to bring the provisions.

"You know my brother, Roman, don't you?" I asked. "We brought some things you'll need. Hard times are coming. I hope this'll carry you for awhile." We handed her our gift and readied to go. "There's really not much I can do or explain. We have to go on, all of us, do our best. The worst is over for you, *Frau* Boost. For me, it's only the beginning."

"We must stay together, Willi. Ernst would have wanted it that way."

"I can't stay. There's so much I must do. There are places I must go and search for my family. There are so many tasks awaiting me, Frau Boost, I'm frightened when I think of them."

"You mustn't be, Willi, you're young, and the young are strong."

"Ah, but I have aged much beyond my years, Frau Boost." I kissed her on the cheek, then Margot and Helene. "Let's go, Roman." I walked away without turning back. She had no time to thank me. It was better that way. I wouldn't have known what to say anyway. She called after us: "God bless you both!"

"Poor woman." I mumbled more to myself than to my silent brother.

"We've all gone through the meat grinder." Roman added.

"You know," I said, "I can't figure this thing."

"What?"

"Well, only a few months ago they had everything. They were the ones who sent us stuff. Suddenly, they have nothing."

"You pity them?"

"Not really, but I can't help wondering."

"They made it happen both ways." Roman said.

"You mean, they were as much victims of circumstances as we were?"

"Something like that." Roman paused. "But they had more choices than we did. After all, they're pure Aryans—the master race, you know."

"And we. . . "

". . . had no choice at all, little brother."

"Except the choice of life or death," I insisted.

"Some did. . .others didn't. . ." I glanced at Roman from the corner of my eye, and I decided not to press on. Some time in the future, perhaps, we might reflect on such sensitive topics. It was still too early for that.

On the eve of our departure for Hamburg, we were called to Captain Weinberg's quarters. My heart sank. "This must be it." I was sure this time. "They're on to us."

"This time there are good reasons for the summons." The Captain began with a grin. He pointed to a man seated next to him. "This is Major Arieh ben Ari, a representative of the Haganah." The Captain introduced his guest unceremoniously.

We examined the stranger with a degree of suspicion. He tried to disarm us with a broad grin, almost a smile, which revealed a row of splendid white teeth. His face and forehead bore evidence of frequent exposure to the sun and wind. He wore a thick mustache beneath the large, grotesquely deformed nose, perhaps the result of a fistfight, which added to the mystery of his presence.

Even without being able to tell his exact height, I figured the man was well over six feet tall. The stranger's appearance suggested the strength of a lion; Arieh meant "lion" in the Hebrew language. When he spoke, he did it softly, yet everyone listened attentively.

"I'm with the Haganah. My mission is to recruit and lead survivors like you to *Eretz*." He used the Hebrew word for Palestine. "The British are getting ready to get out soon, and we expect the worst. The Arabs outnumber us. They have a well trained army, and they intend to drive us into the sea. If we don't resist, they'll claim as much of the land as their force will enable them to grab. The odds are against us."

Arieh's message was compelling. Even the challenge of an adverse bet worked in his favor. He knew us well. Before him, he saw men exhausted from a struggle, eager for another chance at life. What did he offer? Uncertainty and risk.

There was America. It held out a hope for a better future. What this man was offering was a country to be built, perhaps give one's life for "a home where the Jew will walk with his head proudly raised . . . without the fear of being victimized. . ." These were eloquent arguments. They hit against years of degradation and maltreatment which all but extinguished the memory of those ideals upon which human nature is weaned. I gazed at this stranger as he shared his anguish with the rest of us.

We were reluctant, unable to revive those dormant dreams, unwilling to accept the challenge though our sympathies lay with the cause. We felt embarrassed. The messenger might think us selfish and cowardly, at best callous at a time when history itself shouted for action. We remained painfully silent, weary from our encounter with death and eager to embrace life again.

Arieh smiled. "You need not give your answer this very moment. I can wait."

"There isn't much time." The Captain interjected. "The investigation into the deaths of the von Seegers is shaping up." He sounded solemn. "I've already transferred Corporal Blake. The Germans continue to press for the corporal's companions."

I was frightened. My pulse quickened, and I squeezed Roman's arm. "Hey, little brother, calm down," he admonished. "We'll be gone from here soon."

I turned to Abraham for counsel. Tiny drops of perspiration gathered on his forehead. They slowly trickled down his acquiline nose and fell into the open siddur—prayer book—which he held in his lap. He closed his eyes, and he swayed to and fro in the fashion of the pious.

"There's no need to panic, my friends." The rebbe spoke slowly, placing emphasis on every word. "Of course, we know the Germans will pursue this matter to the bitter end. But. . ."

". . . they lack the necessary bureaucracy," Zeviah interrupted.

"It won't take them long to recover," Yacov admonished. "Perhaps going to Eretz isn't such a bad idea after all."

"I've got to look around first. I have the feeling there is someone out there to be found. I want to return to Poland, if only briefly, to see if there's anyone left of the family." I said almost in a whisper.

Yossele's blood rushed to his face. He was angry, and he began to shout. "You heard the man! They'll be fighting for a home for all of us. A home for all Jews! And you go on making excuses!"

"Besides, we made a promise." Zeviah added.

"You can't be held to a promise made under duress," Abraham said.

"A promise is a promise." Saul murmured more to himself than to the rest of us. "And we didn't make it to the living, we made the pledge in the memory of the dead."

"The promise stands. It's Eretz for me, too. Anyway, there's no one waiting for me anywhere, "Moniek said. "That bastard Mengele took care of that." He added. We all remembered his twin brother Lubek who perished under the mad doctor's knife in Auschwitz.

"Wait," Roman interrupted the quarreling. "This is all getting us nowhere. I've made my decision." He paused. "I'm going with the Major." I looked at my brother startled. The decision was so sudden, he had no time to share it with me, and I didn't expect this turn of events.

"They weren't able to separate us all through the war. . ."

". . . you mustn't worry, Vilek, it won't be for long." Roman hastened to allay my fears. "I'll be joining you soon."

"I can't let you do this, Roman."

"My mind's made up." He seemed at peace with himself.

"Let's think about it." I pleaded.

"There's nothing to think about."

"But. . ."

"I'll be fine. . . you'll see."

"So be it." I said gently. "But take care, will you?"

"You sound like it's forever."

"Well?"

"We've been together for so long, it'll do us good to be separated for awhile." Roman was almost cheerful. "When are we taking off?" He addressed the Major.

"With the roosters." Arieh grinned. "We've got to get an early start. There's a lot of territory to cover."

21

The great city of Hamburg was a landscape of ruin; mounds of rubble resembling desert dunes. The larger ones were remnants of apartment houses; the smaller were most likely ruins of private homes. The destruction was so complete, I shuddered thinking that Hitler's prophetic last will and testament, which was broadcast during the Allied siege of Berlin, might have become total reality.

When the war is lost, so is a people!

This fate cannot be prevented! It is therefore necessary to take into consideration the most basic needs which the nation necessitates for its future survival! On the contrary, it is better that we, ourselves, destroy these items! Because this nation had in that case shown itself to be the weaker, and to the stronger, the nation from the East, the future belongs exclusively. Those who are left over after the struggle are the inferior; because all the brave have fallen. . .

The extent of devastation amazed all of us as we made our way atop the military half-truck, moving slowly through the city to our new "home" at the *Marienkrankenhaus*. Borna was behind us, occupied by the Soviets, "the nation from the East," in the Führer's words.

Children ran up and down the makeshift playground, while men and women labored at clearing away the rubble in the hope of salvaging food stored there before the destruction. Somber-faced, the workers scraped clean salvageable bricks and stacked them in orderly cubes. Work proceeded rapidly and efficiently. Only the sound of metal hacking against the surface of stone was heard.

"Clever, these Krauts, aren't they?" I murmured.

"History tells us, they've got a lot of practice at rebuilding." Abraham remarked. "I despise their efficiency and fear their ingenuity," he added with sadness in his voice.

"If they keep up the pace, they'll rebuild this goddamned place in no time at all," Tuviah said. "Only this time they'll have to do it themselves. The slaves have been freed."

"Let's hope this is their last lesson." Yacov chuckled.

"That's hard to foresee." Tuviah mused. "These people have an uncanny propensity for self-destruction."

"Behold everyone!" The rebbe exclaimed suddenly. His eyes were half-open, the tip of his nose produced the familiar drops of perspiration. "The German nation at long last came down from Walhalla to labor in the fashion of their former slaves! Behold, my friends, we have lived to see it come to pass. The Almighty, blessed be He, has smitten the arrogant with His mighty arm."

No one laughed, although we could not take Abraham seriously during his "divinely" inspired moments.

"Behold, the God of Israel is just!" Abraham concluded.

"Where is the justice you speak of, Abraham? The Germans live, and our people are dead!" Tuviah challenged the rebbe.

"Don't blaspheme." Abraham shook his arm menacingly. "We are not to question the ways of our Lord!"

"On your right is Sankt Pauli, lads, the biggest whorehouse in Europe." Came the driver's voice, and we welcomed the interruption.

"There are more whores assembled here than anywhere else on the continent. You've got to see it for yourselves! It's a bloody frightful sight!" The driver, a British Corporal, smacked his lips in approbation. "They got what's coming to them!" He made an obscene gesture.

We came to a sudden halt. The truck moved forward only at the slowest pace. The street wasn't completely cleared for traffic.

German P.O.W.'s made their way through the rubble. Their smooth, haggard faces, betrayed their tender age. Uniformed in rags, some walked on crutches, others with bandaged heads. Frequently, an armless sleeve swayed grotesquely back and forth. There were also those whose one trouser leg cut and sewn up at the hip indicated their own tragic loss.

"*Bitte, bitte*, please, Tommy, a smoke." The beggars repeated plaintively, attempting to keep up with the slow-moving vehicle.

The teenage beggars defied almost all thought of vengeance. I looked on in silence. I wanted to spit in their faces and shout abuses, but the words refused to come. I almost began to pity them. Suddenly, as if it were the memory of the dead, I yelled at the top of my voice.

"I hate you! Do you hear?! I hate all goddamned Nazis!" But just then, I saw a boyish face in a Flak uniform, and I grew momentarily silent. He could have been anybody's son or brother. He was limping slowly.

"Look at the fucking fourteen year old fighter for Adolf!" The driver exploded with laughter. The boy broke out in tears, sobbing convulsively. He was a boy again and he was not ashamed to cry.

Misha pulled the youth by his arm up onto the platform. No one objected. The truck moved on. The driver snapped a cigarette butt from between his fingers. As it fell a short distance away, the beggars threw themselves after it, shoving and pushing at each other.

"Damned Krauts! No pride in defeat!" The driver spat after them.

The boy was frightened. I wanted to yell at him to get the hell off the truck. I wanted to shout insults, but instead I silently remembered the time we were running, my mother and I, the sirens screamed, the Stukas were diving. I begged her to stop and rest. I was out of breath, my lungs were about to burst.

"We mustn't stay in the open!" She said. "It's unsafe! Come, dear, the planes will be here any minute! We must find shelter!" I didn't care. I wanted to die. Then, we found a bench near some shrubs in the park.

We made it just in time. The bombs exploded around us. Each time it seemed they would hit. I pissed into my pants with fright. Only mother wasn't afraid. She pulled me closer to her breast and spoke of things to come, of things we'd do together when this was over, this horrible war.

We lay under a flimsy park bench, but we thought it was safe; like trusting the unknown. God, too, is an unknown.

I was unable then to understand the mysteries of the grownup world. Grownups can reason things out. Children can't. Children are afraid, because they don't understand. I thought grownups don't ever get frightened.

I learned later that I was wrong. They also know how to hate. I never really wanted to grow up.

I turned to the youthful Flak P.O.W., but he was already gone. I must have been talking in my daydream, because everyone looked at me in a peculiar way.

"You think I'm crazy, don't you?" I asked quietly.

"Nothing to worry about, friend. You're in good company." Misha's grin turned into a broad smile.

The truck stopped in front of a massive building with its name printed in bold letters above the ornate door: MARIENKRANKENHAUS.

"Cheer up, Vilek." Misha chuckled. "Things are improving, aren't they? We're in the care of our own Holy Virgin Mary."

I could not forget the hateful, burning eyes of the youthful P.O.W. I'd been thinking about that chance meeting, maybe even dream about it.

"Come on, Vilek! Get it out of your system!" Abraham urged. "It's better than silence!"

"I hate the bastards! I can't stop hating! I can't get them out of my mind!"

"It's obvious," Abraham said gently. "You've hated and planned retribution all these years, now you're being moved to compassion. We Jews are a compassionate people. That's part of our tragic destiny."

"But. . . I. . . I. . . hate the. . ."

". . . yes, I know, you hate the bastards. I often feel the same. I force myself to hate in fear that I might feel pity for my enemy." I listened astonished.

"You must try not to torment yourself, else you'll go mad." Abraham warned.

Misha was obsessed with the prospect of initiating me into man-hood. He offered to pimp for me. Sankt Pauli was full of willing instructors, he said. The more I rebuked him the more insistent the Russian became.

At last, for some unknown reason, I agreed to go along.

"On one condition, if I don't like what I see I'll turn back. Promise?"

"I swear to you on the memory of my mother!" Misha was elated. It was a Wednesday afternoon. Sankt Pauli was quiet, it was too early for traffic.

Women of all ages, of varied shapes, sizes, and appearances surfaced at the sound of footsteps beating against the sidewalks. Some leaned out of the windows as prominently as they could without losing balance. I was shocked though some strange emotion stirred in me.

"Only ten scrip! A bargain! Come up, honey!"

"Like a virgin! Only nineteen, still fresh! Firm breasts!"

"Hey, you there, *Liebchen,* come up! This way, darling!"

"Come up here, handsome! Here! The third story!" The last caller was a fresh, resonant voice, unlike the others. We looked up above our heads. "Here I am, look at me! Am I not beautiful!?"

She was perched on a window sill naked, her slim, shapely legs swinging precariously downward. She could not be over fifteen years old, sixteen at the most. Dark brown hair fell loosely down her frail shoulders. The after-noon sun intruded between the dreary buildings illuminating the lovely girl.

There was something of a child in her; her naive enticements; the disre-gard for danger. We stared upward and I almost forgot my initial fear.

The girl burst out with a carefree, happy giggle. It was the sound of guileless frivolity; not at all an earmark of her trade.

"Come up, honey!" She repeated the invitation. Her thighs spread apart, she pressed her hand meaningfully to her pubic region. She then disap-peared out of sight.

I followed timidly in Misha's path. We knocked. "The door's open, come in!" We entered the small room, and she stood at the door to greet us. She looked fragile. She was remarkably beautiful. There was an aura of inno-cence about her. She doesn't belong in this place, was the only thought running through my confused mind.

Close up, she was even smaller than I expected her to be. Sitting on the edge of her neatly made bed, she was no longer naked. I was relieved, though the negligee left little to the imagination. We regarded the girl in silence.

Devorah might be her age now. She was nine years old then, when they took her away. She, too, might have grown to be a dark-haired beauty, I thought to myself. Instantly, my mind was elsewhere. I recalled the Piotrkow market place, aunt Sabina carrying a bundle of belongings in her right hand, Devorah holding on to her left. There were lamentations everywhere, there was shouting and pleading. Ever-present were the whips of the mercenaries.

I remembered asking Devorah if she would be my wife when we grew up. She only laughed. It was a carefree laughter of earlier years. She said that nothing really mattered when two people were in love. I understood. I often asked her if she loved me. She would always love me, she said. We kissed, to seal the covenant.

Now, this fragile whore whose features bore a striking resemblance to Devorah, observed us without saying a word. With that special instinct of her profession, she sensed the difference of purpose. Customers came unceremoniously to the point. I could see the puzzlement in her face. She spotted my slight build and my shyness. I experienced an urgent idea that she was straining to recall someone. I seemed to remind her of someone she knew.

"I'm Frieda," the girl broke the embarrassing silence. "Come closer. No harm will come to you." She spoke in German.

Misha approached the girl. I was still too frightened to speak. I was glad the girl's name was Frieda.

"I'll leave my young friend with you. Do you understand? Treat him well. Teach him to be a man," Misha said. Without warning or waiting the girl's reply, he left.

I wanted to run. But my feet felt heavy, and I couldn't move.

"Come, don't be frightened. Sit by me, right here." She repeated. I didn't respond. She got up from the bed and took my hand in hers. I followed her hesitantly. Without a word, I sat by her side. She clasped my hand in hers.

Hers was a delicate, small hand of a child. Very much like Devorah's hand. Devorah! I wanted to forget, for the moment at least. I turned my face sideways. She sat very close to me, and she understood my silence; respected my fear.

"How long have you been. . . in this place?" I asked shyly, and she looked surprised. "I mean. . . I mean. . . how long have you. . .?" I stammered for want of words.

"I can not remember how long it's been. What does it matter? I am what I am. That cannot be helped?"

"There are other ways. Better ways."

"*Liebchen*, let us not waste time on silly talk. You heard what your friend said. I don't want to anger him. Here, lie down, relax, make yourself comfortable." She used the word gemütlich, a word which, like her name, sounded softer now than the surroundings. She pushed me gently down till my head touched the pillow. Undressed, she lay beside me very close and very warm.

Gently she caressed my penis and testicles, and kissed them in the process of undressing me. My body shook violently at first, but the feeling was not repugnant. I lay immobile, almost petrified with fear. Her nimble fingers massaged my body. She pressed herself tightly to me, the kissing intensified as she whispered tranquil expressions of love.

"Do you. . . remember. . . your mother. . .?" I stammered.

"Vaguely," she said, without interrupting her pursuits.

"You mean, she left you long ago?"

"I don't know, all I remember is that she was somewhere here in Sankt Pauli, even as I am. She might still be around. I have no way of knowing."

"Don't you ever get to see her?"

"If I did see her, what would I say to her? We must compete to survive. Come now, *Liebchen*, enough talk. Let me make you forget."

I wished to respond to her searching fingers. But I was unable to drown out the past. Suddenly, I rose from the bed, forcing the girl almost violently away from me. I dressed quickly. She looked at me quizzically, hurt.

"Please, you must forgive me. It's nothing personal against you, Frieda." I spoke her name for the first time. "I have nothing against you." I repeated empathically. "Believe me, you must. It's just. . . well. . . it's the language you speak, the language of assassins. It reminds me of too much suffering. I'm unable to accept it as the expression of love!" I almost shouted.

"What do I tell your friend?" She asked with a perplexing innocence.

"Tell him you've kept your bargain. So will I. He'll be pleased." She looked puzzled. "O.K." she said softly. "If you really want it this way. It's all the same to me."

"Then, it's a deal." Quickly, without turning back, I ran into the busy street.

"Come back when you're ready!" I heard her call after me. "Come back when you're a man!"

So this was how it felt to caress fresh banknotes! I wondered to myself. It had been a long time since I had handled money. The Allied Scrip notes had beautiful inscriptions and pleasant color reproductions of the real American banknotes. Each of us received a modest amount of "cash" to cover initial expenses. Clothing had to be bought, underwear, socks, shoes, and other essentials not available in the commissary.

"I'll get sport shoes and a silk shirt," I dreamed, "and maybe some nice looking slacks."

"Is that all you need to be happy?" Misha asked.

"Oh, I don't really know. I'm just thinking out loud," I replied, my fingers crackling the crisp bills in my pocket; two hundred and fifty scrip Dollars!

They responded to my fondling in a most pleasant way. I marveled at the wealth on my person, spending it in a thousand ways mentally. "Are you coming with me?" I asked.

"I'll meet you at the market place at three-thirty. Okay?" Misha seemed preoccupied.

"Fine, take your time. I'll be a while."

The small crowd of hagglers fluctuated in lively exchanges. My prosperity was alien to me. I let my mind wander back to thoughts of my youthful days of lack and denial. "Good Lord!" I thought, "such a fortune!"

There was a commotion, and a crowd quickly gathered around an old vintage BMW; there was a lot of shouting and arguing. "What's going on?" A voice inquired.

"Someone got run over!"

"It was the driver's fault!" Another voice yelled.

"They're driving like crazy!" A third voice shouted.

"It's the old lady, you know, the junk peddler." Everyone there knew Frau Kemp, the grizzly old woman scavenging for all types of discards in the neighborhood which she peddled as "second hand" wares.

"Is she dead?"

"Probably dying. She hasn't moved at all. She slipped trying to elude the vehicle and she got hit squarely on the head," someone explained.

I pushed through the crowd. She lay, motionless, grotesquely sprawled out on the snow-covered street. A traffic policeman was maintaining order, trying to keep the crowd from getting too close. Someone picked up the broken fragments of the woman's glasses; another fetched her purse nearby. The policeman placed the items on the stretcher as the victim was carried away into the ambulance.

Suddenly, I remembered, and I started to look for Misha. I put my hand into my right pocket to feel the banknotes before parting with them. The money was gone! Blood rushed to my head. Now my left hand searched the left pocket. Then, the fingers of both my hands traced both pockets for broken seams. "Damn! Damn! Damn!" It was all I could say for the moment. "How could it have happened? I've been robbed! I, a seasoned *kazetnik*, with the experience of a thousand thieves, a victim of a common pickpocket!" The loss infuriated me.

Following my misadventure with Frieda, coupled by the loss of the scrip, I shied away from Misha and his attempts at "educating" me. Needless to say, he did not let on knowing about my failures, and I was too ashamed to confess. Instead, his visits to the "city of whores" had become more frequent, and I saw gradually less and less of him. Several weeks had gone by, and I noticed a gradual change taking place; Misha was not his "old self anymore.

He came to the hospital for his periodic checkups, and no one was aware that he had spent most of his time at Sankt Pauli with Frieda. Rumors had it that Misha's and Trade's marriage was on the verge of a breakup. Trude was frequently seen in the company of Tommies, provided her through the efforts of Yacov's and Tuviah's pimping. My two Piotrkow friends had established a whole "stable" of Frauleins.

"It's not in the Jewish tradition," Abraham admonished our defiant friends.

"To hell with tradition," they replied, "we'll blow up the whole fucking world, if it comes down to it, it's our turn to repay in kind. 'An eye for an eye,' remember?" They mocked the rebbe.

"But, is there nothing else?" He inquired.

"Look at it this way, rebbe. Most of our living days were spent in slavery. Our mothers and sisters were made into whores, and we fought every inch of the way for our lives. We're so used to fighting, it's our nature. We'd feel sort of naked without it." Yacov spoke for both men.

"It's a dangerous game, prostitution and black market."

"I don't see anyone else feeling sorry for the Krauts," Tuviah said.

"Besides, what better way can we serve the miserable whores. They'd starve to death without us."

"Leave Trude out of it!" I sounded threatening.

"Hey, little poet, don't push your nose into somebody else's business," Tuviah broke into a roar. "She's one of them, isn't she?"

I felt a great sadness that the first Jewish marriage should have also become the first Jewish separation after the war.

Tuesday afternoon was Misha's customary physical. He seemed in good spirits. It was to be his last day as an outpatient.

"Hello Misha." I greeted my friend shyly.

"Hello, Vilek." Misha grinned.

"You're worried?" I asked.

"For the past few days I've experienced a sharp pain in my penis." Misha spoke quickly, as if to himself, his eyes fixed on some imaginary object far away. "It comes when I piss. There were sores on my tongue weeks ago, but I didn't tell the doctor. I even missed two checkups. Then I noticed more sores, and I had occasional fever. Now there is a copper-colored rash all over my body. I was hoping there was no cause for alarm. I told Frieda, and she laughed when I told her. But I couldn't stand it any longer when the headaches came. I was vomiting, and I couldn't sleep. I haven't seen Trude for some time. She'd know what to do. I'm really worried."

For the first time since I knew the Russian, I could see fear in his eyes. We walked to the doctor's office together, and Misha was grateful.

"Strip!" The doctor gave a terse order. Misha stood naked before the examining physician. "On your back, please!" Misha obeyed silently. He watched the doctor's expression. It became serious as the examination progressed.

"Young man," the doctor said while washing his hands, "we must have you hospitalized immediately."

"Is it that bad, doctor?" Misha inquired anxiously.

"Yes, it is," the doctor paused for a moment, "I'm afraid I have bad news for you."

"All right, don't play games with me, what is it!?"

"You're suffering from an advanced stage of syphilis!"

"What?!"

"You heard me. It's syphilis. No doubt about it. I advise immediate treatment." The doctor said dispassionately.

"Why, that dirty bitch! The filthy little whore!" Misha yelled beside himself.

"You mustn't leave!" The doctor tried to restrain the Russian. "You can fight it at this stage, you must get treatment at once!" Misha dressed quickly ignoring the doctor's concern who hurried from the office to summon help. "Stay, Misha, please!" I pleaded in vain. The doctor returned in the company of two male nurses but the Russian was gone.

22

It was too late when the police found Misha. He lay sprawled on the floor in a pool of blood. A forty-five caliber colt automatic pistol was still in his cramped fingers. The barrel pointed at his stomach. Blood flowed gently from the side of his mouth. His eyes were open until an officer pressed down the lids. The girl lay on her bed. "Death by strangulation," the coroner said placidly. He closed Frieda's eyes. It was routine. "I'd say it's murder and suicide. You can put that down sergeant." The coroner's opinion was officially recorded. Date, place, manner of death, all official facts. That, too, was routine.

The funeral the next day was a simple affair. Few friends were present. It was Abraham's first funeral oration. He read about vanity and the destiny of man from Ecclesiastes. The widow was dressed in black. She listened to the rebbe's solemn words, but she did not weep.

In a letter written to his wife, Misha asked that Frieda be buried by his side. No one knew what else he wrote. Trude destroyed the scribbled note as soon as she had read it.

So it was done, and Frieda rested next to Misha. Those present filed past the grave, each mumbled something under the breath, not loud enough to hear. Trude leaned on the rebbe's arm as they disappeared through the gate.

Everyone was gone. I stood at the graveside, staring into nothingness, numb with a renewed pain of knowing death.

"Misha, Misha you fool! Was this necessary? What have you done? You killed my little Devorah! You made her die for the second time! You're now an assassin! You're an assassin and a fool, my friend!"

Slowly, without looking back, I walked away.

"Black market drags on the heels of famine and war." Abraham argued annoyed. "It can upset our plans!" His nose quivered; clear evidence that he was mad. He chastised Tuviah and Yacov, but they continued counting their profits. Lately, they were selling Allied scrip for American dollars, and Abraham was afraid they would get caught and ruin our chances of going to America.

Nine p.m. was curfew time. That, too, was the aftermath of war. The streets of Hamburg were patrolled by M.P.'s and by the newly created German Militia.

"I don't want to seem ungrateful, Abraham, but why shouldn't we cash in? Everyone's getting rich in Europe, why not us?" Tuviah yelled.

"It's just too big a risk, that's all," Abraham insisted.

"One never gets anywhere without taking risks. You ought to know this by now!" Yacov shouted. "Besides, we won't get you in trouble when we're caught!"

"Do we still remember the promises we made on the day the Allies liberated us? Only a few months have gone by, but we've forgotten," I said softly. My remarks had a surprising effect. "Besides, why do we want to get rich all of a sudden? Weren't we grateful for just 'being alive'?"

"I don't want to look for handouts," Tuviah argued. "Let's go, Yacov, we've got business to attend to. A scholar, I've never aspired to be." Tuviah could not refrain from striking out at the traditional Jewish reverence for scholarship and my ambition to return to school.

"Please, my friends," Abraham insisted. "Reconsider, and give up what you're doing. I see no profit in it," he added on his way out.

"We've put a lot of our money and time into this deal. It has to go off well!" Tuviah said, his face aflame.

It was 3:00 a.m. A jeep stopped in front of the house where the two friends occupied a small flat. Through the parted curtains they saw a British staff car. Moments later, the Tommy Sergeant delivered four sacks of flour, which he neatly stacked in the corner of the room.

"Will you have a schnapps, Sergeant? To steady the nerves?" Tuviah asked.

They drank a toast, and then another. "Be in touch, lads." The Sergeant said leaving.

They rubbed the remaining drops of alcohol into their palms for "good luck." Tuviah cast admiring glances at the merchandise anticipating the profits. "We'll have to move it fast," he said.

"You're right. But we can't do it now. It's curfew," Yacov remarked.

"We can't be caught with the merchandise!" Tuviah said emphatically.

"Let's wait a couple more hours. It's almost dawn. We'll be in for twice the trouble if we're caught out there during curfew." Yacov cautioned. "Hold it a second. Isn't that the sound of a motor? The Sergeant must be back." He walked over to the window. "Tuviah! The M.P.'s!"

"It's a trap! Let's get the hell out of here!"

"Let's not panic, Tuviah." Yacov tried to keep his head. "They can't put us back behind barbed wire, can they?" He reasoned.

"Damned if I wait to find out!" Tuviah ran toward the window. "Come on! Yacov, you first. Come on!" He shouted.

Yacov jumped into the street as the M.P.'s burst into the room. Tuviah balanced himself precariously on the window sill, ready to jump. There was a shot. Yacov looked back, and he saw his friend's limp body smash heavily to the pavement.

"Tuviah!!" Yacov yelled, but he kept on running and he was out of breath when he stopped.

By a quarter of seven that same morning, Tuviah's fate was common knowledge. Friends gathered outside the emergency ward.

"Why did they have to shoot? The bastards!"

"Why do you think? To silence him. Tuviah knew too much."

"Will he pull through, doctor?"

"We should be able to tell in about an hour. He's in intensive care now, and his condition is undetermined. We took two caliber slugs out of him. It's a miracle he's made it thus far. It'll be more of a miracle if he survives." The attending physician was less than encouraging.

It was eight-fifteen when we were told the sad news. There were complications; fluid in the left lung and severe infection set in all at once. Tuviah was in a coma. At nine-forty-three Tuviah Moshkovitz was dead.

"It was *bashert*. It was destined." They said. Abraham was unable to hold services. He choked with emotion.

Yit-gad-dal v'yit-kad-dash sh'meh rab-bah. . .

In unison, we recited the kaddish for our departed friend. I wanted to weep, but my eyes remained dry. I felt guilty about not being able to shed a tear for my friend.

"I've drained my tears for those who went before you, Tuviah," I whispered. "Forgive me."

On the following day, I was called to the foyer of the hospital to receive a guest. I recognized her from a distance, though her hair had grown back and she was no longer bent with malnutrition.

"Haya! How good to see you!" I embraced her, lifting her up from the floor and twirling her around.

"Let me down. . . please. . . you're crushing my vertebrae. . ." She laughed.

"But, what brings you to Hamburg?"

"We're on our way to Belgium."

"To Belgium? What's in Belgium?" I was puzzled.

"I'm getting married," Haya said quickly. I sensed the strain, and I knew to give her time. She sat down and I sat down beside her, taking both her hands in my own. My mind went back to our initial meeting in Belsen when the War had come to an end.

"How you have changed," I said with a satisfying smile. "You've grown beautiful again."

"And you have become a handsome man, Vilek. Your mother. . .uh. . ." She caught herself in time, and I understood.

"Let's not talk about that now." I fought against lapsing into melancholy thoughts. I hesitated. "But, tell me about yourself. Who's he? Who's your future husband?"

"He's a Belgian farmer." She grew pensive. "We met in Belsen. He was attached to the British troops guarding the camp." She examined my face with great concern. Her voice was uneven, uncertain. "You sound unhappy."

"Do I? To the contrary, Vilek. I'm as happy as a lark. The happiest I've been in as long as I can remember."

"Even as happy as that day I brought you the toothbrush?"

"Even as that day." She knew I was trying to make her relax.

"Then, why do I have the feeling that there's something you're keeping from me?"

"Oh, it's really nothing important," she hedged anxiously, "nothing."

"If it's nothing, then there's no need to worry, eh?" I insisted.

"Come, look at me. It's me, your cousin Vilek. Eh? Why don't you tell me everything now. I feel kind of responsible. . . we're the only family we have. You and Roman are all that's left to us of the old times." I looked into tearful eyes. I held her hands now tighter, anticipating her response.

"Jacques isn't a Jew." She shot the statement quickly as if trying to free herself from a dreadful burden.

"A *Goy?*"

"Yes, a *Goy*. He was kind, understanding and healing for my torn soul." She talked fast, as if afraid of being interrupted. "I don't expect you to understand, Vilek, only don't rush to condemn me."

"Who's condemning? Whatever gave you that idea?" I hastened to reassure the trembling woman.

"I was so afraid, Vilek. And Jacques loves me very much, and I love him, too." She cried. "God bless you, Vilek, God bless you," she repeated, and her shoulders shook spasmodically.

"Promise me you'll not be afraid again, Hayale." Her pretty face lit up with glee. "Make the best of your life, and don't fear or regret any of your actions. We were all given another crack at it. Let's make the best of what we have."

"Oh, you dear, dear boy!" She embraced me. "You'll never know how much I love you!"

"Yes, Hayale. Indeed, I do."

"I'm leaving for Belgium tomorrow afternoon."

"The trains aren't going yet? Are they?"

"No, it's a British convoy, and I'm getting a ride."

"Can I see you off?"

"Only if you'll promise to visit the farm as soon as you can."

"I promise."

"Here, that's the address." She handed me a small piece of paper with the address scribbled on it. I put it in my breast pocket.

"I won't forget."

"I'll be expecting you. There'll always be a home for you, Vilek." She readied to go. "You've taken a burden from my shoulders. I'm so very happy!"

"I know," I said, kissing her on the cheek. "So am I, for myself as much as for you."

Just then, Abraham approached us as we were about to part. There was no way to avoid the inquisitive rebbe.

"My cousin, Haya—Rav Bachter." I introduced one to the other.

"Nice meeting you. Vilek told me about you."

"Don't believe a word." She laughed. "Now, I've got to run along. You'll have to excuse me." Haya was on her way to he exit. We looked after her as she disappeared in the doorway onto the street.

"My cousin's marrying a Belgian, Abraham."

"Really? There are Jews in Belgium?"

"I guess there must be, though she's not marrying one of them."

"What a shame she's getting married to a Goy. She seems such a nice Jewish girl," Abraham said. I was tempted to respond appropriately, but I restrained myself.

"You might at least wish them a hearty mazal tov, don't you think?" I said. Without waiting for his response, I walked away. Poor woman, I thought to myself. She desperately needed approval. I was glad I was there to give it.

23

The thought of Frieda refused to leave me. I was shocked. I had fearful dreams. I could not think clearly and gloominess and depression set in. Frieda appeared to me as Devorah, encouraging me to set out in search. I woke, drenched in sweat, and decided to leave this place, the sooner the better. Meanwhile, I tried to read, but I became angry with myself each time I picked up a book from the hospital library. I had made the terrible discovery that I was a teenage illiterate, and I felt as though the world had passed me by. I regarded the others with envy, but I would not permit myself to make comparisons.

"My dear Vilek," Abraham said, "I haven't seen you this sad since the Hitler days."

"What kind of a world do we live in?" I said with some annoyance.

"Each time you get your head just enough above water, a new tide threatens to drown you." Abraham listened and I continued, encouraged by his silence. "I won't cry over a lost childhood, if I could only go on from here on in life as if nothing had happened. But the question is how?"

"You're not going to succeed, unless you quit this intense loathing of your own past, and everything and everybody that surrounds you," Abraham cautioned.

There was a saying among the survivors: "If someone's alive, you'll hear about it." Incredible as it seemed, by word of mouth, we had learned of an inquiry to be conducted by the Military Court in Wiesbaden about the wartime activities of SS Commandant Tulka. He was apprehended crossing the Belgian border and brought back to the Allied Headquarters city to stand trial. Witnesses, of course, were in great demand.

I had become a skeptic by experience, not by choice. But news like that I could not shrug off as mere gossip. Whether it was Tulka or someone bearing a resemblance to the "one-eyed monster" of Colditz, I was not going to deny myself the benefit of a reunion.

News of Commandant Tulka's arrest persisted and were difficult to ignore. If only Roman were here, I thought, but in his absence, the responsibility of testifying lay squarely on my shoulders.

"After all, we couldn't stay in Hamburg forever." Everyone agreed.

Captain Weinberg's call from his Headquarters in Wiesbaden confirmed

Tulka's capture. We all felt the urgency of the move. The specter of Leib Glikier's gaunt figure compelled us all to act.

Wiesbaden was a truly imposing city. It wasn't difficult to find the U.S. Army Headquarters, for it seemed every pedestrian we asked knew where the Amis had settled.

"*Kinderlech!*" Captain Weinberg exclaimed overjoyed about our arrival. "You've done the right thing and you won't regret coming here."

The Captain provided us with a spacious villa, abandoned by its owners, and still unclaimed. We talked briefly about pressing matters. There was a sense of excitement when Tulka's trial was mentioned. Why a trial, I thought. Why not hang the fucking assassin without one?

"We conduct trials," said the Captain. "It's the democratic way." He read my mind.

We signed documents pertaining to our eventual emigration to America. Each of us responded to the questions in his own way.

"Age?" The interviewer asked.

"Thirty-nine." The rebbe was the first to falsify his age as did the other "old men," reclaiming the six "lost" years. It was their obsession with time. The world had cheated them, and this was their way of "restoring" their wasted past.

"You're only fooling yourselves," I said.

"It's easy for you to say that, Vilek," said Abraham with reproach.

"You're still young. Time's not your enemy, not yet."

"To make a friend of time is to tame a monster." I said softly, more to myself than to my angered friend.

"There must be things you'd want to do while waiting for the final papers?" The Captain asked with concern. "The time has come for you to make plans for the future."

"The war may be over for you, Captain," I said. "For me, the war still rages on. When's Tulka's trial?" I asked abruptly.

"It's been moved up to Frankfurt." Weinberg looked concerned. "The exact date hasn't been set."

"I should become an assassin," I said quietly. "But that would only prove Hitler was right. I'll fool the bastard and his absurd logic and try to educate myself instead." I recalled my father's dictum: "I don't want you to work as hard as I do for a living, so you must become a doctor." My father's Herculean involvement in eking out an existence nearly used up his entire stock of passion, while mother's supply of love was inexhaustible. They compromised in their almost obsessive care for their children.

"I want to go back to school!" Remembering the past impelled me to shout my decision for all to hear.

"Glad you made up your mind, son." The Captain was delighted.
"We'll take steps immediately."
"It'll have to wait till after the trial," I said, and the Captain understood.
He readied to leave.
"Don't forget, Vilek. Your brother's arriving in Frankfurt tomorrow."
I had almost forgotten Roman's arrival from Palestine. My preoccupation
with Tulka was becoming obsessive. My brother's presence was sorely needed.
I lay awake all night in anticipation.

"Roman!"
"Vilek!"
We collided in a powerful bear hug. The ice was broken. We joked joy-
fully, indulging in trivia. Anything to delay the moment of truth.
"You searched?" I asked.
"I did," Roman replied softly.
"And. . .?"
"It's no use. There's no one."
"You mustn't say that, Roman. You must never say that!" I said stub-
bornly.
"Okay, okay. We'll look some more." Roman was calm. "We must find our
father."
"I've got to look for Devorah." I said with resolve. After a moment's
hesitation, I changed the subject. "Haya married a Belgian. Came through
Hamburg to say goodbye."
"I know. She wrote me. That's how I got your address." Roman smiled.
"They caught Tulka. He'll be tried here soon."
"Tulka?!" Roman exploded. "Tried?! Here in Frankfurt!?" His rage dimin-
ished the joy of hearing the good news. "We'll come, of course!" He almost
shouted.
"We must bear witness, Roman."
The trial of Commandant Emil Tulka was not as exciting an event as it
had originally promised to be. The young, inexperienced attorney from the
U.S. Judge Advocate's Section made the presentation in behalf of the prosecuting authorities of the Allied occupation. Tulka was represented by four
experienced attorneys; all of them familiar with the Nuremberg Laws, members of the NSDAP and making no secret about it. The three Justices repre-
senting the Allied Forces of West Germany were American, British, and French.
It was a solemn occasion. There were no elaborate introductions; a few
words from each of the Justices sufficed. Everyone knew the reasons for

being there. The witnesses seemed anxious; their worried expressions were in obvious contrast to the self-assured manner of the accused.

"State your full name." The presiding U.S. Justice addressed the man on trial. The interpreter echoed the words in German.

"Emil Tulka," came the terse reply.

"State your former rank and position."

"*SS Sturmführer, Lager Kommandant Colditz.*"

"Murderer!" Yelled Zeviah.

"Assassin!" Yacov echoed.

"Order in the court!" Demanded the Bailiff while the presiding Justice rapped the gavel. "One more such outburst and you'll be removed from the courtroom," the Justice warned. He was angry, and the young attorney for the prosecution blushed as though embarrassed by his own inability to control the witnesses.

We sat quietly, listening to the elaborate statements delivered first by the prosecution, then by each of the defense attorneys.

"All this talk about the six million Jews put to death by the Third Reich is emotionally charged, a pack of lies nobody has proven to be absolutely true. Allegations that there were gas chambers for the purpose of killing Jews are also simply hearsay evidence. We will admit that some of the workers died in the labor camps of various diseases, maybe as few as 800,000, but six million? That's a lie, a fabrication of the Zionist propagandists."

"The Third Reich is not on trial here," interrupted the British Justice, "Commandant Tulka is."

"Your Worships," continued the attorney for the defense, "in order to establish the credibility of these witnesses, I must impress upon the tribunal that they lie about the greater crime as well."

"Objection," interrupted the prosecution.

"Sustained," said the presiding Justice. "The witnesses are not on trial here."

Roman became inordinately pale and quiet. At one point, he doubled up as though he was about to retch at his feet. Suddenly, he touched my hand. "I can't stay here any longer. I feel awful." He said quietly. I whispered in the attorney's ear.

"May we approach the bench?" The prosecution requested. Given permission, the young attorney approached the Justices, requesting that Roman be excused from further proceedings in the trial. I wondered about my own capacity to continue. The prosecution, meanwhile, demonstrated stacks of photographs and documents relating to the atrocities committed by the accused. These were procured directly from the *Konzentrationslager Colditz* with the cooperation of the Soviet authorities.

"Only 800,000 victims, the bastard says." The prosecuting attorney whispered to his assistant. 800,000 persons dead from sickness and malnutrition, ONLY! If he were not expected to maintain a certain courtroom decorum, he would himself climb upon the tallest table and shout at the top of his lungs, "assassins!" But that was not the way of the LAW.

The prosecutor knew that concrete evidence was unavailable to prove the alleged assassins' acts of terror. He caught himself thinking "alleged," and he was angry and alarmed to think in these terms. But that was the letter of the law: we must present evidence beyond reasonable doubt. He was troubled about obtaining a conviction against Tulka, and he feared an impending compromise. He glanced at the remaining witnesses. What if they, too, weaken and let him down at the crucial moment? What if the tribunal decides that the evidence presented "falls short of proof?" What then?

The young prosecutor must have anguished over these and other such questions. He tried to penetrate the equanimity of the Justices, and he was almost certain that one of the three, his countryman, had caught his eye.

The presiding Justice was troubled also. "The defense makes sense." He must have thought to himself. What precedent in law do you cite to convict a mass-murderer? "Most of his victims are long dead, some dying in the aftermath of their imprisonment, abandoned and forgotten."

"Under your command at the Colditz Labor Camp hundreds, even thousands of Jewish inmates were liquidated, put to death, at gun-point, gassed in moving vans or brutally beaten." The prosecution carried on.

"I was a soldier, and I performed a soldier's duty," replied Tulka placidly.

"Was it your duty to murder these people?" The young attorney pressed his inquiry.

"Objection." One of the defense lawyers rose to his feet. "My learned colleague is trying to interpret the actions of my client."

"Sustained," said the presiding Justice. "Prosecution will refrain from advancing personal conjectures."

"Sorry, your Honor. I was trying to establish some pertinent data."

"My duty was to make them work," said Tulka.

"Some were unable to work because of illness and were beaten unconscious by you or your subordinates."

"They were pretending to be sick, the filthy swine. . ."

There was repeated rapping of the gavel.

"The witness will confine himself to simple answers. No name calling, no personal views," the presiding Justice said solemnly.

". . . well, they would pretend to be sick so they could go on sick call. The Third Reich couldn't waste food on those who wouldn't work."

"Liar!" Cried the *rebbe* in exasperation.

"Order in the court," demanded the presiding Justice, "the Bailiff is instructed to remove the witness from the chambers until such time when testimony is to be heard."

The attorneys for the defense smiled the inscrutable smile of the expectant victors, while the prosecuting attorney remained perplexed in the light of the apparent disintegration of his case against Tulka. I sensed what was going on in the Prosecutor's mind. He must have thought: "how can the tribunal accept the testimony of my emotional witnesses? Will they be of any use to me when their tim comes to testify? What if they are declared incompetent?" And the prosecuting attorney went on with the routine questioning. Tulka's replies were calm. He was arrogant and cynical.

Endless questions and rebuttals followed. It was a game played by the privileged, a game suffered most by the witnesses who were asked to testify about experiences they had wanted to put behind them. During a brief recess, we speculated.

"From the way things are progressing, Tulka will go free," the rebbe said with bitterness in his voice. "Everything points to it."

"Your outburst in the courtroom didn't help our cause." I remarked

"What did you expect? I'm not made of stone." The rebbe was apologetic.

"Tulka is, and his lawyers know that."

"There's only one thing for me to do," I said with determination.

"Don't do anything foolish," Roman warned.

"I don't intend to go back there, it's a waste of time."

"We have to. Think of the prosecutor," Yacov pleaded. "We can't let him down."

"You go back there. I've got better things to do."

"If there's to be justice done to the assassin, we'll have to help."

"We'll have to find our own kind of justice, my friend." I got up to leave. "Our kind of justice you won't find in that courtroom."

Conceived out of utter helplessness, a bold new plan emerged.

The trial ended. As we anticipated, Tulka was acquitted by the Allied Tribunal. This was done with the clear understanding that he would stand trial before a German Court of Law as soon as the revision of the legal codex of post War Germany took effect. It would take months, if not years. With all my heart, I wanted to direct my energies to resuming my interrupted education. But I was unable to follow my ambition.

Tulka had become a major concern for all of us. We met at the rebbe's place to talk things over.

"You realize, I'm giving up a night of business, don't you?" Zeviah joked. "This is costing me money."

"This better be important." Yacov grinned.

"You can pick up and leave." Roman was irritated. "We can do without your help." He was angry.

"They've set the bastard free," I started. I knew that our common hatred would unite us. "We've got to do something fast," I suggested.

"His release makes a mockery of our existence." We argued long into the morning hours, and we reached an agreement nearly at dawn.

The decision was quick and final; Tulka must die.

It wasn't difficult to trace Tulka to his apartment on the outskirts of Frankfurt. The city was still in ruins, and the only habitable section was near the airport; a section the Allies had had the foresight to spare for their own future use. Tulka was well known to his neighbors. His recent triumph over the Ami prosecution lent him an aura of heroism. They talked about the man with genuine admiration.

Good American coffee and a few cigarettes provided us with the needed information. From the custodian, an old woman who lived directly below Tulka's flat, we were able to determine the company he kept and the time of his coming and going. Soon, a pattern began to take shape.

"We're closing in, boys." The *rebbe* admonished those lacking in patience. "We can't quit now, and we're not ready for the final act. Have patience."

"The *rebbe's* right," I said. "It just wouldn't be right to quit this close to accomplishing our goal."

We found out during the six weeks of February and March that Tulka was not altogether without problems of his own. Each Saturday, he returned to his apartment drunk, in the company of at least two of his barroom friends who literally carried him while he dragged his feet along the pavement. After a short stay at the apartment, the men left. On one occasion, I heard them chuckle, commenting on the condition of their comrade, "he'll sleep like a log, the son-of-a-bitch. Wish my conscience would let me do the same." Then they broke into loud, raucous laughter.

The time had come to buy a weapon. Yacov and Zeviah were assigned that task. They had the connections on the black market. "We'll need a .38 caliber pistol with a silencer. We don't want to wake up the whole neighborhood." Zeviah remarked with the now familiar grin on his face. At first, each of us had thought of getting a weapon. However, as the plan had been carefully thought out, we decided to use a single gun.

"Damn!" Roman exclaimed. "I'd hate to go through life with that bastard on my conscience!"

"Not you, nor any one of us will have to carry that burden," said the *rebbe* with a mysterious twinkle in his eyes. "Be patient, and trust me."

To commemorate the death of our friend, Leib Glikier, and our own day of liberation, Tulka was going to die on the night of May 1, 1946 in the suburb of Frankfurt a.m. Main.

He lay sprawled on his bed when we burst inside. It was only moments after his friends had deposited the drunk Tulka, and he had not had time as yet to fall asleep. He looked at us, and his eye told us that he was quickly sobering up. There was fear in that one good eye; only the glass eye would not betray his emotions.

"Get up, dog!" Said the *rebbe*.

Silence.

"Make it fast, *Herr Kommandant*! You son-of-a-whore! You're going for a walk!" Yacov ordered the bewildered Tulka. Slowly, he sat up in his bed. He was fully dressed, and as he stood by his bed, Yacov and Zeviah grabbed him by his arms and led him outdoors. Once there, the two friends propped him up against the side of the building. Tulka stood, silently obedient, meek in his fear, waiting.

Until then, the gun was in the *rebbe*'s coat pocket. It was the *rebbe*'s idea how to proceed with the execution, and he was to fire the first shot. Now, the *rebbe* drew the gun, and Tulka became aware of the seriousness of the situation, by then having sobered up completely. The former SS Camp Commandant knelt before his executioners.

I read the brief verdict informing Tulka he was going to be executed for the crimes he had committed against humanity. "The death penalty was mandated to you by our friend, Leib Glikier, your last known victim, whom you murdered a year ago in Colditz in front of us; the witnesses."

"Have mercy. . .give me a little more time. . . I have a wife. . . and two small boys. . .," begged Tulka with tears running down his cheeks.

"You'll get the same treatment you gave our friend, *Herr Kommandant*."

". . . they're arriving tomorrow morning from the East. . ." Tulka pleaded.

"Just in time to bury you, swine!" Yacov landed a kick to the German's kidney, and Tulka toppled to the ground. He quickly got on his knees again.

"Don't, Yacov," I said resolutely. "We haven't come to play *their* games. We have serious business to do."

"Please, give me a little time to explain why I did what I did." Tulka pleaded.

"The dog will lie even when facing death." Zeviah ground his teeth together.

"Especially when facing death," Yacov remarked.

The gun was aimed at the German.

"No. . . please. . . I had no other choice. . . except to do my duty. . . please
. . ." sobbed Tulka.

"Pull the goddamned trigger!" I yelled at the rebbe who stood looking at
Tulka, hesitating. I, too, became aware that listening to the assassin's pleas
would rob us all of the courage we needed to pull off our act.

The *rebbe* squeezed the trigger, and Tulka fell back against the building.
A large red spot appeared on the victim's shirt above the right elbow. He fell
backward, and his body went into a convulsive motion not unlike that of an
epileptic. The gun was passed to me. It was my turn to squeeze off a round.
I did, quickly, hitting the German in the stomach. Then it was Roman, and
several large red spots became visible on Tulka's shirt as blood began to flow
profusely. In quick succession, two more shots were fired. Yacov and Zeviah
had done their share and the gun containing the last round of ammunition
was returned to the rebbe. His eyes half closed, pearls of sweat appearing on
his prodigious nose, the rebbe fired the last round at close range directly
into the German's chest.

The bloody, twisted body lying before us did not resemble the once arrogant *Lagerkommandant* Emil Tulka. No one of us was sure which of the
shots had killed the one-eyed assassin of Colditz. His body lay still at last,
and the magazine was empty.

". . . *but if you refuse and rebel, you shall be devoured with the sword*," the
rebbe quoted the prophet Isaiah as he dropped the empty gun into a nearby
gutter.

Another glance at the lifeless Tulka and I turned to go, whispering inaudibly to myself: "That evens things up, Leib." I was suddenly not altogether
certain that Tulka's liquidation had given me the sought-for satisfaction. I
observed the somber faces of our small band. No one laughed. Don't people
laugh when they're happy? I questioned silently. We have forgotten how to
be happy, and that was cause for much concern.

"Let's get out of here." I said.

24

The German press speculated that the victim might have been a former German intelligence agent, executed by his own associates, having endangered their anonymity. The intimation was that perhaps a much larger framework of international intrigue was at play than surface circumstances had indicated.

"Arrests have been made, and more are yet to come. The authorities will get to the bottom of this matter and criminals will be brought to justice." The papers concluded. The matter was finished for us as well.

My ambition to learn was dampened by the treatment I had received from my schoolmates. Here I was, a seventeen-year-old man placed into a learning situation for twelve-year-olds. No doubt, the former Hitler Youths were now firmly rooted in their belief that a Jew's mind was inferior, and my appearance in the sixth grade did nothing to discredit that theory. They almost rioted, laughing at my Polish accent when I handled *their* language, and they scorned my feeble attempts at pronouncing French.

It was not my physical appearance that placed a distance between me and my classmates. At five feet and six inches, my height was compatible with theirs. But in their understanding I was an intruder. From the day of my admission to the *Realgymnasium am Zietenring*, a science oriented High School, the Jew had become the butt of their frequent mockery. But I came to learn, and I wouldn't be provoked. I reasoned to myself with increasing impatience. I tried to conceal the hatred I had felt toward them. That, too, had become more difficult with each time my classmates enjoyed themselves at my expense and their keen instinct made them see through my forced equanimity. Nor did they try to hide their own feelings of resentment toward me.

"Goddamned Nazis!" Roman raved. "They'll never change. There's no way to purge them except by blowing their heads off!"

"That's exactly what they've been taught to expect of us. I cautioned my brother. "The war is over now, you said so yourself, Roman."

"Still I'd like to. . ."

"Calm down, brother. Sure, I feel strange sitting next to boys six years younger than I, ahead of me in every school discipline, but killing every last one of them wouldn't give me back my lost years of learning."

"Well, you can tell them you're a midget, and that's why you look older than they." Zeviah tried humor, but no one laughed.

"I hate the *master race*," I said quietly. "Wish I could at least humiliate the bastards in some small way."

"I'm afraid you'll have to tolerate all this for awhile, Vilek. In fact, we'll all have to live with it," said Abraham with seriousness.

"They'll laugh at us, but there's no laughter in our hearts. There are no children left among us, no infants crying for a mother's breast, no games to play, and dreams have turned to nightmares." I sobbed.

"We must try to understand, Vilek. I know it's hard, but we must try." The *rebbe* put his arms around my shoulders tenderly. "It's a strange thing this hatred of theirs and their feeling of guilt. Like an inherited sickness, it comes from the fathers on down to the children. The disease visits mankind time and again without cure, without mercy; one generation's sins become the legacy of the next." Abraham spoke in his sing-song manner while cradling me lovingly in his arms.

"When will it ever end, Abraham, this hatred of theirs?"

"They have no monopoly on persecuting the Jew, Vilek," answered the *rebbe*. "The same sickness plagues half the world."

"What'll I do? I can't go on like that."

"Let's have a talk with Captain Weinberg. Maybe he'll think of something."

Captain Weinberg was reluctant at first to remove me from the classroom. He saw defeat in withdrawal. But after much arguing and vain threats, there was not much else he could do. "We'll have to discuss the matter with the good principal," said the Captain.

The "good" principal of the High School for Boys *am Zietenring, Herr Doktor* Ehrlich Hobel, must have anticipated my visit. He was polite but not overly cordial. He was friendly without the genuine abandon of sincerity.

Like most German academic supervisors, the principal held himself in the highest esteem, aloof from students and faculty alike. Herr Hobel was not a malevolent person. When he acted with an absolute degree of dogged determination in the pursuit of academic goals or in meting out academic justice, he did so more out of sheer sense of duty than evil intent. "Obedience to duty," said the principal quite often, "is the highest form of civilized behavior in man."

Oftentimes, parents would visit the principal's office to plead a case of a delinquent child. They would appeal to the conscience of the stern *Oberstudienrat* begging for a "second chance." On such occasions, he would look down at the tips of his well polished shoes silently, fold his hands in pious gesture in front of his enormous belly, and he would speak in his routinely kind manner: "I am very sorry, but we cannot break the rules. Regulations have been set up. They apply to everyone. It is our duty to uphold the law. All we can do is forgive the child. I shall forgive him. Let us pray for the youngster."

Mine was a special visit. I did not come to plead; I came to demand my due. I enjoyed the protection of the Amis, and *Herr Doktor* Hobel never was one to challenge authority.

Though I felt humiliated in visiting the German principal to discuss the nature of my problem, events of recent days led to my predicament. One particular happening convinced me that our differences were irreconcilable.

On Wednesday of the previous week, I had excused myself during the 9:00 a.m. algebra class to go to the bathroom. No sooner had I sat down with my pants on the floor, when my archtormentor, Heinrich Dummler, entered. There was only one other unoccupied commode available, and Heinrich took it with a sigh of relief.

"You have a stomach ache?" I inquired politely.

Silence.

"Must have eaten something rotten?"

More silence.

"Well, anyway, I hope you'll get to feeling better."

We shit in silence though each could hear the other's labored breathing. Maybe I shouldn't have talked? I asked myself silently. Dummler was caught off guard, and I embarrassed the poor fart. I reasoned.

Our business done, we buttoned our trousers and proceeded to wash our hands, our shoulders almost touching. It suddenly occurred to me that this might be the time to break the ice. After all, if you can't talk to a man in the bathroom, where can you talk to a man?

"You know, Dummler?" I started slowly but without hesitation. "We have something in common after all. You're a Nazi, and I'm a Jew, but we both take a shit sitting down."

There was silence.

No longer patient for Heinrich Dummler's response, I slammed the door on my way out, vowing to heed the lesson.

But that was last Wednesday, and now I faced the principal. *Doktor* Hobel was forebearing, almost kind, to the only Jew under his charge. Indeed, the principal remembered the days when there were no Jews among the students of his school; learning was the attribute of the pure, the Aryans. My anger grew while contemplating the past, and I knew that I must not betray that anger, else I might antagonize the principal. I must guard against betraying my thoughts.

Sitting there, I suddenly imagined rows of long black-white-red- banners that must have hung all the way from the ceiling of the school auditorium to the floor below. I could see a white circle in the middle of each banner, and inside that circle there was a black swastika, the emblem and spirit of the Third Reich. The students must have sat stiffly in the many rows of seats, and up in front of them, on the large, festively decorated stage, there sat the dignitaries, *Herr Doktor* Hobel most likely among them.

It must have been an impressive spectacle. There were horizontal banners that stretched across the vast wall of the auditorium. Those were special banners; they contained catchy slogans that read clearly the party's views to be remembered by all:

DIE JUDEN SIND UNSER UNGLÜCK! THE JEWS ARE OUR MISFORTUNE! FRAUEN UND MÄDCHEN! DIE JUDEN SIND EUER VERDERBEN! WOMEN AND GIRLS! THE JEWS ARE YOUR RUIN!

Many speeches would follow, and all were dressed up in festive oratory. The *Führer* was absent but the fervor of those present was a tribute to his popularity and a token of his people's dedication to his ideals. The ever-present brass band entertained in marching tempo between the oratorical deliveries, and the audience clapped their hands and beat the rhythm with their feet against the wooden floor. They loved it. They sang the ballads and songs telling the bravery of the Aryans.

Another patriotic speech was delivered followed by the *Horst Wessel* song which reveled in the shedding of Jewish blood; *wenn das Judenblut vom Messer spritzt. . .*

As an appropriate climax to the festivities, the audience stood and sang their national anthem *"Deutschland, Deutschland über alles. . ."* a deeply moving episode which brought tears to many eyes.

The day following the rally, all non-Arian teachers were summarily fired from their jobs, and all non-Arian children were sent home from school, never to return.

"You know how terribly unpleasant it is for me to let you go. All of you, with whom I had worked for so many years, and whom I had learned to respect professionally," *Herr Doktor* Hobel must have recited from a prepared statement. "Worst of all, where will I get qualified staff to replace you in the middle of the school year? I want you to know that I have been ordered to do this. It is my duty to fulfill these orders. I hope you'll understand, and I'll pray for you." He wrung his hands, and he bid all a brief "good bye, and God be with you."

The principal cleared his throat with a loud "uhumm," which startled me from my reverie. He smiled one of those inscrutable, benevolent smiles. I sat silently, unable to speak my mind though I had planned carefully beforehand what I was going to say to him.

"Now, my young *friend*, how can we be of service to you?" The principal addressed me.

"I came to ask for a private tutor. This will help me to enter classes with students of my own age," I said as calmly as I could. "I hate sitting in a classroom with small children," I added hurriedly, afraid that my true feelings had revealed themselves. But Hobel did not interrupt, nor did he let on that he was aware of my emotions. The sympathetic expression never left his features.

"We know exactly how you feel, young man," said the principal. "Going to classes was a worthy try, however, and I am sorry it did not work out. But I think we now have just the right place for you." He spoke with the characteristic slowness of a person deliberating each thought. "Let us see. . ." He turned toward his secretary. "*Fräulein* Lindemeier, do we have the address of *Fräulein* Paula Kaiser?"

"It's on your desk, *Herr Oberstudienrat*. . ."

"Ah. . . indeed. . . here it is. *Taunusstrasse* 21." The principal paused. "Miss Kaiser will be expecting you tomorrow morning at eight o'clock sharp. Good luck and God bless you, child."

The cab left me off in front of a small house on *Taunusstrasse* 21. I knocked. A deep, pleasant voice called in German, "*Moment, bitte!*"

Soon, the door opened and Paula Kaiser, a woman in mid-thirties, appeared. "Won't you come in?" Though her eyes did not meet mine, she somehow sensed my hesitation. "You don't mind if I call you Willi, do you?" She asked, extending both her hands in the general direction where I was supposed to have stood. It was only then I noticed the empty look in her blue eyes. Good Lord, she's blind. I thought to myself. I grasped her hand, and she led me inside. She felt more self-confident leading me through the room-full of furniture and skattered bric-a-brac of her living room. Her shoulder-length blond hair reminded me of Trude. *Fräulein* Kaiser was more serenly beautiful, I thought. I was puzzled and suspicious about the choice the principal had made for me. Can the blind lead the blind? I asked myself in silence.

"You're probably wondering how we will get along, Willi?" said Paula, as if reading my thoughts. "So, before we'll begin the lessons, I'll have to explain a few things." I was silent. I blushed, and I was angry at myself for having so easily revealed my embarrassment. Paula squinted her eyes as though making an effort to catch a glimpse of my expression. I was no longer certain she could not see.

"Really, Miss Kaiser, you don't owe me an explanation," I said apologetically. She dismissed my protest with a gesture of her hand.

"But I insist. If we are to become good friends, we must put some things behind us, bad things; things that affect both of us in a very strong way."

"I'm only interested in learning, Miss Kaiser," I insisted.

"What I have to say to you is also part of learning, Willi." She strained her sightless eyes again in the direction of my voice. "The things of the past must be forgotten."

"That won't be an easy task, Miss Kaiser," I said sadly. "I've suffered too many losses."

"My own losses won't compare to yours, Willi, I know." Paula's voice was soft, almost plaintive, and it had a low, gentle pitch. "I, too, have lost some loved ones."

Silence.

"Two years ago, our old home burned down with the V-1 attack," Paula continued. "My father was bedridden then with pneumonia. Help was too late, and he died of asphyxiation." Paula narrated slowly, and I was surprised at her self-composure. I listened silently.

"A little more than three years ago, I was to marry a nice young man." She continued outlining her past as if to an old friend. "Just then, I received notice from the Ministry of War; he was killed at Tobruk, that's Africa, you know?" Here, Paula hesitated, and I feared she was finally going to break down, but she regained composure quickly. "I, too, have suffered losses," she repeated more to herself than to me.

I was not sure why she should have confessed to me, a perfect stranger.

"I'd like you to know that I was a member of the NSDAP." She paused. "I had to join the National Socialists or lose my permit to teach. But I was not aware of the terrible goings-on in the Concentration Camps. This is the truth, as God is my witness." Paula madea sign of the cross. I was bored with yet another assertion of innocence.

"I believe you," I said softly. "And I don't blame you for anything." Two lies in a single sentence which were not meant to surface but did anyway. Paula surely knew I was lying, for I cannot have sounded too convincing. She sensed the veiled resentment in my voice with that special perception of those afflicted with her infirmity, but she did not let on. They're all the same. I thought to myself. They all deny any *knowledge* of that embarrassing enigma. I was reminded of the one-eyed Tulka. Would she have approved of our deed? I wondered silently.

"No good will come of it, Willi," she said. "You'll suffer more than you'll inflict." I was startled. Was this woman able to read my mind?

"But justice has to be done," I said, referring to Tulka's liquidation. "It was for my friend, Leib Glikier." I heard myself say, though I knew full well Paula would not understand. "The one-eyed monster killed my friend in cold blood. He had to be punished."

"He'd have been punished, Willi," Paula continued. "We all pay sooner or later," she said in her soft, deep voice, and she blushed while inadvertently touching my arm. "We'll stand trial every day for the rest of our lives." She paused. "But you must no longer suffer, Willi. You must seek out the beauty of man, else hatred will consume you."

My desire to learn became a source of joy for Paula. She showed genuine delight with each conquest on my long road back. Sponge-like, I absorbed each utterance she made. I translated Rousseau's *Emile* and Caesar's *Gallic Wars*, and I committed to memory the Pythagorean principles much in advance of the desired deadlines. Once again, it seemed, I had become obsessed with the passage of time. Paula was worried.

"Do you play an instrument?" she asked suddenly during a morning session.

Silence.

"I used to. . . the violin."

"The violin? Really? It's a beautiful instrument. Do you still play?" Paula was excited. "You must play for me!"

"I'm afraid I can't," I said. "I've been away from it far too long. I don't believe it would do any good to start now."

Paula sensed the sadness in my voice, and she insisted. "Anything beautiful is worth pursuing," she said softly.

"There are so many things I must start anew," I said without the intention of being cynical. "I don't know where to begin."

"Well, we'll have to start at the beginning and advance from there," said Paula, her gentle fingers touching my shoulder as if by accident. Her touch was not altogether unpleasant.

"I'll never really catch up with the rest of the world, Paula."

"That depends on how you look at it."

"The truth is, no matter how much I'll accomplish in the life ahead, I could have done more were it not for the time lost," I insisted.

"It doesn't really matter how long it takes a person to reach his goal. All that matters is that you get there." She smiled innocently.

I grinned, though I knew she could not see my face. I was silent.

"I know how this must sound to you, but I also know it's the only way for you, Willi. You must believe. Save yourself and save us all." She blew her nose loudly into her handkerchief and then reached up to dry her eyes.

"I won't promise miracles," I said in almost a whisper.

"You owe it to yourself," said Paula gently. Suddenly, a thought occured to me, and I couldn't hold it back.

My life's a lie, and I live among assassins. I only tolerate it, because still it's better than being burried alive."

"You mustn't continue being negative, Willi. It will lead to nowhere." She reasoned in her peculiar logic.

"There's no future for me, because there's no past." I said stubbornly.

"Don't ever give up, Willi." She said softly. "You haven't been singled out by fate for a hard childhood. There were others. Yet they grew up to be successful." Paula's arguments echoed all of the cliches I had heard long ago, but, somehow, I wanted to listen, to make them concrete.

"I understand that only too well, Paula." I replied. "But I also know that it will be harder for me to overcome this accident of my youth. Especially its loneliness. There are none of my people left to lend support, to lift me up when I fall, to encourage when I doubt, to priase when I succeed." A sudden sadness took hold of me, and I was nearing tears, only I held them back for fear I'd reveal another me to Paula. I wasn't ready, not yet.

"I know only too well that you have suffered unspeakable injustice during the time of war—it hurt terribly, and it left deep scars. There are those, however, who are suffering injustices during the time of peace. The question is. . ." she hesitated, not being able to read my face, ". . . which injustice goes deeper?" She argued vainly, for I was in no mood or condition to empathize with any of the "suffering" she was alleging.

"Another time, Paula. . . perhaps another time." I said leaving hastily.

Summer was upon us, and we spent a major portion of time on various activities in anticipation of my exams to enter the *Oberprima* the final semester prior to my graduation from high school. There were moments during my quest for knowledge when I had become so totally absorbed in learning that I permitted myself the luxury of forgetting my past. On occasions, triggered by an inadvertent remark or a study assignment, old memories would jolt me into melancholy brooding.

It was then, Paula would softly squeeze my hand or touch my face as if by accident. Such was the nature of our occasional intimacies, and it was with some degree of pleasure that I had begun to anticipate them for they had brought me relief from my usual preoccupation. On one occasion, emboldened by my passive acceptance of her caresses, Paula lifted my hand in hers and pressed it gently, as if not to frighten me, to her breasts. She held it there, and I felt the mighty heaves of Paula's pulsating bosom.

"Paula. . . please. . . no. . .," I said without withdrawing my hand from the warmth of her soft body.

"Why. . . Willi. . . is anything wrong?" She asked innocently.

"I must. . . I have to. . . concentrate on my studies," I said, a smile brightening my face, trying to conceal my embarrassment. I withdrew my hand.

"Why don't you visit with nature occasionally?" asked Paula. She always knew how to change the subject at crucial moments; how to avoid embarrassment.

"I haven't the time for such things now."

"You must make time. Go out and enjoy the beauty of the tulips in full bloom. Have you seen the tulips on the *Kaiser Friedrich Ring*?" She mentioned the proudest display of Wiesbaden's landscaping; the imported Dutch tulips. "Would you like to take a walk with me on Sunday?"

"If you wish." I hesitated. "I'll be glad to see the tulips with you, Paula." I placed special emphasis on the word see to let her know I understood. I, too, suddenly realized how completely insensitive I had become to nature's beauty; I was only aware of its cruelty, remembering the mountains of Buchenwald in their wintry majesty not for the rare glimpses of enjoyment and childhood snow games, but for the frostbite suffered during morning roll-call and the frozen bodies of my comrades piled up in heaps at the side of the barracks.

And the many springs and summers recalled only for the ghastly sweat and thirst I had suffered in the quarries and steel mills of the Third Reich without food or water.

Nature was not a kind mother to my childhood and early adolescence. But I was willing now to forgive her, to give myself a chance at reconciliation. If there was beauty present somewhere beneath that layer of indifference which I had thus far experienced, I was eager to seek it out; if there was joy in finding that beauty, I was anxious to embrace it.

I looked forward to Sundays with a kind of ritualistic anticipation. The Dutch tulips were in full bloom. Paula went down on her knees, caressing their petals, and I patiently described their color in detail. She was like a child delighting in newfound pleasures, and I, too, had begun to respond.

"One needs this sort of thing in order to get away from human imperfection," Paula said softly.

"You don't learn to appreciate flowers behind the barbed wires of a concentration camp." I remarked gloomily.

We argued long hours. At times, the assigned lesson was forgotten. Paula would pick up a heavy volume and cite a few lines from *Lessing's Nathan* the Wise, as the drama's protagonist beseeched the stubborn *Tempelherr*:

. . . We must be friends? Though you may feel contempt for my people. We did not, each of us, choose our people. Are we our people? What is a people? Is Christian or Jew rather Christian or Jew and not a human being?

It annoyed me that Paula would quote the *good* Germans whenever she wished. I refused to listen, because I felt my hatred melting away, and wished for it to remain. From earliest memory, I recalled being persecuted and despised. I didn't know whether I was capable of forgiveness or even whether I wanted to forgive.

"Beware of an emotion you cannot control!" Paula warned.

"I'm not a saint!"

"You mustn't dignify the guilty by hating them," she insisted. It will ease their conscience and justify the dastardly acts they've committed."

I sensed that Paula was trying to tell me yet more. I was not ready to listen. Not yet.

Once again my thoughts were with Devorah as I strolled through the colorful gardens, and I wished that she were here by my side. There it was again, that gnawing sense of resentment against the entire world.

Suddenly, a G.I. caught my eye.

"Paula!" I took both her hands in mine, and it must have hurt because she grimaced. "That G.I. across the tulips! It's Blake! My liberator!"

"Go to him, Willi." Paula rubbed her palms together to relieve the pain. "I'll hail a cab."

"Sure you don't mind, Paula?" I was concerned. "I hate leaving you here like that."

"No, silly." She was amused. "I wasn't altogether helpless before you came into my life. Go now! Go after your friend!"

Blake was still there. I recognized my friend by his heavy stride, swaying from side to side, as if he were lifting a heavy load. There was no doubt about it. "See you later, Paula!"

"Bill Blake!" I yelled. I ran toward him, leaving a path of broken tulips in my wake. I heard Paula's voice and I was unable to determine whether it was a frightful shriek or a fond farewell. It didn't matter.

"Barbarians!" Someone shouted in our direction. But we were oblivious to the world around us. Bill lifted me up in a breathtaking bear hug while repeating "Vilek. . . Vilek . . ." I was glad that Blake remembered my name.

We settled on a vacant bench to rest and talk, each trying to bring the other instantly up to date.

"Trade's here in Wiesbaden!" Blake announced suddenly.

"Who?"

"Trude, you know the blond nurse from Borna. The crazy Russky's wife." Blake explained, though it needed no explanation.

"How do you know?"

"She's been here for some time now. Got work at the dispensary in my unit. She's friends with Mona, my wife."

"It's hard to believe." I let out a shrill whistle through my teeth.

"She's as pretty as ever, Vilek. Everyone in the unit's been after her."

"And she's been generous, I presume."

"Want to see her? I can arrange it."

"Not interested."

"Don't be a fool."

"I've got things to do right now. She can wait."

"Anyway, she's here and you're bound to run into her sooner or later. And when you do, don't pass judgements. Nobody's perfect, you know?"

"Okay, okay, maybe we can all get together soon for old time's sake."

"By the way, Vilek, she's different now. Not like she used to be, remember? Nobody's been able to get into her pants since that day in Hamburg."

"You've heard about Hamburg?"

"We sure did. More than that, Trude confessed it was she who had given V.D. to Misha, not the poor little whore Frieda. He killed the prostitute for nothing."

"Son of a bitch!"

"You mean. . . you didn't know?"

"How would I?"

Images of the Hamburg events went through my mind rapidly. Little Frieda who reminded me so much of Devorah. "Poor creature." I said louder than I had intended.

"Who? Trude?" Blake asked.

"No, not that slut. She was having too much fun fucking every Tommy who'd have a hard on. Not her. I'm thinking of the girl Misha killed, Frieda, you know?"

"Hey. . . pal. . . let's go home." Blake said. "Want you to meet the family."

"Mona! Hey, Mona, I'm home!" Blake yelled entering the hall. We could hear footsteps. Two small boys ran toward him, jumping onto the sergeant's outstretched arms and hanging on to him as he held them tightly. Their small blond heads contrasted with his ebony appearance as they hugged his neck. Blake fell playfully to the floor, and the boys fell on top of him, wrestling his massive frame, tickling his arms, biting his ears and laughing hilariously.

"They're Mona's boys." Blake tried to explain between sporadic laughs. "This one's Hans. . . he's going on ten." Blake pulled one of the boys up by the belt into the air. "And this little rascal's Jurgen." He pointed at the smaller of the two. "Jurgen's six." Another burst of laughter.

The sound of Mona's footsteps separated the combatants. She was tall, blond and in her late twenties with milk-white skin. Her blue eyes hid behind long eyelashes. Her figure curved in noticeable places when she bent over to lift up the two boys.

"Hello *Liebchen*." Blake addressed her shyly.

"I didn't expect you home this early." She stopped abruptly noticing me at the entrance. "*Mein Gott!* Bill! Why do you let the boys mess you up like this? You dirty up the uniform faster than I can wash it. Hans! Jurgen! *Auf! Schnell!*" The boys sprang up from the floor. "Get busy with your homework!" She added threateningly.

Blake stood as if rooted to the spot, finally finding his voice. "Vilek, meet my Frau Mona. Isn't she something else? Eh, little pal? Isn't she?"

"Don't embarrass the young man, Bill!" Mona admonished Blake.

"I'm pleased to meet you." She turned toward me.

"Same. . . here. . ." I managed to stammer my reply. She was pleased at noticing the impression she had made on me. She seemed accustomed to a similar reaction from the opposite sex and her eyes softened. "But I'm intruding on your time, am I not?" I said clumsily.

"Intruding?" She exclaimed laughing. "My dear, this is such a fine, unexpected pleasure. Any friend of Bill's is our friend. Say, it's almost twelve o'clock. Have you eaten yet?" She turned to Blake without eliciting my reply. "Why didn't you let me know you were bringing along a friend for lunch? You and your surprises." When she did not shout directives, her voice sounded almost pleasant. "You will stay for lunch, of course?" She insisted. "We can always prepare another plate. Or maybe you have another appointment?" She added when noticing my hesitation.

"Oh, no, but really, you needn't bother."

"Please feel at home," said Mona, leaving to attend to her chores. I couldn't understand why I was apologetic or why I tried to refuse an invitation even though I felt compelled to stay.

"I'm going to tell you something you won't want to believe." Blake whispered as if he were afraid of being overheard. "Your rabbi Abraham has been seeing Trude." Blake interrupted to observe my reaction. Pleased with what he saw, he added, "She wouldn't see him at first, but he kept coming, bringing stuff, pleading. She finally gave in, and Abraham's a frequent visitor in her flat."

"The hypocritical son-of-a-bitch!" I seethed. "And he goes on lecturing me about duty and morality."

"That's life, pal. Need has little to do with morality nowadays. Never really had." Blake grinned. "You've got lots to learn about life, little buddy."

"Give me time, Bill. I'm getting the hang of it." I admitted.

Though I had hoped Abraham would go on being a good friend."

"Things don't stay the same, pal. Men don't think or act the same as they did before women came between them."

"I would have understood."

"You sure?"

"I'd have tried."

"Maybe he didn't want to risk it."

"But he was such a pious Jew."

"Maybe he still is."

"How will I ever know?"

"Just give it time, little buddy, and don't try to be the judge and jury." I discovered the philosophical side of my friend Blake. "You know, it must be awful hard to go through life with a deformed leg, at his age trying to make it with women, young and beautiful, who refuse better offers."

"Still. . ."

"Just mind your own business and behave like you did before. Things'll work out between you."

"It's going to be hard to keep a straight face."

"It's worth it if you really care."

"I'll try. Promise."

25

The military Chapel was festively decorated. It was a first for the Wiesbaden Jewish community; *Rosh Hashanah*, our New Year and the symbolic beginning of a new life. Abraham Bachter cut an imposing figure in his white robe, the prayer shawl draping his shoulders, as the officiating rabbi. An ancient Torah was borrowed for the holidays from the Frankfurt synagogue; Major Weinberg's expression of thanks for his recent promotion.

I hadn't prayed for a long time without pleading for some concession or another, and I was out of practice. A young cantor was hired. This, also, was Major Weinberg's contribution for his good fortune. While the cantor sang, Abraham turned his eyes toward the center aisle where Trude sat in the front row. I had seen her briefly at the entrance and exchanged a few words as we walked into the narrow vestibule. There was no way I could have avoided her, as much as I tried. She looked stunning, and I couldn't help but approve of Abraham's taste.

Abraham lifted his face piously toward heaven and recited the holy liturgy. I looked at the *rebbe* with feelings of guilt for not having warned him about Trude's condition. Abraham wanted to be an important man some day and give Trude the respectability he thought she deserved. She would be a beautiful *rebbitzin* and make him the envy of his profession. I knew what he wanted, and I respected his wishes. He confessed, in his excitement, of his plans to change Trade's name to Hannah, his mother's name. By then, even if I had the intention to prevent him from proceeding with his plan, I lacked the courage to destroy his obsession.

After several weeks of courtship, Trude accepted Abraham's proposal, and the Franfurter rabbi arrived to officiate at their wedding. She would try her best, she said. Abraham said she would never regret her decision. In witnessing their apparent bliss, I forgave myself for my cowardice in the betrayal of my friend. "He's a grown man," I rationalized to myself, "and should know what he's getting into." Trude looked radiant in her wedding dress, virginal veil and all. Abraham's excitement was evident in the appearance of large drops of perspiration on his huge nose.

"Will you Abraham take Hannah. . ."

"I will. . ."

"Will you Hannah take Abraham. . ."

"I will. . ."

They took each other for "better or for worse." It would be for the best, Abraham thought to himself.

The festivities extended into the early morning hours. Champagne flowed freely, provided by the good *Bürgermeister* of Rüdesheim, a town famous for its vineyards. There was dancing and there were hugs and kisses.

"Attention! Attention everybody!" Major Weinberg shouted at the top of his lungs. He climbed on top of one of the tables from which he tried to quiet everybody. From his breast pocket he drew a letter. Waving it in one of his hands, the other raising a glass of champagne, he motioned for silence. "This is a matter of great importance to all of us!" He shouted. "I have in my hand a copy of an important document! Let me read some of it to you." Others joined in quieting the restive crowd. "This is a letter from The President of the United States, Harry S. Truman, to the King of Saudi Arabia. Listen, and it may change your lives!"

THE GOVERNMENT AND THE PEOPLE OF THE UNITED STATES HAVE GIVEN SUPPORT TO THE CONCEPT OF A JEWISH NATIONAL HOME IN PALESTINE EVER SINCE THE TERMINATION OF THE FIRST WORLD WAR. . .THE PEOPLES LIBERATED SHOULD BE PREPARED FOR SELF-GOVERNMENT AND A NATIONAL HOME FOR THE JEWISH PEOPLE SHOULD BE ESTABLISHED IN PALESTINE SO THAT THE DISPLACED JEWS IN EUROPE MAY CONTRIBUTE THEIR TALENTS AND ENERGIES TO THE UP-BUILDING OF THE JEWISH NATIONAL HOME.

The Major's voice trembled as he read, and those who listened quickly sobered up. Glasses were raised and toast followed on toast.

"To Harry Truman!"

"A great President!"

"Long live the United States of America!"

"Long live Harry Truman!"

"A man of compassion and justice!"

The Major enjoyed the effect of the announcement. "Where is Abraham?" He shouted. "Let him say a few words." The Major insisted. Yacov whispered into the Major's ear causing a burst of hilarity. "Already?" Yelled the Major. There was more laughter. "Okay. I feel generous tonight." Major Weinberg carried on, "let someone else apologize in Abraham's behalf."

"I'll do it," said Yacov in a clear loud voice. "I want to apologize for the unkind words we have spoken about your homeland. We all know that the people of the United States and their President Truman are our loyal friends. President Truman shows a great deal of courage."

Applause. More champagne. More speeches and much laughter. I didn't drink, nor did I feel like laughing. An eerie forboding had told me that now a new struggle would begin; the struggle of my people to gain their identity.

All was not well with the Abraham Bachters. Only one week into his marriage, and Abraham looked a defeated man. I had only seen him that way once before; during the afternoon of April thirtieth, lined up against the wall in Colditz and facing the barrel of a machine gun.

"It can't be all that bad, Abraham," I said reflecting on his thoughts.

"It is, Vilek. It's worse than you can imagine."

Silence.

"I've waited for this moment, Vilek, oh. . . how I've waited." Abraham's voice quivered with emotion. "When nothing happened during the wedding night, I thought it was too much champagne. But I was sober on the second, the third night, and also the following. God, I'm so embarrassed." The *rebbe* buried his head in his hands.

"Maybe it was overexcitement, Abraham?"

"Not likely. The first night, perhaps, but not the whole week."

Silence.

"We tried everything. Everything. Poor Hannah, she's so loving. It's not fair to her. I'm ashamed. I had to tell you or I would have gone."

"Why don't you see a doctor?"

"I even prayed for an erection, Vilek. Can you imagine me praying for an erection?" Abraham repeated to emphasize his sacrilege. "Don't you see the absurdity of it? Can't you see? An old man like me trying to live the life of a young buck? God is not concerned with trivialities. You see? It was easy for me to lie on paper, but it's difficult to convince my genitals that I am a young man in bed."

"It's probably a temporary condition, Abraham." I tried to assuage my friend's despair. "After all, where's your faith?" If he only knew, I thought to myself, how lucky he was in his misfortune.

Here, Abraham closed his eyes halfways looking up into the heavens, as he recited from memory:

"And the Lord remembered Sarah as He had said, and the Lord did unto Sarah as He had spoken. . . and Sarah conceived, and bore Abraham a son in his old age. . ."

We waited patiently for the test results. "It may take some time," the nurse told us, "the doctor will be glad to call when the results are in." But we prefered to stay and wait.

"I'm really grateful you've come along," Abraham said.

"Glad to be here."

It was nearly three hours later when we returned to the doctor's office. The doctor began, wearing a serious, almost grim expression, on his face. "I'm afraid, I don't have good news for you, Mr. Bachter."

"No! No! You can't mean this!" Abraham was nearing hysteria.

"Let the doctor talk, Abraham. Let him say what he has to say." I attempted to restrain my friend.

"I won't lie to you, Mr. Bachter. There's one in a million chance to restore your sexual virility. Mind you, not one hundred percent at that, but you may never get your wish of a child in your marriage."

"What are you telling me?" The doctor seemed to have rekindled Abraham's faith.

"The damage is mental as well as physical, it will require prolonged treatment."

"I'll do anything, doctor."

"Science isn't magic, Mr. Bachter. What you have experienced during the last few years cannot be waved away by a magic wand. Too much stress. . ."

"I know what I've experienced, doctor, you don't have to tell me that. Just give me the treatment."

"You'll spend a few months in Taunusheim under strict medical supervision, follow my instructions to the minutest detail, and we'll see."

"When do I leave?"

"As soon as possible." The physician was scribbling on a pad. He handed his patient the note. "Present this to the head physician at the resort hospital. I'll visit regularly. The rest is up to providence."

"Thank you, doctor. Thank you." Abraham could contain himself no longer. He wept like a small child, tears rolling down his cheeks, repeating "*Gotenyu*, dear God, please don't let me down now. What have I done to deserve such punishment?"

I bent down to Abraham's ear to tell my friend that we must leave. He stood up and leaned heavily on my shoulder. As we walked toward the exit, once again, I was tempted to tell him of my fears concerning Trude. Then, I glanced at the weeping, broken man, and quickly abandoned the thought.

26

I went about a relentless pursuit of my studies to prepare for the approaching exams. It seemed like only yesterday I had first come to Paula's doorstep, an illiterate survivor of the War. Now, a few months later, I would be admitted to the *Oberprima* as an equal of my peers.

"You must pass the examination to be admitted," Paula said.

"I know, I know." I was painfully aware of the *Realgymnasium*'s academic rigors.

"The time has been set for next Wednesday at nine o'clock in the morning."

"I'll be ready."

When Wednesday arrived, I was at Paula's an hour before the examinations.

"Let me look at you," said Paula examining me with her nimble fingers to check that all the buttons were in place, that my tie was on properly, that my hair was not ruffled as usual. "Are your shoes clean?" She asked.

"They're clean and polished," I answered slightly annoyed. "What do my shoes have to do with the entrance examination?"

"You'd be surprised, young man, appearance means much to your teachers."

"I thought knowledge was what they were after."

"First impressions are important, Willi. So don't complain. Now go." She tried to sound stern, but she did not succeed in her attempt. Suddenly, as if by accident, she stumbled onto me, her arms stretched out in an embrace. She hugged me tightly to herself, murmuring endearments. Her face was close to mine and our lips touched lightly. I lingered longer than I had intended to, but it was not at all unpleasant.

"Remember the hexameter!" Paula called after me as I walked out the door. "And keep the algebraic formulae apart! Concentrate!" I heard her voice after me as I turned the corner. "Good luck, Willi!" I knew how much she cared though she pretended unconcern. I was going to succeed, not only for myself but for Paula as well.

The examination went better than I had anticipated. I was able to compensate for my lack of mathematical skill with the essays in literature and philosophy. The oral and written sessions began in the morning and lasted well into the evening hours. When it was all over, I was satisfied that I had done my best. Now, all that was left was several days of evaluation to be completed and I would be notified of the results.

I was admitted to the *Oberprima* "conditionally." Paula was elated despite the condition that I was to repeat a routine examination for Algebra II. Then, I'd get permission to continue with the study of Trigonometry.

"I hate math," I said quietly.

"You need it to develop your mind."

"I thought that was what Latin did for me?"

"Don't argue, Willi. The school term is upon us and there is really no sense in arguing the point. The committee decided that for you."

For the first time, I was among students of my own generation. I was summoned to Dr. Hobel's office to receive the customary congratulations and blessings from the principal of the Realgymnasium. "Young man," said the principal, "we are pleased to have you among us. We wish you good fortune and success in your endeavor." He handed me a congratulatory letter.

I was once again the butt for my classmates'jokes. Almost a year after Hitler's demise, his spirit lived on. They would not accept the reality of a Jew in their midst, laughing at me and mocking my people.

"Is it true the Jew never does an honest day's work?"

Laughter.

"Aren't the Jews best suited for money lending?"

More laughter.

"They'll quit," said Paula. "They're no more mature than the twelve-year-olds." She tried to assuage my rage.

"Why should they have fun at my expense?" I asked. "They won't allow me to come close to them. Even at exam time, when everyone's expected to do his part in cheating, I'm alone. I'm probably the only one in my class who's being honestly tested."

"You're better off after all, don't you see?"

"I really don't think I am, Paula." I tried to explain. "I can't let them go on thinking that the Jew can't fight back. The world will someday say that the millions of our people were led to the gas chambers without resistance. They'll forget the heroic resistance in Warsaw, the thousands of brave partisans who fought against Nazi occupation and the treachery of their Christian countrymen."

"It will do no good to open up old wounds, Willi."

"They're not old wounds, Paula. They're still very fresh and bleeding and the behavior of these Hitler Youths does nothing to heal them."

"I feel what you felt, my Willi." She held my hands in hers and tears trickled down her cheeks. "I had no idea that even your own Polish people betrayed you."

"Some did. Many did. There was a price for a Jew's head." I was very angry. "And now, you tell me to 'turn the other cheek?'"

"Give them a little more time." Paula pleaded.

"My dear friend, their time has run out with the fall of the Third Reich, only they don't know it yet. It's time someone told them."

"You have more important tasks to perform for your future, Willi. They don't deserve your attention," said Paula, hoping to disuade me from whatever I was planning for my classmates.

"I've tried so very hard to be fair, not to be judgmental. I did that, because I had experienced not only friendship and love but also snatches of happiness during the War. Who can tell, were it not for those few courageous individuals who gave me shelter amidst an insane world, I might not be here today. When the War was over, I was not out for a bloody vengeance like many of my comrades. I wanted to tell the story of good and evil Germany; of good and evil people. I'm just not very good at hating." I was not sure she had heard me. I looked up at her, she sobbed without restraint and her whole body shook convulsively. We embraced and comforted each other. "Okay, okay, I won't go out and kill one of them to set an example, though the idea did occur to me briefly," I said, half in jest.

Paula smiled through the tears. "You're a fine boy. . .uh. . .man."

Three weeks into the school term, *Herr* Schroeder, our math teacher, took ill. *Herr* Dr. Hippie, a substitute math teacher and an amateur astronomer, was given the temporary teaching assignment. He had many stellar discoveries to his credit. One distant star was named for him: the "Hippie" star.

Herr Hippie carried a silver plate in his skull a few centimeters above the right ear; the result of an injury he had sustained in World War I. On humid days the metal would expand slightly, exerting pressure on the brain lobes. That pressure in turn caused Herr Hippie to suffer racking pain, forcing his whole body into all manner of grotesque contortions.

The temporary teacher was a welcome diversion from the routine of everyday assignments. There was no indication of a quiz, and the class progressed in a relaxed manner. We applauded Herr Hippie's witticisms or explanatory remarks with the traditional pounding of knuckles on our desks.

It happened halfway through the class period. The rising humidity caused *Herr* Hippie to suffer one of his seizures. Suddenly, his mouth remained grotesquely agape but he was unable to emit a sound. He reached with his right hand to his silver plate and pressed hard to relieve the pressure. His whole body twisted and throbbed in pain.

The performance was real though it appeared contrived. The students could not contain their laughter.

"Great show, Herr Hippie!"

"You've missed your calling!"

"Stop it, my sides are aching!"

The Verdun hero listened to his students' catcalls helplessly, his eyes bulging and his face purple with pain. Then, as suddenly as it had started, the attack subsided. Herr Hippie took out a large handkerchief from his trouser pocket and wiped the froth from his lips. He folded the handkerchief neatly and placed it back in his pocket. There was a somber hush in the classroom.

Hippie's eyes searched each row slowly, challengingly. Ernst Gemmer snickered into his desk a few seats from where I sat.

Gemmer was not known for exemplary scholarship. He was a huge boy, weighing over two hundred pounds, whose goal was to someday join the police force and become a detective. He was the class clown, and he enjoyed his immense popularity.

During the brief period of his recovery, Hippie's eyes fastened on me.

"You there." He addressed me. "You up there, in the upper row." Hippie repeated. I tried to appear nonchalant. I looked away, but Hippie persisted. "Do you find me funny?" He asked. "Come down here in front of the class." I maintained silence. "You will come here this very minute!" Hippie shouted. Right then and there, I decided to leave the classroom. I had almost reached the exit door, when *Herr* Hippie blocked my way.

"I'll tell you when you can leave the room, young man."

Silence.

"Have you nothing to say for yourself?"

Silence.

"You see?" Hippie addressed the class. "Your funny friend here suddenly seems to have lost his capacity to speak." He paused. "Perhaps I might help him out a bit by improving his circulation?" Then, with a quickness no one would have suspected of the veteran teacher, *Herr* Hippie slapped my face twice in rapid succession; once with the palm to the right cheek, and then another strike with the back of his hand to the left. My head was jarred by the violent impact to one side and then to the other. I hesitated. My fists clenched, but the rage within me was quieted by a flash vision of Paula.

I ran past Hippie, and only when I was on the street did I slow down. The cool autumn air hit my nostrils inducing a sudden chill in the afternoon haze beneath the autumnal, almost barren, trees.

"I'm not going back there!" I shouted more at myself than at Paula.

"You must, Willi, think of the future." Paula pleaded. "All this is just an unfortunate circumstance."

"Circumstances. Circumstances." I repeated impatiently. "Life's full of unfortunate circumstances. So why do I have to get caught up in most of them?"

"I'm really sorry about what has happened, Willi." Paula was nearing tears. After all, "*Herr* Hippie isn't your regular teacher."

"I'm not worried about Hippie as much as I'm about my classmates. Their suspicions have been confirmed. I'm a coward."

"Quite the contrary, Willi." She trembled with excitement. "It took great courage on your part to have restrained yourself." Paula sobbed unabashedly.

"I'm sure no one will see it that way, Paula."

"You shouldn't care." She pleaded.

"I shouldn't, but I do."

Only the morning after did I learn that I had become an overnight celebrity; the most talked-about student *am Zietenring*. My handling of the "Hippie affair," as the case was referred to, was admired by almost everyone; skeptics were easily spotted by their persistent silence. My company was sought after even by those who had previously avoided me.

That afternoon, I was summoned to Dr. Hobel's office. Here, for the first time since my arrival at the *Realgymnasium*, the principal received me with an almost genuine smile and a cordial welcome.

"Young man, we are all so very proud of you," said the principal, rising slightly from his chair as a sign of deference. "You have displayed a remarkable degree of restraint. Indeed, we are pleased." The principal extended his hand and I accepted the gesture reluctantly and without a word.

"In fact," the principal went on, "your behavior as well as your significant achievements in academic matters might merit early graduation."

The statement caught me completely off guard. I didn't know what to say at first. Finally I uttered an awkward "thank you," muted to a degree of incomprehensibility. The principal was pleased with my reaction. He grinned from ear to ear. "In the entire history of our school only four men graduated with such high honors, only four," said the principal, repeating the important number.

"I. . . I. . . don't. . . know. . . what. . . to. . . say. . ." I managed to stammer.

"You don't have to say anything, young man. The honor of an early *Abitur* is well-earned." He went on to say how he had known, before anyone else, of my special attributes, my fine character and superior intelligence. I heard the principal only vaguely, as I turned my head away and gazed at the clear blue sky through the open window. "Of course, there is still the matter of the comprehensive examinations, but I am sure this will be only a mere formality in your case. *Fräulein* Kaiser reports that you are ready. . ." The principal went on as though indulging in small talk, and I listened entranced only to the echo of his initial statement: "Early graduation. . ."

By mid-afternoon all of my classmates knew about it.

There were congratulatory handshakes. Even Ernst Gemmer, the mischievous giant, put his arm around my shoulder. "This calls for a celebration!" He exclaimed enthusiastically. Everyone agreed.

I momentarily forgot the wastes of War, its stupidity and barbarism. Something told me to visit *Herr* Hippie on my way home, and I found the professor still thoroughly shaken by the recent events.

He gripped my hand in his, seeking reassurance. I was taken aback by the professor's emotional outpouring. I found myself staring into the man's clear blue eyes, and only now I noticed how they were surrounded by a hue of dark greyish skin, and the whites were reddish, perhaps caused by a sleepless night. I thought of withdrawing my hand from Hippie's grip, but decided against it. There was a residue of moisture in those sad eyes of a man thrice my age, and I shook Hippie's hand saying, "It's all right, *Herr* Hippie, it's all right."

"I promise to name my next discovery in your honor, *Herr* Willi," said Hippie, refusing to let go of my hand. I smiled at the frightened man.

"Thank you, Herr Hippie, but you needn't bother."

"But I insist!" cried Herr Hippie. "That's the least I can do to try to rectify my horrible behavior," he paused for a moment, "my inexcusable behavior." He added resolutely.

There was silence. The teacher regarded me plaintively.

"It will be a bright star," he continued excitedly, "the brightest I can find: And I hope it shall follow you around wherever you might go!" He anxiously observed the impression his proposal had made on me; his face reflecting fear of rejection. I stood silent, somewhat embarrassed by the effusion of undeserved homage from a man I had scarcely known a few days ago. I knew there was no use in trying to dissuade him from paying his self-imposed debt, and I nodded my head in silent approbation.

"If you insist, *Herr* Hippie. . . if you insist." I said at last. I shook the professor's hand once again before leaving. I practically ran to Paula's, my chest pounding with the newly found freedom.

"Well, that was very nice of you." Paula was happy. "To accept the man's offering of a star." She added with a smile.

"After all, Paula, Hippie saved me, didn't he?"

27

I t was my graduation, birthday, and going away celebration on a wintry
October night. Several days ago, a letter arrived from my father's second
cousin, Elizabeth, from London. She had recently received news from Henryk,
she wrote. His letter was postmarked in Poznan, and he said he was on his
way to Berlin with the Kosciuszko Division as part of the Soviet forces. We
immediately agreed that one of us would travel to Poland to search for our
father. It was my turn now. Roman had done enough traveling already.

My departure for Poland was very much on my mind even as I was
greeting my classmates who had come to help me celebrate. There were
congratulatory handshakes and back patting. "You really made it, Willi."
They commented with admiration. "Wish old man Hippie had slapped me
in the face so I'd graduate a half year ahead of my class!" They joked with
some degree of concealed envy.

The *rebbe* was in Augsburg for the weekend performing a wedding ceremony, and Hannah had brought my teacher along. I was glad Paula could
come, though I wasn't altogether sure of Hannah's motives. But she insisted
she came only "to help with the chores." It disturbed me that I should still
notice how beautiful she was. I promised myself to keep my distance.

It was a successful party after all. My guests were in a jovial mood. I was
pleased. They danced and sang to recorded music. They recited poetry, both
serious and comical, for their own amusement. Paula played the piano, and
Gemmer displayed his talents on the guitar. I looked at them with envy.
Curious memories of my own musical endeavors stirred inside me. How I
would have liked to impress them with my own virtuosity! But the sounds
of distant music were no longer resonant. There were more urgent matters
to attend now. Perhaps someday in my strange existence I might again be
destined to caress the strings of a violin. Not now. Not here, I thought. Later.
Patience.

"A toast to the beautiful *rebbitzin!*" Major Weinberg exclaimed, and everyone knew that the American was deliriously happy and totally drunk.

It was nearly 2 a.m. when the last of the guests had left. Earlier in the
evening, Paula had complained of a headache and Gemmer volunteered to
take her home.

Only Hannah remained to "clean up."

"Lock the door after yourself, Hannah!" I called out from my bedroom. "I'm too tired to help!"

She didn't answer, and I was too weary to attribute any significance to her presence. I was undressed and under the blanket in a matter of minutes.

In the total darkness I could only smell the scent of her perfume. As it grew stronger, I knew that she was approaching the bed. My conscious mind rejected the *rebbitzin's* presence, and I began to think of the woman in terms of her former self; Trude the Borna whore. I opened my eyes, squinting toward the door.

The promise of the moment was not only erotic; it had been a long time since Trude had initiated me to sex, and that was a bond we now shared.

I was unable to resist the touch of Trade's fingers on my chest. I tried to hold my breath for fear my pounding heart would reveal too much. Her hands now caressed my hair. I trembled. She spoke, but I did not listen. I only felt the softness of her voice.

Driven, I reached for her skin. Probing the texture of her breasts, I whispered, "Trude. . . you're a bitch. . . you shouldn't be here. . ."

"I had to. . . *Liebchen*," she whispered, calling me by that endearment of professional whores that had brought curious echoes of the past.

"You're a damnable whore! You gave a case of VD to Misha, and he killed himself. Now, you want to repeat that with me. . . and with the *rebbe!*" I shouted.

"You can relax, *Liebchen*. That's long past. I was treated. . . I'm okay now . . . relax. . . . everything will be okay. . ." She whispered softly, her skin now pressed to mine. We touched. It was so new, for I was now a willing participant. Her body was firm yet soft to the touch. There was a tender symetry, pliant and electrifying.

I closed my eyes better to feel the moment. A fever consumed me as Trude gently guided me inside her. I gloried in the new experience even to the moment of ultimate relief.

We lay a good while in repose when suddenly the telephone returned us to reality.

"Who? Abraham? Is it you?—Yes, she was here. Left a good while ago. Yes. Yes.—No. I don't know. Guess she must have slept over at her friend's house. What?—She has no close friends? Don't worry. She'll be okay. Glad you're back. See you soon, Abraham."

I was unable to see Trude's face in the dark but I felt the mischievous grin. "Still the frightened little boy, aren't you?" She laughed. I felt shame and remorse at having betrayed the trust of my friend.

"Not frightened. Guilty. He's my friend and I'm sleeping with his wife!" I almost shouted.

"Believe me, you're doing him a great service, dear boy."

It annoyed me that she should call me "boy," but I wouldn't reveal my anger. "You'd better leave now. I need some rest," I said rudely. She cried softly now. "I need some rest, Trude. I'm leaving for Poland this week, and we won't see each other when I'll get back. It's better this way," I said in one breath. I was able to understand why I had so suddenly decided to leave on my journey.

"Goodbye my Parzival," she whispered.

I was angry. "Wish you'd stop calling me by that stupid name." I couldn't resist insulting the Wagnerian myth which brought back memories of the *Führer*'s own mad adulation. "I don't like playing games."

"But it's not a game at all, *Liebchen*." She was apologetic. "Like you, Parzival once left his safe sanctuary in search of. . ."

". . . a foolish dream." I interrupted defiantly.

"Not at all, Willi." She called me by the name Boost had invented for me, and I felt as if she had no right to do that, but I was silent sensing her urgency to speak. "It wasn't foolish at all." Trude continued. "The hero journeyed in search of a better humanity, of man unscarred by evil."

"Foolish dream after all," I said. "All I want to find is a part of my past, my family, anyone who might still be alive."

She stood fully dressed now. "Have a safe journey," she said softly while walking out of the room. When she left, I wasn't at all certain that I was alone along with my bold imaginings.

That Sunday morning, I walked with Paula along the *Kaiser Friedrich Ring*. We had taken a taxi there early to avoid the crowds. It was an unusually bright and sunny day for October, and we knew the weather would attract many. The air was cool but pleasant. The light from the brightly shining sun reflected itself on the thin layer of snow which had fallen during the night. The snow was dry, almost fluffy, and each step was accompanied by the sound of its crispness.

We walked silently beneath the bare sycamores and elms, holding hands, past the massive brick apartment houses. I confessed my plans. She kept asking questions as usual, I answered at length, first explaining my plans, later describing what I saw; it was then I knew full well how much Paula would miss my eyes. The leaves were gone from most of the trees that lined the avenue. Only the giant birches—allegedly planted there more than one century ago on Napoleon's orders to commemorate his march to Moscow— had retained some of their greenery.

"It's the first really pleasant day," remarked Paula. "Isn't it exhilarating?" She had a way with big words. "Why must you leave now?"

I was silent. Then I spoke.

"We'll stop at *Schönemann's* for a cup of hot chocolate," I said. "Aren't you getting weary?"

"I could walk all day," said Paula. I knew she was only pretending. "But I'll take you up on your offer."

We returned to Paula's late that afternoon. When we entered, the grandfather clock on the wall struck five. As if I were in a great hurry, I looked up at the clock, then on to my wristwatch. "I've got to get going now," I said. In my mind, I had made up an imaginary date somewhere with someone; a kind of deadline. It was easier to say "good bye" when facing deadlines and imaginary appointments. "I really have to get going." I repeated as if to myself.

Paula trembled a little, she moaned and began sobbing softly. When she was like that, there was nothing I could do to assuage her. "You just get up and go," she spoke plaintively. "Just disappear never to be heard from again."

"My roots are not here, Paula." I tried to speak. "My roots were unearthed by your people long ago and . . ."

". . . they were not my people, Willi. I wish you wouldn't. . ."

". . . I wanted to say that my roots had died somewhere in the East as did my dreams."

"This is not the time, my dearest friend," she pleaded.

"And why not? Why not now or any time? I haven't told you that before, my dear Paula, but I must tell you now because I don't know what the future holds. When I was a young boy of eleven they put me in a labor camp, a prison by any name, and like a hollow grave it enveloped me, and swallowed all my human instincts and hopes and aspirations."

"My dear, dear boy, how you must still suffer remembering."

"Worse yet, I suffer trying to forget the unforgettable."

"All right now, young man," she spoke resolutely. "This is no time to be sad, no time to spend on self-pity. I want you to remain happy. I want you to conquer the world, your new world." Paula stopped her chatter for a moment, her hands fondly enfolding mine. "And you must not forget your Paula Kaiser, promise!" She added as if in afterthought. I readied to go.

"I won't forget. I promise." I said softly. There was a moment of self-conscious silence.

"Come closer," she squinted, as she always did when straining to catch a glimpse of something that meant a great deal to her, "let me look at you." I approached into her outstretched arms. She felt my shoulders, touched my cheeks and then my shoulders again. "My, how you have grown into a man,

Willi, indeed, how you have grown in every way." Her voice trembled again and she began to weep quietly. "Oh, how I shall miss you. I shall miss you sorely, my dear." She cried without restraint.

"For God's sake, Paula!" I was close to tears myself. "Please, control yourself. You know how I dislike tears. It isn't the end of the world!" I choked a little. I desperately tried to avoid her tightly shut eyes.

Suddenly, perhaps because of our closeness or the impending departure, I knew it was Paula not Trude whom I had wanted. Yet it was the traditional reverence for the learned which stopped me. I was Paula's student and could not become her lover.

"After all, you've taught me to write." I said, and she smiled faintly.

"You will, won't you?" She needed a promise, a desperate resort of a terribly lonely person.

"Of course, I shall." I asserted, using the German expression *selbstverstädndlich* to please my teacher.

"Only when you need to chat, Willi. Write when you need to talk with your old friend," she added.

We walked toward the door arm in arm.

"I want to thank you for all. . ." I stammered suddenly in a scarcely audible voice. "I will continue to learn. I won't give up, and I will succeed. Surely, I will succeed. Thanks again."

We walked outside into the winter breeze. She buttoned my overcoat caressingly, lovingly. "You always forget to button up, and you catch cold so easily."

I ran down the few steps not looking back. Moments later, I turned. She stood in the doorway, probably shivering in the cold, waving at someone she could not see, throwing kisses.

"It isn't long till spring, Paula!" I called out to her. "Good bye Paula, stay well!"

"Good bye, Willi. Take care," she called in the direction of my voice. She walked inside, closing the door, and I was glad she did just then. It was hard to walk away. The temptation to run back was there, lingering for but a brief moment. I raised the collar around my neck and tightened the wollen scarf Paula had knitted for this occasion. My steps became firmer the more distance I put between myself and *Taunusstrasse* 21.

The next day, I left for Poland.

28

"Why am I here?" I asked the NKVD agent who had brought me to the detention center after arresting me at the railway station. The prison, a former hotel, was filled almost to capacity with "political" prisoners.

The guard pushed me into a small room, then bolted the door outside. I looked around the room thinking that nothing could be as bad as it was then; these people were not the same as those where I came from. The room was filthy, still there was a small lightbulb near the window; there was a window, after all. The only furniture in the room was a narrow bed, more like a military cot, against the wall on top of which there was a thin mattress. What luxury! I thought silently, seeing a toilet built into one corner. Several crumpled sheets of toilet paper lay beside the commode.

I lay down in the dark room trying to recall everything that had led to my confinement; the journey through Bavaria to the Czech border on an American refugee train; crossing the border with new identity papers; traveling through Czechoslovakia and visiting some friends in Prague who accompanied me to the Polish border where I crossed into Zakopane. That's where it all started with some seemingly trivial questions by the border guard.

I must sleep, I thought, but worry about my fate prevented sleep. I wanted to imagine myself free and somewhere with my father, but I couldn't. I had no reason to be frightened; after all, I was innocent. I would maintain my dignity, the only thing left me after my jailers confiscated all my belongings. "These'll be returned to you later." They said. I had no reason to believe them.

Next morning I was awakened by the clanging of the keys opening my door. The guard ordered me out: "Are you going to confess today?" He laughed raucously.

"I haven't done anything that I could confess." I responded calmly.

I became aware of the seriousness of my situation when the interrogators began questioning me about "subversive activities against the state."

At one point, the door to the interrogation quarters opened and three men burst inside. They stood over me, glaring down. Suddenly, each man hit me with a karate chop. Within seconds, my lips were cracked, my nose bled profusely, and my eyes were almost blinded. Soon, I could not see at all. When I was no longer able to stand up, the three men used my limp body as a punching bag. The last thing I heard before passing out was their abusive laughter.

I recovered in a cell full of other battered "political prisoners." A guard tossed some ice water on my face, ordering me to *confess*. Although I had nothing to confess, now I made up stories to avoid being beaten to death.

I could not remember how many times they beat me into unconsciousness. Once, one of the guards drove his knee into my abdomen which made me faint with unbearable pain. "He's not ready to talk," a voice sounded through a reddish haze. "Let's give him a few days to think. We'll get back to him when he's ready."

Back in the cell, I was kept on a diet of bread and water. After three days, they started again; this time it was psychological. A guard strolled casually into the cell, turned abruptly and pointed arbitrarily at one of the prisoners. The doomed man was dragged into the courtyard and shot.

These torments began to take their toll. The climax came when I was in conversation with a fellow inmate and a guard fired into the man's temple at point blank range. The noise was overwhelming. "These are my liberators!" I thought. "Clean up the mess," the guard commanded. He uttered some threats about shooting me but finally went away.

While I was scrubbing the floor clean, I began to think that I've seen this sort of behavior elsewhere, under different circumstances; men in different uniforms and speaking a different language. Could they be the same people? What kind of people were they, these assassins who killed with such ease? After all, killing is not an easy task; killing without reason made no sense at all.

Why did I still care to go on living? I wished what had to happen would happen fast. Like the man whose brains I was now mopping up, I felt already dead. They had shot him because he had told them that he was born in Lodz, but when asked about that city's main street, he wasn't able to remember. That lapse cost him his life.

On the fifth day of my detention, I was transferred to another of Zakopane's hotels which had been converted into a prison to hold the repatritaes from the West as well as the swelling ranks of "political prisoners."

An NKVD agent told me that very serious charges had been leveled against me. I was determined to resist for as long as I could.

From my cell, I caught a glimpse of the distant Tatra mountains. I had been there with my parents before the War. My mother was ill with consumption and my father had brought her to the sanatorium.

On the sixth day of my detention, a high-ranking officer joined the interrogation team. Joseph Goebbels would have described him as "typically Semitic." He had a prominent nose, fleshy, sensuous lips, and dark penetrating eyes. I chuckled mentally at this observation.

The interrogation continued without the newcomer's interference. He sat in the corner; an aloof observer. Questions came at a rapid succession, without time for reflection, meant to overwhelm, not to elicit response.

"Talk!—Damn you, swine! Talk!"

"Why were you in Germany?"

"You were a collaborator, weren't you?"

"We've got the goods on you. Better admit it now and we'll go easy on you."

"You're a *Volksdeutscher*! Talk!" A blow might have followed were it not for the presence of the silent observer.

"I know you won't believe me," I said quietly, "but I was born in Sosnowiec of Jewish parents. You can check out the family name. The Nazis persecuted our family, killing most of them because we were Jews. After six-and-a-half years of hell, I was liberated in the concentration camp Colditz by the Americans. You can check that out, too, if you don't believe me." I tried to speak calmly, without emotion.

"Don't tell us our business, pig. We know your kind!" The interrogators leered at me. "Only collaborators went to work for the Germans. Your kind turns with the tide. You join the enemy when he's on top, and you return when he's vanquished. And you don't have the courage to admit it. You're a liar, a damned liar! Admit it!"

My resistance was near its end. My strength was almost gone. I could not face another day of interrogation, especially since the interrogators worked in shifts, relentlessly pursuing their goal: admit to a crime I never committed.

"I returned to my homeland in search of my family. It's God's truth," I said. "If any of them are alive, I want to find them."

"It may be *your* God's truth. But is it *our* kind of truth?"

"How about testing my ability to speak *Yiddish*?"

"You talk *Yiddish* like a *Goy*."

"That doesn't prove anything."

"If you continue to be stubborn, we might lock you up and throw away the key." There was hilarious laughter.

"How can I prove my innocence?"

"Admit you're a collaborator."

"Guess it's no use trying to convince you I'm not."

"You're lying, *sobaka*." They used the Russian word for dog for the first time. The observer stirred in his corner, then rose and approached.

"Where were you born?" He asked quietly.

"I've told them twice already."

"Never mind what you've told them. Tell *me*."

"In Sosnowiec."

"Look, young man. You don't have to be afraid. We need your help. If the things you tell us will help us identify other agents of the imperialists we'll go easy on you."

"I'm not afraid of you," I answered. "Why should I be? I've seen everything already."

"Were you a member of the Hitler Youth?"

"No."

"Where's your father?"

"I came here to look for him."

"Why did the Americans send you here? Are you their agent? Are they sending more of your kind?"

"I'm not an agent, and I don't know anything about agents."

Out of my bloodshot eyes, I looked at the inquisitor. His face betrayed no emotion. Suddenly, I was overcome by total despair.

"Why don't you just go ahead and shoot me. You might earn yourself a medal for killing a boy of eighteen!" My desperation had given me new courage. I was prepared to die.

"Comrade Vilek," my tormentor said in a voice a shade more gentle, "I believe you."

"Then why do you torment me so?"

"It's our job to catch spies. I feel for you because I am one of your people, though I'm no longer of your faith. It doesn't pay to be a Jew in the new Poland."

"Was all this necessary? Beating me half to death?"

"There's no other way. We're threatened every day by the imperialists. It's my *duty* to defend what's ours."

"The Americans are your allies, aren't they?" I asked.

"Appearances are deceiving comrade. Our ideologies are on opposite poles; one is destined to destroy the other. Only one of us will emerge alive."

"I don't understand."

"You will, comrade. Some day, you will." The man looked at me somberly, made a resigned gesture with his hand, and then abruptly left the room.

The following day, I received papers that permitted me to travel all over Poland. My backpack was returned to me on orders of the Commissar who had last interrogated me.

The document instructed me to report to the NKVD offices on every stopover. The Commissar's words echoed ominously in my mind.

The same evening, I boarded the first train to Czestochowa, clutching my backpack in front of me. The compartment was filled to capacity, and I was lucky to find a seat though I could barely breathe.

I could not quite believe that I was free. The pain from the NKVD "inquiry" was still in my bones. My fingers searched inside the backpack, containing all my worldly treasures. I smiled to myself, the carton of Camel cigarettes was still there. American cigarettes were at a premium in Poland. I also fondled the G.I. winter clothes given to me for the trip by Bill Blake. The thought of Bill caused me to smile some more. Hitler would turn in his grave at the prospect of Mulatto Krauts running around in his Third Reich. I relished the thought, and my smile turned into a mischievous chuckle.

The train negotiated a sharp curve, winding its way serpent-like, rapidly into the valley. I observed the sudden change of color and appearance of the mountains. They turned gradually a soft blue, before disappearing completely from view as they fused into the early evening fog and the low lying clouds.

As it grew dark, I placed the backpack on the seat using it as a pillow. Believing it to be safe, I fell into a deep sleep.

I woke up with a sharp pain in my right hand. Someone was tugging violently at the backpack. The sudden shock of pain made me release it, as I noticed that my hand was covered with blood. The thief was running down the corridor and, as I hesitated, he disappeared from sight.

Shit! I ground my teeth together. I had to get it back! I had to! The success of my journey depended on the contents of that backpack. I pushed my way ahead desperately trying to pursue the fugitive.

Out of breath I reached the last compartment. Beyond that was an empty track. The train was moving too fast for the thief to have jumped off. I searched frantically, but he was nowhere to be seen. I banged at the lavatory door. It was locked. I banged harder.

"Come out, or I'll call the conductor!" My voice trembled, and I prayed that I was addressing the right door. "We'll break in the door. I know you're in there. Hand over my backpack, and I'll forget the whole thing!" I pounded at the door, then heaved my body into it hoping to break it open. "You'll have to come out sooner or later." Hopelessly, I leaned against the solid door. "I'll wait," I said resigned.

"Can we make a deal?" A voice suddenly said from inside.

"What kind of a deal?" I asked, trying not to sound anxious.

"A deal, you know."

"Give me my backpack, and we'll talk."

"No tricks?"

"Look who's talking." My relief was giving way to fury. Why was I bargaining with a thief?

The door opened a crack, and I kicked it in. I looked at a boy my own age. I jumped on him and pushed him down on the floor.

"I should cut your throat from ear to ear!" I shouted, pulling a knife from my pocket. "Talk about deals, will you?" The knife drew a trace of blood under the boy's ear. "You see this?" I yelled, showing him my bleeding wrist, "I'll make you a deal and give you back your miserable life; show me your face again, and you're dead." I picked up my backpack and left the lavatory.

My compartment seat had been taken. But I didn't mind. I had recovered my property. Without it the trip would be doomed to failure. I sat on the floor, not daring to fall asleep.

An hour later, the train pulled into Czgstochowa. I looked at the desperate, shoving, shouting people, much like those who not long ago had fled the Nazi invasion. Only this time, they were returning home, not running from the enemy.

Suddenly there was a great commotion at the door to our compartment. "Out! Everybody out!" a Corporal shouted in Polish. "Get out! All of you! *Sobak!l Ya vas osvabodil!* Dogs! I liberated you!" The Corporal commanded in Russian, the language of the liberator. He lifted an elderly man near him and heaved the unsuspecting victim through the open door. The man fell heavily to the snow-covered ground and remained there, motionless, moaning softly. The snow cushioned his fall. He was lucky.

The Corporal's action was a signal for his companions. Laughing uproariously and shouting obscenities, they proceeded to evict the passengers. Men, women and children were brutally thrown out of their compartments. I was no exception. Clutching my recovered backpack, I jumped into the snow. The cold was Arctic. Our Soviet guests took over the entire compartment. I got up from the ground and hid behind the last car, waiting for my opportunity. The train began to move again on its journey to Piotrkow and I jumped onto the stepping board. Soon it gained momentum, and I realized that I would not be able to hold on very long. There were seven hours of travel ahead, and one slip of a hand could kill me.

Holding on with one hand to the door handle, I cautiously loosened my G.I. belt. I pulled one of the gloves from my stiffened fingers, and I lost my grip. I grabbed the handle, but one of my gloves was carried off by the howling wind. Within minutes, my exposed hand began to lose all feeling.

Suddenly the train came to a jarring stop and I slipped one end of the belt through the door handle. I managed to tie a knot around my waist before the train began to move again. Then I inserted both my hands into the one remaining glove. Now, I felt more secure and one hand would warm the other for the remainder of the journey.

It was almost dawn when the train rolled into the Piotrkow railway station. Exhausted with pain and cold, I fell to the ground. With my last strength, I got up as the train was pulling out of the station. I've come home at last.

29

I checked into the only hotel in town. I woke in the morning to a bitter cold. The heating system wasn't working, and I dressed quickly.

On the surface, Piotrkow remained unchanged. The rabble had been cleared from the streets. Here and there I saw remnants of houses, mute reminders of the violent past. I also noticed new buildings that I didn't recognize. Progress, I thought.

Street vendors were peddling their wares. It was Sunday, and the market place was buzzing with festively dressed peasants. Not one of the vendors was Jewish. The traditional Hasidic merchants were missing. "Who had taken their place?" I questioned silently.

Who would take the blame for the cheating and conniving? Against whom would the peasants' passions be aroused?

It was difficult to imagine Piotrkow *Judenrein*, completely without Jews.

"Street names are different now." An elderly fruit vendor said to me with a conspirational wink. "You're a newcomer, aren't you?" He scrutinized me from head to toe, examining my G.I. clothes.

"Not really."

"You've been here before?"

"Yes." I ventured. Suddenly I remembered the day the *Stukas* had swooped down. My grandmother scurrying toward the mikvah with us in tow; the first victims of the *Stukas* scattered around us dead and dying.

"Did they rebuild the armory?" I asked, pointing to one of the modern buildings.

It was the first thing they did," the old man replied. "The country must be kept strong, you know?" He added, winking again. He looked over his shoulder. "Got some trading for me?" He nodded toward the backpack.

"No, not really," I said cautiously. "You're here all the time?"

"That's where you can find me, comrade."

"If I get some trading, I'll look you up."

"Don't forget. Franek's the name."

"I won't forget."

Piotrkow was still the small *shtetl* with its own peculiar grapevine. Word spread quickly of my return.

"You came to stay?"

"What brought you back?" They asked.

"Trying to find my family. Have you seen my father? He's been through here with the Kosciuszko Division."

"No, haven't seen him."

"You'd better go back to where you came from. You won't find anyone here. No one's returned."

They spoke in half sentences. Strangers. Suspicious and hostile, perhaps feeling guilty.

"The Jew came back to dig up his treasures." I overheard an old woman say.

"You need any help digging?" Another one asked. When I turned around without reply, she whispered: "The filthy Jew wants it all for himself."

Slowly, fearfully, I walked down the familiar street toward my grandparents' home. Their kind and loving faces came back to me. They had never hurt anyone. They worked hard and saved for a future that never came.

Still deep in thought, I suddenly stood in front of the old building, barely recognizable. I walked up to the staircase, to the familiar door and knocked. There was no answer. I knocked again, this time impatiently, but it would not yield.

"Anyone in there?" I called. "Open up, please!"

The door opened a crack. In the dim light, I saw a stranger's face, a young man in his thirties.

"You're making a lot of noise," he whispered, "and you'll wake the baby."

"Who are you?" I asked, trembling. "This is my grandparents' home."

The man hesitated. "Come inside," he motioned finally. I followed him into the kitchen. There was an odor of urine and vomit.

"Tell me, what happened here?" I asked with emotion and nausea.

"What do you mean? Nothing happened. After the war the housing committee assigned these places to us Poles."

"Janek. . . Januszek. . . who is it?" A female voice inquired from the bedroom.

"It's my wife," explained the man. "Just someone inquiring about the old owners, dear!"—"She has a bad cold, poor thing," he said a little awkwardly. "We came from the East and the government put us here," he then repeated. "We weren't expecting you. We were told the owners were all dead."

"How tactless of me to have returned," I said in a whisper.

"What?" the man asked, cocking an ear. He had not understood my sarcasm. "Would you want to sleep here overnight?"

Stunned, I turned around without replying and walked away. Outside, I sat down on the staircase. Unable to move, my body shook convulsively. I broke into uncontrollable sobs. I didn't want the stranger in the house to hear me, yet I could not stop. I was homeless. I was free. I was human once again. But I was also naked in my humanity. And I was alone.

I got up and walked aimlessly through the streets trying to put as much distance between me and my grandparents' home as possible.

On my return to the hotel I was told that there was someone waiting for me. "Is it a young person?"—"Yes, about your age."— "Blond?"—"Yes." "Tadzik!" I ran toward my childhood friend. The only friend who stood by me. To my immense pleasure, I saw his slight figure sitting on a sofa in the vestibule.

"Tadziu!" We hugged. "Tadziu, how good of you to have come here! Oh, Tadziu! What memories!"

"Sorry, we have to meet this way." Tadzik glanced anxiously over his shoulder. There was no one. Only the wind whistled through the empty, ghostlike, hall. "You know how it is," Tadzik added.

"You mean. . .?"

"They're everywhere. We've got to be careful."

"But why?"

"You wouldn't understand."

"It's bad, uh?"

"Worse. You've heard about my father?"

"No, I haven't."

"He's in prison."

"Why? What was his crime?"

"Remember? We were *Volksdeutsche*. Even though he helped save some Jews, they said he was a collaborator. Nothing we could do."

"That's terrible. I'm sorry. Prison, for how long?"

"Fifteen years."

I fell silent. "Fifteen years? That's severe," I said.

"Could have been worse, you know."

"How's that?"

"Death."

"How's your mother?" I asked hesitatingly.

"She's okay. Say, listen. . ." Once again, Tadzik looked over his shoulder. "I suppose you didn't come to stay. Did you?"

I hesitated.

"Well, did you? You'll be going back to Germany. Won't you?"

"Well. . . I. . . don't. . . really know. . ." I wondered why Tadzik was pressing me.

Suddenly, Tadzik grabbed my arm. "I want to go with you. Mother knows. She agrees."

"You?" I gasped.

"Yes. You are my only chance. There's nothing here for me."

"What'll you do? Where'll you go?"

"First, I want to get out."

"Why not apply for an exit visa?'

"There's no way for us to get one."

"You mean? You're stuck?"

"There's no way. Only the dead are free to get out."

Some more hesitation followed.

"I'd have gone already, by myself." Tadzik looked at me imploringly. "But it takes two to be successful. My father gave me the route. It's safe, if we do it right. Look, I'll be with you. You can trust me. If they catch us, it's Siberia for both of us." He was pleading now. Suddenly, I became aware of the effect my lack of trust had on my friend. I was ashamed. "God!" I thought, "what have they done to me?"

"Wait till you've been here for a while." I heard Tadzik say. "I've heard of children turning in their parents just to earn meritorious citations from the government."

"That'll make my search harder." I said.

"You mean, for your father?"

"Yes."

"He came through some time ago."

"Where to?"

"West."

"And my mother. . .Felusia?"

"Treblinka."

"You're sure?"

"Absolutely."

"Have you heard from Devorah?" I asked. My voice quivered.

"I've got things to tell you about her. Not now, though. Someone's coming." Two men entered the hall. Tadzik pulled away. "Same place, tomorrow night. Same time," he whispered as he walked quickly toward the door.

"You have a visitor." The clerk warned me later that evening. "I let him into your room. He wouldn't wait down here."

In total darkness, a man was sitting on the only chair in my room. I switched on the light and looked at the stranger cautiously. I didn't recognize him. "Who are you?" I asked. I was now frightened. "What do you want?"

"Mlynarz is the name, Franek Mlynarz. I apologize for intruding."

He was a man in his late fifties, paunchy and balding. His features started to look familiar. I had heard that voice somewhere.

"Perhaps it'll refresh your memory if I introduce myself as Franz Müller."

I stared at him.

"Müller from the big furnace," the man said.

Suddenly I remembered.

"*Herr* Müller!" I hissed. "Hortensia!"

"I only want to take a moment," Müller stammered. "Can we talk in private?"

I nodded.

"I know why you're here," Müller continued. "You've come to fulfill your promise, didn't you?"

I waited, saying nothing.

"What do you want with me? I'm an old man with a wife and grandchildren and I'm terribly sick." Müller was shaking. "God. Sweet Jesus. Let me die in peace."

I was silent.

"I've lived with your threat all these years. Had nightmares about your return."

"Did you, *Herr* Müller?" I asked quietly. "Do you remember my mother? My little sister? All those people you sent to the ovens? Do you remember them?"

"What I did, I did because it was my duty," Müller said, still shaking. He sat down again. "I paid! I stood trial, and I paid! Don't you understand? It was my duty. If I hadn't done it, someone else would have."

Without a word, I took my switchblade knife from the dresser drawer, opened it and began toying with the naked blade. "What else do you remember, *Herr* Müller?"

"Sweet Jesus, Holy Virgin Mary, you're not going to kill me! Are you? Put that thing away! Please! Let's talk." Müller's face had turned ashen. He was breathing heavily. Suddenly, he slumped to the floor. His lips moved without sound, and he pointed to his breast pocket. "Take. . .one. . .pill, please. . .some water. . ." he whispered.

"What did you say, *Herr* Müller?" I asked. "Speak louder, please." Müller's fingers gripped his chest convulsively. "I'll run and fetch some help." I turned toward the door.

"No. . . time. . . for. . . that. . . please. . ." Müller moaned. His eyes glazed over and he lay motionless at my feet. I placed my ear to his chest, but there was no sound. I felt neither rage nor pity. Only relief that fate had intervened. "My mother would have envied you this kind of death, *Herr* Müller," I said softly. I folded my knife and put it back in the drawer.

Like in the old days, we met behind the great furnace. I was reluctant at first, but I came. There was an eerie silence in the once noisy place; the furnace was cold and in ruin. The retreating Nazis made sure that Hortensia didn't recover long after they'd gone.

We looked at each other in silence, and neither knew how to begin. "There's trouble, Vilek." Tadzik said at last. "Big trouble."

"What do you mean, Tadzik?" I asked. "What kind of trouble?"

"They've murdered some Jews in Kielce yesterday." Tadzik whispered sadly. "I'm afraid it's coming this way."

"Murdered? Jews? What Jews?" I shouted disregarding the secrecy of our meeting. "I didn't think there were any Jews left in Poland!"

"There weren't." Tadzik replied sadly. "Until they've returned, like you, to look for family and relatives who may have survived."

"Instead, they found death!" I shouted in anger. "After going through all the Nazi hell, they come home to be killed by their countrymen!" I was close to tears.

"I don't know what to say, my dear friend." Tadzik seemed crashed. "Except that you have to leave."

"The sooner the better!" I agreed. "Nothing could keep me in this God forsaken country!"

"I don't blame you for feeling the way you feel, Vilek." Tadzik was apologetic. "Only please don't judge us all by the few."

"Be careful, Tadzik, my friend." I warned. "You're beginning to sound like all the Germans."

"Sorry if I've offended you, Vilek. I know how you must feel."

"Forget it, Tadziu." I was composed now. "We've got more important things to think about. Like how do we get out of here?"

Tadzik began mysteriously. "Next Friday will be our last chance. We travel east to the village of Terespol. The Moscow-Berlin Express stops there to make the switchover to the narrower western gauge. An empty train waits in Terespol overnight for the switch. There are no sentries to guard it." Tadzik took a deep breath. He grinned satisfied. "We'll find a way to get on that empty train.

"Before the guards and dogs get there?" I asked, remembering Terespol.

"That's hard to forsee," Tadzik hesitated. "If we're caught. . .you know. . ."

"We'll make it, Tadzik," I insisted. "We can hide in the mail wagon, and let them load the mail on top of us."

Tadzik smiled. "Seventy-two hours later, and the Almighty willing," he said, making the sign of the cross, "we'll be in Berlin."

"If it's that simple, why aren't more people doing this?" I asked anxiously.

"There aren't too many who know," Tadzik said.

I was satisfied with my friend's plan, yet something was still bothering me.

"What about Devorah?" I asked suddenly. "And my aunt Sabina?"

"Uh?" Tadzik looked up startled.

"You were going to tell me."

"There isn't much to tell." He seemed evasive.

"Tell me what you know."

"They were on the Auschwitz transport. It was the last one my father was chief engineer on."

"Auschwitz?"

"I'm sure."

"And I thought they were taken to Treblinka."

"Your mother and Felusia went there. Your aunt and Devorah went South."

"What happened then? Go on." I pressed on.

"You're sure you want to hear?"

"Yes."

"They were making one of those latrine stops. My father stopped the train and the SS ordered the people off into the woods. One wagon at a time. Lithuanian guards escorted them."

Tadzik glanced at me with concern.

"Go on. . . go on!" I insisted.

"As my father was watching, he saw three guards leading your aunt and Devorah away. He followed them."

"Sure it was my aunt and Devorah?"

"He saw them clearly from where he stood." Tadzik hesitated again. "You want me to go on?"

"Yes, please go on, Tadziu," I urged, trying to hide my terror.

"One of the guards put his rifle on the ground and lowered his breeches. The second guard grabbed Devorah from behind, placing one hand over her mouth. Your aunt pleaded with the guards to spare her daughter. My father heard her clearly, as she begged, 'I'll do anything, only let the child alone.' The guard laughed. One of them threw himself on top of your cousin. He forced himself between her thighs."

"Oh God," I moaned.

"She offered no resistance, even as he lunged into her with a wild scream. The second guard, excited by this spectacle, attacked your aunt, impatient for his own gratification.

"He took a little longer, deriving added pleasure from hitting your aunt in the face each time he lunged into her. Soon, he, too, was spent. By that time, the third guard had his pants off. My father, unable to watch this any longer, ran back to the train. He blew the train whistle which marked the end of the stop-over.

"Before pulling out, my father watched for your aunt and Devorah. He never saw them." Tadzik was silent.

"My God, they must have killed them." I was sobbing.

"There were no shots," Tadzik reassured me. "Maybe they fainted, or the guards just left them there for dead. Who knows?"

"The bastards probably strangled them or beat them to death," I wept.

"That's only guessing, Vilek. When my father returned from that trip he told us of its final destination: Auschwitz. If they're alive, they could be somewhere near here. Possibly in Radomsko. You've got to look there, Vilek."

"If they're alive, I'll find them," I said. "I've got to go there before we leave for Berlin."

"You've got two days to do it." Tadzik reminded me. "It's Tuesday. I'll expect you back on Thursday morning."

"I'll be back on time, Tadziu," I promised. "I'll be back with them or without them."

I hitched a ride on a sleigh traveling south to Radomsko. I rode alongside the driver, deep in thought. The day was tranquil, and the sun reflected from the snow and made my eyes water.

"You're new in these parts?" The driver wanted to know.

I nodded.

"What's the place you're looking for," the driver asked.

"The Wisiak farm." I looked up at him. "I'm looking for the Wisiaks. They told me there's a young girl working there as a farmhand. About my age. They picked her up during the war in the woods. Half dead. Summer of forty-one." I talked quickly, more to myself than to the driver.

From my inquiries, after I left Tadzik, I had learned that a young girl had been found near the Wisiak farm. She had been badly beaten and left for dead. Near her, beaten to death, was a middle-aged woman.

I had also heard from the same sources that the foundling was unable to speak. No one knew her name nor that of the dead woman. The Wisiaks, a childless couple, cared for the mute girl affectionately, and after a year or two, she regained her voice. Still, she would shun strangers and only spoke to her adoptive parents. The Wisiaks called her Maria.

"The Wisiaks are nice people," the driver said to me, "she's well off with them. They lost a son and their daughter Maria in a Nazi raid." He spat into the snow. "The goddamned bastards left their evil mark on everybody." He spat again. "The Wisiak farm is just beyond that hill."

I got off the sleigh and thanked the driver, handing him two cigarettes.

My heart raced as I walked toward the farmhouse. Despite the bitter cold, I was perspiring as I knocked at the door.

A peasant woman in her late fifties opened the door.

"Who is it?" A man's voice called from inside.

"I don't know."

The man came to the door. He, too, was middle-aged. His eyes were blue, yet soft.

"What brings you to us, young man?" He asked.

"I'm looking for a girl, a relative of mine. We were separated during the war. She's about my age, eighteen. She and her mother were on their way to Auschwitz, Oswiecim," I repeated the Polish designation. "They told me in Radomsko that you saved a young girl during the war. She would be my age now. If she's here, I'd very much like to talk to her. Please, will you let me?" My whole body trembled. The couple looked at me, exchanging a glance. The woman was the first to answer.

"My husband, Andrzej, found the girl in the woods some years back. He was on his way to the market." She stopped as if to collect her thoughts. "She lay there in the thicket where they left her, half crazy, starved, and mute.

"Andrzej tried to touch her, but she was like a frightened animal. A dead woman lay nearby. Clubbed to death, most likely." The woman spoke mournfully. "It was her mother, we learned that later. We gave her a good Christian burial, poor soul." The woman piously made the sign of the cross.

"The girl. Where can I find her?" I asked still trembling.

"Where she usually spends her days. Working in the barn."

"May I go there?"

"Yes, you can, but please be gentle."

"I've come a long way to speak to her."

"Good luck, young man," the farmer said with a tenderness I didn't expect from one of his sort as I walked toward the barn. "Be gentle!" He cautioned once again. "She's gone through enough already!"

I entered the barn door, trying to see in the dim light. Suddenly, I saw her, kneeling. She was silent, stroking a small calf. She looked at me as I approached. There was no sign of recognition.

It was Devorah. There was no doubt. With every fiber of my being, I yearned to embrace her. Yet, I restrained myself and stood there drinking in her familiar features.

"Devorah?" my voice quivered. She looked up at me, for what seemed an eternity.

"I don't know you," she said finally. "My name is Maria. I don't know you."

I scrutinized her face. Dismay swept over me. Her eyes were haunted, with the knowledge of years of suffering. The pain flooded over me. I had to turn away for a moment.

"Don't you know me?" I asked desperately. "I'm Vilek, your cousin Vilek." I looked at her persistently, and I thought I understood. Unimaginable events had turned this soft creature to granite. Claiming ignorance was her protection. Now, momentarily safe, I was afraid for the first time. What if I can't convince her? I began to tremble. Knees beat against each other. My tongue curled throatward: teeth chattered until I thought they would break into small fragments.

"My name's Maria." She repeated mechanically.

"It's me. . . Vilek. . . your cousin. . ." I repeated slowly.

Another eternity passed.

"I've come from far away to see you, Devorah. I've come from Germany and looked for you everywhere. Don't send me away," I was pleading now. I felt that my very life was hanging in a balance.

"Leave this place," Devorah said suddenly. "There's nothing here for you. Go as far as you can from here!"

"Please, Devorah." The tears were rolling down my cheeks. "Come with me."

"I have a good home here. The Wisiaks treat me like their very own. I'm fine." She looked away.

"But. . . I love. . .you. . .Devorah." I stammered. "The. . .thought. . .of. . .you. . .kept me. . . going. . . through all these years. . ." I was sobbing uncontrollably.

"I'm not for anyone. . . unclean. . . blemished." She said harshly. "They raped me," she added quietly. "I've not kept myself pure."

"You couldn't help that, my darling." I sobbed. She didn't respond.

Then, with a small smile, she added: "The Lord Jesus never lets me down. I ask him for strength, and He gives it to me."

"Devorah. . . don't. . . please." This sudden revelation, shocked me to my very bones, and I didn't know why.

"I wasn't always that way," Devorah continued. "There were times when I doubted God's existence, like the time when those evil men did the horrible things to my mother and me. But then I learned not to hate myself anymore. I'm fine here. Can't you see?" She looked at me again imploringly.

"Devorah. . . please come with me. I love you."

"There's no love here for anyone, except from Jesus," she said without emotion. My heart stopped with anguish. "Leave me and never come back!" Devorah was screaming now. "I am with the Lord Jesus now!"

"But. . ."

Blinded by my tears, I turned around to leave. I reasoned silently. I had no choice but to respect her privacy, the mystery and pain of a survivor. Suddenly I realized that no one really survived. We were all doomed to carry those dark years with us to our graves. It would not be easy for me to escape the past either. I knew that I would not see Devorah again.

"I hope you're happy," I said without conviction. Then, my strength gave way to the love of all those years. "Please," I begged, "just one last time, let me hold you, just for a moment." I took her into my arms, and felt her body stiffen as if in a sudden spasm. Then she went limp, like a rag doll. I kissed her hair and let her go.

"Go now," Devorah said quietly, "and forget you ever saw me. If you find my father, tell him I'm dead."

"Goodbye, my love," I said softly, more to myself than to Devorah. "Your secret will stay with me." I walked into the howling wind, grateful that it drowned out the sounds of my sobs.

Walking through the storm, I proceeded to bury my past: first my grandfather, then my mother, and now Devorah. And my father? Was he dead, too? I wondered. Or was he mad with grief, like Devorah? I still wasn't free. I would look for him. Somewhere in Poland? Or perhaps even in Germany? I didn't know. Yet, I was sure that I must try to find him. Life, after all, was the answer to death.

30

Three days later, on a Friday morning, we were on our way to Terespol. We changed trains in the large and noisy Warsaw railroad terminal.

I looked around at the bustling crowd. The War had involved everyone; it made of us a generation of refugees. People spoke in hushed voices, often glancing anxiously over their shoulders. I listened intently. Many thought they would never see their homes again. Once the Soviets moved in, they didn't let go. That was common knowledge.

"They've been uprooted again," said Tadzik. "First the Nazis, now the Soviets."

"Where are they all going?"

"They're being resettled in East Germany."

"What happens if Germany rises again?"

"She won't. The Soviets are there. They'll see to it."

Suddenly the dreary railroad station resounded with the strains of a mournful Russian tune. I recognized the Ukrainian ballad Katyusha. It was a popular melody, common in times of war. It told the story of a young woman left behind by her soldier lover who promised to return but never did, and she goes on waiting, endlessly.

"The Russians have always had a way with music," Tadzik said. "I suppose, that's the way they atone for their crimes."

I was about to reply that the Russians weren't any different from the Poles or the Germans nor from any one else, for that matter, concerning national conscience, when three Red Army soldiers came to view. They walked toward us, their arms around each other's shoulder, singing at the top of their voices. I was strangely moved. As I stole a glance at Tadzik, I thought there were tears in his eyes. *Katyusha* was a sad song. "Why did my enemies have the power to move me?" I wondered to myself.

Soon, we went past the city of Minsk. It seemed only yesterday over one hundred thousand Jews lived there. Now, all that was left of them was an unmarked mass grave in a quarry minutes from the railway station. I could see it plainly from the train window.

"I must visit the grave," I suddenly heard myself say.

"We don't have the time. We'll miss the train!" Tadzik shouted.

"There'll be another train if we miss this one," I insisted. "I must say kaddish."

Tadzik knew that there was no arguing with me. He followed me in silence.

The huge snow-covered hillside rose up before us. We stood there, Jew and Christian, silent in the howling storm. Then, with a great effort, blinded by the snow and by my tears, I recited the sacred words:

"*Yitgadal v'yitgadash shmay rabah, b'alma divrahirusay. . .*

. . . Let the glory of God be exalted, let His great name be hallowed in the world whose creation He willed. . .

Treblinka, Majdanek, Sobibor, Belzec, Auschwitz—they were all a short distance away from here. Which of them had devoured my mother, my sister, and my paternal grandparents? I would never know. And so I spoke the kaddish for them all.

Losing track of time, I repeated the prayer several times. Tadzik was becoming impatient.

"You've done your duty now," he said, nudging me in the ribs. I ignored him.

"Shouldn't we move on? The train might still be at the station." Tadzik pleaded.

Quickly, I turned around and walked away from the place of death as rapidly as I could. We made the train just in time.

I stared out over the frozen landscape, as the train thundered across the countryside. Not long ago, I had been here with the partisans, blowing up Nazi munitions trains bound for the Russian front.

Soon, we passed Biala Podlaska on our way to the border town of Terespol. We arrived at dawn. Now, we had to cross into Russian territory. We didn't keep to the main road, but went across the fields and through the woods. It wasn't the first time I had done it. Luck was on our side; we didn't meet a single soul. The river Boug was frozen over, and we crossed it on foot, avoiding the Soviet border patrol. We were nearing our target.

In the distance, we could see the lights of the Moscow-Berlin Express. "So far, so good." I whispered as I poked Tadzik with my elbow, pointing to the mail wagon at the front end of the train. No more than twenty yards from the vacant train, there was a poster: OFF LIMITS ZONE. IT IS FORBIDDEN TO APPROACH CLOSER THAN 15 YARDS. SENTRIES WILL SHOOT ON SIGHT WITHOUT WARNING.

We looked at each other not daring to break the silence. On our bellies, we dragged ourselves as far as the first wagon. We stood up and made a dash for the mail wagon at the head of the train.

"Let's get inside," I whispered. In the howling wind Tadzik could not hear me, but he understood my motion.

"Come on, Tadziu, it's open," I urged him on. We slid the door open and Tadzik jumped aboard first. I was about to follow, when Tadzik uttered a loud cry, high and plaintive with desperation.

"Holy Madonna, dear God in heaven. Sweet Jesus, not now."

"Off to the tundra with you, dogs!" It was a growling voice. A huge bearded man in uniform appeared at the door, holding Tadzik by the neck. I stood there, rooted to the spot, speechless.

"You dirty vermin thought you'd get away with it, did you? This means a one-way journey for you." The sentry laughed uproariously, pointing his rifle at me with one hand while clutching Tadzik with the other.

"Lie in the snow! Head down!" He barked, throwing Tadzik into the snow, and placing a boot on his neck.

Desperately, I tried to think. The guard's uniform seemed old and tattered. "Can we talk?" I asked timidly. "We were only trying to hitch a ride."

"A ride, eh? A first class ride at that." The guard snarled. His foot pressed down hard on Tadzik's neck.

"Could you please point the gun elsewhere?" I pleaded. "It might go off by accident."

"It'll only go off when I pull the trigger," the guard grimaced. He took his foot away, and Tadzik was able to sit up. "Now, let's see, what have we here?—I see two beggars who want to lead the lives of princes." His voice sounded a shade more human.

"Listen, comrade," I suddenly took courage. "We'll make it worth your while if you let us go on our way."

"I make no deals with bums." The man laughed harshly. "And you're not in any position to offer any bargains."

"We'll share fifty-fifty what we have, if you'll let us go."

"Let's see what you've got." The guard reached for the backpack and looked inside. "Get inside," he said gruffly after a moment's hesitation. Tadzik now stood on his feet. "Get in," the guard repeated. We obeyed. The guard slung my backpack over his shoulder.

"Let him choke on our sausage. The bastard." Tadzik whispered. I was resigned to the loss of our supplies, crouched in the darkness of the wagon, ravenous with hunger.

Just then, the hatch opened slightly and my backpack was thrown at me. I examined the contents quickly. "One bottle, one sausage, five packs of cigarettes, and one blanket." I almost shouted for joy. "He only took half of everything . . ."

". . . and gave us half a chance," Tadzik added.

Daylight streamed into our hideout beneath the floor. We heard the noise of clanging metal. A new locomotive was being hooked up to our car. Soon afterward, to our immense relief, the car shuddered. We were moving. Toward the West! Toward Germany!

It was light outside. Through the cracks of the metal, we could see people moving objects and hear voices speaking in Russian. It was the crew of the

Soviet train. Soon, the passengers would also transfer onto our train, and we'd be on our way. It was the first dawn of our journey to freedom.

"Are you asleep?" I asked my friend.

"No."

"Let's smoke one. It's so damned cold in here."

"Good," said Tadzik. "But only one. We may need the rest later. And. . . for God's sake. . . be careful. . . we could all go up in smoke!" he added as an afterthought.

"Sure, I'll be careful. What do you think, Tadziu, how many kilometers did we put behind us last night?"

"At least two hundred fifty."

"When do you think we'll get to Berlin?"

"If they run on schedule, in two days."

"I'll be an icicle by then," I said, warming my palms on the glow of the cigarette. "You know, Tadziu," I continued, "I don't care anymore. Outside it's like Siberia, but here we have a blanket and cigarettes. I'm in no hurry." I laughed for the first time in weeks.

"Not so loud," warned Tadzik. "Someone may hear. And be careful with the ashes. We don't want to finish the job the Nazis started."

"That's not funny."

"Wasn't meant to be funny. One spark and we'd burn like cinder."

The frequent check-points had become a great source of anguish to us both. Now, we were approaching a major check-point on the border between the "New Poland" and the "New Germany" on the Oder-Neisse line. Crossing this border was the final obstacle before reaching freedom.

We listened to the slightest noise from within the mail compartment as well the shouts of the railway personnel directing the train.

"If you want to know, Vilek, the worst thing that can happen to us is being sent back and then. . ." Tadzik whispered fearfully, ". . . sentenced to fifteen years of hard labor in Siberia." I shuddered. "That's the usual punishment for those who seek freedom in this manner by crossing the border illegally."

"It's very nice of you to try to cheer me up, Tadzik." I tried to sound jovial though my voice trembled.

"Most likely they won't take the trouble to empty the cargo till we arrive in Berlin." Tadzik speculated.

We lay breathlessly still, and my limbs were getting numb. There wasn't any space to move them and get the circulation going. I got into the habit of feeling my pulse every now and then for fear it would stop at one point altogether.

When such worries crept into my mind, I experienced flashbacks of my recent past and, were it not for the prospect of the approaching freedom, I might have wept in utter resignation. "You're in the right place, Vilek, maybe by accident or by design, but you're here for a reason." I thought to myself as an infusion of courage.

We could hear the guards. One of them referred to Frankfurt-on-the-Oder by its new name: Slubice.

"They're coming this way." Tadzik made the sign of the cross. I could feel his trembling body. "We're in for it."

"Don't be silly. We're well hidden in this coffin." I tried to reassure my friend.

Suddenly the hatch opened. A brilliant light poured into the car, and we were temporarily blinded.

We crawled into the farthest corner as the cargo was being moved. The dust made my eyes water as it tickled my nasal passages, and I had to muster all my willpower to avoid sneezing or coughing. It was a most painful effort but the thought of being discovered by the searchers aided me in my resolve. And just as I thought I could no longer hold the dust within me, the hatch above us closed. As if by some secret agreement, we both luxuriated in letting out with powerful coughs and sneezing.

After what seemed an eternity, the sentries left. Tadzik made the sign of the cross again. This time it was a gesture of thanksgiving. I recited the *shema*.

"We make a damned pious team, don't we?" I said.

"It can't hurt, can it?"

"Pretty hypocritical, if you ask me."

"Force of habit, I guess." Tadzik chuckled.

"Does it matter?" I asked.

"Not really."

"Let's try to get some sleep now," I suggested. "We'll be in Berlin by morning."

"You're right. We'll need the rest."

We awoke with a start as the brakes gave out a metallic hiss. We were dazed at first, half-conscious. We could feel it; it was one of Berlin's railroad stations. Straining to look through the cracks in the hold, we saw people running back and forth, shouting orders, pushing carts.

"They're bound to discover us when they empty the mail wagon," Tadzik whispered.

"Let's keep shoving the parcels toward them and they won't find us," I said without much hope.

A thin stream of light pierced the hold. They must have spotted us. The light lingered, but no one spoke. In the pit of my stomach, I felt doomed. It was a familiar fear, and I wondered if I would ever be able to shake it. With the instinct of the persecuted, we cowered in the farthest reach of the car, but the searchlight followed us relentlessly. At long last, a deep basso voice cursed loudly in Russian.

"*Sobaki! Idy syuda!* Dogs. Come out here." The voice commanded. My fear deepened into panic. I lost control of my bladder and felt the wetness run down my legs. I began to pray.

"*Sobaki!*" The man became visible now. He was a giant. Lurching toward us, he held us by the crop of our hair. "There's only one place for the likes of you, Siberia!" He growled. A puddle had formed under me. This man would hardly settle for what was left of the contents of my backpack. I thought silently.

"Anna!"

The man suddenly called toward the adjoining compartment. "Anna, come here and see the rats we caught hiding in the hold."

Incongruously, a woman appeared in the doorway. Her frail figure stood in stark contrast to the huge frame of her male companion. She touched his arm and he released us from his grip. She wore a dark dress and a scarf was drawn over her head. I judged her somewhere between twenty-five and thirty years of age. Her features were regular, almost beautiful. She vaguely reminded me of my mother.

"What is all the noise about, Vanya?" She asked. Her voice was gentle.

"Can't you see? We have two stowaways on board. I must report them to the authorities."

"Let's not be too hasty, Vanya." The woman smiled. There were no lines on her youthful face. She was attractive. Vanya's voice seemed to mellow.

"They could have gotten us in trouble, and they must be punished." He insisted. "Let me deal with them, Anushka."

"This could get us all in trouble, Vanya," the woman said calmly.

"Let's not talk about Siberia. Why should you want to send these two miserable boys to such a dreadful place?"

"Still, I'd like to. . ." The woman nudged him.

"Come on now."

He grinned broadly at his female companion, took her dainty hand in his own and kissed it gently.

"As always, you make sense, Anushka." He turned toward us sternly. I wanted to run, but both my feet seemed rooted to the spot.

"Get the poor devils out of here before the inspector arrives," the woman urged.

Vanya was still unconvinced.

"You tried to make a fool of me," he said loudly. "Now you must pay."

"We haven't got anything to pay with," I retorted. "But if you give us a chance, we'll come back and bring you some American cigarettes."

"*Khorosho!*" The man nodded, putting his arm around his wife. "Get the hell out of here, before I change my mind."

"God bless you both." Tadzik said in Russian.

We jumped off the train. Soon we were wading in the knee-deep water of the flooded Berlin subways; Hitler's departing gift to his Thousand Year Reich's capital. The total darkness of the sewer was like a gigantic maze. We were afraid that we might never see daylight again.

"Give me a hand, Tadziu. It's so dark, I can't see a thing."

At that moment, I felt something bite my right ankle. I knew full well what it was. "Rats!" I screamed. I kicked frantically and glimpsed a huge black rodent scurrying away.

"They're as scared of us as we're of them," Tadzik said. His voice was shaky.

"I wouldn't bet on it, Tadziu. If they're hungry enough, they'll have us for lunch."

The water made it difficult for us to move and we fought our way through the rat-infested sewer. Finally, almost exhausted, bleeding from rat bites, without hope, we glimpsed a light in the distance. Daylight at last. Half blinded, we found ourselves in the middle of the rains of a railway depot. I took a deep breath.

"Vilek, what day is it today?"

"I think it's Thursday."

"The date?"

"July thirteenth, I believe."

"That's what I thought. It's Bastille Day tomorrow, and we're free! Do you know what that means? Vilek, my friend, we'll celebrate!"

"I'd be contented with a hot bath and an equally hot bowl of soup."

"So would I. . .so would I, my friend. My stomach's shrunk to nothing."

Gothic lettering on the wall informed us that we were at the GÖRLITZER BAHNHOF. Everything was in shambles.

There was not an undamaged building in sight. Hitler had kept his promise; he left nothing for the people who "were cowards unworthy of life."

"Jesus have mercy," Tadzik whispered. "So this is the capital of the Thousand Year Reich. I hope there's a place left for us to spend the night."

I said nothing. The city of terror, I thought to myself, had now become a place of hope.

It had been nearly three weeks since my arrival in Berlin, and I was becoming restless. I was free, yet I wasn't free. Berlin was an island surrounded by a Russian sea. The refugee compound near the picturesque *Wannsee* offered little opportunity for amusement, and the Zone borders were guarded by a new breed of sentries; the newly organized German militia known as *Schupo*.

"It's time I left this place, Tadziu."

"I'm not sure I want to leave as yet, Vilek."

"My mind's made up."

"Why don't you wait till spring? It'll be easier to cross the border."

"My father may already be in Wiesbaden. I'm certain, if he's alive, he'd be in touch with our Aunt Yetta in London. We've written her first thing on arriving in Wiesbaden. He must know it by now. I have to look for him here in Germany."

"In that case, you'd better go."

"Sure you won't come? Watch out, Tadzik!" I jerked my friend out of the path of a jeep. It was too late. The driver, a young G.I., turned the steering wheel desperately. The jeep swerved to a screeching halt, and Tadzik was hit broadside. He had suffered a slight cut on the forehead when he fell, his head hitting the right front fender.

"I know that every bone in my body ought to be smashed to pieces," Tadzik moaned, "but I'm not hurting." Cautiously, he first moved his right arm, then his left, then his legs. "I suppose I'm in one piece as long as I can move them." He smiled faintly. The youthful driver appeared concerned. A crowd of curious onlookers gathered quickly. The G.I.'s female companion—a stunning red-head—bent over the victim. She spoke in the inimitable Berliner dialect.

"Are you all right, *Liebchen?*" The crowd was becoming restless. They shouted insults at the American and his Fräulein.

"*Verfluchte Amis!*" Damned Americans!

"*Ami* drivers! There ought to be a law!"

"They're madmen! No one's safe anymore!"

"*Ami* go home!"

The redhead's eyes searched the crowd for sympathy. "*Meine Damen* und *Herren!*" She pleaded. "Please, I beg you. Give the man some air." She knelt beside Tadzik, applying her water-soaked silk scarf to his bleeding forehead.

"Listen to the *Ami* whore talking like a lady!"

"You're no better than your *Ami* friend, bitch!"

"Is it chewing-gum or does he buy your arse for silk stockings?" The crowd jeered.

"Let's get the hell out of here," the American pleaded. "The mob's in a lynching mood and we've got to get the guy to a medic."

Tadzik's head rested in the woman's lap as the jeep made its way slowly through the hostile crowd. Someone hurled a rock and a small trickle of blood appeared under the woman's left eye. She let out a muffled cry and Tadzik tried to comfort her. It was his turn now to apply the scarf. "Keep calm, *Liebchen*." He drew her head down toward him. "*Danke*." She whispered softly and kissed his hand quickly.

"Are you okay, Tadziu?" I asked.

"Very well indeed." He winked.

Their injuries were attended by the medics at the Headquarters dispensary. The G.I. driver excused himself with a meaningful wink toward us.

"My name's Greta." The redhead introduced herself. She offered me her hand. I hesitated. "My hand is clean. I'm not a whore." She blushed violently. "That's not what I was thinking about," I lied embarrassed. "See you tonight, Tadziu?" I asked as I turned to go. I remembered Misha. "Tadzik Bosiacki," my friend introduced himself as he walked on with his arm round the woman's waist.

"See you tonight, Tadziu?" I called after him again.

"Don't wait up for me!" Tadzik responded from a distance.

"It's been days. Where the hell have you been?" I asked concerned. Tadzik grinned at me.

"I was with Greta. She insisted I stay at her place to rest up."

"To rest?" I laughed. "You should see yourself in the mirror!" Tadzik looked like a wreck.

"Go on, laugh all you want." Tadzik glanced at the floor. "I've never been alone with a woman before."

"You don't owe me an explanation," I said.

"It's an old house. The bombs didn't destroy it completely. Greta's mother lives with her. You've got to come out, she said."

"I don't know."

"You'll sleep on fresh linen, I promise."

"It's tempting."

"Say yes."

"It's time to move on, isn't it?" I asked.

"Not for me, Vilek. Not yet."

I looked at my friend. I knew there was no use in arguing. "What the hell, we couldn't stay together forever, could we?" I said shrugging my shoulders.

"Come on. Don't take it this way."

"I've got to be on my way. I have a feeling that my father's waiting in Wiesbaden. You'll write, won't you?" My eyes were becoming moist and I turned away.

"Let's go to Greta's and have a celebration," Tadzik pleaded. Reluctantly, I nodded agreement. "O.K.," I said. An hour later we arrived.

"We'll uncork the best bottle of *Rüdesheimer* for our guest!" Greta breathed deeply with excitement.

"*Liebchen*, why don't you ask your mother to join us?" Tadzik suggested. "I'm sure she'd want to meet my old friend."

"Let's not disturb her. The war, you know?" Greta pointed to her head. "It left her very bitter." She poured wine into glasses. "Papa will be tried soon. He was pretty high up among the Nazis, a real big shot, as they say, a *Bonze*. Mama's bitter. She says papa did his duty, that's all. Now they treat him like a common criminal. Mama says she expected this kind of treatment from the *Russkys*, not from the *Amis*. Papa gave himself up to the *Amis* because he trusted them. Now mama hates the Amis because they betrayed us. That's why I won't let her out of my sight. She's sure to cause trouble," Greta explained.

Toward midnight Greta's mother, Frau von Lutzow entered the room. She had scarcely glanced in my direction, seating herself at the table while Greta poured her a drink. "Don't expect sympathy, young man," she said without taking her eyes off her glass. "We didn't know what went on in the concentration camps."

I was silent. My eyes met Tadzik's. Greta was worried. Frau von Lutzow became talkative under the influence of the Rüdesheimer. "Nothing has changed, nothing, I tell you!" She shouted. "Everything is now as it was with the Führer. Only the names are different. We Germans fear change! We fight change! Pure Aryan blood flows in our veins, you know!"

"*Mutti*. . . don't talk like that, please. . . mama. . . It's not good for you to get excited. Call it a night, yes? You've had enough, mutti." The old woman ignored her daughter. She went on.

"Maybe I'm wrong!" *Frau* von Lutzow shouted in her shrill, staccato tone. "Maybe one thing did change. The young have no respect for the old. Now they tell us what to do!" She was approaching hysteria. "Just look at her! This is my daughter, you're nothing but a piece of trash." She turned toward Greta. "You cheap whore. You trashy bitch! So this is what you've been up to. I try to keep the honor of the von Lutzow name, do things becoming an Aryan aristocrat—then here I find you! Fucking a Slav! Associating with a . . .with a. . . *Untermensch*! A non-person!"

Her lips kept moving though no further sound came out. She was trembling violently. Suddenly, she rose from the table and slapped Greta across the cheek. Tadzik placed himself between the women to absorb the second slap. Greta's eyes filled with tears.

"It wasn't respect, mother. It was fear that made us do things we hated to do." Now, the daughter shouted. "Fear of you and your *Führer*. You told us to die for the fatherland! Now we want to live and we don't intend to die for anyone!"

I looked at the two women. "My mother is dead," I thought, "and this witch is alive and well." *Frau* von Lutzow found her voice again.

"It's your way to defy tradition, to mock me, to spite me, you're in bed with this. . . this. . . animal, letting him defile someone of pure German stock.. . just to shame me. . . your mother who goes on slaving for you. . ."

"Mama, please." Greta begged tearfully.

"Don't ever call me 'mother' again. You should be killed for committing *Rassenschande*. I should have had a son. He would have given his mother respect. German daughters are all whores."

"Where would I be if I were a man?" Greta challenged. "I'll tell you where I'd be. I'd be where most of our young men are today: in Soviet labor camps or buried under foreign soil."

"I'd rather see you dead than whoring with an enemy of the Reich. The only wrong the *Führer* did was not to win the war. You hear? That's the *only* wrong he did!" Her mother was shouting again. "Do you see those holes up there?" She pointed at shrapnel holes in the ceiling. "We will repair everything else, but the holes will stay!" Suddenly, she let out a mad chuckle. "We'll leave those ugly holes there to remind us of the *Amis* and the Communist Jews."

I got up from the table. "If I stay, I'll kill the old bitch. I'd better leave now, Tadziu. Goodbye." We embraced. "You'll write, won't you?"

"Goodbye, my friend."

I closed the door behind me, and I fled into the open. The Nazis had obviously outlived Hitler. It was a clear night and the snow was fresh and crisp under my feet. I spotted a shooting star leaving a brilliant trail. It was time to get on with my life.

That night, I lay awake in my tiny quarters at the refugee center. I thought of a plan to cross into the British Zone. Once again, I found myself surrounded by Soviet sentries; Berlin was situated inside the Russian sector, and free travel across was severely restricted. Late that morning, I went to talk to one of the smugglers. The man laughed uproariously when I told him that I had no money.

"American dollars!" The man slapped his thigh. "If you want to come along, American money will get you across the border!"

The next party to leave for the border was scheduled for the following morning before dawn. I was desperate. "If you won't take me along, I'll follow you anyway." I said to the man. "I'm getting out, and I don't care how I'll do it."

"Suit yourself, punk. I don't run a charity."

That evening, at the cafeteria, I spotted a man sitting at the far end of the hall. I carried my tray toward his table. On coming closer, I recognized the familiar features.

"Jossele Barnblatt!" I exclaimed.

"Velvele!" He clasped my hand.

"What in hell. . .?" I looked at my old friend quizzically.

"Don't ask, Vilek, don't ask."

"But. . . weren't you in. . .?"

"Palestine. . .? Yes, I was." He paused. "But that's another story. Now, I'm on my way to Poland."

"To stay?" I was surprised.

"To search. There must be someone there."

"I've just returned from there, Yossele. There's no one left in Piotrkow." I took a deep breath. "Except, the Goyim, that is."

"Still, I want to see for myself," he insisted.

"It's tough getting out, Yossele."

"I know. I've heard." He looked at the floor.

"How's Roman? Have you seen him?" I asked anxiously.

"He's okay. So's your father."

"Father!?"

"Yes, he was here in Berlin with the Soviets, deserted and found Roman in Wiesbaden. Been waiting for your return ever since."

I trembled, tears filling my eyes. "That's wonderful. . . wonderful," was all I was able to whisper.

"Hurry up and get going, will you?" Yossele urged, smiling happily.

"I'm leaving in the morning."

"So am I, Vilek." Yossele smiled again. "Hope to see you soon."

"Have a safe trip, my friend." We hugged.

I was excited. I lay awake all night, and I was resolved to depart when morning came.

I would not ask my friend how my father was, what he was like. I wanted to see for myself. Soon, I would be with him.

The refugees gathered at dawn. They talked in hushed voices, afraid the woods might carry the sound. There were two large Army tracks ready for loading. From a distance, I recognized the guide's voice. "Get inside, all of you, quickly!"

I waited in hiding and watched the people climb obediently into the tracks: twenty persons into each.

The leader signaled the driver of the first vehicle to move out.

He, himself, took the wheel of the second. I ran breathlessly after the two vehicles. I managed to grab the tailgate of the second truck and climbed aboard. I looked at the twenty occupants who had paid 100 American dollars each. "You betray me, and I'll yell so loud the border sentries will come running," I hissed, out of breath. No one said a word. I climbed in and settled in the corner. The truck rattled along for hours. By nightfall, we reached Halberstadt, the border town of the British Zone.

There was a full moon. The guide ordered the huddled fugitives off the tracks. I had jumped off before and was now watching the proceedings from behind a nearby bush. The forty men and women carrying their belongings in small bundles, ran toward the safety of the dark woods and huddled nearby. The full moon was their enemy.

"West of here, about three kilometers is the British Zone," the guide whispered. "I'll be back in a few minutes to take you across. Wait here, and don't make a sound."

I wished I could have joined the others, and I was trembling with loneliness and fear. I felt like the last man alive on earth.

The full moon, beautiful and treacherous, continued shining relentlessly. I was able to hear the frightened whispers of the fugitives, waiting for theirguide to take them to freedom.

The minutes seemed like hours.

Finally, I heard a muffled voice. "Let's not just stand here like idiots. We must get going. Can't you see we've been betrayed?"—"No," another voice was pleading anxiously. "Give him a few more minutes. Maybe he's in trouble?"—"It's taking him too long," the first voice said resolutely. "We've got to move. It'll be daylight soon."—This final argument was convincing. All of them picked up their belongings and, shadow-like, emerged from the woods into the open. I, too, came out from behind my bush and followed at a safe distance.

Suddenly there was shouting and cursing in Russian. Sentries had appeared as if from nowhere. I counted six in all. Shepherd dogs were growling menacingly at the cowering victims. Shots echoed into the night. The violent noise was deafening. I crouched down in the underbrush as cries of agony filled the silence. Between the salvos, the wind carried sounds of prayer and death. And then, all I heard was the barking of the dogs and their masters' brutal voices fueling the animal rage.

The sentries marched the captives off into the woods leaving me alone in the night. I lay still for a long time, trembling, afraid to breathe, fearful that the dogs might catch my scent carried toward them by the wind.

I've got to get going, I thought to myself. I rose cautiously, like the hunted animal, ready to blend into the protective darkness of the woods at the slightest danger. In the distance I saw a farmhouse, a thin wisp of smoke curling up from the chimney. I ran, my lungs aching and gasping for breath. Perhaps this farmhouse was my deliverance.

I collapsed at the doorstep. The door opened a crack and a woman's voice spoke in German.

"British Zone?" I managed to pant.

She smiled. "*Ja. Ja. Die Britische Zone.*" I was free now, really free. I had reached a farmhouse inside the British Zone, and I felt safe. The farmer and his wife were generous people and spared me nothing.

31

Compared with the crossing of Poland and East Germany, the journey across the British Zone was uneventful. Hitching rides on military vehicles, trucks making deliveries to markets, and on empty freight trains, I traveled from Berlin to Wiesbaden, some 330 kms., in three days' time. I ran the distance from the railway station to our apartment on the Kaiser Friedrich Ring, hoping that all was well; that my father and Roman were there to welcome me.

"Vilek!"

"Roman!"

We hugged each other. "God! I thought you'd never come back!" Roman exclaimed.

"You weren't the only one."

"He's in the kitchen, eating supper." "He" was the way we referred to our father.

"How is he? Is he expecting me? Is he okay?"

"He's been asking for you every day. He's okay. A little deaf, but okay."

"Is there anything I should know?" I studied Roman's face. He lowered his eyes.

"No. . .well. . .yes. . .he's been through his own private hell. Go inside and be kind to him."

"Come with me. Please." I begged.

"I'd rather let you do this by yourself, little brother. It's better this way. Go now. He's been waiting a long time for this day."

My father sat at the table eating. His back was turned and the bright tiffany lamp shone upon his thick gray hair. I would have recognized him anywhere by the slightly hunched back, a clear giveaway of the tailor's trade. God, how old he had become! I swallowed hard because of a sudden dryness in my throat. What could I say? What *should* I say?

My father turned around. Our eyes met for a moment and then he turned back to his supper. I was a total stranger to him. I wanted to run and hide from the pain of this reunion, to weep for the irretrievable, lost years. Then, I felt Roman's hand touching my shoulder. "Don't go, Vilusiek, he'll come around. You must look at him when you talk, else he won't hear you." My brother was whispering. I wondered why.

I stepped in front of my father. He looked up at me, with renewed interest. "Father, it's me, Vilek, your son," I said softly as if trying to justify my presence before my unsuspecting father. "It's me, your son," I repeated, since there was no reaction.

"Velvele!" My father rose with outstretched arms calling me by my Yiddish name.

"Father!" We embraced and kissed each other on both cheeks. I swallowed the saltiness of my father's tears when my lips touched the hollow cheeks. I was still weeping and I felt the weight of my father's body in my arms. I helped him back into the chair, and knelt next to him, trying to embrace him and to stroke his head. My father was sobbing convulsively, his entire body shaking. Finally, he stopped. He wiped his tears away, apparently embarrassed by his behavior. His shoulders stooped, he looked at me searchingly.

"You have grown."

"Yes, father."

"How old are you now?"

"Don't you remember?"

"Well, yes. I think you're seventeen."

"More like eighteen, father. More like eighteen-and-a-half to be exact."

"Has it been that long?"

"Over seven years, father."

"Has it been that long?" He repeated the question incredulously.

"I've been shaving for over five months now, father."

"Yes, yes, I can see that, my son. And I've heard many good things about you, Velvele. I'm proud of the things I've been told."

"Have you met my teacher? My friends? The *rebbe*?" I asked anxiously.

"Indeed I have. They've made me feel at home."

"I'm glad, father. They're good people."

We talked into the early morning hours; father and son trying to pretend that all was well, waiting as long as possible with questions that ultimately had to be asked and hoping against hope that the answers would come without too much pain and anguish.

There was a new family in town. Though I couldn't believe that any Jew would voluntarily return to live in Germany, I met the newcomers— save *Herr* Tiegel who stayed home with a cold—at a social gathering, a sort of welcoming party for me.

The Tiegels, Werner and Luti, had recently returned from their self-imposed exile in Bern, Switzerland with their two grown children Heinz and Rita. Werner was a man of slight build and medium height, in his fifties perhaps, with thinning white hair and deep blue eyes. He wore a goatee and steel-rimmed glasses.

Luti, short for Luitigarde, in her late forties, appeared fragile and thin-boned, with light tanned skin on her face and hands. Her dark-brown eyes were sad, surrounded by dark shadows.

Rita, a vivacious brunette of eighteen had inherited her father's blue eyes. She had no memories of Wiesbaden which the family had left fifteen years ago. She seemed to be the only one in the family who was capable of laughter.

Heinz, twenty-one, was a loner.

I felt immediately attracted to Rita. Her happy disposition was a welcome change from the experience of the recent past. Moreover, young Jewish women were scarce. Eighteen-year-olds, unaffected by the war, were non-existent.

I wasn't at all surprised to see Hannah present at the party. She was, after all, the *rebbitzin*, expected to accompany the *rebbe* to most community functions.

To my annoyance, she drew me aside, away from Rita. "It's four months now. Here, feel it." She took my hand in hers and placed it on her belly. To my horror, I felt a slight movement. Dear God, I prayed silently, let it be Abraham's not mine. "Abraham happy?" I asked innocently.

Hannah didn't reply. Instead, she smiled ambiguously.

"He knows nothing?" I pressed.

"Absolutely not, *Liebchen*." She winked and squeezed my arm.

"He must never know. Do you understand? Never!" I was perspiring with a new anxiety. Greatly upset, I walked off to join Rita.

"Are you ready to call it a night?" I asked.

"Will you walk me home?" She smiled.

"You want me to?" I was overjoyed.

"I wouldn't ask if I didn't."

She picked up her coat and I helped her get into it. In the process, my right hand brushed her breast. She didn't object. We walked down the deserted street, holding hands in silence. The snow had almost melted and there were large puddles on the pavement, heralding the approaching fall. Happily, I guided her through the puddles. Gradually, I grew bolder.

"There, look! A falling star!" I whispered, holding her close.

"Did you make a wish?" She asked quickly.

"I've quit making wishes long ago." I said.

"But you mustn't. You mustn't ever stop dreaming, Vilus." She called me by the diminutive of my name, and I wondered where she had learned it. I looked at her again. She was beautiful. Suddenly she smiled. Apparently, she had sensed my admiration.

Herr Tiegel's voice greeted us at the threshold. "Is that you, baby?"

"It's me, daddy. Go back to sleep!—Wish he wouldn't treat me like his baby anymore." She sounded angry.

"We'll always be children to our parents," I said, soothingly. I, too, was annoyed at the intrusion. Yet I was pleased with her displeasure.

Inside the house, we sat next to each other, on the couch. The old man, mercifully, had gone upstairs to bed. Rita snuggled up to me. There was urgency in her voice.

"Could you love me?" She whispered suddenly. "Could you love me just a little?"

"I wish I could say yes, Rita," I said sadly without looking at her. "I really don't know if I'm capable of loving."

"I'm glad you won't lie."

"Please don't misunderstand. You're a wonderful woman. Any man ought to feel fortunate to have your love. Only, I'm not sure I know what love is any longer." Searching for the right words, I realized with horror that I still was not free of Devorah. She was silent, breathing heavily.

"Go now," she said suddenly. There was a quality in her voice I had not heard before. There were tears in her eyes. I reached for her hand, trying to explain: it was still too early for me. The pain of memory was still too strong. It was of no use. "Go," she repeated.

I walked out into the bustle of the Kaiser Friedrich Ring. Soon, imported Dutch tulips would appear in the flower beds and children's playgrounds would be filled with carefree shouts and laughter. I wondered how I could explain to someone of Rita's innocence the terrible void left by the absence of my little sister Felusia and the countless other Felusias murdered by the Third Reich.

Things weren't sitting well with my father; I tried to probe, but I was unable to identify the problem.

He kept to himself most of the time. Gradually, he took to drinking heavily, occasionally muttering under his breath words no one was able to understand. They were obviously meant for himself alone.

There was a time when my father was strong. In my youthful adulation, there was nothing my father couldn't accomplish; no wisdom he didn't possess. He was the ultimate authority in family matters, but he governed with love and understanding. In return, I played my violin for him. The War changed all that.

Throughout the War years, a time of serious problems, I was in desperate need of his support. In his absence, I had built him up to greater than life proportions. I grudgingly justified that absence. Soon, I fantasized, he would return and rescue me, not unlike the sleeper hero coming to the aid of those distressed.

As the years went by, my father's image grew in proportion to my longing
for him. As I grew old and shed the mantle of innocence, only the hope of
a distant reunion remained. Not much else was left.

When I had finally found my father (or was it he who found me), he was
only a shadow of the man I once knew and venerated; a fraction of the
person I had created in my imagination. He had grown distant and disagree-
able. He now lacked understanding and strength. Only his eyes still carried
the fire of vengeance, though his heart beat the rhythm of Jewish compassion: *rachmones.*

He found an old Newsweek article while going through my dresser drawer.

Attracted by a group photo of some emaciated Evansee concentration
camp survivors, my father asked for a translation of the text accompanying
the picture. Though reluctantly, I explained with the little English I knew,
improvising wherever necessary.

THE UNITED STATES OF AMERICA, THE FRENCH REPUBLIC, THE UNITED KINGDOM
OF GREAT BRITAIN AND NORTHERN IRELAND, AND THE UNION OF THE SOVIET
SOCIALIST REPUBLICS AGAINST HERMANN WILHELM GOERING, RUDOLF HESS,
JOACHIM VON RIBBENTROP. . .

So began the title of the briefs at Nuremberg for the trial of war criminals, enumerating all of the names of the accused. The international war-
crimes tribunal wrote a new chapter in international law as it opened the
case of the Allies versus the archcriminals of Germany. The accused were
charged with four crimes, of which one count interested my father in particular:

CRIMES AGAINST HUMANITY constituted the last count, unique in legal
history. Denying the right of the German leaders to abuse their own
people, it branded them criminals for persecuting and murdering their
minority groups, especially Jews; for persecuting on political, racial and
religious grounds within Germany; and for the singling out of individual
opponents for imprisonment and murder. . .
Newsweek, October 29, 1945

"There's no justice! There's only vengeance!" Ten months after the
Nuremberg Trials had begun, my father broke his brooding silence. I welcomed his anger as a sign that the period of melancholy had ended.
Nuremberg was a great disappointment to all of us, but my father took the
defeat harder than I had expected. Even the news of my recent admission to
the University of Heidelberg failed to cheer him.

"We've been betrayed by everyone! I want you to remember that! You
must avenge your mother! Swear to me on her soul of blessed memory that
you'll never forget, never forgive!"

"We cannot go on fighting the world forever," I tried to reason.

"Then you must prepare. You must study. Become a learned man, a doctor, and use your knowledge to punish the traitors!"

"Why do you want me to spend the rest of my life fighting, father? Haven't I fought enough already?" I asked.

"As long as any of them are free, we cannot rest! The Nazis must pay!" My father yelled. "Nuremberg was only the tip of the iceberg. It's never finished while the assassins live!"

I listened in silence, knowing that to argue was useless.

"Can't you understand?" My father shouted perplexed. His eyes focused on my lips. "Did you say something?" He repeated. Only then did I realize that my father didn't hear me at all. His hearing problem must have increased in severity, but he was too vain to admit it.

"I said, I didn't want to study medicine, father."

"Is that what you said?"

"It's no use, father. I'm not made for it." I spoke slowly, painfully, studying my father's face.

"How do you know you're not suited to be a doctor if you haven't even tried?" My father insisted stubbornly.

"I just know, father. It takes a special person to practice medicine. I'm not that special person."

What are you talking about? A special person? Not suited?" He mimicked me. "You give up before you try. Is that the right way for a son of mine?"

"I'm sorry you're taking it that way, father."

"Which is the way I should take it? Tell me, which way? You are an educated son, and you seem to know things better than I do, so tell me! I should maybe let you waste your life away? Should I?"

"Is there no other respectable profession for me, father?"

"For you, there isn't."

"Why, father?"

"Because I want you to make a good living. Is it wrong if I want you to be a successs?" He was on the verge of a breakdown. I didn't know what else to say. To my father, the medical profession offered a high degree of material security as well as prestige.

"When a doctor talks, everybody respects what he's got to say," my father added, strengthening his argument.

"I'll do my best, father," I said on a sudden impulse. "I'll be in Heidelberg for the coming semester." My father beamed, having gotten his way.

I felt the urge to share the evening with Rita. I hastily washed the supper dishes, dried them, and put them away on the shelf. Then, I wiped the table and swept the floor. I wasn't sure about fulfilling my promises to father, but I was pleased about making him happy. At least for the moment.

Rita was glad to see me. *Herr* Tiegel was in the middle of a heated argument with his son, and Rita thanked me for coming to her rescue. We left quickly, as I was anxious to share with her the news about Heidelberg, my dreams about the future, and inquire about hers. We talked late into the night, and I felt a great closeness toward her when we said goodbye at the door.

I returned home to find my father in a black mood. On the kitchen table before him lay several parts of a luger pistol he had recently purchased. He was cleaning and oiling each part meticulously as Roman watched.

"Why the gun, father? Why are you cleaning it?" My father looked up at me. I turned to Roman. "Why the gun?" I repeated. "What's he doing that for?"

"He didn't tell me." Roman shrugged his shoulders. "He seldom talks to me nowadays since we don't agree on his plans for my future."

"About what?" I asked.

"He wants me to be more like you." Roman grinned.

"Like me?" I was astonished.

"Yes. Like you. A scholar." Roman chuckled.

"He wants me to be a doctor."

"He thinks you're a brain." There was another prolonged chuckle.

"So why can't you go along with him." I urged.

"I've never been good at it. It's too late to learn now." He replied sadly.

"What made him angry?" I asked.

"I told him that I was going to join the Army as soon as we get to the States."

"What did he say?"

"He didn't say anything. He slapped me twice."

"Damn!"

Roman suddenly looked depressed. "Hasn't spoken a word since."

"Oh, God!"

"Let's not talk about it anymore."

Suddenly, my father rose from his chair. He hadn't heard a word of our conversation. "We've got to kill the Nazi bastard!" He spoke into the air. "I won't rest till he's dead!"

I faced my father. "Tell us about it, father. Please, sit down and let's talk. This can get us all into big trouble."

"I saw him this morning at the entrance to the Military Police Headquarters! It was him! I never forget a face! It was Gestapo Chief Galfe! The same scarred face, the same arrogant eyes! I tell you he was at the NKVD training center at Kutchinsk!"

"Who is this Galfe?" I asked.

"Who is Galfe, he asks? The bastard is a Soviet agent!" My father shouted again. "Kutchinsk is only one of many camps where they are trained. Most of the former Gestapo and SS officers are trained by the Soviets for fifth column work. When they're ready, a clever escape into the West Zone is improvised, with all the trimmings. They're even pursued and shot at by the border guards. Some are sacrificed to make it look real. The rest is simple."

"Nobody'll believe it."

"Here he is, working at the M.P. Headquarters, with access to classified information. He's a spy. It's as simple as that. Part of the NKVD network. Believe me, I know what I'm talking about." My father trembled with excitement. "The Kremlin plays its game. The assassins have their assignments."

"But the Soviets are allied with the Americans." Roman dared to interject.

"The Soviets are nobody's allies. They're all thieves, *ganeveem*. He emphasized with the Jewish equivalent. They want you to think they're your friends before they steal your guts. That's why it works for them. Because nobody'll believe it. The police are in control in the Soviet Union. At first it was the *Cheka*, then they called it the GPU, now it's the NKVD. The czarist *Okhrana* was a kindergarten compared to the professionals of today."

"Okay, father, calm down. We'll go see Major Weinberg," I suggested. "It's his Headquarters, after all. He ought to know about it."

Major Weinberg was in a jovial mood. He was leaving Germany soon, and he was in the middle of marking boxes for shipment to the States. The anticipation of seeing his bride had infused him with renewed vigor. He smiled to himself as he marked one of the boxes "Malke." "You know what's in there?" He asked us. "It's a set of Meissen china. It was a bargain, and I couldn't resist it. My Malke will be ecstatic over it."

I smiled. I couldn't understand why this American placed any value at all on such things as dishes. "We have some important news for you, Major. Of grave concern," I said calmly.

"Okay. What is it? I'm busy." The Major continued his activity.

"I'll give you exactly five minutes. They're picking up the boxes in three hours and I've got a million things to pack."

"It won't take but a moment of your time, Major."

"Okay. . . I'm listening."

"You have a former Gestapo chief working for you, Major!" My father exclaimed in Yiddish, unable to contain his anger. "His name's Bruno Galfe, and he's a Soviet spy!"

"Father. . . please."

"One hundred percent sure, Major." My father pressed on.

"That's very unusual, to say the least," the Major mused. "Our people are thoroughly screened before they're hired."

"I saw him at the M.P. Headquarters. The same man. Has an ugly scar on his right cheek. I'd recognize that man among a million. He was at the NKVD training center in Kutchinsk when I was a prisoner there. He's an assassin! He belongs on the gallows!" My father shouted again.

"Calm yourself, Henryk." The Major scrutinized my father not without compassion. "This is a serious charge. We've got laws to take care of matters such as these. How can you be so sure?"

"You can investigate. I'm telling the truth." My father asserted.

"Okay. The man was at Kutchinsk. So? He could've been a prisoner like yourself. Couldn't he?"

"He's a Nazi, and I'm a Jew."

"You're a Jew, I know, Henryk. Do you think that being a Jew places you above suspicion?"

The Major's line of reasoning was taking its toll on my father's already tattered nerves. "The bastard's an assassin! I tell you he is!" My father yelled.

"I'm sure he was thoroughly investigated before being hired. Besides, you wouldn't want a man put in jail just because he resembles some criminal you knew. Would you?" The Major reasoned.

My father regarded the Major, with incredulity. I knew this was the wrong time to argue with the Major, but I was cut short again by my father.

"I know he's the same man, Major, but you don't believe me. You think I'm mad or making up the whole story." My father was suddenly calm. "Well, believe what you want, Major. We'll find another way."

"Come to think of it," the Major recalled, "I received word from the document center. Your Displaced Persons application for immigration to the States has been processed. From now on it's only a formality, I'm sure. You'd all better get ready for the journey."

"Are you sure, Major? It has been processed already?" Roman asked.

"You'll be leaving shortly." The Major smiled. "And leave all those spy stories to the professionals." He was busy marking cartons again. "Things like that can only cause you trouble."

"Sorry we disturbed you, Major." I apologized. "Thanks for the good news."

Back on the street, my father didn't seem the least bit cheerful.

"You don't have to worry about anything," he repeated stubbornly. "I'll take care of it myself."

That night my father insisted on taking a walk. His pistol was in his raincoat pocket. Roman and I looked at each other. "We'd better keep him company." I said.

Rain was falling torrentially. Huge puddles of muddy water were forming on the sidewalks. The streets were deserted, save an occasional M.P. patrol or military vehicle.

We waded through the puddles, past the *Zietenring* and the school from which I graduated, it seemed an eternity ago.

"We have to surprise him," my father muttered. "Before dawn is the soundest sleep. He will offer the least resistance." I listened, terrified. Only a few short months ago, I would have welcomed the idea of killing a German with great enthusiasm; it mattered little whether he was a Nazi or not. Now, however, flanked by my father and my brother, I was worried that there might yet be another murder.

My father played with the luger in his coat pocket. I studied his face. Apparently, the weapon gave him courage. He needs a victory,

I thought; even a small one, but a victory. There had been too many defeats in his life, laced with more than his share of grief. "No one has a monopoly on grief," I thought to myself, "as no one does on joy."

My father was adamant. He knew what he wanted and no amount of reasoning was going to dissuade him. "The killer must pay . . . he must die a worse death than those he murdered . . ." He kept muttering under his breath. To my dismay, Roman nodded in agreement. In him, father found an accomplice. Failure was their common bond. The present venture was bringing them closer together than they had been in a long while. The bridge was hatred.

"That idiot Weinberg." My father broke the silence once again. "All he could think of was going home." He paused. "Can you imagine him implying that I could be a spy? Because I rotted in the dungeons of Kutchinsk? Me, a spy? Makes me wonder how in hell the Americans won the war with officers like Weinberg!"

"What do you expect, father," Roman tried to assuage him. "After all, the Major is an American Jew. They don't think the way we do. Try to understand."

My father didn't hear Roman's last remark. He stopped in front of number thirty-seven *Zietenring*. "We're here," he said. "That's where the Nazi lives."

We walked silently up three flights of stairs. Apartment 4B was at the end of the hallway. My father opened the door with a pass key and we entered the vestibule. My eyes pleaded with him in a final effort to dissuade him. He didn't relent. Flashlight in his left hand and the luger in his right, he kept opening door after door until he had found the bedroom.

Galfe was in bed, asleep. "There's a woman, too," Roman whispered. It was too late. Perhaps it was instinct that woke them, or else perhaps it was the flashlight. I touched my father's shoulder.

"We didn't expect a woman, father. Let's get out of here."

"Have you forgotten your mother?" Father hissed. He turned the light on the German's face, and Galfe squinted helplessly. He was still groggy with sleep.

The woman awoke with a start, sitting up in bed. She was in her mid-thirties and looked rather pretty. My God, I thought: we have to kill both of them.

"Not a sound out of you, Nazi, or I'll take your head off!" My father pointed the gun at the German. "You ought to know how it's done, *Herr* Gestapo *Chef* Galfe. You shot people often enough, didn't you?" My father pronounced the man's name slowly, emphatically. "There must be some mistake." The man's voice trembled. "Tell them our name, Tradi." He addressed the woman. "Tell them who we are, dear."

"This is my husband, Gustav Fritzke, and my name's Trudi." The woman sounded almost formal. Her voice had the quality of innocence. My father burst out laughing. "We're pleased to meet you both." He said cynically.

"Take what you wish and leave." The man pleaded and his voice shook. "You'll find money on the dresser drawer. My wife's jewelry is in the small chest next to our family picture on the dresser. Take it and go."

"For a condemned Nazi, he sounds awfully confident, don't you think?" Roman grinned.

"Maybe he isn't the one we're after." I dared to suggest.

"Can't you see they want to put doubt in your minds?" My father spoke calmly. "We're not ordinary thieves. What do you take us for? You goddamned Nazis have some nerve." He addressed the couple. "You've always been a bunch of clever sons-of-bitches," he used the German word *Schweinehunde*. "We came to try you, swine, for all the misery and death you caused." He cocked his pistol and pointed it at the head of the trembling German. There was a pause and only labored breathing could be heard. But my father didn't pull the trigger. Perhaps, I hoped he had changed his mind. The woman was sobbing hysterically, and the man's voice pleading for his life, had become shrill and plaintive.

Roman turned toward my father. "Well? What are you waiting for? Shoot, and let's get the hell out of here!" He urged.

"My husband is telling the truth. He's never been out of Germany. He's a cripple. One leg's shorter than the other." The woman wailed. "Show them, Schatzi." She implored her husband. "Get out of bed and show them," she cried.

"Father." I touched my father's shoulder again. "Let's get out of here."

"Get out of bed, Nazi!" My father barked. The German complied clumsily. "Walk!" The man limped a few steps. The woman pleaded desperately as the man knelt in front of my father's pistol begging: "Please. . .there are two small children in the other room. . . Hans is three and Monika two years old . . .I never heard the name Galfe before. . . I swear."

"Admit it! You're Gestapo Chief Galfe!" My father shouted at the top of his voice.

"My name's Gustav Fritzke," the man repeated.

"You were trained in Kutchinsk. It's clever the way they trained you to walk with a limp. But you don't fool me one bit!"

"Either we finish him off or we leave, father." Roman was growing impatient. "We can't spend the night arguing."

"I swear, I've never been in the Soviet Union. This is all a terrible mistake." The man was on his knees.

Large beads of sweat had appeared on my father's forehead. "What if he's telling the truth, after all." Roman whispered to me.

"Show your underarm!" My father ordered the kneeling man. The man took off the nightshirt and extended his arm obediently. My father shone his flashlight on the man's underarm. There was no telltale tattoo common to SS and Gestapo agents nor was there any indication of surgical removal. My father examined the skin carefully. Then, he shook his head. His face ashen, he turned toward me. "Goddamn it, he's clean," he said.

We walked home in silence. I was the first to talk. "You may have made a mistake, father." I looked at the old man's face. "We did the right thing leaving as we did."

"They made fools of us once more, Velvele." He shook his head, still unbelieving. "They're specialists in deceit. He's the one, I'm sure." "But what if you're wrong, father?" Asked Roman.

"I'm not wrong. My only mistake was to take the two of you along. You're too soft. And what if they go to the police?"

"Don't worry, father. They haven't seen any of us in the glare." I assured him.

"I can see him rolling on the floor with laughter," my father said gloomily.

"After all, father, we're not assassins of women and children," I said.

"We're sentimental people. There's too much pity in us Jews. We have to learn to be less sentimental, less merciful with our enemies or we'll not survive," my father insisted.

"Don't worry, father. What I've seen in Palestine will surely survive," Roman said. "The only sentiment those pioneers feel is for the land they cherish more than their own lives. No man on earth will wrest it from them, I assure you."

"Besides, think of it father. We could have killed an innocent man," I added.

"Never! Do you hear? Never will there be an innocent German! They all have bloody hands, and the guilt of this generation will visit them for a thousand years!" It began to rain torrentially again, and my father shouted his curses into the howling wind, while we plodded once more through the puddles. I looked at my father again, shivering: a total stranger.

"It seems only yesterday, my dear William, we said goodbye when you were on your way to Poland." Paula paused for a moment. "And here you are leaving again, for better things, I hope." The day I had told her of my intention to emigrate to the United States, Paula took it upon herself to address me by my new name "William." "In America, Willi translates into William," she told me. "The sooner you'll get used to it, the better."

So it happened that I became William to please Paula, and was about to leave for the University of Heidelberg to pursue the study of medicine in order to please my father.

"Is anything wrong?" Asked Paula, taking both my hands in hers.

"Is there something you're not telling me?"

"I. . . I don't really think the medical profession is for me, Paula," I said.

"You had better decide right now or you'll waste a lot of precious time."

"I promised my father I'd try."

"Then try."

"I'm frightened."

"Everyone's afraid of the unknown."

"It's not that, Paula." I thought for a moment. "It's more like I'm deceiving myself."

"If you feel you are, then you should do something about it. Level with your father."

"I haven't the courage to break it to him. He's set on my becoming a physician."

"The longer you put it off, the more you'll hurt him later. You've got to learn to live your own life. Now's a good time to begin."

"What would you have done in my place?"

"I'm not you, William. But if you ask what I'd do regarding my own father, all you have to do is look around you. Look at me, an old maid, virtually blind, living with the memory of having eased the aging years of my father."

"Do you regret it?"

"Regret? Do I give that impression?" She asked. "I've never regretted anything I've done. Not even having taken you under my wings." She forced a nervous laugh. Yet, I noticed a tear rolling down her cheek.

"Forgive me for asking silly questions, Paula." I put my arm over her shoulder. "I should've known."

"You must always remember me as a cheerful woman, my dear William. Because. . . that's what I am." She added with a smile.

"Your heart tells you to follow your father's bidding. You're a fine young man. Go and do your very best. Who knows?" She kissed me on both cheeks. "And come to visit your Paula soon, will you?"

"Like a criminal returning to the scene of the crime." I chuckled.

Before I left, I tried to make her laugh once more. I did not succeed.

"Abraham's in intensive care. A heart attack, they say." Roman blurted out on my return home.

"What? How did it happen?"

"Nobody knows," Roman said.

The bitch, I thought, she must have told him. I trembled at the thought that I might be the cause of Abraham's anguish. No. She couldn't have. She couldn't be that vindictive.

"Better go see your friend while there's still time." My father suggested.

"You're right," I said. Leaving the soup on the table untouched, I turned around and ran all the way to the hospital.

"Your friend is very weak," the head nurse said. "You may see him only for a few minutes. No longer than ten."

Abraham lay motionless under the sheet. He opened his eyes when I touched his hand. A fleeting smile passed over his emaciated features. "I'm happy to see you, Vilek." He whispered. "Come, sit close by me." I sat on the edge of the bed and took his hands in mine. Guilt and relief in equal measure swept over me.

"Tell me, what happened?" I asked. "Why haven't you called?"

"Calling you would have accomplished little, my friend." Abraham spoke slowly and with great effort. "These are difficult hours, Vilek. I'm glad you could come." He spoke slowly in a dignified manner. Even now, Abraham sounded very much the *rebbe*.

"Please don't concern yourself with trivialities, Abraham," I said.

"I came because I want you to get well. You've got a lot of living to do, my friend."

"This is no time for deception, Vilus." Abraham tried to grin. Instead he grimaced. "We mustn't pretend. Not now."

"Silly talk, old friend. Remember what you've always told us? We stayed alive because God meant for us to bear witness, didn't we? You can't leave me alone with that responsibility now. Can you?"

"No, Vilus. I know when my time's up. There's nothing for me here. Nothing."

"You mustn't give up, Abraham."

"You've been like a son to me, you know?"

"I know, Abraham, I know," I said. "But you mustn't talk any longer. Doctor's orders. I'll be back tomorrow."

"Tomorrow will be too late. We must talk now. Open the shades, Vilus, it's so dark in here."

It was early morning and the sun shone through the window. The *rebbe* was dying. My eyes filled with tears, as I bent down to hear my friend better. Abraham gasped for breath.

"The other night. . .after *Shabbat* service. . .we had an argument. . .Hannah was mad. . .hysterical. . .she hasn't been herself lately. . ." He stopped and took a deep anguished breath.

"Please, Abraham, not now." I pleaded. "I'll be back."

"There's no time. . .she said. . . the baby. . . my little. . . Isaac. . . she said . . . Isaac. . . was. . . his. . . the Nazi soldier's. . . who came back. . . not mine . . . I. . . I. . ." Abraham began to choke. He coughed spasmodically and clutched his chest, his face contracted painfully.

"Doctor!! Oxygen!!" I yelled into the hallway. "Help!! Someone help us!! My friend's dying!!" I sank to the floor, sobbing convulsively. Nurses ran in. One applied oxygen, the other attempted vainly to get a reading on Abraham's pulse. A young resident doctor ran to Abraham's side, pressing down on his chest with both fists. It was all in vain. Abraham was dead.

I sat quietly staring at Abraham's face. I had seen death before, but not like this one. This one was different. My friend had survived Hitler, only to succumb to a woman.

"He died peacefully." The young doctor put his arm over my shoulder. "We did all we could," the doctor added before saying goodbye.

I took Abraham's hands carefully into my own. They were already cold. I folded them on his chest. Then, I silently recited the kaddish. Finally, I asked the dead man's forgiveness, but I knew that the guilt would stay with me.

I brought Hannah the news. If she had any feelings at all for her dead husband, they didn't show.

"What are you going to do, Hannah?"

"What do you mean?"

"About your future, and your son's?" I asked as gently as I could.

"Oh. . . the kid? He's driving me crazy. The truth is," Hannah continued, "I'm confused; about my own name and about the Jew bastard in the next room. . ."

"What. . .?"

"All I want is to be Trude again. I want to be myself, not some kind of Jewess, a rabbi's widow. Maybe getting rid of the kid will bring me luck. The Tiegels want to adopt him."

"Hannah! I. . ."

"Don't act so shocked, *Schatzi*. I'm not getting any younger. That's the way life is. It'll work out better for everybody this way. I haven't been getting a good night's sleep lately, and neither has Walter, you know." I gasped at her. Her husband hasn't been buried properly and already she was screwing a Nazi, fresh back from Stalingrad.

"So what kind of a future would the kid have around me?" Hannah asked me reproachfully. She noticed my dismay.

"You're his mother."

"But who's the father? Do you know?" Hannah asked with a cynical grimace. My face reddened. I studied the floor, feigning indifference.

She had struck a raw nerve.

Hannah smiled conspiratorially.

"You don't have to worry, Schatzi," she suddenly reassured me.

"There's no chance he's yours."

"But. . .?"

"I'm sure."

"How can you be?"

"There are ways of telling, Willi. And you had better learn about those ways for your own good." As I prepared to leave, I didn't know which emotion was deeper; my shock or my relief. At any rate, I was sure of one thing. Hannah had always remained Trude.

I enrolled in the Heidelberg Medical School in September, 1946. It was already unusually cold. Each morning, I rose before daylight and went to sleep past midnight. I took my task seriously. No one was going to say that I didn't try.

My father was pleased to see me so earnestly trying to become a useful member of society. Each passing month, my father asked the same old question: "When are you going to be a doctor?" I explained patiently that doctors didn't grow overnight, like weeds: "It'll take patience on both our parts, and a lot of hard work on mine, before I receive my diploma."

Secretly, however, when I had completed my medical assignments, my interest turned to philosophy. Only Paula and I knew that I would not become a doctor. Gradually, I was trading fossils and skeletons for Spinoza, Kant, and Hegel. Most of all, I immersed myself in the works of my philosophy teacher at Heidelberg, Karl Jaspers.

I became one of the many hundreds who had filled the auditorium, called the *Aula*, to capacity each day as Jaspers lectured on philosophy and ethics. I sat fascinated by that old philosopher whose intellect had been banished from Hitler's Third Reich along with thousands of scholars, including half of Heidelberg's faculty. Jaspers, and others like him, I felt, endeavored now to return the basic values and moral foundations of western civilization to their ravaged home. As far as I was concerned , I would do all in my power to nourish the idea of an all-embracing unity of the human race.

I loved Heidelberg. It lay between hills covered with vineyards and forests on the banks of the Neckar river. I roamed the cobblestoned streets, along the *Hauptstrasse*, from the quaint railway station to the *Karlstor,* the famous gate. I walked the old bridge crossing the river, and marveled at its architecture which had carried traffic since 1788.

During the second week of my studies, I realized that medicine was not for me. As was customary, each student was given a cadaver to be dissected. "You'll study the right leg," the Dozent said, as I approached a pool filled with cadavers floating in formaldehyde. Instantly, the sight filled me with grief and horror reminiscent of my recent past. That corpses of Nazi victims are used for medical instruction at German universities was more than I thought possible. Clearly, they brought with them the shame of the past six long years.

Lorries filled to capacity with corpses of ghetto victims. . .inmates resembling skeletons tossed unceremoniously on top of each other in front of the camp barracks. . . *Sonderkommandos* extracting valuables during "mouth and rectal inspections" . . . I stood immobile and terrified, trying to fight off these specters of the past, but the talkative attendant only confirmed my suspicions.

"Don't be shy, young fellow," he joked, "there's enough of them floating here to last us a hundred years or more." He harpooned a decapitated cadaver near the edge and immediately proceeded to saw off the right leg. I retched pathetically. The attendant, ignoring my distress, handed me the severed leg.

"Nothing to worry about, young man," he chuckled, "you'll get over it. Others did." He grinned broadly. "If it weren't for some of your friends, you'd have fallen into the pool and wound up like the others." He pointed to his saw. Retching in the nearby lavatory, I made up my mind. I was finished with medicine before it would finish me.

A few days later, I found a cryptic note in my mailbox. It was scribbled on a small but delicate piece of stationery, lavender in color, its fragrance exuding the familiar scent of violets. I read: "Staying at *Zum Ochsen*. Need an escort. Medium height man, dark and preferably handsome. Pick up at 7:00 p.m. promptly." I smiled happily while inhaling the pleasant smell. I bathed more meticulously than usually, and got myself a quick but elegant haircut.

It was a clear evening when I set out for the hotel. The stars were out. Rita waited for me in the lobby, and I walked quickly toward her. We embraced and I kissed her lightly on the lips. She did not withdraw, and I savored the fragrance of her cologne as much as the taste of her lips.

The town carnival was a show of pageantry. There was much to see and to enjoy. Heidelberg had been spared from the ravages of war and its charm and scenic beauty had largely been preserved. We drank a lot of wine and by midnight it had gone to my head. Arm in arm, laughing and chatting about nothing in particular, we walked along the river bank.

"I want to offer a toast to the most beautiful woman in the entire world!" I exclaimed. Rita giggled. "At this moment," she laughed, "you'd toast a goat."

I was about to propose another toast when a woman approached us. She startled us with her sudden appearance, but she seemed harmless. She wore a colorful scarf which covered her right ear. The other ear was adorned by a huge earring that reached almost to her shoulder and produced a pleasant chime each time she moved her head.

"Won't you come in?" She motioned toward a nearby wagon. "For a few coins I'll tell your past and your future."

Rita looked at me provocatively, a mischievous twinkle in her eyes. Sufficiently emboldened, I accepted the challenge.

"Come inside, and be welcome," said the Gypsy. Just then, it started to rain and we were grateful for the unexpected shelter. Inside, we noticed porcelain pieces, ginger jars and other exotic objects. The wagon was partitioned by a screen which separated the living quarters from the "consultation" room.

"You're a fortune teller?" I asked rhetorically.

"If you wish, you may call me that, young man," the woman said. "I'd prefer if you looked at me as an advisor, a counselor of sorts. Is there anything in particular you'd like to ask?"

"I wouldn't know where to start," I began. "I'd like to know everything, if you don't mind."

"I won't promise everything, but I'll tell you things you know already and things you don't." She smiled and gently took my hand in hers.

"You have beautiful, strong hands. . .strong fingers," the Gypsy said. "The hands of a musician. A violinist, perhaps?" She looked into my eyes. I exchanged a glance with Rita. "But you're no longer playing." The woman continued. "Maybe you should. You may need it now more than ever. The talent is there, it'll always be there." She looked me straight in the eyes again, and I felt as if I were naked. "Another coin, please," she said. I placed a silver coin in her extended palm.

"I see much misery in your past. Much trouble and sadness. There's a little girl. . . her mother. . . both dead at the hands of satanic people." She hesitated. By now, I was stone sober. It was thundering outside. I quickly placed several more coins in her palm. "Go on, please." I entreated her.

"Many people cross your lifeline, some good, many bad." Her voice had become hushed.

"Even now, I can see a force telling you to do one thing while you want to do another." She paused. "There's a conflict here. Beware of that force, young man."

"What shall I do?" I asked almost inaudibly. My voice had begun to tremble.

"I see talent, my young friend. I see much talent and the will to develop it further. You could succeed in almost anything you seriously undertake. Follow your intuition and your heart. Nature does not betray man; it is man who betrays nature." She nodded thoughtfully.

"And what of that other force?" I asked, almost in a whisper.

"Live your own life and let the rest fall into place. You're responsible for your actions to yourself alone." The Gypsy folded my palm. There was compassion in her eyes. The rain had stopped outside.

"Is there anything else?" I asked, reaching into my pocket.

"There's more, of course. Much more. Remember, my young friend," she said almost tenderly, "you've a lot of living ahead of you. Make the best of it. And . . ." she hesitated, "love one another." I produced another coin. "No," said the Gypsy, "that won't be necessary. You've paid me enough." She withdrew her hand and motioned us to go. "Go in peace and make each other happy."

Rita and I walked back to the hotel in silence, holding hands. It was nearly dawn when we entered the lobby.

"Won't you come up?"

"Why. . . uh. . . why?" I looked at her.

"I want to be with you."

"Really?"

"You've got to have more confidence in yourself, Vilek." She sounded serious.

I stammered for lack of words.

"And now you even take to stuttering." She burst out with one of her carefree laughs.

"The hell I have!" I took her into my arms and held her body tightly. I kissed her on the lips and she trembled. I was startled at the surge of passion in my body.

"Vilek! Please, Vilus!" Rita tried to pry herself loose. "Not here! Come up to my room."

We pulled down the window shades. Then we undressed, and stretched out under the covers. I felt Rita's body pressing against my own. "Rita," I whispered, and gave myself up to her completely. Soon only our soft moans broke the stillness of the night.

During my absence, a message had been delivered from my father. "Come immediately," it said. We left for Wiesbaden the following morning. "Don't be so glum," Rita tried to humor me. "I bet it has something to do with going to America." "I hope so," I replied. "Besides, I'm going with you," she added coquettishly.

EPILOGUE

32

"I t's the medical checkup," Roman said quietly, as I burst into the room. "Father's frightened out of his wits."

"Does he have a reason?" I asked.

"He thinks he does. He's got a spot on his lungs. Siberia had a lot to do with it, and the horrible tobacco there did the rest."

"How was he able to serve in the Soviet army?"

"They'd have put a dead man into a uniform in those days. It was tough going for the Russians."

"When's the checkup?"

"Tomorrow afternoon."

"That soon?"

"Does it matter?"

"If we had the time, we could have him checked out by a local doctor." I suggested.

"There's no time. It wouldn't matter anyway. A spot's a spot." Roman shrugged his shoulders resignedly.

My father looked up from his lunch and hugged me. "He's aging rapidly." I thought to myself.

"I won't make it," he said in answer to my unspoken question. "They'll see the spot."

"It must be healed by now, father. I'm sure it is." I said slowly, articulating my lips for emphasis.

"I'm not so sure, *Velvele*." My father's hands trembled and he hid them quickly behind his back. "They told me to quit smoking long ago, but I kept it up anyway."

"But the American tobacco is much cleaner than the crap you used to smoke in Russia." I said soothingly.

"I hope you're right, son," my father said slowly. "If I were a man of religion, I'd sure as hell have reason to pray right now."

"It won't hurt to do it anyhow. God is so busy listening to everybody, you might be taken for somebody else." My father didn't see the humor in my remark.

"One thing I want you to know. If they won't let me go, you and Roman are going regardless, you hear?"

"Let's not make rash decisions, father. We'll see what happens. You worry too much, and it's all for nothing."

"You've got to promise me you'll go without me." My father was getting excited.

"Okay. We promise," Roman said. He was anxious to prevent an argument.

"Then, it's agreed." My father tried to smile, but managed only an awkward grin. "You go first and I'll follow later."

"Agreed."

The following day, we reported for the medical examination. "Don't worry, father," I pleaded in the waiting room. "Things will go okay, you'll see." I put my arm around his bent shoulder.

The examination was long and thorough: from head to toe, every joint and muscle were tested, blood was drawn as well as urine specimens. Then came the dreaded x-ray. It was late in the evening when we were finally released. Results would soon be available, we were told. How long was "soon," nobody knew.

"Did you see the way the x-ray technician looked at me?" My father asked. "I tell you he knew something, he knew."

"Don't be foolish, father. He's like everybody else. He has to wait for the x-ray negatives," Roman said annoyed.

"How long did the doctor take to listen to you when he put that cold metal on your back?"

"They do that routinely to everybody." I said.

"Yes, I know. But how long did he listen to you?" My father insisted.

"Oh. . . about five minutes."

"You see? It's me they're after. The doctor told me to breathe in, and then he told me to breathe out. Again and again the same thing, breathe in, breathe out for over fifteen minutes. Can you tell me why he took so much time with me?"

"We'll just have to wait and find out, father," Roman said resignedly.

"And there's no use getting excited about it while we wait." I added.

"It's my stupid luck, I tell you. I had to get some doctor who's a specialist in lung disorders. That was *bashaert* for me. It was." My father carried on.

"It has little to do with luck, father. Every doctor would approach the problem the same way." I said, lacking conviction.

"I want you to remember if you ever have to do the same, have some *rachmones*. You must be a doctor with compassion." My father reminded me. "What's a little spot on the lung when a whole future depends on it?"

Though experiences had taught us that waiting was as indispensable to life as breathing, the months following the medical examination proved to be an exercise in endurance. Each day at mail delivery, my father held vigil near the mail box hoping that the results of the examination would arrive. Every day, he was laying in wait for the mailman—to the latter's great annoyance—to ask the same question: "Are you absolutely sure there's nothing more for me?"

"Absolutely." Answered the mailman.

"You couldn't have mislaid it?" My father insisted. "It's an official letter. Very important."

"I couldn't have mislaid it."

"Would you look again, please?"

"I've looked twice already. There's nothing else. Here, look for yourself." The mailman grew more impatient with each passing day, but my father did not relent.

On the eleventh day of January, even before my father was able to make the usual inquiry, the mailman approached waving a large manila envelope above his head, a big grin of relief on his face. "Here it is! Your official letter from the Amis!" He called at the top of his voice from a distance.

Overcome with emotion, his hands trembling, my father took the letter from the mailman and held it to his chest. "Well? Isn't this the letter you've been waiting for?" The mailman asked. "Go on! Read it!" My father did not respond, and long after the mailman had left, he stood there, leaning against the doorway, lacking the courage to open the envelope. He kept examining it against the light, as though he had intended to see through the mustard colored surface.

"Father, if I didn't know that you're not a man of religion, I'd say you're praying." I startled him from his reverie.

"Here. Take it," my father said stubbornly. "Read it and tell me what's *bashaert*." He practically threw the envelope at me as we entered the living room. "It arrived?" Asked Roman. "It's really finally here?" He exclaimed excited. "You realize, it's the eleventh day of the month. A lucky day for all of us!"

"You're beginning to sound like father," I remarked. "Keep talking about good luck and bad luck as if there were some sinister forces involved in a medical examination." I glanced at my father whose facial expression was not unlike that of a person anticipating a final judgement.

"Well? What does it say?"

"Nothing definite, father," I paused. "We've been scheduled to see the doctor again the day after tomorrow. Seems like they want to take another look at us."

"What did I tell you?" My father shouted. "I know the way these things work! I know!" He yelled. "It's my goddamned luck! After two months of waiting, they want to take another look?!"

"It's not only you, father. We have to come as well," I said. "You're jumping to conclusions."

"I know what I'm talking about!" My father yelled. "And the doctor is probably an anti-Semite!"

"I've heard he's a Jew," Roman interrupted.

"So much the worse. A Jewish anti-Semite!" My father was implacable.

The examining physician secured my father's x-ray negative against the view-box. He made a detailed examination of the negative, from every possible perspective. Now and then, he muttered under his breath. My father scrutinized the doctor's lips intensely but was unable to understand.

At last, the doctor snapped off the light switch. He turned toward my father, smiling. "The spot's completely healed, my friend," he said slowly. My father's eyes filled with tears. He reached out for the doctor's hand and shook it, not letting go of it for a long time. "Thank-you, doctor. Thank you from the bottom of my heart." He kept repeating himself, weeping. His shoulders were shaking spasmodically. The doctor patted the weeping man gently on his back. "It's all right, my friend. It's all right. Everything's fine now. You can go home and start packing for the trip to America. Good luck to all of you."

My father wiped the tears from his face. But his reddened eyes betrayed him. He smiled, and I knew that his tears, at long last, were tears of joy.

On October 24 came the long-awaited communication from the United States Military Government. It read:

Displaced Persons quota for immigration to the United States of America completed. Visas granted. Report at Bremen Headquarters on January 17, for processing. Embarkation February 22, 1948, S/S Marine Marlin. Departure February 27, 1948. Port of entry, New York, N. Y., U.SA.

It was a time for rejoicing, but, for my father, still a time of disbelief as well. "Read it again, *Velvele*" he demanded, and I complied several times, until he fully understood. He took the document in his hands caressingly, his eyes blinded by tears. I realized that my father had at last accepted our good fortune: dreams and expectations fulfilled, we would now have a chance for a new life in America.

Saying goodbye to Paula had become a melancholy habit.

"My dear William," she said with tears in her empty eyes. "I have two great dreams: one is to stand on top of the Neroberg and look down upon the city, fully enjoying the beautiful view; the second is to see my dearest William successful and happy in his endeavors." She paused for a moment and reflected on what she had said. "Put these in reverse order, on second thought." She managed an awkward smile and I realized how much this had cost her.

"I'm only going across the great Atlantic lake," I tried to sound cheerful, "and it isn't forever, Paula."

"There'll be an immensity of water and space between us from now on, my dear, and time will be very scarce in the United States."

"I'll write often."

"You'll be fortunate if you're able to write every now and then. And your Paula will be very grateful when you do." There was sadness in her voice. "Most importantly, I want you to write only when you feel like talking with me, only then, and not out of a sense of obligation."

"I will," I promised.

We took our customary walk along the Kaiser Friedrich Ring to admire the Dutch tulips which were still in bloom, and Paula made the usual inquiries about their size and fullness, about their hue and color contrast. I took pains to inform her about the flowers in a minuscule detail, sensing a foreboding that this would be our last walk together. And then Paula asked to be taken up to the *Neroberg*. I hailed a taxi and in ten minutes we stood at the top of the mountain. Beneath it lay the city of Wiesbaden.

We stood there a long time in silence. "I love this blind woman looking sightlessly into the valley," I thought to myself. "She, more than anyone else, had given me back my life."

We returned to Paula's in silence. For a long time, I sat in her library. The pain of this farewell was great and it was hard for me to leave.

"You've always favored Theodor Storm, my William," Paula said, interrupting my train of thought. She reached unerringly for a green, leather-bound, two-volume set of Storm's collected writings. "You've especially admired this set, William." It was a rare annotated edition of the great North-German story teller. "You may take the first volume with you, my dear William," she said softly. "On your return visit to your teacher, you'll receive the second. What do you say?" She asked with apparent lightheadedness.

"Agreed," I said happily, and Paula released the book into my hands. With her keen sense of hearing, she was able to experience the sound of my fingers caressing the soft leather of the treasured tome. She opened the door. I walked outside, and Paula followed. She came very close and her palms enveloped my face. I felt a sudden shame for lack of tears. "Wait, William." Her fingers grappled with my coat collar. "You'll catch your death of cold, William." She scolded me lovingly. "You know how sensitive your neck is to this dreadful weather, don't you?"

"Paula!" We locked each other in a strong embrace. Our cheeks touched, and I felt her tears once more. "And if you should need the second volume sooner than your next visit, just write me a few lines and I'll send it to you anyway," she whispered in my ear.

33

Two weeks before our departure for Bremen, my father rose early in the morning and began to pack. Having set aside a suitcase for himself, he began to pack another, smaller one for me.

My father had been brooding lately, and we did all we could to stay out of his way. We had learned from experience not to interfere with his melancholy mood. He would work things out in time by himself. Then on the morning of January fourth, he spoke up.

"You're coming with me, *Velvele.*"

"Where are you taking me, father?"

"To Dachau."

"What for?"

"To remember."

"I remember, father."

"You're beginning to forget."

"That'll never happen, father."

"I want you to remember and to hate."

"I shall remember, but I cannot continue to hate, father."

"You don't want to hate?"

"I don't want to become a solitary avenger of my people, father."

"What do you mean, an avenger?"

"Okay. I just don't want to go on hating."

"And what about your mother? Your sister?"

"They're dead, father. Nothing'll bring them back."

"And it doesn't bother you that their assassins are free and alive?"

"It bothers me a lot."

"So you know who killed them?"

"Yes, father, I know who killed them."

"Tell me. Who killed your mother and your sister?"

"The Nazis killed them, father."

"And you will not. . ." he hesitated, ". . . cannot hate them?"

"I'll always hate the Nazis, father," I replied. "Wherever they are."

"We will go to Dachau, *Velvele.* This one last time, we must go and see again what happened there. It may be the last chance we'll have to see it with our own eyes."

"Why must you see it again, father?" I asked incredulously. "Why must you torment yourself so?"

"Your mother tells me to do it, *Velvele*. She talks to me in my nightmares. Her vision stays with me." My father was on the verge of tears.

"All right, father. We'll go to Dachau, if it'll make mother rest easier."

It was a seven hour journey. The German railroads ran again with their proverbial punctuality.

Between Augsburg and Munich lay the little town of Dachau. We joined one of the many tourist groups. No one would have guessed that this horror was set against such a pastoral landscape. Dachau Concentration Camp was founded here in the year 1933.

The return train to Munich was scheduled in three hours. "We must be alone," my father said, solemnly. "We're not tourists." I understood. We spotted the ghostlike cattle-cars that stood on an isolated rail spur not far from the main terminal. There was a plaque nailed to the boards of the first car, but my father did not wish to read it. "These are the cars the Americans found, filled with corpses." I spoke as if reciting some kind of an eerie testament from memory. "Half of them were dead, the other half dying. The stench caused some of the less-hardened soldiers to vomit. Those able to observe, had a hard time holding back their tears." My father stood silently, and I led him by the arm toward the camp gate. "Let's go on, father, or we'll miss the train."

The sun was descending and the sky was cloudy. A small mongrel dog approached and cautiously sniffed at us. A sharp wind caused a sudden chill and we quickened our steps as the dog ran for shelter, tail between his legs.

We stopped at the gate to read the arched inscription: ARBEIT MACHT FREI. WORK MEANS FREEDOM. My father lit a cigarette. He had been chain smoking nervously. "You're smoking too much, father," I said, "against the doctor's orders." It was of no use. My father has grown sullen, and I knew not to pursue this line of conversation. He would only ignore it. We followed a group of Germans who walked solemnly through the compound listening to the guide in silence, occasionally interrupting to ask a question.

"It's getting cold." I said. "We should have brought a coat."

"I've packed one. We'll get it out of the suitcase when we get back to the station. It's for you, *Velvele*, so you won't catch cold." I was startled at his concern for my welfare.

"How about you, father?"

"I'm not worried about the cold."

I looked at my father's face. His eyes expressed a terrible harshness I had not seen before. "We should be going back, father," I said. "Yes, we should." His voice was as cold as the glare of his eyes.

The Munich train arrived on time and we boarded it along with the multitude of sightseers.

"We'll spend the night in Munich," my father said.

"There's a train leaving for Wiesbaden tonight, father. We should be on it."

"No. We'll spend the night."

"Is that necessary?" I tried to reason.

"It's necessary." He closed his eyes and clenched his fists.

It was late when we checked into the hotel. We bathed and freshened up.

"Why don't we go down and have supper? Aren't you hungry, father?"

He nodded.

At the hotel restaurant, we ordered some food, and he asked for a bottle of vodka. Some of the other guests were laughing and drinking beer. "Damned Nazis." My father growled repeatedly. "The Americans aren't much better," he went on, more loudly now. "Just look at them. Fraternizing with Nazi whores."

"Father, please," I whispered. "Someone's bound to hear you. Let's leave."

"We're not leaving!" He shouted. "Not till we've eaten."

Just then, the waiter arrived with our food. I kept glancing at my father from the corner of my eye. He ate slowly, swallowing his food with much effort, clearing his throat occasionally, and serving himself generously from the vodka bottle.

"Don't you think you've had enough, father?" I asked. My father's eyes had a glassy stare and drops of perspiration had appeared on his forehead as if he had a high fever.

"I can hold my alcohol. Don't worry, son."

We finished the meal in silence, and then my father carried the half-full bottle to his room. He sat near the window, and continued drinking until there was nothing left.

"Now, we must go," he said finally.

"Go? Where?" I asked.

"You're not to ask questions. You're to obey."

"It's way past midnight, father. You ought to get some rest before our trip back. We've got an early train to catch."

"There'll be plenty of time to sleep. And there'll be other trains." He slurred his words drunkenly. "Let's go." He picked up his jacket.

"Please, father. Can't we talk?"

"There's nothing to talk about. You can stay here, if you want to. I'll do what must be done." He was calm now. The slur was gone and he was in complete control of himself. He walked a straight line toward the door as if to prove his sobriety, and I followed more out of curiosity than filial duty.

His tolerance for pure alcohol did not surprise me, knowing that frontline soldiers made common practice of mixing their scarce supplies of vodka with high octane gasoline to keep warm during inclement weather. "Are you coming?" He sensed my hesitancy.

Without a word, I followed him outside.

The streets were deserted but for a few hurrying pedestrians. The cold, northern wind scattered the snow, which was beginning to stick to the ground.

Several blocks down the street, we turned the corner. On the sidewalk, in front of us, we spotted clearly visible footprints. Down the road, in the distance, we saw a man in uniform. "Damn! We're in luck! A cop," my father whispered. "Hurry up!" He walked faster now, and I had a hard time keeping up with him.

"Hurry up, son. This is our man." My father's voice was hoarse with excitement. The footprints in the snow were of little importance now. The policeman was a few yards away. He turned toward us as we approached, and looked at us quizzically. He was on a routine check of this deserted back alley. But we were too obvious not to arouse his suspicion. He stood silently, looking us over.

The policeman's back was against the wall. It was a dead-end alley. He was a man in his late forties. "Are you lost?" He asked with apparent concern. "This alley ends here," he added, "if you follow me, I'll show you the way out." He prepared to go, but my father blocked his way. Suddenly, the policeman's smile vanished. "Have you got any identification?" His voice now sounded formal.

"Sure," my father said, reaching into his coat pocket. "This is it." He drew his luger and pointed it at the astonished man.

"I'm unarmed." The policeman's voice trembled. "All doors here have security alarms and you'll never get away with it."

"You dumb Nazi," my father hissed. "So you think we're common thieves?" He spat at the man. With his left hand he screwed the silencer onto the barrel of the gun. The policeman cowered with fear. "Why do you say that?" He asked quietly. "Wasn't everybody a Nazi?" He added with an unsuccessful effort at humor.

"You hear that, son? Hear what the man said? Now, do you believe me?" My father shouted.

"Sure, everybody was a Nazi in Hitler's Germany. Now we're free, and the devil's gone," the man said. Perhaps he thought my father was joking.

"Well, then. I intend to send you to your master," my father said icily. "I'm sure there's a place waiting for you in his new Reich."

The policeman knelt down before my father. He had just become aware of the seriousness of the situation. He began to plead for his life.

"Father. Haven't you carried this far enough?" I, too, was pleading. "Now that you've frightened him out of his wits, we've got an early train to catch."

"He's an assassin! They're all assassins!" My father screamed. "He must die for his crimes!"

"No, father. You've tried this once before without success. Killing him won't bring anyone back. Don't do it, father. I beg you, let's leave the bastard."

"He must die." My father spoke calmly now. He held the gun steadily aiming it at the kneeling man before him. The man suddenly reached into his breast pocket, but before he was able to withdraw his hand, a bullet struck him in the face. His body fell back violently, head striking the wall with full force. Blood rushed from the gaping wound.

"Did you see that? Did you see? He was going to kill me!" My father shouted at me, "that damned Nazi was trying to kill me." He repeated.

"He was unarmed, father."

"And you believed him?"

"Yes, I did, father." We were running now. "What matters is that you picked a German at random and you killed him," I panted. My father stopped in his tracks, and faced me. He placed both his hands on my shoulders. "I had to do it, son. Isn't that the way they killed our people? At random?" He asked.

"So why did you have to do likewise?" I turned my face toward him. "The Nazis took this country down into the abyss of the deepest spiritual crater in German history," I continued, "and in your blind vengeance you've managed to follow them below."

"Some of us have to remember, when there are those who try to forget." My father said defiantly.

"By doing what you just did, you've brought the Nazi demons back to life again, father." My voice trembled with sadness. "The ghost of Hitler is dancing a jig each time you kill one of his erstwhile subjects." I reflected. "The sooner we'll leave this graveyard, the better."

"Your mother's soul will rest easier."

"You're using mother's memory as an excuse to kill."

"All right. I killed a Nazi just to kill a Nazi."

"What if you killed an innocent person?"

"There are no blameless Germans, son. They're all Nazis and they're all assassins of your family." We walked to the hotel in silence.

"Vengeance is mine, says the Lord." I quoted a long forgotten passage. My father stared at me intensely, somewhat hurt, as if reproachful for the unfairness of the argument.

"It also says somewhere 'an eye for an eye,' *Velvele*" he said sadly.

"But the God of Abraham and Isaac is a merciful God."

"Why do you say that, my son?"

"He delivered us from the ovens, didn't He?"

"After the sacrifice of many." My father's hands trembled, and he tried to steady them by rubbing them together.

"It was a test," I said softly and without conviction.

"A test? A test of what?"

"A test of obedience. Obedience to His laws."

"You mean. . . like he tested Abraham and Isaac? And such a test was worth so many victims. . . so many sacrifices?"

"Who is to judge?" I asked.

"Do we judge if we say that God made a mistake? Just this once?"

I was silent. Then he spoke again.

"This whole story about Abraham being tested, it's all a fake. It was all made up by men to serve their scheme, to fool other men. God is merciful, has compassion, *rachmones*. A merciful God would not allow one man to be sacrificed for all mankind. He would not accept the anguish of one to redeem the corruption of all." My father paused. "No, my son," he cried, "it wasn't God who tested man. What is there to test?"

I looked at my father shocked, stunned at what he had said, hoping that God was too busy to pay attention to him at this very moment.

"It's all right, father. I understand."

"I don't think you do, *Velvele*" my father insisted. "I ask how we are to go on and accept this God's blessing 'to multiply like the sand in the sea and the stars in the heavens?' What for? To conduct another test? Another Hitler?"

By the time we returned to our hotel room, it was early morning.

"Get some sleep, father. It doesn't do any good to continue this way."

"This has been on my mind for too long, and it's not easy to forget," he went on. "Men were dying around me, being killed, killing. God was absent. He was also absent as I marched through Europe, fighting the Nazis, death and famine everywhere; there was no God.

Only men; cruel, vicious men, killing or being killed." He interrupted his train of thought momentarily as if reaching into the far recesses of his mind for some missing pieces, to fit them into the fabric of his story. "And then, one day, we took Treblinka. When we arrived, the furnaces were still fired, the smoke was everywhere, and the smell of burning human flesh will forever haunt me. When I discovered that your mother and your sister ended their lives there, I went crazy and I wanted to die. I can't remember how many of the assassins I killed in the days that followed." He stopped briefly. Suddenly, as if recalling an important event, he reached into his pocket. "See this?" he asked. "They gave it to me for valor at Vyazma. I've killed those bastards before." I looked at the medal he put on the table before me, but I wasn't convinced.

"That was war, father. It wasn't like. . ."

"It's war everyday, *Velvele*. As long as the assassins live, it will be war," my father interrupted. "There was no God in Treblinka; one of the many Nazi killing factories. There was no testing. Only human assassins. Murderers who blamed God for the things they did so that they could go on doing them. They made God human and wanted Him to share their guilt. Do you realize what I am trying to understand myself, son? Am I making any sense?"

"I think you do, father," I sat silently. My father was peaceful now, his hands folded in his lap, breathing evenly. I reflected on my father's words, trying not to allow my own thoughts to interfere, to accuse. "And that is why I had to do what I did, son. Why I had to kill, to take revenge in a human way for what the other humans did to us," he added softly. "I'm sure God looked the other way."

Why had my father not told me that he had planned to kill a German if he had carried the idea all along in his mind? I looked at him as if he were a stranger, one never to be trusted again. "But then, neither did God reveal His plans to Abraham until the very last moment of the journey." I thought to myself. It was all too puzzling, too perplexing, for the moment at least. I glanced at my father and images of my childhood appeared in my mind in rapid succession; the love and the understanding, the punishment and the rewards. I thought I knew this man well enough. But now, there was a question: was this the man who once was my father, my mother's husband? Was it the same person whose revered memory had sustained me throughout the many years of hardship in captivity. I was frightened at the thought of having to refashion an ancient and treasured myth.

34

It was our last journey through the German countryside. My father, Roman, Rita and her parents, we all occupied the small train compartment. We were on our way to board the ship that was to carry us to the United States. My eyes were fixed onto the rolling hills in the distance and the beautiful German countryside. I was overcome with melancholy. That beauty meant nothing to me anymore. I would never see it again.

During the long train ride, I studied my father's face while he was sleeping. My fingers played with the medal in my pocket. It would be hard to forgive the Germans and the Russians for having murdered his soul. This stranger before me was still my father, and I would not abandon him. I had no right to judge him.

We were taking few material possessions with us to the New World. "We'll buy everything in America," my father had said. "We'll buy the best, and we'll be rich like all Americans."

"Not all Americans are rich, father," I had warned him.

"Oh yes, they are," he insisted stubbornly. I wouldn't argue. He'd have to find out for himself.

Bremerhaven was a rubbleheap. Yet, in the harbor, the small ship was waiting for us, glistening in the sun. Rita and I walked on the dock, hand in hand trembling with anticipation. As we looked over the ship, our home-to-be for the next two weeks, I spotted some wild flowers nearby growing in the midst of the rubble, clinging for their dear life on to a barren sand dune.

By force of habit, I looked around in all directions, fearful that I might be spied upon. Quickly, I plucked one of the flowers and handed it to Rita. "A bouquet for my lady love," I said. She smiled and lifted it gently upward to her face, enjoying the tender fragrance of the early-blossomed wild flower. "Where there was life, there will be life." I recalled my grandmother's saying. "When flowers can thrive on barren ground, reason may yet come to visit this world void of sanity." Rita observed wistfully. She kissed me tenderly.

"Can you spare a little something for a widow of the war?" A high-pitched voice jarred us out of our reverie. Annoyed, we turned around. Behind us stood a haggard old woman, bent over with age and wearing clothes made of sack-cloth.

Her sunken eyes gave her face an eerie appearance.

The woman extended her hand toward me. "Medals. See? I sell them cheap," she shrieked.

"I don't need your medals," I said harshly. I threw her a coin.

"Take it!" The old woman called out, tossing the medal at my feet.

"My son gave his life for it at Vyazma! Damn the Bolsheviks!" She was gone before we were able to respond.

"Vyazma! A most curious coincidence." I thought to myself. I examined the medal as I bent down to pick it up from the ground. "God!" I exclaimed. I was looking at the Distinguished Service Cross! The highest Nazi military decoration. I reached into my own pocket. "Father got this one at the same place, Vyazma." I handed Rita my father's Polish medal which I had kept with me ever since that fateful day in Munich.

"You didn't tell me your father got the *Virtuti Militari*" Rita said reproachfully. "It's the highest honor Poland can confer on any living soldier for bravery and valor."

"Would you have loved me more?" I laughed.

"Probably not. But I might have understood your father better."

"It's not the medal, but his many wounds that makes my father who he is today." I suppressed a sigh. "He was with the Kosciuszko Division when they broke through at Vyazma. It was there he suffered so horribly."

"I am terribly sorry. I had no idea." Rita pressed my arm tenderly.

"Who knows? My father might have been the one who killed this old woman's son," I said softly as I placed the German medal into Rita's hand.

"They belong together," she suddenly said, trembling. "Let's dig a grave and bury them side by side." She knelt down among the wild flowers and I knelt beside her. We scooped up the loose earth with our bare hands until the tiny grave had become sufficiently deep.

"That'll do," I said, and Rita dropped the two medals into the shallow pit. They fell inside with a metallic sound.

"See? It's only tin, nothing else." Rita said quietly.

"Not a compelling reason for killing or dying," I agreed.

Together, we replaced the earth over the two buried medals. And then, we walked toward the ship lying in the harbor.